Simulation Modeling Methods

Other McGraw-Hill Books by H. James Harrington

- *The Improvement Process: How America's Leading Companies Improve Quality* (1987)
- *Business Process Improvement: The Breakthrough Strategy for Total Quality, Productivity, and Competitiveness* (1991)
- *Total Improvement Management: The Next Generation in Performance Improvement*, written with James S. Harrington (1995)
- *High Performance Benchmarking: 20 Steps to Success*, written with James S. Harrington (1996)
- *The Complete Benchmarking Implementation Guide: Total Benchmarking Management* (1996)
- *ISO 9000 and Beyond: From Compliance to Performance Improvement* (1997)
- *Business Process Improvement Workbook: Documentation, Analysis, Design and Management of Business Process Improvement*, written with Erik K.C. Esseling and Harm van Nimwegen (1997)
- *The Creativity Toolkit: Provoking Creativity in Individuals and Organizations*, with Glen D. Hoffherr and Robert P. Reid (1998)*
- *Statistical Analysis Simplified: The Easy-to-Understand Guide to SPC and Data Analysis*, written with Glen D. Hoffherr and Robert P. Reid (1998)*
- *Reliability Simplified: Going Beyond Quality to Keep Customers for Life*, written with Les Anderson (1998)*
- *Area Activity Analysis: Activities and Measurement to Enhance Business Performance*, written with Glen D. Hoffherr and Robert P. Reid (1998)*
- *ISO 14000 Implementation: Upgrading Your EMS Effectively*, written with Alan Knight (1999)*
- *Project Change Management: Applying Change Management to Improvement Projects*, written with Daryl R. Conner and Nicholas L. Horney (2000)*
- *Performance Improvement Methods: Fighting the War on Waste*, written with Kenneth C. Lomax (2000)*

*Titles in the Harrington Performance Improvement Series

Simulation Modeling Methods

H. James Harrington
International Quality Advisor
Ernst & Young LLP

Kerim Tumay
Vice President
CACI Products Company

McGraw-Hill

New York San Francisco Washington, D.C. Auckland Bogotá
Caracas Lisbon London Madrid Mexico City Milan
Montreal New Delhi San Juan Singapore
Sydney Tokyo Toronto

McGraw-Hill

A Division of The ***McGraw-Hill*** *Companies*

1 2 3 4 5 6 7 8 9 0 DOC/DOC 9 0 9 8 7 6 5 4 3 2 1 0 9

ISBN 0-07-027136-4

Library of Congress Cataloging-in-Publication Data

Harrington, H. J. (H. James)
Simulation modeling methods / H. James Harrington, Kerim Tumay.
p. cm. (Harrington's performance improvement series)
ISBN 0-07-027136-4
1. Production engineering. 2. Simulation methods. 3. Design, Industrial.
I. Tumay, Kerim, 1959- II. Title. III. Series.
TS176 H368 1999
658.5—dc21 99-045944

The sponsoring editor for this book was Catherine Schwent. Manuscript development and production by CWL Publishing Enterprises, Madison, WI, John A. Woods, President (www.cwlpub.com).

Contents

About the Series

Simulation Modeling Methods is one title in McGraw-Hill's Harrington's Performance Improvement Series. The series is designed to meet an organization's need to understand the most useful approaches now available to bring about improvements in organizational performance as measured by:

- Return on investment,
- Value-added per employee, and
- Customer satisfaction

Each title in the series is written in an easy-to-read, user-friendly style designed to reach employees at all levels of an organization. Our goal is to present complex methodologies in a way that is simple but not simplistic. The following are other subjects covered in the books in this series:

- Statistical process controls
- Process redesign
- Process reengineering
- Establishing a balanced scorecard
- Reliability analysis
- Fostering teamwork
- Environmental Management Systems ISO-14000
- Simulation modeling
- Rewards and recognition
- Performance improvement methods
- Creativity tools
- Statistical analysis simplified
- Area activity analysis

We believe that the books in this series will provide an effective way to learn about these practices as well as a training tool for use in any type of organization. In each title in the series, you'll find icons in the margins that call your attention to different points. Use these icons to guide your reading and study:

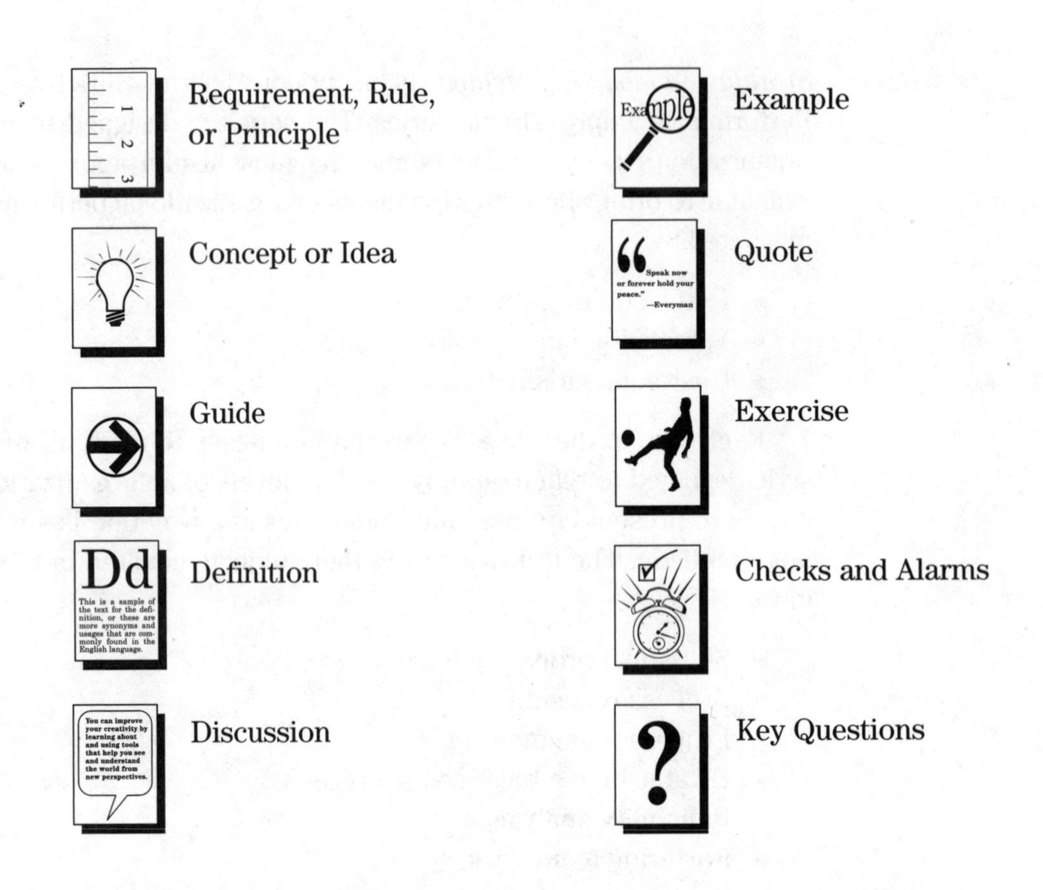

It is our hope that you will find this series of Performance Improvement books enjoyable and useful.

H. James Harrington
Principal, Ernst & Young LLP
International Quality Advisor

About the Authors

Dr. H. James Harrington Dr. H. James Harrington is one of the world's leading process improvement gurus, with more than 45 years of experience. He has been involved in developing management systems in Europe, South America, North America, and Asia. He currently serves as principal with Ernst & Young LLP and as International Quality Advisor. He is also chairman of Emergency Technology Ltd., a high-tech software and hardware manufacturer and developer.

Before joining Ernst & Young LLP, he was president of the consulting firm Harrington, Hurd, and Rieker. He was a senior engineer and project manager for IBM and, for almost 40 years, he worked in IBM's quality function. He was chairman and president of the International Academy for Quality and the American Society for Quality Control. He has released a series of videos and CD-ROM programs that cover ISO 9000 and QS 9000. He is author of a computer program on benchmarking, plus 14 videotapes on performance improvement. He has written 14 books on performance improvement and hundreds of technical reports.

The Harrington/Ishikawa Medal was named after him in recognition of his support to developing nations in implementing quality systems. The Harrington/Neron Medal was also named after him to recognize his contributions to the quality movement in Canada. China named him its Honorary Quality Advisor. He has also been elected honorary member of nine quality professional societies and has received numerous awards and medals for his work. Recently, Dr. Harrington was elected into Singapore's Hall of Fame. To contact Jim Harrington, please refer to his Web site at www.hjharington.com or call his office at 408 358-2476

Kerim Tumay is the Vice President of Modeling and Simulation Solutions at CACI Products Company in La Jolla, CA. He has over 15 years of hands-on simulation experience as an analyst, trainer, marketer, and consultant. He has been involved in various applications, such as manufacturing, enterprise modeling, supply chain, transportation, and data communications. Tumay has contributed to the successful use of simulation tools and methods by hundreds of commercial organizations, such as Boeing, DuPont, Ford, Ernst & Young, and Union Pacific, and academic institutions, such as Arizona State University, MIT, San Diego State University, the University of Michigan, and the University of Wisconsin.

Tumay holds an M.S. degree in Industrial Engineering from Arizona State University. He is a co-author of the popular book titled *Simulation Made Easy*, published by Industrial Engineering and Management Press. He has also authored 32 papers and conducted over 50 seminars on simulation modeling and analysis. To contact Kerim Tumay, please refer to his Web site at www.simmodel.com.

Preface

It has been said, and we agree, that a picture is worth a thousand words. Well, if this is true, a picture that logically simulates tasks and collects data has to be worth a million words. Simulation models provide a picture that gives the appearance that it can think for itself. It has the capability of considering complex interrelated tasks and structurally projected outcomes by exercising the many alternative combinations in a matter of seconds, which would normally take months to do in the real process, and providing its user with validated results that can be very reliable. Truly, simulation modeling is a weapon of mass destruction in your war on waste and performance improvement.

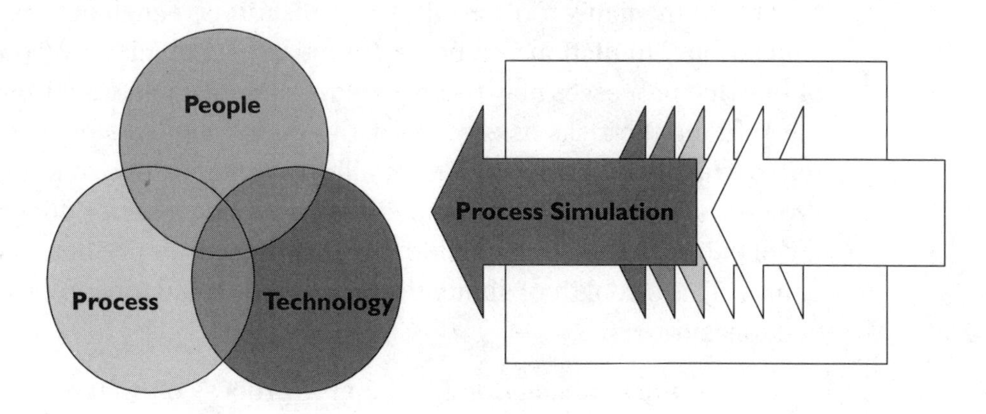

Process improvement enablers

What Is Simulation?

"Simulation is a means of experimenting with a detailed model of a real system to determine how the system will respond to changes in its structure, environment, or underlying assumptions." (Charles

Harrell and Kerim Tumay, *Simulation Made Easy: A Manager's Guide*).

Simulation, by definition, allows for experimenting with a model of the system to better understand processes, with a goal of improving performance. Simulation modeling incorporates various inputs to a system and provides a means to evaluate, redesign, and measure or quantify customer satisfaction, resource utilization, process streamlining, and time spent.

Process Simulation in Reengineering

Process reengineering, or *process innovation* as it may sometimes be called, is a means by which organizations attempt to almost reinvent themselves. This effort involves redesigning processes, finding new and innovative and therefore more effective, efficient, and productive ways of doing business.

One of the many tools used to organizations reengineer is process simulation. Simulation is a powerful means by which new processes or existing processes may be designed, evaluated, and visualized without running the risks associated with conducting tests on a real system. Dynamic process simulation allows organizations to study their processes from a systems perspective, providing a better understanding of cause and effect in addition to allowing better prediction of outcomes. This strength of simulation allows for evaluating, redesigning, and measuring:

- customer satisfaction for the new process or system
- resource utilization in the new process or system
- processes, in order to streamline them
- time, in order to minimize it

All these capabilities make simulation an ideal tool in a reengineering effort.

Organizations use process simulation to help reengineer their businesses. Simulation plays a powerful role in the analysis of the cur-

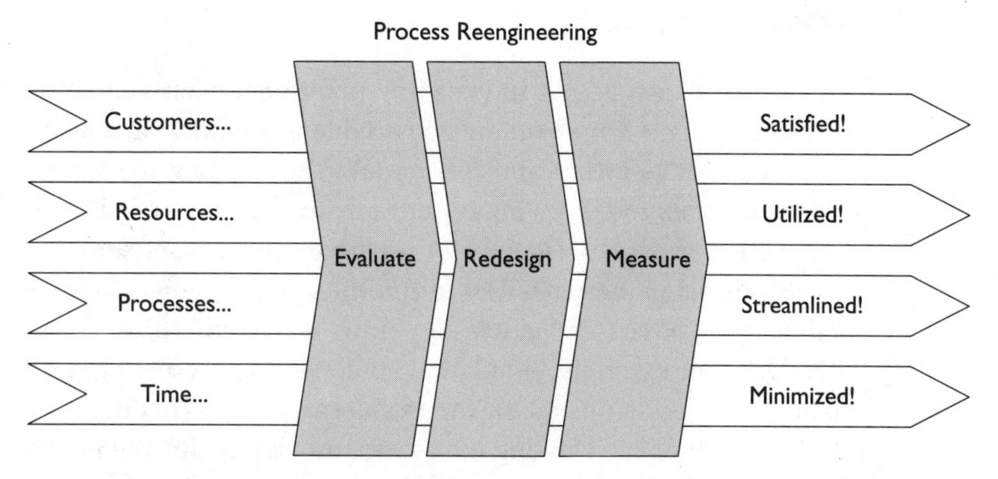

The benefits of simulation

rent state as well as the future-state vision for the reengineered processes.

Simulation could assist in the following areas in a reengineering effort:

- feasibility analyses: examining the viability of the new processes in the light of various constraints, conducting a cost/benefits analysis or process evaluation.
- visioning: exploring the possibilities for the system in the future state.
- performance characteristics: examining the performance metrics of a system in either the current state or the future state, thus providing an understanding of performance.
- prototyping: applying the future-state vision in implementation planning and risk assessment, beginning detailed process design.
- communication: disseminating the working of the new reengineered process to the organization.

Why Simulate?

Simulation can assist in creative problem solving: Fear of failure prevents people from coming up with ideas. Simulation will allow creative experimentation and testing and then selling the idea to management, thus encouraging an optimistic "Let's try it" attitude. Thus simulation provides a means for creative problem solving.

Simulation can predict outcomes: Management is prediction. Simulation educates people on how a system might respond to changes. For example, simulation could help in predicting response to market demands placed on the business system. This allows for analyzing whether the existing infrastructure can handle the new demand placed on it. Simulation can thus help determine how resources may be efficiently utilized. Simulation thus helps in predicting outcomes for various changes to system inputs.

Simulation can account for system variances: Conventional analytical methods, such as static mathematical models, do not effectively address variance as calculations are derived from constant values. Simulation looks at variance, in a system incorporating interdependence, interaction among components, and time. This approach allows for examining variation in a broader perspective.

Simulation promotes total solutions: Simulation allows modeling entire systems, therefore promoting total solutions. Simulation models provide insight into the impact that process changes will have on input to and output from the system as well as system capabilities. Simulation models can be designed to provide an understanding of the system-wide impact of various process changes. Thus simulation provides a means of examining total system-wide solutions.

Simulation can be cost-effective: As organizations try to respond quickly to changes in their markets, a validated simulation model can be an excellent tool for evaluating rapid responses. For example, a sudden change in market demand for a product can be modeled using a validated system model to determine whether the existing system can cater to this need. Additionally, simulation modeling allows for experimenting with system parameters without having to tamper with the real system. Simulation provides more alternatives, lowers the risks, increases the probability of success, and provides information for decision support without the cost of experimenting with the real system. Simulation thus provides a cost-effective way to rapidly test and evaluate various solutions to respond to market demands.

Simulation can help quantify performance metrics: Simulation can help quantify performance measures for a system. For example, the aim of a system may be to satisfy the customer. Using a simulation model, this requirement could be translated into time to respond to a customer's request, which can then be designated as the performance measure for customer satisfaction. Simulation can help measure trade-offs associated with process designs and allow for further analysis on parameters such as time to market, service levels, market requirements, carrying costs, SKU levels, and so forth. Simulation thus provides a quantitative approach to measuring performance.

Simuliation serves as a means of communication: Simulation is an effective communication tool. A simulation model can be used to communicate the new or reengineered process in a dynamic and animated fashion. This provides a powerful means of communicating the function of various components to those who will use the new system, helping them understand how it works.

Process Simulation at Work

Organizations use process simulation as part of their approach to business process innovation and performance improvement. Simulation is used to understand and analyze the current state of a system as well as to vision the future state of the reengineered system. Simulation provides a powerful means of generating suggestions for improving or innovating systems.

For example, Ernst & Young has used simulation to help clients improve parts of systems or entire systems. Examples of processes in which simulation has been used include:

- Order processing/management, with a purpose of improving service and shortening time to respond to customer requests.
- Inventory management, to help evaluate various options so as to select a cost-effective system and layout.
- Customer support/service, to help redesign processes so as to shorten response times and improve service.
- Service delivery, with a purpose of improving the quality of service delivered with efficient utilization of resources using streamlined processes.
- Claims processing, with a view to minimizing cycle time through streamlined processes so as to improve customer satisfaction.
- Critical path evolution, to help improve system response to external market requirements.

In each situation, process simulation provided a means to analyze the system and allowed for a innovative approach to arriving at better solutions.

Acknowledgments

We would particularly like to acknowledge the excellent work and effort of Stacey Burkholder, who converted and edited endless hours of dictation into this final product; John Osborne, who created the storyboard for the CD-ROM; Melissa Hsaio-Ching Mido, who helped Kerim Tumay develop and put together his part of the manuscript; and Greg Gossler, who was instrumental in the preparation of Chapter 10 (Simulation Exercise) and the multimedia CD-ROM.

John Woods and Bob Magnan of CWL Publishing Enterprises have worked closely with us in giving the manuscript one final review and managing the production, turning it into the book you now hold. We would also like to acknowledge the efforts put forth by the personnel at SystemCorp in preparing the CD-ROM: Richard Rosenbloom, who brought the storyboard to life, and Ari Kugler, who provided the resources to create the CD-ROM free of charge. And last, but not least, Jaimie Benchimol, who managed and followed the process that created the CD-ROM.

We would be remiss if we did not recognize our wives, who put up with us while we spent many nights preparing the manuscript. We love them for many reasons, one of which is for being so patient with us.

—H. James Harrington
—Kerim Tumay

Simulation Modeling Methods

CHAPTER 1

Introduction to Process Simulation

A simulation model can open the door to what was thought to be impossible.

Process Simulation–What Is It?

Process simulation is a technique that helps organizations predict, compare, or optimize the performance of a process without the cost and risk of disrupting existing operations or implementing a new process. Process simulation is a technique that allows representation of processes, resources, products, and services in a dynamic computer model. A model, when simulated, mimics the operations of the business: it steps through the events in compressed time while displaying an animated picture of the work flow. Because simulation software keeps track of statistics about model elements, performance metrics can be evaluated by analyzing the model output data.

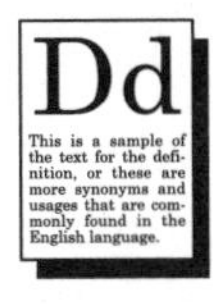

Process simulation—A technique that pictorially models or represents processes, resources, products, and services in a dynamic computer model.

Peter Senge, in his bestseller, *The Fifth Discipline*, defines situations "where cause and effect are subtle, and where the effects over time of interventions are not obvious as 'Dynamic Complexity.'" He illustrates the concept of dynamic complexity with Jay Forrester's Beer Game (a typical supply chain). Senge adds that conventional forecasting, planning, and analysis tools are not equipped to deal with dynamic complexity.

Business processes such as supply chain, customer service, and new product development are much too complex and dynamic to be understood and analyzed by flowcharting and spreadsheet techniques. The interactions of resources with processes, products, and services over time result in a large number of scenarios and outcomes that are impossible to comprehend and evaluate without the help of a computer simulation model. Although flowcharts and spreadsheets are adequate in answering "what" questions, they are inadequate for answering "how," "when," and "what if" questions.

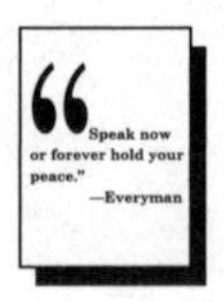

"No airline would dream of sending pilots up in the real thing before they had extensive training in a simulator on the ground ... yet managers are expected to fly their organizations into unknown skies."

—*John Sterman, MIT Sloan School*

Business process improvement approaches such as process reengineering, process redesign, and benchmarking are often unsuccessful if the present- and future-state solutions are not proven out in a simulation model. It is often impossible to understand the as-is process through simple flowcharting techniques, due to the number of dissection points and variation of cost and time required to process individual items through a simple point on the flowchart.

In the 1980s, average cost, quality, and cycle-time figures were sufficient to do activity-based costing, process redesign, and process reengineering projects. This is no longer true today. Major errors were made when processes were changed based upon averages. Organizations don't usually lose customers due to the average performance of their processes. They lose customers when customers are subjected to the negative end of the process output variation. This means that for each critical measurement at each activity, the average, the +2.5 σ, and the -2.5 σ points should be defined and used to evaluate the total process average performance and performance variation over time.

We recommend that at least the ±3 σ limit point of a proposed future-state solution should be acceptable for 99.99% of your customers when the proposed process is approved. World-class organizations are developing processes that meet customer expectations 0.0000003% of the time, or 3 errors per million transactions. Being right 99.9% of the time is inadequate. For example, if these processes were correct 99.9% of the time, then:

- 22,000 checks will be deducted from the wrong bank accounts in the next 60 minutes.
- 1,314 phone calls will be misrouted by telecommunications services every minute.
- 12 babies will be given to the wrong parents each day.
- 103,260 income tax returns will be processed incorrectly this year.
- 18,322 pieces of mail will be mishandled in the next 24 hours.
- 880,000 credit cards in circulation will turn out to have incorrect cardholder information in the magnetic strips.
- 114,500 mismatched pairs of shoes will be shipped this year.

(From *Training*, March 1991 Supplement)

Remember that by the time the process is changed to better satisfy your customers, their expectations will be much higher than they are now. With this in mind, it's easy to understand why flowcharting and spreadsheet approaches to improving process are wholly inadequate today. It's as if a person were trying to design a bridge knowing only addition and subtraction, compared with an engineer who has mastered trigonometry, calculus, and stress analysis.

His customer satisfaction level is above average.

Today, 5% of management decisions are considered bad decisions, while 85% of management decisions are considered good decisions. Only 10% of management decisions are considered "the best" decisions. We believe that process simulation is an essential tool for businesses to make "the best" decisions. The ability to visualize how a process would behave, to measure its performance, and to try "what ifs" in a computer model makes process simulation a necessary tool for decision making, "a crystal ball for dynamic complexity."

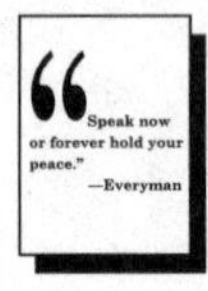

"The nice thing about 'what iffing' is that it allows you to suspend a few assumptions, and get into an imaginative frame of mind."

—*Roger Von Oech*

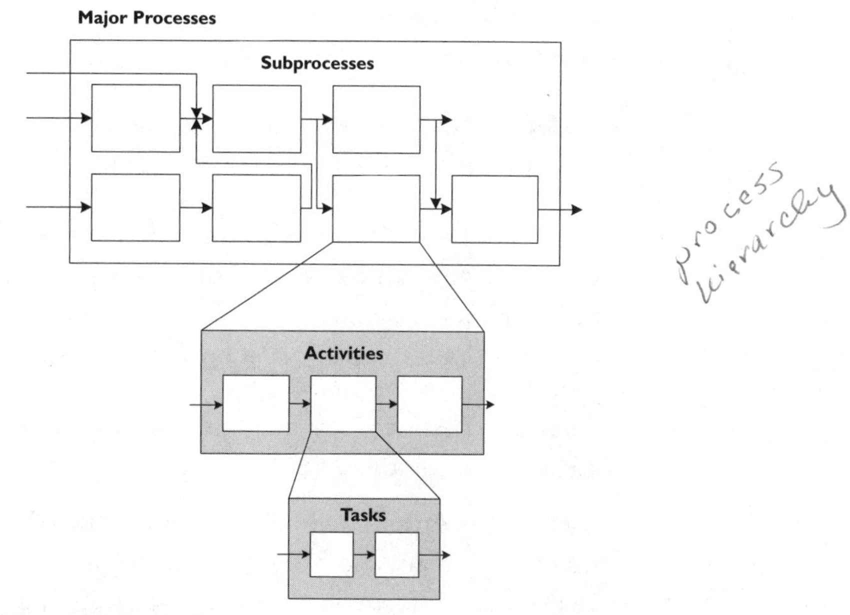

FIGURE 1-1. Process hierarchy

What Is a Process?

If we are going to simulate processes, we first need to agree on what a process is and what it is made up of. Figure 1-1 shows the process hierarchy.

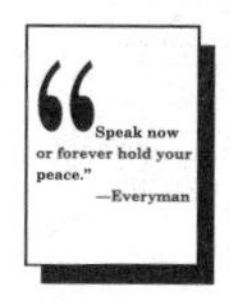

"If companies are serious about measuring performance beyond simply bean counting for isolated business units, processes are the obvious alternative."
—TOM DAVENPORT

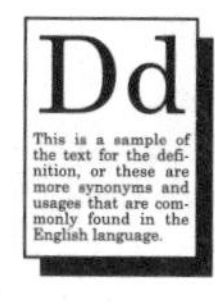

Process—A logical, related, sequential (connected) set of activities that takes an input from a supplier, adds value to it, and produces an output for a customer.

Major process—A process that usually involves more than one function within the organizational structure and that has a significant impact on the way the organization functions. When a major process is too complex to be flowcharted at the activity level, it is often divided into subprocesses.

Subprocess—A portion of a major process that achieves a specific objective in support of the major process.

Activities—Things that go on within a process or subprocess. They are usually performed by units of one (one person or one department). The tasks that make up an activity are usually documented in an instruction, in terms of the tasks that make up the activity.

Tasks—The individual elements and/or subsets of an activity. Normally, tasks relate to how a resource performs a specific assignment.

System—An assembly of components (hardware, software, procedures, human functions, and other resources) united by some form of regulated interaction to form an organized whole. It is a group of related processes that may or may not be connected (see Figure 1-2).

Organization—Any group, company, corporation, division, department, plant, or sales office.

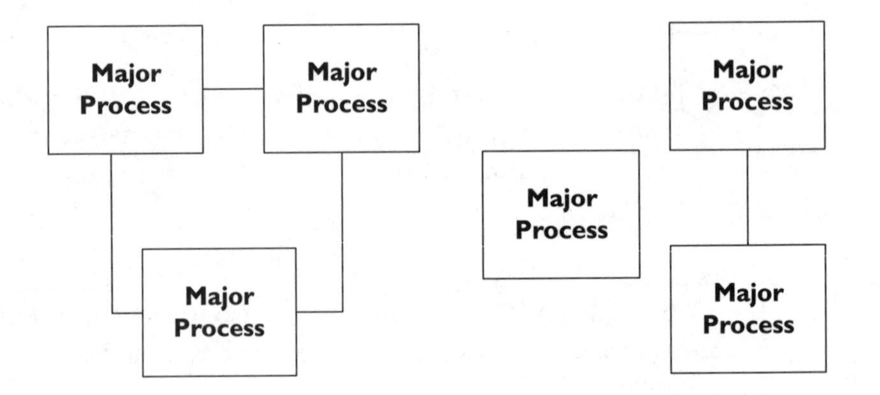

FIGURE 1-2. Systems

History of Simulation

Computer simulation was first used in the defense industry in the 1950s. Early simulation models were built using programming languages such as FORTRAN and run on mainframes. In the early 1960s, the use of simulation spread out to other industries, including manufacturing and finance, with the invention of general-purpose simulation languages such as SIMSCRIPT and GPSS. The availability of personal computers in the early 1980s and new simulation languages such as SLAM and SIMAN that ran on personal computers made the technology more usable for staff personnel, engineers, and managers.

In the late 1980s and early 1990s, graphics capabilities of personal computers enabled software developers to create graphical model development tools and to use animation with simulation. Another major development for simulation was the explosion of personal computer users running Microsoft's Windows operating environment. Simulation tools like Witness, ProModel, Arena, and iThink provided menu-driven user interfaces, visual interactive modeling, and impressive animation capabilities. These developments significantly affected the widespread use of simulation languages.

The first half of the 1990s brought another very exciting development to simulation—object-oriented modeling and analysis. There is a natural fit between object-oriented modeling and simulation. Simulation languages such as ModSim and Simple++ provide yet another breakthrough in simulation by taking advantage of object technology and enabling reusable object libraries. This development is facilitating the development of domain-specific simulation solutions, thus making simulation available to a greater number of end users.

No matter how different each development of the past and present may be, it is apparent that simulation has always been a powerful tool. The future of simulation, in our opinion, lies in our ability to distribute models on a network. The most pragmatic application, of course, is the use of the World Wide Web. There is already plenty of research and development taking place in these areas. Paul Fishwick, a recognized researcher on Web-based simulation, suggests that "there are two

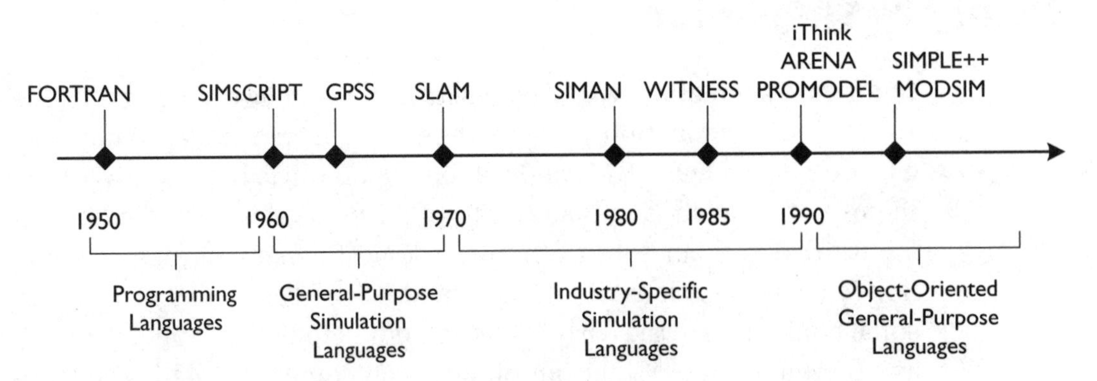

FIGURE 1-3. History of simulation tools

directions for creating a marriage between the Web and the simulation field: 1) parallel and distributed model execution, and 2) distributed model repositories." He believes that both of these avenues are fruitful.

Web-based simulation would depend upon the extension of the classical object-oriented framework, including the organization of model information. Because the Web is similarly concerned with how to effectively and efficiently organize information, this seems to be a reasonable means to combine the Web with simulation.

"We will see a tremendous increase in the use of simulation during the next decade. Object technology, data warehousing, distributed simulation, and the Web will dramatically change the way we will use simulation in the future."

Process Modeling Stairway

Process modeling has evolved over time to become one of the most important weapons against waste. Figure 1-4 is a pictorial view of this evolution.

Block Diagramming

Block-flow diagramming is the simplest and most prevalent type of process modeling approach. It provides a quick, uncomplicated view of the process.

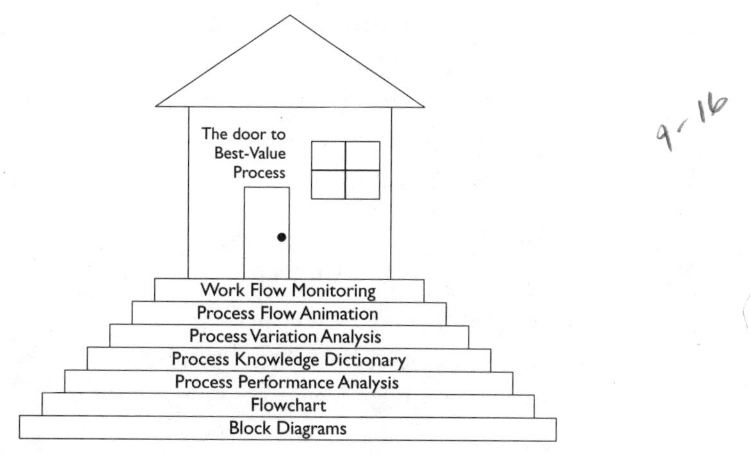

FIGURE 1-4. Process hierarchy

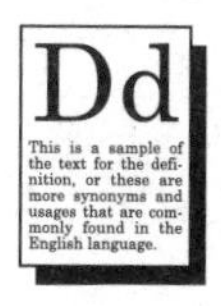

Block diagram—A pictorial method of showing activity flow through a process, using rectangles connected by a line with an arrow at the end of the line indicating direction of flow. A short phrase describing the activity is recorded in each rectangle.

The block diagram serves as the foundation of all the other process modeling approaches. Block diagramming usually provides a starting point for all of the more complex process modeling approaches.

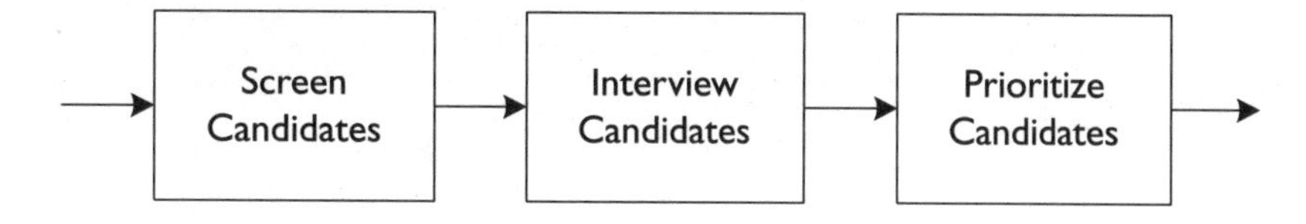

Flowchart

Flowcharting is one of the oldest of the process visual aids available today. It is a degree more complex than block diagramming.

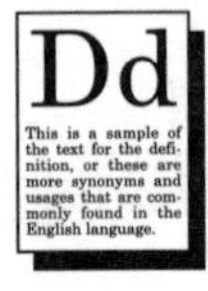

Flowchart—A method of graphically describing an existing process or a proposed new process by using simple symbols, lines, and words to pictorially display the process activities in sequence.

Flowcharts graphically present the activities that make up a process in much the same way that maps represent a particular area. Some advantages of using flowcharts are similar to those of using maps. For example, both flowcharts and maps illustrate how the different elements fit together.

There are many types of flowcharts, including:

- ANSI standard flowchart
- graphic flowchart
- functional flowchart
- functional timeline flowchart
- electronic circuit flowchart

Each type of flowchart has its own unique rules and symbols. For example, the ANSI standard flowchart uses the following symbols to represent the indicated activities:

operation
movement or transportation
decision point
inspection
paper document(s)
delay
merge
direction of flow
connection point

Flowcharting provides the fundamental base for all of the simulation modeling activities. It is essential that anyone considering using simulation modeling have an excellent understanding of the flowcharting technology. Figure 1-5 is an example of a flowchart. Figure 1-6 is a description of each block in the flow diagram.

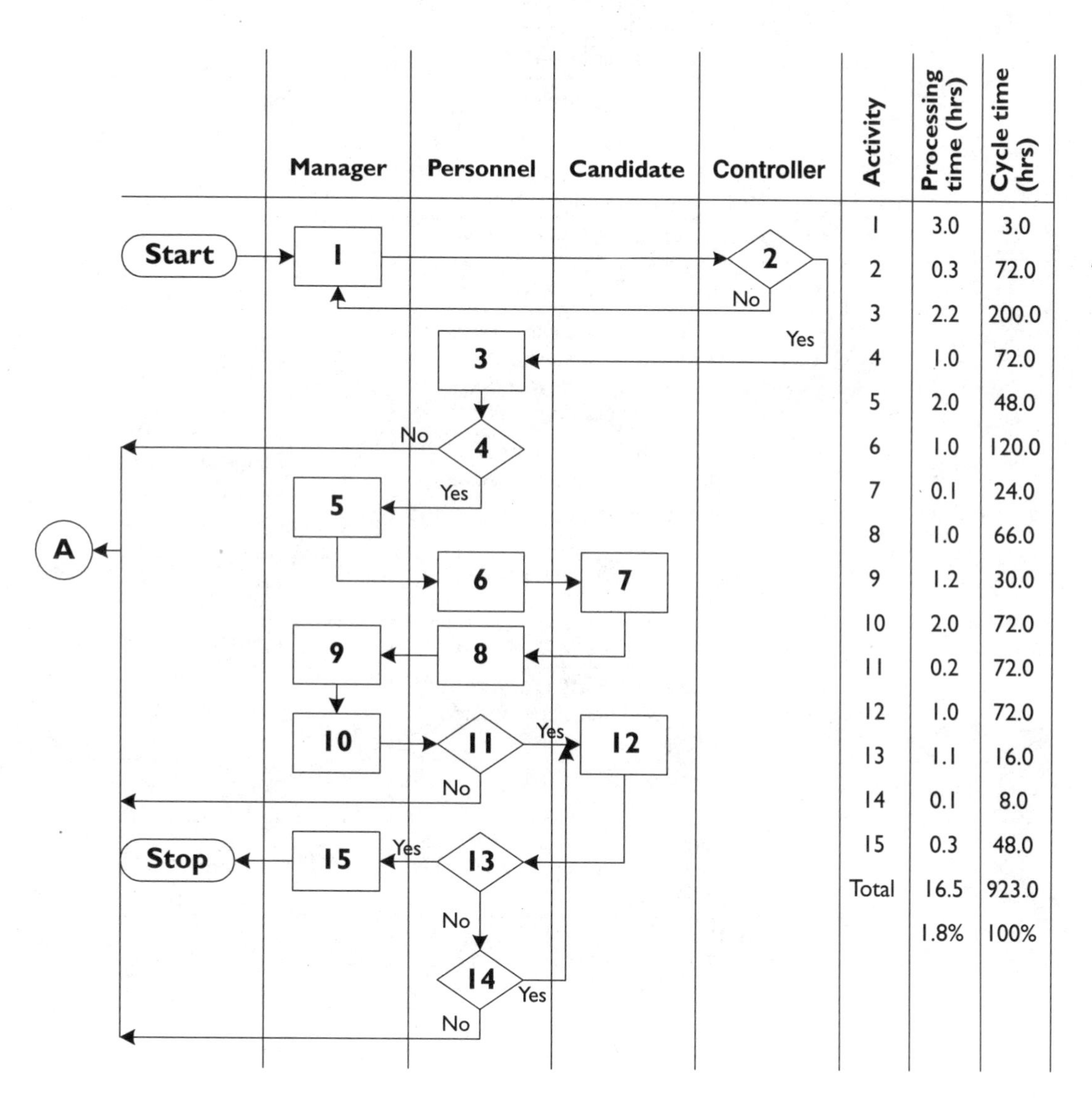

Activity	Processing time (hrs)	Cycle time (hrs)
1	3.0	3.0
2	0.3	72.0
3	2.2	200.0
4	1.0	72.0
5	2.0	48.0
6	1.0	120.0
7	0.1	24.0
8	1.0	66.0
9	1.2	30.0
10	2.0	72.0
11	0.2	72.0
12	1.0	72.0
13	1.1	16.0
14	0.1	8.0
15	0.3	48.0
Total	16.5	923.0
	1.8%	100%

FIGURE 1-5. Functional flowchart of the internal job search

Activity	Responsible Area
1. Recognize need. Complete payback analysis. Prepare personnel requisition. Prepare budget request.	Manager
2. Evaluate budget. If yes, sign personnel requisition slip. If no, return total package with reject letter to manager.	Controller
3. Conduct in-house search.	Personnel
4. If in-house candidates exist, provide list to management. If not, start outside hiring procedure.	Personnel
5. Review candidates' paperwork and prepare a list of candidates to be interviewed.	Manager
6. Have candidates' managers review job with the employees and determine which employees are interested in the position.	Personnel
7. Notify personnel of candidates interested in being interviewed.	Manager
8. Set up meeting between manager and candidates.	Personnel
9. Interview candidates and review details of job.	Manager
10. Notify personnel of interview results.	Manager
11. If acceptable candidate is available, make job offer. If not, start outside hiring process.	Personnel
12. Evaluate job offer and notify personnel of decision.	Candidate
13. If yes, notify manager that the job has been filled and go to activity 15. If no, go to activity 14.	Personnel
14. Were there other acceptable candidates? If yes, go to activity 12. If no, start outside hiring process.	Personnel
15. Have new manager contact candidate's present manager and arrange for the candidate to report to work.	Manager

FIGURE 1-6. Description of the blocks in Figure 1.5

Process Performance Analysis

This approach was developed to collect performance data related to each activity in the process and then to use this data to calculate the performance of the total process. Typical information that would be collected related to each activity is:

- cycle time
- processing time
- cost
- wait time
- yield
- quantity processed per time period

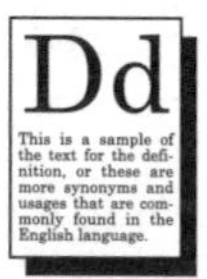

Process Performance Analysis—The collection of efficiency performance data at the activities or task level of a flowchart that are used to calculate the performance of the total process.

Along the right side of Figure 1-5 are the processing and cycle times for each of the activities in the flow diagram. It's very easy to understand that the processing time is not the sum of the individual processing times (16.5 hours), due to the number of recycles that are designed in the process. In this case, the processing time can be as short as 5.2 hours and as long as 49.7 hours.

A computer program is often used in support of a process performance analysis because of the complexities involved when the flowchart includes a number of decision blocks.

Process Knowledge Dictionary

This methodology is an extension of the process performance analysis. In addition to the performance data, all of the other information related to the activity is also collected. Typical additional data collected are:

- operating procedures
- drawings and blueprints

- work instructions
- training documents

The process knowledge dictionary is normally kept online and is accessed by management and the employees performing the activity. The process knowledge dictionary is organized so that it is accessed through each of the activity blocks in the flow diagram.

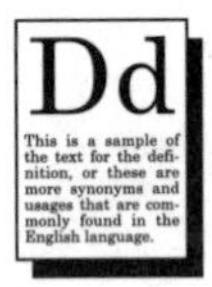

Process knowledge dictionary—A way of storing online the information related to a process that is organized according to each activity/task in the process.

Process Variation Analysis

As people began to understand the true complexity of processes, it became apparent that customers were lost not over average values of the process measurements, but as a result of the extreme negative part of the population measured. For example, the repair cycle for the average TV is 1.5 hours, but 5% of the time it takes two weeks or more. Well, few customers are going to be really unhappy about not having a television for 1.5 hours, but if you have to wait for two weeks to get your TV repaired, you will probably look for another repair shop the next time. There are many things that can cause variation in the process, including:

- uneven work flow
- differences in complexity of the individual work item
- changes in the input drivers
- workload buildup because people are out
- equipment downtime
- seasonal variation

Variation is occurring simultaneously in each activity and the variation is occurring in random patterns. It is unrealistic to calculate the total process performance by using the -2σ limits of the process measurements because of the low probability that all measurements will be at their low point (-2σ) at the same time. Process variation analysis uses random number generation tables to calculate a realistic total process performance distribution for each of the key measurements.

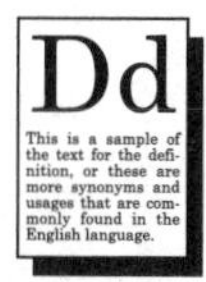

Process variation analysis—A way of combining the variation that occurs in each task or activity in a process, in order to make a realistic prediction of the total variation for the entire process.

Process Flow Animation

Until the development of process flow animation, the process designer was limited to a static picture of the process. But with process flow animation, the flowchart on the computer screen comes to life. It can show the flow of transaction through the process and how bottlenecks affect the process performance. For example, animation can show customers waiting in line while the service agents are busy or idle resources with unused capacity due to transportation delays.

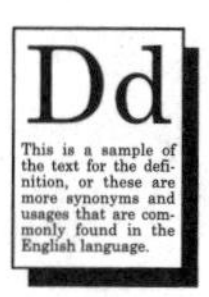

Process flow animation—A process model that pictorially shows the movement of transactions within the process and how variability and dynamics affect process performance.

Workflow Monitoring

This is an online model that is used to track transactions through the process. Each time a transaction enters an activity, it is logged in; when it leaves the activity, it is logged out. The information is computer-analyzed so that the exact status of each transaction is known at all times. Typically, the maximum time for a transaction to be in each specific activity is preset in the computer program so that exceptions are highlighted and priorities reestablished.

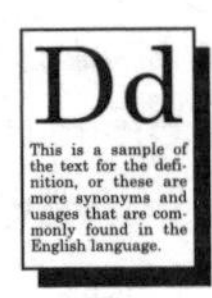

Workflow monitoring—An online computer program that is used to track individual transactions as they move through the process, to minimize process variation.

Depending upon the complexity of the simulation software package that you select, these seven steps of process modeling that open the door to best-value processes are partly or totally integrated. As an organization develops its process focus, it will progressively step up through each of these seven levels.

How Is Simulation Used in Business Process Improvement Projects?

The business process improvement breakthrough approach to improve an individual process's performance includes three methodologies—process reengineering, process redesign, and process benchmarking. In each of these three methodologies, a future-state solution is developed that is intended to represent the new process after the suggested changes are installed. The problem is that with all three methodologies the process improvement team (PIT) that develops the future-state solution has to make a number of assumptions that may or may not be correct. These important assumptions are then used to estimate the benefits for the organization as a result of implementing the new process.

It is important to realize that the processes to which these breakthrough methodologies are being applied are the critical processes that can make or break the organization's performance. Because of this, no organization can afford to implement the future-state solutions that are developed by a PIT without some way of verifying that the underlying assumptions are correct before the organization commits the resources required to implement the recommended changes. Often management is betting the organization's future on the results of these changes.

Because these changes are critical, simulation models of the future-state solution are a critical part of each of these three methodologies. Modeling allows the PIT to evaluate its assumptions. These simulation models put the complex paper model into a virtual operating mode that verifies workflow and identifies bottlenecks. It also allows the PIT to adjust the proposed process to correct for weaknesses in the design and to quickly collect data to measure the effectiveness of any change made to the process.

Simulation modeling by itself is not adequate to evaluate the correctness of the new process design, because the model is created using estimates generated by the PIT, as only the first step in the piloting process. A typical piloting process for a reengineered process is:

- simulation modeling
- conference room pilot
- in-process pilot

It's a good idea to try something out before you make a final commitment.

Although the gurus for process reengineering claim that the members of the PIT do not need to understand the present process because the team starts out with a blank sheet of paper, we don't agree with that assumption. We believe that it's hard to define a route to get to a desired destination if you don't know where you are. As a result, we believe that all three methodologies should construct a simulation model of the present process (as-is state) in order to understand the process and to measure the variation that takes place in key measurements such as cost and cycle time.

The single most important weapon in the breakthrough arsenal is simulation modeling. In a later chapter in this book, we will look in detail at how simulation modeling is used in the breakthrough methodologies.

Target Processes for Simulation

Industrial and service enterprises face increasing pressures to minimize the time it takes to service customers, develop products, and fulfill demand. Today, customers demand and expect quality products and services with custom features at affordable prices. More important, they want the products and services now! Marketing windows that used to last for years are now measured in months. We can remember in the early 1980s when IBM slipped the announcement and shipment of a new random access drive by four months due to internal technical problems, and it had no effect on the market projects. Today if IBM slips a product four months, it could mean that the company will lose 40% to 50% of the market and the product will no longer be viable to put on the market. This puts tremendous pressure on business managers to maximize profits while minimizing risks.

The International Benchmarking Clearinghouse divides business processes into two classes: *operating* processes and *management and support* processes. *Operating processes* range from product development to production, from supply chain to customer service. *Management and support processes* range from human resources to information management, from financial management to environment management.

A business manager's ability to successfully design or manage a business process depends on his or her ability to quickly evaluate alternatives. Whether a process is an operating process or a management or support process, process simulation can help businesses evaluate the impact of change with accuracy and speed. The following examples describe three specific target processes for simulation—product development, supply chain, and customer service.

Product Development

Life cycles of product and services are becoming shorter and shorter. The up-front costs of developing and testing a product are not recouped until revenue is generated. Therefore, minimizing "time to market" is a key competitive advantage for industrial enterprises. Understanding and estimating the time and cost to complete a product development process is a key business challenge. Traditionally, managers have relied on project management tools. However, variable activity times and interdependencies among resources make it very difficult to analyze activity costs and resource requirements using project management tools.

When Boeing was trying to shorten the time required for design changes in its product development process for the Boeing 777, it turned to process simulation. The design changes involved resources from designers to process engineers to purchasing agents. First, a project management tool was used to create process maps and simulations of the current process. Then, proposed alternatives—including policy changes and workflow automation—were simulated to determine impact on cycle times.

Supply Chain

One of the key business processes for an industrial enterprise is the supply chain. Integrated supply chain management means managing the flow of products and information from your supplier's suppliers to your customer's customers. The primary goal of supply chain management is to maintain high service levels while minimizing costs and inventory. The key problem in supply chain management is balancing inventory. Variability in demand and process times, complexity of the supply chain objects, and system dynamics create uncertainty that cannot accurately be modeled and analyzed with spreadsheets and flowcharts.

IBM was faced with a problem in one of its computer products businesses due to high inventory and low service levels. The proposed solutions included reducing channel inventory and building product to order. Process simulation was used in the reengineering project that resulted in a 50% reduction in inventory and a 63% increase in service level.

Customer Service

Today, customers are much more demanding and cost-conscious than they were five or 10 years ago. Increasing competitive pressures make it a tough challenge for service enterprises to maximize service quality while minimizing costs. The service industry is faced with a double standard metaphor. Customers want the service provider to serve the person in line ahead of them rapidly, but then to take all the time necessary to serve their needs and answer their questions. Such performance metrics as waiting time and activity costs are critical to providing quality service and strategically pricing services.

Microsoft Corporation made extensive use of process simulation in preparation for the launch of a new operating system. It used simulation models to design its customer service processes so that service levels could be maximized with proper staffing levels. Alternative demand patterns were evaluated to predict the impact on waiting times.

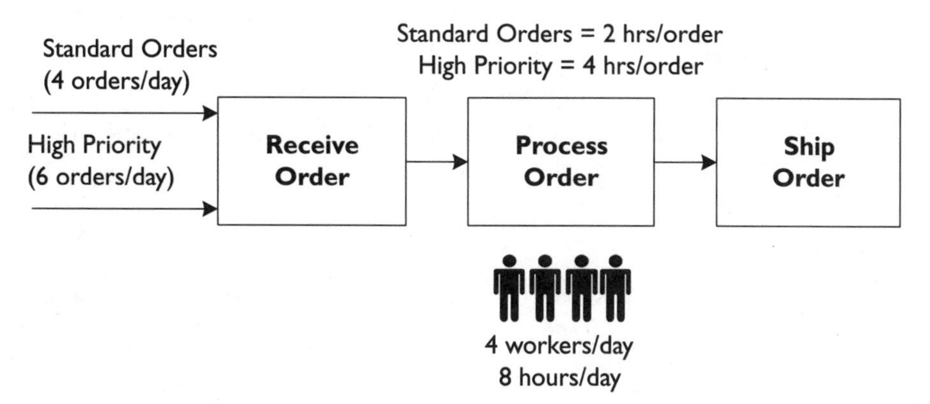

FIGURE 1-7. Order processing example

Why Do You Need Process Simulation?

Let's take a look at a very simple order fulfillment process and see the reasons why process simulation is needed. The process map shows three activities: where orders are received, where they are processed, and where they are shipped.

Let's define some parameters about how the process works.

- On the average, 10 orders are received every day.
- There are two types of orders, standard and high priority: 40% of the orders are standard and 60% of the orders are high priority.
- On the average, a standard order takes two hours to process and a high-priority order takes four hours.
- Four workers process orders in eight-hour shifts.

Based on the simple calculations shown below, we can quickly conclude that the customers will always receive their orders on time and that the order fulfillment process is optimized with its resources at 100% utilization!

standard orders = 4 orders/day × 2 hours/order = 8 hours/day
high-priority orders = 6 orders/day × 4 hours/order = 24 hours/day
total capacity required = 32 hours/day
total capacity available = 4 workers/day × 8 hours/day = 32 worker hours/day
percent utilization = capacity required/capacity available = 32/32 = 100%

Now, let's look at a typical day's activities where the order arrival rate is somewhat random, that is, customers place their orders at various times throughout the day. A manual simulation of the process for 10 orders is shown in Figure 1-8. The table includes the event times (receipt and shipment) of each order, the order number and type, and the event type.

Event Time	Order Number	Order Type	Event Type	Number in Queue	Number in Process	Time in Queue	Time in Process
9:00 A.M.	1	Standard	Receive	0	1	–	–
9:00 A.M.	2	Standard	Receive	0	2	–	–
10:00 A.M.	3	Standard	Receive	0	3	–	–
11:00 A.M.	1	Standard	Ship	0	2	–	2 hrs
11:00 A.M.	2	Standard	Ship	0	1	–	2 hrs
11:00 A.M.	4	Hi-Priority	Receive	0	2	–	–
12:00 P.M.	3	Standard	Ship	0	1	–	2 hrs
12:00 P.M.	5	Standard	Receive	0	2	–	–
12:00 P.M.	6	Hi-Priority	Receive	0	3	–	–
12:30 P.M.	7	Hi-Priority	Receive	0	4	–	–
1:00 P.M.	8	Hi-Priority	Receive	1	5	–	–
1:00 P.M.	9	Hi-Priority	Receive	2	6	–	–
1:00 P.M.	10	Hi-Priority	Receive	3	7	–	–
2:00 P.M.	5	Standard	Ship	2	6	–	2 hrs
3:00 P.M.	4	Hi-Priority	Ship	1	5	–	4 hrs
4:00 P.M.	6	Hi-Priority	Ship	0	4	–	4 hrs
4:30 P.M.	7	Hi-Priority	Ship	0	3	–	4 hrs
6:00 P.M.	8	Hi-Priority	Ship	0	2	1.5 hrs	5.5 hrs
7:00 P.M.	9	Hi-Priority	Ship	0	1	2 hrs	6 hrs
8:00 P.M.	10	Hi-Priority	Ship	0	0	3 hrs	7 hrs

FIGURE 1-8. Manual simulation of the order processing example

The first two orders arrive at 9:00 a.m. The third order arrives an hour later, at 10:00 a.m. The first three orders are standard orders. At 11:00 a.m., the first two orders are shipped. Also at 11:00 a.m., a high-priority order is received. At noon, the third standard order is shipped while two new orders arrive, one standard and the other high priority. At 12:30, another high-priority order arrives. At 1:00 p.m., three more high-priority orders are received. By 4:30 p.m., the workers have shipped seven orders. Three workers stay on and complete the remaining three orders by 8:00 p.m.

The last four columns of Figure 1-8 contain the vital statistics that are recorded each time an event takes place in the simulation. For example, the number of orders in queue reaches its peak of three at 1:00 p.m. At the same time, the total number of orders in process peaks at seven. The last three orders spend 1.5 hours, 2 hours, and 3 hours in queue, respectively. Let's summarize the performance measures of the manual simulation.

average cycle time for standard orders = 8 hours /4 orders = 2 hours/order
average cycle time for high-priority orders = 30.5 hours/6 orders = 5.08 hours/order
average queue time = 6.5 hours/10 orders = 0.65 hours/order
maximum queue time = 3 hours.
average service level = 7 orders on-time/10 orders = 70%
3 workers had to work a total of 6.5 hours of overtime to complete orders
total queue time = 6.5 hours

Although the process appeared to be designed perfectly, the random arrival rate of orders caused queuing and subsequent delays in processing time. Now, let's take a look at three other possible scenarios.

- Scenario #1: What if the daily demand varies in a way such that the business receives anywhere from eight to 12 orders a day (most likely daily demand remains at 10)?
- Scenario #2: What if the time to process high-priority orders is anywhere from 3.0 hours to 5.0 hours (most likely processing time remains at 4.0)?
- Scenario #3: What if the order mix is random?

How long will it take to fulfill an order (cycle time) given the new demand, process times, and product mix? The answer is even more difficult to compute by hand. Why? More variability in the process means more variability in performance. Possible results for the cycle times for three scenarios may look like the outcomes in Figure 1-9. The table shows the average values as well as the values for the mathematical variance (σ) in terms of the 2σ variance.

Scenario	Avg. Cycle Time	Max. Cycle Time (2σ)	
1	5.26	7.13	Variable demand
2	5.35	9.23	Additional variability in process time
3	5.77	10.84	Additional variability in demand

FIGURE 1-9. Outcomes of cycle time measures

Mathematical variance is a very important consideration when analyzing the performance of a process. Figure 1-11 shows a normal distribution curve with one, two, and three σ variances. (See *Total Quality Control* by Armand V. Feigenbaum for calculating σ.) Assuming that observations are from normally distributed population, the 2-σ band contains 95.46% of the observations and the 3-σ band contains 99.73% of the observations.

Organizations lose customers most often because of exceptionally bad performance, not because of average performance. In the potential scenarios described above, the maximum cycle-time values are outside the 2-σ band, representing exceptionally bad performances. That is, the likelihood of a high-priority order taking 7.13 hours (in Scenario #1) is less than 5%. Even though this seems like a small percentage, that is all it may take for a major customer to consider doing business with a competitor.

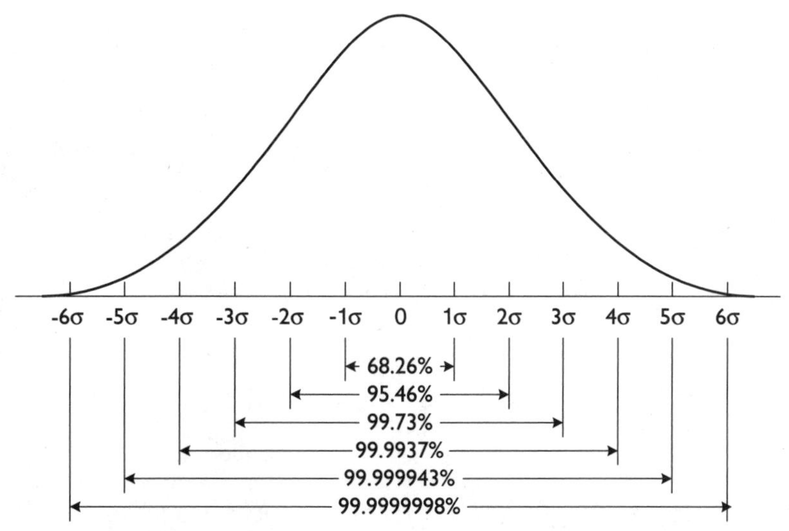

FIGURE 1-10. Standard deviation width of a normal distribution

Of course, when such a rare event as an exceptionally bad performance occurs, management begins asking questions like "How many customers were lost? What additional costs such as overtime were incurred to recover from the situation? How much will be spent in marketing to lure back customers who were lost?" Based upon our research, the following are typical cost ratios:

- Cost to keep a present customer 1x
- Cost to get a new customer 10x
- Cost to win back a lost customer 100x

Your priority should always be on keeping your present customers because you cannot afford to try to win them back.

Although this exercise presents an overly simplistic view of an order fulfillment process, it clearly demonstrates the effect of process dynamics on cycle time, service level, and process costs. It also demonstrates clearly why complex processes cannot be adequately analyzed without the use of process simulation modeling. In other words, as randomness of behavior and interdependencies of resources increase in a process, it becomes impossible to predict performance without process simulation.

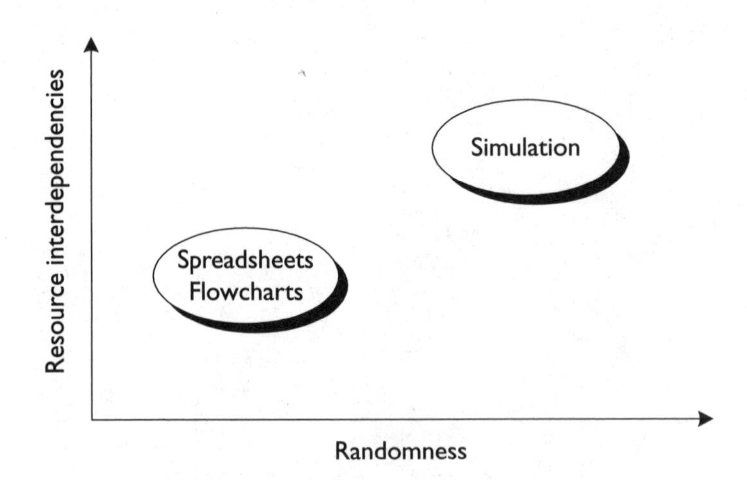

FIGURE 1-11. When do you need process simulation?

A Phased Approach to Successful Implementation

27-28

Successful implementation of process simulation requires a three-phase approach (Figure 1-12):

Phase I—Assessment and Planning
Phase II—Implementation
Phase III—Measurement and Continuous Improvement

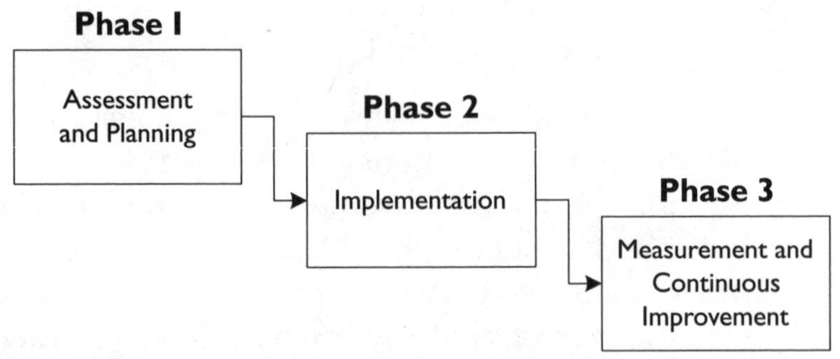

FIGURE 1-12. Phases of a simulation project

A brief overview of these phases is provided in the following sections of this chapter. An in-depth description of these phases is provided in Chapters 2 through 7.

Phase I: Assessment and Planning

The assessment and planning phase involves such activities as selecting a process simulation champion, identifying critical processes, and assigning owners to those processes. For example, *critical processes* may be defined as needs analysis, software selection and acquisition, training, customer support, and modeling services support. Resources with training expertise may be assigned to planning training activities, while resources with modeling expertise may be assigned to planning customer support activities. Phase I consists of nine steps:

1. Identify the process simulation sponsor.
2. Appoint a simulation assessment project manager.
3. Determine modeling needs.
4. Estimate resource requirements.
5. Assess current simulation technologies.
6. Review related tools and methods for synergy.
7. Evaluate and select simulation software.
8. Appoint a simulation champion.
9. Receive training and conduct pilot project

The pilot project includes such activities as data collection and analysis, model building, design of experiments, and output analysis. In this stage, it is often helpful to consult with experts and to partner with suppliers to ensure early buy-in and enthusiasm.

Phase II: Implementation

As the organization enters the implementation phase, simulation is applied to an individual process as defined in the project plan or as assigned based upon business needs. Once a suitable application or project has been confirmed and a project team is assembled, the implementation steps can begin.

Phase II consists of six steps:

1. Plan the simulation project.
2. Collect and analyze data.
3. Build the model.
4. Verify and validate the model.
5. Conduct experiments.
6. Analyze, document, and present results.

Each step need not be completed before moving on to the next step. The implementation steps are iterative, in that activities are refined and sometimes redefined with each iteration.

Phase III: Measurement and Continuous Improvement

There are eight steps in the measurement part of this phase:

1. Review important goals.
2. Review measurement principles.
3. Conduct a brainstorming session.
4. Discuss and debate.
5. Develop a scorecard.
6. Develop a baseline.
7. Establish reporting and feedback procedures.
8. Reward and recognize outstanding performances.

There are seven steps in the continuous improvement part:

1. Assess today's process simulation capability.
2. Establish environmental vision statements.
3. Set performance improvement goals.
4. Define desired behavior and habit patterns.
5. Develop a three-year plan.
6. Develop a rolling 90-day implementation plan.
7. Implement the continuous improvement process.

Benefits of Process Simulation

Significant value of process simulation and analysis comes from the dynamic analysis of costs based on the event-driven simulation. Because the simulation model keeps track of resource interdependencies and captures the random nature of processes, the process performance statistics are far more accurate than results obtained from static analysis.

Focus on Cycle Time

Successful companies understand that minimizing waste can make real process improvement. Non-value-added activities such as queue, hold, and review sometimes waste as much as 95% of the total cycle time. Process simulation makes it easier to focus on cycle time by modeling non-value-added activities and showing their impact on total process time.

Strategic Pricing

Life cycles of product and services are becoming shorter and shorter. The up-front costs of developing, testing, and marketing are not recouped until revenue is generated. Understanding the cost trade-off between life-cycle stages is critical to strategically pricing the products. That is, understanding when the total investment in product development can be recouped is valuable information for strategic pricing. Process simulation allows simulation of the process changes during the life cycle of a product or service for strategic or time-based pricing.

Process Variation

Process simulation allows organizations to study and reduce performance variation by defining the activities that have the greatest impact upon the total process variation. Understanding the impact of variability on customer demand or activity times on cycle time can help managers minimize waste.

Evaluation of Capital Investments

Reengineering business processes requires a trade-off between the benefits and costs of making process improvement changes. Without the trade-off, executives and managers are faced with making large investment decisions based on gut feel. Process simulation provides an analytical tool for accurate evaluation of capital investments.

Evaluation of Organizational Changes

Decisions about centralizing, decentralizing, or even eliminating an organizational function are difficult management decisions that impact customers, employees, and stakeholders of a business. Mergers and acquisitions require corporations to constantly evaluate these alternatives and make quick decisions. Powerful resource and hierarchical process modeling functions of process simulation allow visualization and evaluation of alternatives before making these risky organizational change decisions.

Limitations of Process Simulation

Like any other technique, process simulation has its limitations. These limitations are usually overcome with the application of other techniques, such as project management, scheduling, or optimization.

- Process simulation is a *process* management technique, not a *project* management technique.
- Process simulation is a *planning and analysis* technique, not a *scheduling* technique.
- Process simulation is primarily a technique for measuring process *efficiency*. It does not measure *effectiveness* or *adaptability*.

"Don't simulate life. Live every day to its fullest."
—H.JAMES HARRINGTON

Summary

Process simulation helps organizations predict, compare, or optimize the performance of a process without the cost and risk of disrupting existing operations or building a new process. The interactions of people with processes and technology over time result in a large number of scenarios and outcomes that are impossible to comprehend and evaluate without the help of a computer simulation model. The ability to visualize how a process would behave, to measure its performance, and to try "what ifs" in a computer model makes process simulation an invaluable technique for decision making.

Successful implementation of process simulation involves a three-phase approach:

- Assessment and Planning
- Implementation
- Measurement and Continuous Improvement

"Simulation modeling is the best way to visualize, analyze, and predict process performance."

References

Davenport, Thomas H., *Process Innovation: Reengineering Work Through Information Technology* (Boston: Harvard Business School Press, 1993).

Feigenbaum, Armand V., *Total Quality Control*, revised edition (New York: McGraw-Hill, 1994).

Fishwick, Paul A., "Web-Based Simulation," in *Proceedings of the 1997 Winter Simulation Conference*, eds. Sigrún Andradóttir, Kevin J. Healy, David H. Withers, and Barry L. Nelson (Piscataway, NJ: Institute of Electrical and Electronics Engineers, 1998), pp.100-102.

Hansen, Gregory A., *Automating Business Process Reengineering: Breaking the TQM Barrier* (Englewood Cliffs, NJ: Prentice Hall, 1994).

Harrell, Charles, and Kerim Tumay, *Simulation Made Easy: A Manager's Guide* (Norcross, GA: Industrial Engineering and Management Press, 1995).

Harrington, H. James, and James S. Harrington, *High-Performance Benchmarking: 20 Steps to Success* (New York: McGraw-Hill, 1996).

_____, *Total Improvement Management: The Next Generation in Performance Improvement* (New York: McGraw-Hill, 1995).

"Is 99% Good Enough?," *Training*, March 1991, Supplement.

Ostrenga, Michael P., Terrence R. Ozan, Robert D. McIlhattan, and M.D. Harwood, *The Ernst & Young Guide to Total Cost Management* (New York: John Wiley & Sons, 1992).

Senge, Peter M., *The Fifth Discipline: The Art and Practice of the Learning Organization* (New York: Doubleday, 1990).

Watson, Gregory H., *Business Systems Engineering: Managing Breakthrough Changes for Productivity and Profit* (New York: John Wiley & Sons, 1994).

CHAPTER 2

Phase I: Assessment and Planning

Be sure you know where you are before you define how you're going to get to where you want to go.

Introduction

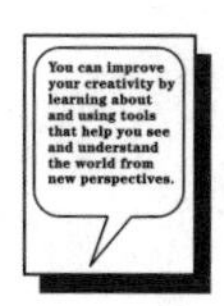

Many simulation efforts are doomed to failure from the outset because of poor assessment and planning. Prior to using simulation on any project, the proper tools, skills, and resources must be in place. Assessment of simulation needs must precede assessment of state-of-the-art simulation technology. Review of related tools and methods can provide synergy as well as integration opportunities. As with any process improvement technique, selecting the right people and training them are critical success factors for process simulation. It must be made a high-priority task in the planning phase. With proper training and a focused pilot project, an organization can greatly increase the likelihood of a successful implementation.

The purpose of this chapter is to provide guidelines for assessing the contribution that process simulation can make to the organization's operating performance and for planning once the decision to adopt process simulation has been made. We discuss the importance of management commitment along with the other steps necessary to successfully incorporate simulation into decision-making processes. We present guidelines for identifying a simulation champion, determining simulation needs, and estimating resource requirements. Then we provide an overview of simulation technology, followed by a discussion of related tools and methods. Software evaluation, training, and pilot project activities are also described.

If you don't know where your island is from where you are, you will never get your dream even when you have defined what you're dreaming of.

Management Commitment

As with any new technology, the most important ingredient for successfully incorporating process simulation into a company's decision-making processes is management commitment. It takes time and patience to begin reaping the benefits of new technology. Without the commitment and support of management, technologies such as process simulation stand only a slim chance of succeeding. This commitment has to be more than just lip service. It must take the form of positive, sustained action by providing the necessary planning, resources, funding, and follow-up to make it happen.

One of the best ways for management to become committed to process simulation is to become informed both about the benefits and the limitations and about the process of implementation. This understanding will help prevent any misguided expectations with regard to the technology. It's impossible and unrealistic to succeed with process simulation if management expects a three-month implementation project to be completed in three weeks. Other failures occur because management does not understand the need to involve qualified people in modeling and analysis. Untrained or unqualified staff members who are assigned to simulation projects typically reduce the chances of success.

Assessment and Planning Activities

Once management has a basic understanding of the technology of process simulation and recognizes the need for adopting it within the business, assessment and planning activities can resume. Figure 2-1 lists the assessment and planning activities.

1. Identify the process simulation sponsor.
2. Assign a simulation assessment project manager.
3. Determine modeling needs.
4. Estimate resource requirements.
5. Assess current simulation technologies.
6. Review related tools and methods for synergy.
7. Evaluate and select simulation software.
8. Appoint a simulation champion.
9. Receive training and conduct pilot project.

FIGURE 2-1. The nine assessment and planning activities

Activity 1: Identify the Process Simulation Sponsor

In every business where process simulation has been successful, there has been at least one *sponsor* involved who had the vision of what process simulation could do and who internally promoted the technology. This should be an individual with good analytical skills whose enthusiasm is contagious—one who not only has the aptitude for understanding the technology and how to apply it, but also is capable of winning over the skeptics. The enthusiasm and vision of the sponsor are crucial to ensuring that the conservative, resistant forces in a company do not hinder or prevent acceptance of the technology. The process simulation sponsor keeps everyone in the business informed of progress with the technology and helps identify opportunities for applying simulation within the company. This individual promotes development of internal training programs and user groups and publicizes success stories both inside and outside the organization. Simulation sponsors like Dr. Hal Scott of Boeing, Dr. Hwa Sung Na of Ford Motor Company, Dr. Charles White of DuPont, and Dr. Terry Ozan of Ernst & Young have institutionalized process simulation in their organizations. They have made significant contributions to successful

Sponsors make things happen.

implementations not only within their own companies but also with their suppliers or customers.

The sponsor is usually a manager who has the ear and respect of top executives. This person will either fund or get upper management to fund an assessment to determine if the organization should use process simulation.

Activity 2: Assign a Simulation Assessment Project Manager

As a result of the sponsor's efforts, a project manager is assigned to form a team to make the process simulation assessment. This team can be made up of process owners who are completing or have completed process redesign, benchmarking, or process reengineering activities. It is also beneficial to have someone from information systems on the team.

The assessment team's mission is to evaluate if the organization should be using the process simulation techniques and to identify typical processes that would benefit if a process simulation model were developed for their present or proposed future-state process. The members of the simulation assessment team will need to be trained in the basic simulation modeling techniques so that they can evaluate potential applications and prepare a business case (return on investment) and preliminary implementation plan. A three-day training program is usually adequate for the simulation assessment team. If the decision is to go ahead with the process simulation project, more training will be required for the individual responsible for its planning and implementation.

Activity 3: Determine Modeling Needs

The simulation assessment team should begin by assessing the organization's needs for using simulation. It should consider the following questions for both the short term and the long term:

?

- How often will simulation be used?
- Which applications will it be used for?
- Which related tools and methods are being used or will be used?
- What are the characteristics of the processes to be modeled?
- Who will be the end users?
- Who will be the customers?

Each of these questions has important implications for the way in which simulation should be adopted.

Frequency of Use

Although process simulation modeling can be applied to all the processes within the organization, there are some processes that benefit more than others. To identify these high-potential processes, look at the following:

- Processes that are already flowcharted.
- Processes that are being reengineered or redesigned.
- Any place where benchmarking is being applied.
- All processes that impact the supply chain.
- All processes to which new or updated software applications will be applied.
- Any process that is having cycle time, scheduling, or cost problems.
- Any process that is being analyzed using activity-based costing.

As the simulation team identifies potential processes, the applications should be reviewed with the process owner(s) so that the owner(s) can estimate how the process would improve if a simulation model were prepared for it.

In some organizations simulation is used no more than once or twice a year, such as when a change in a major process is being considered. In this situation it may be preferable to hire a consultant to do the modeling. If simulation software is purchased, it should be a product that is easy to use, to avoid repeating a steep learning curve with each simulation project. In organizations that plan to use process simulation more frequently, it may be desirable to involve more than one individual in the use of simulation. Likewise, it may be necessary to acquire several software licenses and possibly even a network license, which can usually be obtained at a considerable discount over individual licensing.

Types of Applications

The types of applications will have a significant impact on choosing the software as well as determining the people to be involved in the modeling projects. If the applications are extremely diverse, it may be desirable to have multiple software products and various skill levels in the organization. If the applications can be classified into a dozen or so types, then a single tool with reusable component technology and a dedicated, highly skilled modeler are more appropriate. With object-oriented technology, the modeler can create components that can be saved and reused over time.

Process Characteristics

The characteristics of the process to be modeled should have a significant influence on the software that is selected. For example, processes with high transaction rates and a fairly straightforward flow have quite different characteristics than processes with low transaction rates but multiple and complex flows. Therefore, it is important that the software selected be capable of handling the size, complexity, and issues associated with the processes to be modeled. Chapter 3, “Selecting Process Simulation Software,” will discuss how to match simulation software to a particular set of process characteristics.

Users

The time, skills, and commitment of the simulation users will have a definite impact on the extent to which simulation gets implemented in an organization. Simulation experts can abstract and develop complex models using sophisticated simulation tools. It has been estimated by Robert Shannon of Texas A&M University that it takes over 3,000 hours of training and practice to become a skilled simulator. Since simulation is an experimental tool, its effectiveness lies largely in the modeler's ability to quickly identify the cause-and-effect relationships in the system and conduct appropriate experiments.

The recent emergence of easy-to-use and graphical simulation software intended for use by analysts and managers rather than the simulation specialist has put simulation within the grasp of the ordinary user with little or no simulation experience.

The most effective decision tools are those that can be used by the decision makers. Often, improvements suggest themselves in the very activity of building the model that the decision maker would never discover if someone else were doing the modeling. While an analyst or a manager may not be as capable as a simulation expert, using someone who has an excellent understanding of the process usually outweighs the disadvantages because he or she understands the process better and will acquire skills in conceptualizing process dynamics.

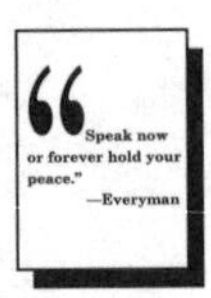

"Companies spend a tremendous amount of time and money evaluating different simulation tools, but seldom spend enough time choosing the person who will use the tools. This can be a big mistake."

— *Matt Rohrer, Vice President of Simulation, AutoSimulations, Inc.*

Identifying the potential users helps determine the level of training. Easier simulation tools have largely eliminated the need for programming skills, but they will always rely on the modeler's ability to abstract the real world in a model, design an experimental procedure, and interpret the final results. Given the fact that process simulation primarily involves gathering data, building models, and experimenting, a modeler will also benefit from having:

- organizational skills
- communication skills
- data-analysis skills
- modeling skills
- familiarity with one or more modeling tools
- a background in statistics and design of experiments
- strong analytical skills
- basic programming skills

As you can see, a skilled simulation modeler is a very special person.

Customers

The customers of process simulation are those for whom the simulation is being performed, whether it be management or the modeler. The ultimate measure of success is whether the customers are satisfied with the results. Therefore, it's important to understand the customers' needs, educate them about the benefits and limitations of process simulation, and set their expectations so that they are realistic.

Like many other technologies, process simulation serves two types of customers: internal and external.

Internally, almost every function in an organization is a potential customer. A chief executive officer (CEO) may need simulation for evaluating the impact of a merger or acquisition on the customer service level. A chief operating officer (COO) may need simulation for workforce planning. A chief information officer (CIO) may need process simulation to evaluate the impact of proposed business process requirements for a client-server enterprise management application. Marketing or sales executives can use process simulation to demonstrate the enterprise's or system's adaptability to fulfill new customer demand.

Externally, the customers for simulation technology may be suppliers or customers. Suppliers may need simulation models to understand the supply chain process and expected service levels. Customers may need simulation to see how capable an organization is of meeting promised delivery dates. Banks or financial investors may need simulation to help convince them to provide financial backing for expansion projects or new facilities.

Both internal and external customers should be involved in understanding the benefits and drawbacks of simulation. Some innovative companies are now using their simulation experts to educate their customers about quality management and continuous improvement. For example, DuPont provides process simulation expertise and modeling support to its suppliers and partners to improve the performance of its entire supply chain. Another example is the SABRE Decision Technologies Division of American Airlines. SABRE uses simulation to assist organizations such as Port Authorities, Immigration and Naturalization Service, Customs Service, and even other transportation companies to minimize the delays and inefficiencies associated with travel.

Activity 4: Estimate Resource Requirements

Investing in a new technology like process simulation requires a financial plan and a budget. In order to receive the anticipated benefits from simulation, the organization must understand that there are both initial costs and ongoing costs related to applying the technology and make sure to budget sufficient money. Costs include software and support costs, training costs, hardware costs, and user wages. A typical breakdown of these costs by percentage is shown in Figure 2-2.

The exact amount to budget depends on the degree of expertise, hardware availability, price, and ease of learning the software. A recommended budget for a single user is shown in Figure 2-3.

We will briefly examine each of these costs.

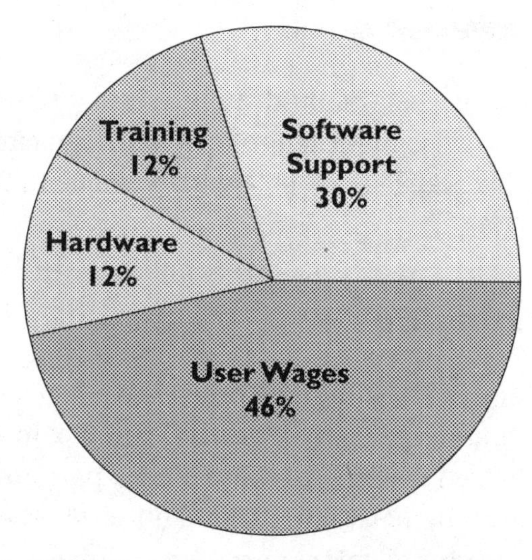

FIGURE 2-2. Typical breakdown of simulation start-up costs

Item	1st Year	Annual Cost After 1st Year
Software Support	\$10 - \$20K	\$1 - \$3K
Hardware	\$3 - \$5K	\$1 - \$2K
Training	\$3 - \$5K	\$3 - \$5K
User Wages	\$50 - \$75K	\$55 - \$75K
Total	\$66 - \$105K	\$55 - \$85K

FIGURE 2-3. Recommended budget for a single simulation user

Software and Support Costs

Of course, software costs vary depending on the product. However, the software costs should be divided into initial costs and ongoing costs. Initial purchase costs can be estimated between \$10,000 and \$20,000 per license and annual maintenance and support costs can be estimated between \$1,000 and \$3,000.

Hardware Costs

Hardware costs should include not only the computer but also the peripherals (monitor, network interface card). These costs can be estimated at $3,000 to $5,000, with a $1,000 to $2,000 annual allowance for upgrades.

Training Costs

Training costs should also be viewed as initial and ongoing costs. Initial training costs cover general training in simulation and analysis and specialized training in the use of a particular product. These are estimated to be between $3,000 and $5,000 per person. Ongoing training costs are for advanced product training and participation in an annual simulation conference. These costs should be estimated between $3,000 and $5,000 annually.

User Wages

Most people who are involved with simulation will agree that the most overlooked cost in a simulation project is time, especially if a company has no previous experience with simulation. We have seen as much as eight to 12 months of engineering time go to waste because of steep learning curves with simulation software or delays in completing the study. Engineering time for conducting a simulation study can easily reach $50,000 to $75,000, without factoring in overhead. This is one reason for seeking an outside consultant's help in conducting the initial project.

Time Requirements

It is difficult to estimate exact timelines for various activities in getting started with simulation. Many factors, such as the organization's experience with simulation, the size of the organization, and the simulation software used, affect the duration of these activities. However, we provide some loose ranges for the most common processes involved in getting started. Figure 2-4 shows tasks and estimated times for preparing to do the first simulation project. Figure 2-5 is a timeline chart for these tasks.

Task	Estimated Time
Assign a person to be responsible for simulation	2 weeks
Become informed on simulation technology	6 weeks
Assess needs and define requirements	4 weeks
Evaluate and select software	12 weeks
Purchase software	8 weeks
Purchase hardware	4 weeks
Become trained in using the simulation software	2 weeks
Conduct a pilot project	4 weeks

FIGURE 2-4. Time estimates for preparing for first simulation project

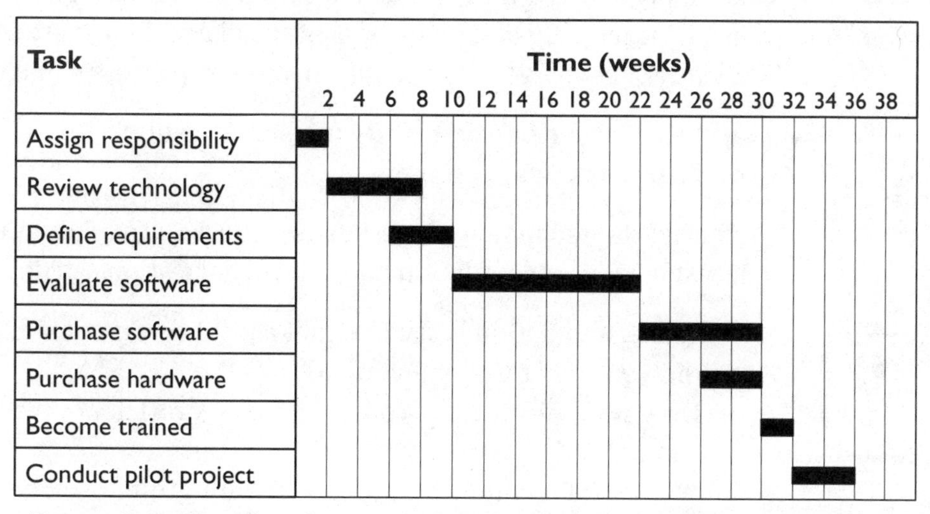

FIGURE 2-5. Timeline for preparing for first simulation project

Note that some of these activities can overlap, such as defining requirements, which can be performed while reviewing technology. The questions to ask that will impact the budget and schedule include the following:

- Use in-house engineers, hardware, software, or outside consultants?
- Use existing hardware or acquire a new computer?
- Use corporate simulation group or use project engineers in this facility?
- Single-user or multi-user modeling environment?

Activity 5: Assess Current Simulation Technologies

With advancements in hardware and software technology, this step is essential to making sure that you are taking advantage of the newest developments. It also helps determine the cost and time that will be required to come up to speed on the latest tools. Old tools should not be used simply because they worked in the past. Organizations will benefit by using the most up-to-date technology available. Below are some of the Web sites for sources of current information on process simulation tools.

- http://lionhrtpub.com/software-surveys.shtm
- http://www.wintersim.org

During the technology assessment process, you should try to find successful users of simulation and ask such questions as the following:

- Which simulation software packages did you consider and why did you select the one you did?
- How long did it take you to achieve proficiency with process simulation?
- What kind of support did the software group provide?
- What kinds of problems did you encounter in using the technology (not the software package)?
- How much was your total investment?
- Have you achieved the benefits you anticipated?
- What kind of expert help did you use in model development and analysis?
- To what do you attribute your success or failure?

Once you have gotten answers to these questions, you should prepare a technology assessment report to summarize your findings. If simulation is not new to your organization, it is a good idea to review the most recent applications of simulation in the firm. This review should address questions such as the following:

- What specific benefits were realized?
- Were the results implemented?
- What related tools and methods were used in conjunction with process simulation?
- Is the person who developed the last simulation model still with the firm?

Process Simulation Methods

Assessing the state of the art in simulation technology will give you a good idea of what to look for in simulation software. It may even revise some of your initial conclusions about the types of applications that you intend to use it for. This section describes the four common types of simulation modeling methods:

- Analytical
- Continuous
- Discrete event
- Object-oriented

Analytical Simulation

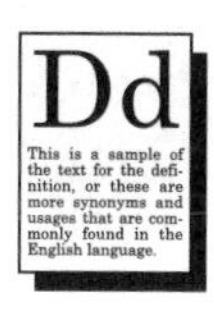

Analytical simulation models—The effects of process dynamics are pictured using queuing theory. The models consist of nodes that are connected with each other in a queuing network. Each node is analyzed as a GI/G/m queue, with an approximation for the mean waiting time based on the first two moments of the arrival and service time distributions.

Analytical simulation addresses several aspects of dynamic complexity, such as multiple customers competing for the same resource and some variability associated with arrival and service processes. Analytical models provide estimates of aggregate steady-state performance with far more accuracy than spreadsheet analysis. Figure 2-6 illustrates the concept of steady-state performance. Advantages of analytical simulation are rapid modeling and fast simulation execution.

Analytical models are not appropriate, however, for modeling non-optimized processes or transient phenomena (recovery from an emergency situation or the start-up condition for a new process). They are also unable to effectively deal with processes where blocking occurs (when limited queue sizes for downstream activities cause resources to stop an activity). Another limitation of analytical simulation is the lack of animation.

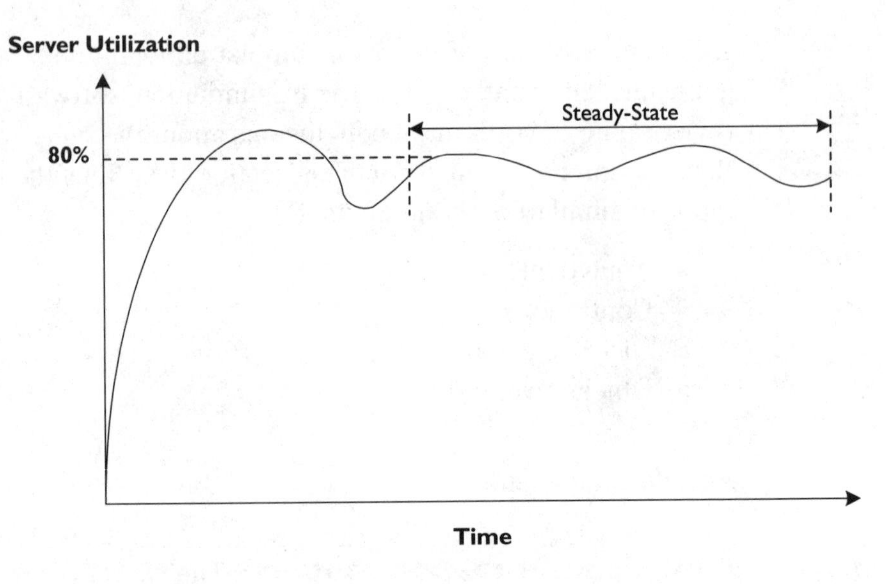

FIGURE 2-6. Steady-state performance

Continuous Simulation

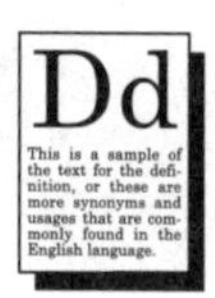

Continuous simulation models—This approach involves the characterization of process behavior using differential equations. The equations calculate the change in a state variable over time. A state variable may be the arrival rate of orders or the processing rate of a resource. In continuous models, the state variables change continuously over time. Differential equations are usually used in small time-step increments to determine the current values of state variables until some threshold is reached that triggers some action.

Continuous simulation can capture process dynamics with differential equations and can contain random behavior. Continuous models are capable of modeling both steady-state and transient phenomena. Animation of continuous models is more meaningful than analytical models because bottlenecks and flows can be visualized with dynamic gauges and dials. They are most appropriate for modeling high-volume or continuous-production processes.

Continuous simulation is not as appropriate for modeling ad hoc, low- to medium-rate production, logistics, or service processes where the behavior of the transactions are more suitable for characterization by discrete-event simulation. Two major challenges for continuous

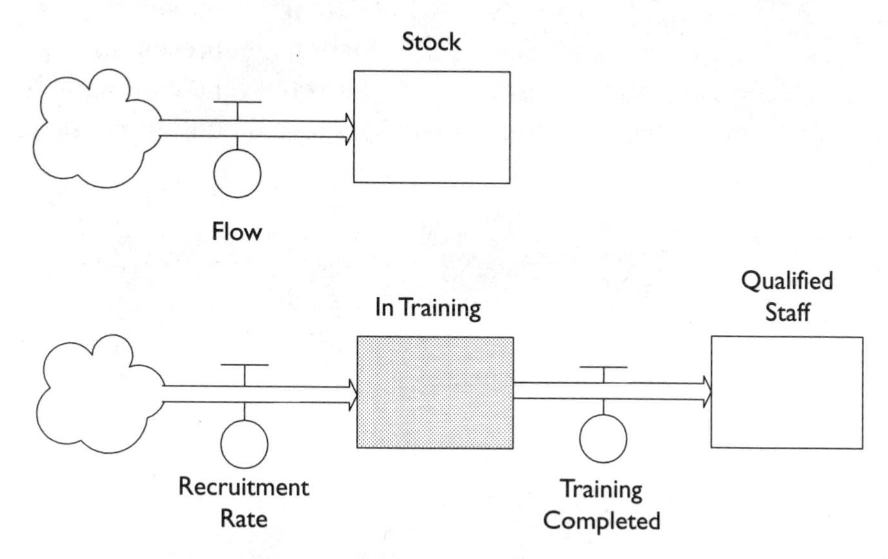

FIGURE 2-7. Continuous simulation

simulation modelers are developing equations and events that describe the time-dependent, random behavior and evaluating the equations to obtain results.

Discrete-Event Simulation

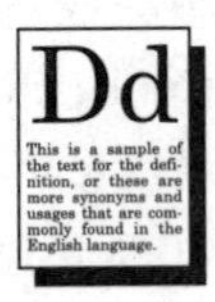

Discrete-event simulation—In this type of simulation, the state of the model changes only at discrete (possibly random set of points) event times. Transactions (or entities) in discrete-event simulation flow from one point to another point (in time) while competing with each other for the use of scarce resources.

Discrete-event simulation allows definition of random behavior with probability distributions and expressions. Discrete-event models produce output that is random and therefore is only an estimate of the true behavior of the model. Multiple replications must be made and the composite average results must be obtained to get an estimate of the expected performance measures.

In a discrete-event process simulation, entities representing products or services are induced into the model, they compete for resources that perform activities, and they are disposed of. Therefore, discrete-event simulation is the most natural simulation technique for process modeling and analysis. Animation of discrete-event models can be very impressive and useful for validation and presentation purposes.

One of the drawbacks of discrete-event simulation is that it usually takes longer to run than analytical and continuous simulation models.

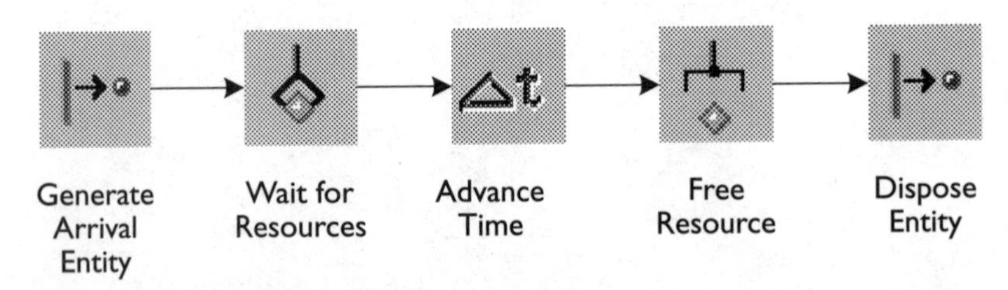

FIGURE 2-8. Discrete-event simulation (Note: The definition for each of these activity objects can be found in Appendix A.)

Another challenge with discrete-event simulation is the skills required to create valid models.

Object-Oriented Simulation

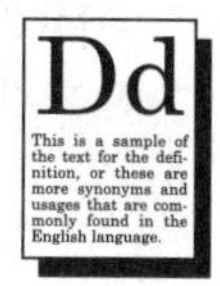

Object-oriented simulation—This type of modeling views processes, products, services, and resources as objects. Object-oriented modeling can be applied to analytical, continuous, or discrete-event simulation. The purpose of object-oriented modeling and simulation is to enhance the modeler's ability to create complex models, to maximize the life cycle of the model, and to allow for integration with other models. The most visible aspects of object-oriented simulation are the graphical user interface and the process flow animation.

Objects consist of information (attributes) and procedures (methods). Both are combined to create an "instance" of that object. For example, an object called "customer" may have age, credit worthiness, and years of education as attributes. In a mortgage-processing process, loan applications are routed through the process based on certain rules. Using an object-oriented model, you can define unique information about an individual customer and the procedures applied to his loan application.

The ability to define a process model in terms of objects offers real productivity gains for business management. Rather than re-creating process models from scratch, you can start with templates and reuse them. This radically reduces development time. Templates may include reference models or benchmarked process models that can be used to compare the performance of your own process. For example, a template that includes the process simulation of centralized, decentralized, and hybrid purchasing processes may save you lots of development time, if you are about to redesign your purchasing process.

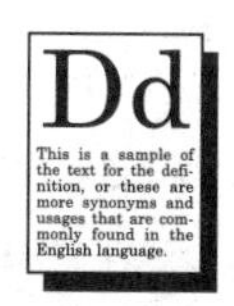

Object-oriented—A system that combines information and procedures in a single object.

Instance—A unique individual member of a product, an activity, or a resource class. For example, if the product class vehicle contains cars, trucks, and vans, an instance of the class cars would be a car with a unique serial number.

Polymorphism—Characteristic of a group of objects that share common ancestry. They can also share a method, with each method implemented differently.

Activity 6: View Related Tools and Methods for Synergy

Process simulation is closely related to a number of tools and methods, such as process mapping, activity-based costing, workflow automation, object-oriented design and analysis, and design of experiments. It is essential to understand the interactions among process simulation and these related technologies in order to completely appreciate the value of process simulation.

A significant development in the past few years is the integration of related tools and methods with process simulation products. For example, flowcharting, activity-based costing, input and output data analysis software, and design of experiments are some of the tools that are now integrated with process simulation software. Although some tools include such functions, it is important to obtain the latest versions of supporting software products and to make sure that they are compatible with the selected process simulation software. This section provides an overview of the tools and methods related to process simulation and how they can be used in conjunction with simulation.

Process Mapping

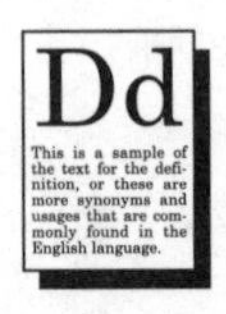

Process mapping—Understanding what a business does and how it does it, which requires documenting inputs, processes, outputs, and resources. Process mapping combines the simplicity of flowcharting with the documentation features of word processing.

Typically, executives and managers of industrial and service enterprises have managed their businesses by executive summaries and organization charts without understanding the processes and their performance. However, executives and managers who are successful now are the ones who understand their business processes in detail. Process mapping includes several pieces missing from the organization chart: the customers, the products, and the workflow. Process mapping enables you to see how work actually gets done, which is through processes that cut across functional boundaries. The definition of boundaries allows managers to define customer-supplier relationships through which products and services are produced.

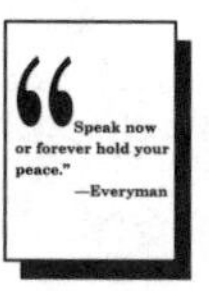

In his book *Process Innovation*, Tom Davenport states, "Process modeling tools are useful for documenting a common understanding of current processes. But a tool that has simulation capabilities can play more than the role of artist and publisher. It can take account of current operational variables in designing and running a model that illustrates the operation as well as the structure of a target process."

ISO 9000

ISO 9000 is a quality management system created by the International Organization for Standardization (ISO) to establish an international standard for ensuring process quality by providing third-party registration for supplier certification schemes. According to an article in *ISO 9000 News* (June 1998), surveys show that companies seeking ISO or QS-9000 certification spend only 20% of their time designing and up to 80% of their time writing quality system documentation. And once these quality manuals are completed, they are seldom used in daily management of the business, due to the sheer volume and impracticality of text-based documentation.

Gladwin and Harrell note that flowchart-based simulation can help companies seeking ISO 9000 certification in three ways:

1. The simple act of using flowcharts to document quality processes saves time over the traditional method of text-based documentation. It is not uncommon to be able to shrink a 10-page written procedure into a two- or three-page flowchart.
2. The predefined flowcharts eliminate the need to "reinvent the wheel," since most companies perform many of the quality processes in a similar way. The predefined charts are simply modified to match the specific ways in which a company does business.
3. The simulation allows the processes to be analyzed for inefficiencies and reengineered for increased performance.

Activity-Based Costing

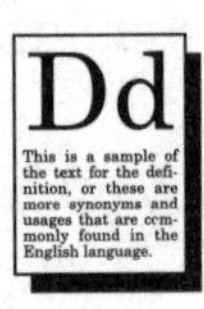

Activity-Based Costing (ABC)—A technique for accumulating cost for a given cost object (i.e., product, service, customer) that represents the total and true economic resources required or consumed by the object.

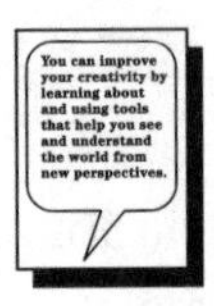

Activity-based costing occurs in two phases. First, cost data are reorganized into activity cost pools. In other words, costs of significant activities are determined. This first phase is sometimes called *activity-based process costing*. Then, the amounts in the cost pools are assigned to products, services, or other cost objects. The second phase is called *activity-based object costing*.

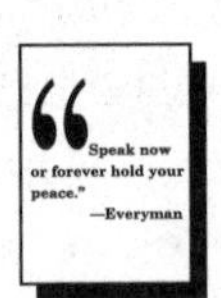

The goal of ABC is to model the causal relationships among resources, activities, and entities in assigning overhead costs. "The fundamental belief behind this costing approach is that cost is caused and that causes of cost can be managed. The closer you can come to relating the costs to their causes, the more helpful your accounting information will be in guiding the management decisions of your business" (Ostrenga et al., *The Ernst & Young Guide to Total Cost Management*).

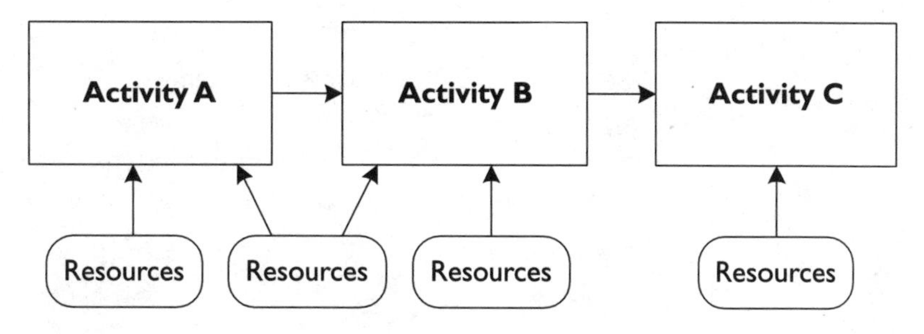

FIGURE 2-9. Activity-based costing

Enterprises use resources to conduct activities. Resources perform activities to benefit products and services. The key to understanding cost dynamics in any enterprise is modeling the relationship between activities and their causes and the relationship between activities and costs. If cost dynamics are not modeled (which is usually the case with traditional management accounting information systems), the performance information provided is incomplete or misleading. Like ABC, process simulation embodies the concept that a business is a series of interrelated processes, and that these processes consist of activities that convert inputs into outputs. The building blocks of process simulation—namely processes, resources, and entities (products or services)—provide a nice bridge between process mapping, discrete-event simulation, and ABC.

Workflow Automation

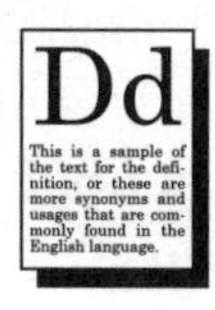

Workflow automation—A tool set for the proactive analysis, compression, and automation of information-based tasks and activities (Tom Koulopoulos, *The Workflow Imperative*).

Workflow applies many of the same concepts and benefits of factory automation and industrial engineering to the process of work management in an office environment. The basic premise is that an office environment is an information factory or, more specifically, a process factory.

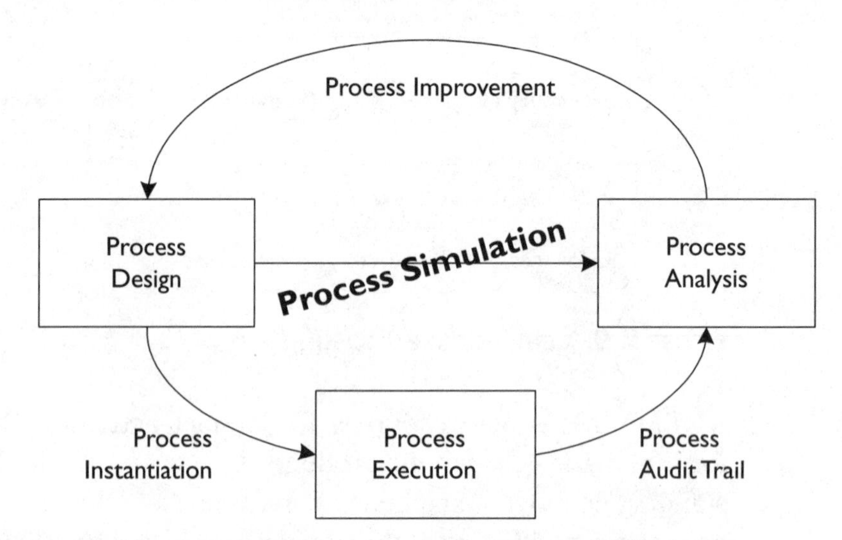

FIGURE 2-10. Process design, execution, and analysis cycle

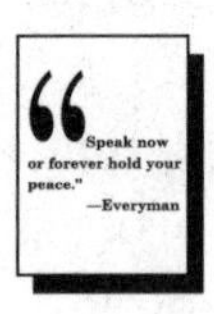

Koulopoulos states, "Workflow simulation tools allow designers to test workflow processes and to identify problems with the process before the workflow application is implemented." This can save substantial time and money in designing an efficient workflow. Once the process is automated and executed in real time, data collected from the workflow management system can be used as input into the simulation.

Object-Oriented Design and Analysis

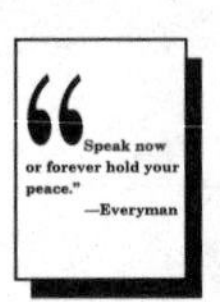

"When we analyze systems, we create models of the application area that interest us. We can manipulate the model and this helps us to invent systems or redesign business areas. Enterprise modeling is important in planning enterprise automation. With object-oriented analysis, we model the world in terms of object types and what happens to these objects" (Martin and Odell, 1992, p. 68). The genesis of object-oriented technology dates back to the early 1960s. It rose from the need to simulate a variety of phenomena, such as nerve networks, communication systems, traffic flow, production systems, administrative systems, and even social systems.

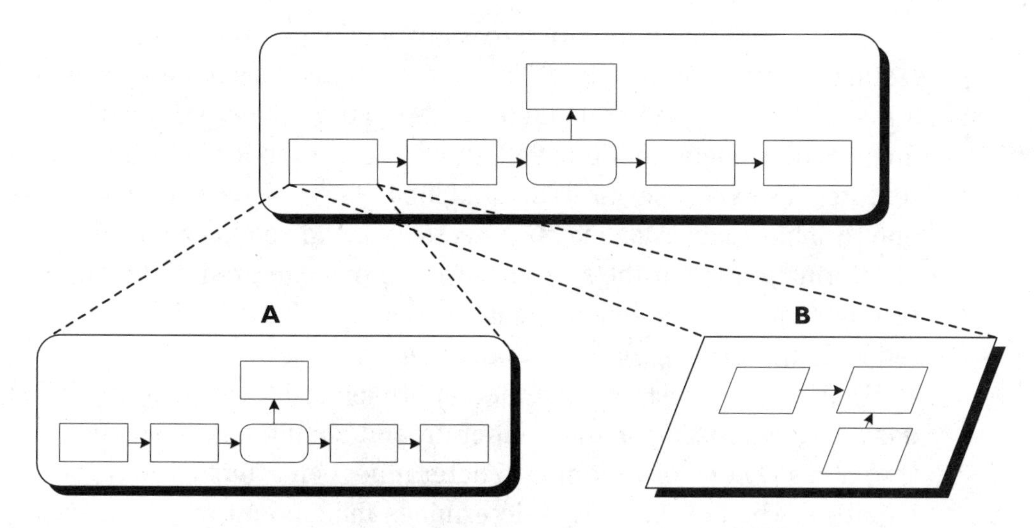

FIGURE 2-11. Object-oriented design and analysis

Figure 2-11 shows a typical object-oriented design and analysis model that has one delay activity laid out to show the current design (A) and the new design (B). (Standard rectangles represent delay activities. Rounded rectangles represent decision activities.)

Design of Experiments

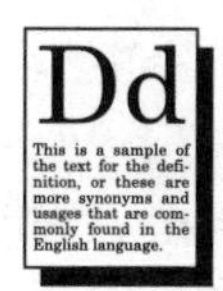

Design of experiments (DOE)—A set of statistical methods for yielding the most information with the fewest possible number of experiments. An experimental design systematically and simultaneously changes input values to study the effects on the model's performance.

A simulation model is built from components that are well understood. The interactions among all of these components, however, are complex and not so easily understood. DOE is based on the assumption that variables interact in synergistic or antagonistic ways. DOE reveals how these variables combine to influence the performance of a system.

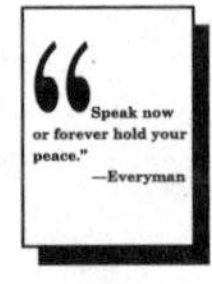

"The traditional alternative to statistical experimentation involves testing one variable at a time. This approach involves holding constant all variables except the one under investigation. The traditional experiment is dependent not upon statistical principles but on the individual researcher's expertise, intuition, and luck. Since each run only looks at one variable, many runs may be necessary to gain a reasonable amount of information about the system. Also, no one can predict the number of runs that will be needed" (Quality Management & Technology Center, DuPont, *Strategy of Experimentation*).

DOE, by contrast, is a planned approach to experimentation. The design is organized for the deliberate and simultaneous changing of the values of control variables to determine their effect upon response variables. The design chosen determines the amount of experimentation that will be necessary to achieve the experimenter's objective. The investigator thus knows in advance how much effort and time an experiment will require. Because the design is based on statistical principles, the greatest amount of information will be extracted from the fewest number of simulation runs. As a result, both time and resource costs can be anticipated, controlled, and reduced.

Activity 7: Evaluate and Select Simulation Software

Most companies evaluate software without having well-established criteria. Much time is wasted examining software products with little or no guidelines on what to purchase except that it should generally be easy to use, flexible, and inexpensive. As a consequence, many organizations get stuck with a product that falls short in meeting their needs. Since software selection is such an important step in getting started, we devote all of Chapter 3 to this topic.

Activity 8: Appoint a Simulation Champion

The process simulation expertise in an organization need not reside in a single individual. It is often wise to involve more than one individual, if for no other reason than to provide a backup in case the principal specialist becomes unavailable. In bringing simulation technology into an organization and continually improving its use, the simulation champion is responsible for identifying user needs, continually evaluating software and new developments in technology, and making sure that the proper processes and resources are in place for successful implementation. On an ongoing basis, the champion acts as an advisor to individuals in the organization who may require modeling assistance.

Although major corporations have developed one or more simulation modeling groups, most businesses do not have the luxury of dedicating a full-time staff to process simulation. For organizations with few or no experienced simulation users, it may even be best to use consultants, at least initially. There are many qualified experts in the field who can provide not only modeling and analysis services, but also training services. A consultant with years of simulation expertise will likely charge high fees. However, the benefits of meeting project deadlines and educating your organization while getting your project done will more than pay for the consultant's fees.

In recent years, a growing number of highly skilled professionals have become available for process simulation consulting. These professionals provide corporations with assistance in all phases of a process simulation implementation from assessment and planning to auditing and continuous improvement. If an organization retains such a consultant, it must ensure that proper technology and knowledge transfer activities take place regularly, in order to protect its assets. After all, the knowledge of the processes for successful implementation is a corporate asset.

A tendency among some managers is to appoint a process simulation champion without providing that person with the needed resources in time and budget for investigating and promoting the technology. These managers give "growing" the technology a low priority;

Be sure to get the right simulation champion.

the champion must work it into an already busy schedule. With this approach, the process of implementing simulation technology could drag on indefinitely.

Another poor practice is to assign personnel who are really not the best suited for the job, simply because the best people are too busy. Some businesses attempt to use summer interns or co-op students to implement the technology. Although this approach seems cost-effective, it rarely provides the commitment and consistency necessary to succeed. When a co-op student, who took a simulation course in college, is given a process simulation product and is expected to try it out on a simulation study of the whole enterprise in two months, it is inviting failure. This is especially true if the student is not familiar with the day-to-day operations of the company or has not gotten formal training in using that simulation package.

Activity 9: Receive Training and Conduct Pilot Project

Training for process improvement methods and tools is often equated with software training. Unfortunately, this is a major mistake. There is a clear distinction between method and tool training, especially for process simulation. Receiving tool training without proper knowledge in simulation modeling and analysis can lead to costly mistakes. In fact, this is one of the primary causes of failures with simulation.

At least a one- to two-day formal training in simulation methodology is an absolute prerequisite to receiving training in a particular software tool. Such formal training must cover such topics as modeling, validation and verification techniques, statistical analysis of input and output data, and design of experiments. Only with a clear understanding of these concepts can a person be effective with process simulation. Although instructors of tool training courses are knowledgeable about these concepts, they focus on teaching how to use the tool. For example, you may learn how to run multiple replications of a simulation in a tool training, but the instructor will assume that you know how many replications to run.

Tool training is usually offered by the software vendor or an authorized representative. Unless the training is a customized training session, the training is designed to cover all of the functions of a particular tool. Although this general training approach is convenient for software vendors, it may not be the most effective training for your needs. The ideal tool training provides exercises and hands-on sessions relevant to your process. A useful tip on training is to prepare the description of your pilot project and take it to the training course. If the instructor becomes familiar with your pilot project early on in the training, he or she will be more sensitive to your questions. Consequently, you will get much more out of the tool training.

The purpose of a pilot project is to go through an actual exercise in process simulation. For this project, your application needs to be small yet realistic (e.g., a process with at least a dozen activities and least as many resources and products). A common mistake made at this stage is to put too much emphasis on building a model. The emphasis at this point should be to go through all the typical activities in simulation deployment.

The pilot project should be completed within two to three weeks and the findings should be summarized. You should track the time and resources consumed during the pilot study so that you can provide good time and budget estimates for the actual simulation study.

Conducting a pilot project is very much like a warm-up exercise. It should be treated as a learning experience as well as a means of building confidence and momentum.

Summary

Proper assessment and planning tasks are very critical in deploying process simulation. The assessment phase begins with the confirmation of management. This is followed by appointing a sponsor whose primary responsibilities are to create enthusiasm, promote the technology, and manage expectations. Identifying simulation needs and resource requirements is often overlooked in software evaluation and pilot project tasks. However, without clearly defined needs and proper resource allocation, process simulation can easily become an exercise in futility.

Developments in hardware and software technologies naturally influence improvements in simulation technology. For example, object-oriented modeling technology and Web technology are making a significant impact on simulation as this book is written. So, it is recommended that you assess the latest developments prior to deployment.

It is also a good idea to assess the related methods and tools so that benefits of process simulation can be enhanced by integrating similar applications, sharing data, etc. Although most organizations underestimate the value of training, training in both simulation methodology and simulation software is absolutely necessary in the planning phase.

"Remember the five P's: Proper Planning Prevents Poor Performance."

References

Brooks, Frederick P., Jr., *The Mythical Man-Month* (Reading, MA: Addison-Wesley, 1975).

Davenport, Thomas H., *Process Innovation: Reengineering Work Through Information Technology* (Boston: Harvard Business School Press, 1993).

Gladwin, Bruce, and Charles Harrell, "Introduction to ProcessModel and ProcessModel 9000," *Proceedings of the 1997 Winter Simulation Conference*, eds. Sigrún Andradóttir, Kevin J. Healy, David H. Withers, and Barry L. Nelson (Piscataway, NJ: Institute of Electrical and Electronics Engineers, 1998), pp. 594-600.

Koulopoulos, Thomas M., *The Workflow Imperative: Building Real World Business Solutions* (New York: Van Nostrand Reinhold, 1995).

Mabrouk, Khaled, "Mentorship: A Stepping Stone to Simulation Success," *Industrial Engineering*, February 1994, pp. 41-43.

Martin, James, and James J. Odell, *Object-Oriented Design and Analysis* (Englewood Cliffs, NJ: Prentice Hall, 1992).

Mott, Jack, and Kerim Tumay, "Developing a Strategy for Justifying Simulation," *IE Magazine*, July 1992.

Norman, Van B., "20 Questions for Your Simulation Consultant," *Industrial Engineering*, May 1993, pp. 39-40.

Ostrenga, Michael P., Terrence R. Ozan, Robert D. McIlhattan, and M.D. Harwood, *The Ernst & Young Guide to Total Cost Management* (New York: John Wiley & Sons, 1992).

Quality Management & Technology Center, DuPont Engineering Technology, *Strategy of Experimentation—Planning and Analyzing Efficient Experiments* (Wilmington, DE: DuPont Engineering Technology, 1988).

Tumay, Kerim, "Business Process Simulation," *Proceedings of the 1996 Winter Simulation Conference*, ed. John M. Charnes, Douglas J. Morrice, Daniel T. Brunner, and James J. Swain (Piscataway, NJ: Institute of Electrical and Electronics Engineers, 1997), pp. 93-98.

CHAPTER 3

Selecting Process Simulation Software

Understand what you need, then find someone who wants to do it.

Introduction

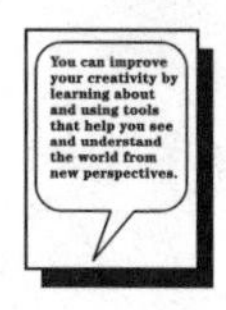

This chapter covers the activities of Phase I, Activity 7—Evaluate and Select Simulation Software. We have dedicated an entire chapter to this one step because it is so important and so critical to the success of the entire simulation project.

Often, software products are evaluated on only two or three criteria, such as price, ease of use, or impressive demonstration. As a result, it's easy for an organization to end up owning software that does not meet its needs or for a large organization to own more than one simulation tool. Diverse organizations with various types of processes and user requirements prefer a best-of-breed approach with simulation software.

This chapter focuses on evaluating process simulation tools and vendors. First, software and vendor evaluation criteria are described. Then, a weighted-scoring selection method is applied to the evaluation criteria.

Software Evaluation Criteria

The Software Engineering Institute (SEI) is a federally funded research and development center sponsored by the U.S. Department of Defense and operated by Carnegie Mellon University. One of SEI's primary functions is to perform technology evaluations. The SEI provides guidelines for evaluating software and up-to-date information about current software engineering best practices and technology trends (http://www.sei.cmu.edu). Software evaluations can be either *product*-oriented or *process*-oriented:

1. *Product*-oriented is evaluating a set of products with similar functionality (e.g., analytical simulation tools or discrete-event simulation tools).
2. *Process*-oriented is evaluating a new technology to assess the impact on existing practices (e.g., object-oriented simulation tools or Web-based simulation tools).

SEI's Capability Maturity Model (CMM) and ISO 9000 standards provide excellent guidelines for software evaluation techniques and criteria. For example, the ISO 9126 standard proposes the following criteria for evaluating software:

- Functionality
- Usability
- Reliability
- Efficiency
- Maintainability
- Portability

Although these criteria are common for all software products, it is difficult to design a single set of criteria that can be used for evaluating all types of software products. For process simulation software, it is especially important to develop additional criteria, such as scalability, vendor services, and cost of ownership. Below is a brief overview of a complete set of criteria that we developed for evaluating process simulation tools.

- Functionality: Does the tool exhibit required functions to satisfy particular needs?
- Usability: How much effort is needed to learn and use the software?
- Reliability: How capable is the software product in maintaining its level of performance?
- Maintainability: How much effort is needed to secure, transfer, interface, and upgrade?
- Scalability: Does the tool come in multiple levels of functionality that are compatible?
- Vendor quality: Does the vendor have a proven track record and established user base?
- Vendor services: What training, technical support, and consulting services are provided?
- Cost of ownership: What are the total costs (licensing, maintenance, training, run times, etc.) associated with the use of the tool over a three-year period?

These criteria are described in detail in the upcoming sections. Appendix B provides a complete checklist of these software evaluation criteria.

Functionality

Functionality of a process simulation tool can be evaluated in terms of five functions:

1. Process mapping
2. Modeling
3. Simulation and animation
4. Analysis
5. Input and output

1. Process Mapping Functions

A process model is created graphically by dragging and dropping shapes from a palette onto a layout space and linking them with connectors to represent workflow. These shapes usually have dialogs with predefined fields such as activity name, duration, and cost. The shapes may also have predefined alternatives representing different types of behavior. For example, a START shape may have different fields than a DELAY shape, a BRANCH shape, or an END shape. To define a process, it's desirable to be able to use alternative icons for a model object, to color-code connectors, to hide certain objects, to label the connectors, etc.

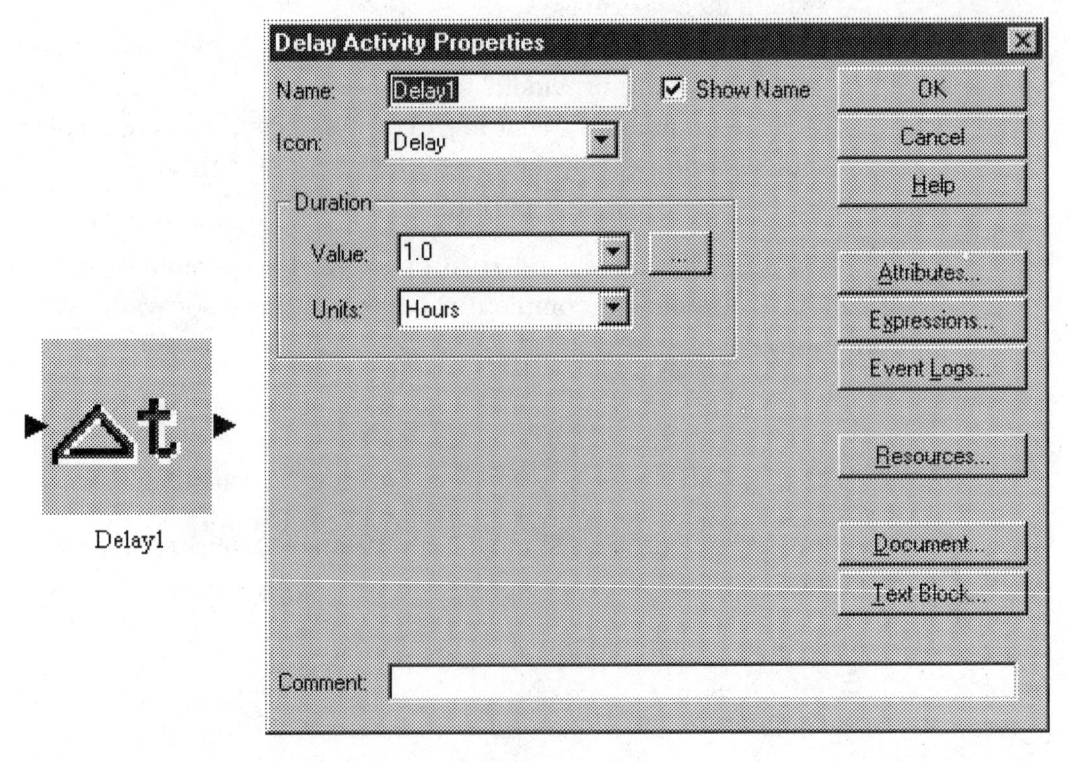

FIGURE 3-1. An activity dialog

Perhaps the most important requirement for process definition is hierarchical decomposition. For example, a production process may consist of receiving, fabrication, assembly, test, and shipping activities. The top view of the production process would simply show a single object, while the detailed view would show the hierarchical decomposition of the production process in terms of its activities. A good process modeling tool must support both a top-down and a bottom-up modeling approach. It is also desirable to create alternative representations of a process and encapsulate those alternative behaviors in a process template. These functions are best supported in object-oriented simulation tools. For example, a modeler defines a purchasing process template that contains centralized, decentralized, and hybrid representations of the purchasing process. When users of that template wish to model their purchasing application, they can select the representation that best fits their process requirements.

In terms of defining the process, some process modeling tools are methodology-specific (e.g., systems dynamics, IDEF, Rummler-Brache) when it comes to defining the process. iThink from High Performance Systems, Inc., and Powersim from Powersim Corporation are based on systems dynamics. IDEF (Integrated DEFinition methodologies) provides a framework for developing functional, information, and process flow models. IDEF was developed by the U.S. Air Force in the late 1970s and became a popular methodology within the Department of Defense. Rummler-Brache is a methodology that promotes functionally deployed process modeling.

Methodology-specific tools offer unique benefits, such as standard process documentation throughout an enterprise. On the other hand, the same methodologies confine the user to a specific world view that is not beneficial for simulation analysis. For example, it may be suitable to use IDEF methodology for graphically defining a transaction-based process, but that methodology imposes rigid rules for describing a supply chain process in which the graphical layout looks more like a network of nodes connected with links.

Other process simulation tools are methodology-independent. These tools provide a set of basic shapes representing model objects.

For example, SIMPROCESS from CACI Products Company, Work-Draw from Edge Software, Inc., and ProcessModel from ProcessModel Corporation are methodology-independent. Users can select any shape to represent any type of object. Users can also define the process flow without any restrictions on the graphical layout. These tools are commonly used because they offer the flexibility to customize diagrams. A drawback of this approach is potential communication problems throughout an enterprise if many symbols and flow conventions are adapted.

The ideal process definition capability is one that is methodology-independent yet adaptable. This offers the user the best of both worlds—a flexible approach that allows importing or customization of a specific methodology.

A graphical definition of the process model is very useful in the early going and for communication purposes after the model is complete. However, an alternative, tabular representation of the model is much more efficient for browsing or editing a complex model with multiple layers of hierarchy and many activities and resources. Process Charter (now Scitor Process) from Scitor Corporation provides a nice tabular user interface for editing large models.

2. Modeling Functions

A process simulation tool must have a set of robust modeling functions and flexibility for representing various types of behaviors in a model. These functions enable the modeler to schedule entities or resources; to model activities such as branching, splitting, and joining; to assign resources to activities; and to model complex rules and routing. If a process simulation tool has a rich set of constructs for defining commonly encountered situations, the time and effort involved in model building can be greatly reduced.

Scheduling refers to the generation of multiple transactions or entities. A powerful process simulation tool should offer built-in templates for periodic, cyclical, and calendar-based schedules. Some tools allow the ability to import scheduling information from external files.

Others provide a user-friendly interface to define schedules. Ideally, a tool should support both functions. Initially, a user may define schedules using the graphical interface. Once the model is validated for a set of schedules, it's more convenient to update schedules in a spreadsheet or database and import them into the model.

One of the greatest strengths of process simulation over other process analysis methods is its ability to realistically represent the resource constraints in a model. Resource modeling involves the definition and allocation of resources to activities. When modeling a resource, a user first defines the attributes of a resource such as cost, availability, and down times. Then, resources are assigned to activities where they will be used during the simulation. A process simulation tool should provide built-in functions for defining resource availability schedule as well as down-time schedules or random interruptions. A tool should provide assignment of multiple units of a resource to an activity. For example, an assembly activity may require two or three workers. Another desirable resource assignment capability is the assignment of multiple types of resources to an activity. For example, a review process may involve one unit each of three resources.

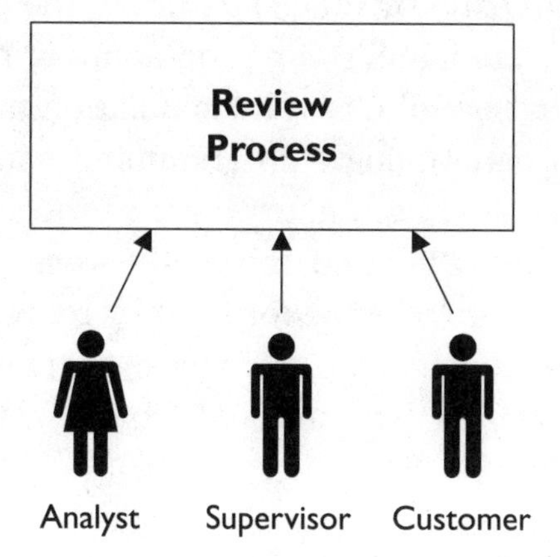

FIGURE 3-2. A review process with three resources

Another critical resource modeling capability is costing. Resources accrue various types of costs, such as usage costs, setup costs, or fixed costs. A powerful process simulation tool should enable definition of various cost elements and keep track of these costs as products and services flow through the activities in the process model.

Activity modeling constructs contain the functionality for modeling the unique behavior of business processes. For example, an activity that receives a customer inquiry as input and produces a qualified buyer has different behavior than an activity that receives a purchase order as input and produces three copies of that order, each copy destined to a different activity. A powerful process simulation tool includes a set of flexible activity modeling functions that can be used in defining the dynamic behavior of a business process.

In many cases, the user will want to consider the distribution of key measurements at each activity (e.g., cost or cycle time). The use of averages does not address the process variation that is often a major problem. Some process simulation tools provide a limited set of basic activity modeling functions, while process simulation products, especially the ones that are domain-specific, provide built-in functions for quickly modeling certain types of processes. However, sometimes the complexity or special nature of the processes being modeled may require extendability or programming capability. Banks and Gibson argue that building a valid simulation model of real systems requires some programming: "Programming simply refers to the process of designing, coding, and testing the procedures necessary to imitate real system activities and logic—the real behavior of the system. This process could take the form of any representation that a computer can interpret and execute, such as an 'if-then-else' type ordered logic written by the user, or selected from a list—even using point-and-click operations."

"Speak now or forever hold your peace." —Everyman

Extendability should be evaluated based on four aspects of the simulation tool.

1. *User-defined attributes.* The software should provide the capability to define user attributes or variables for a model object. For example, the modeler should be able to define order type as

an attribute of an order, learning curve as an attribute of an activity, or in-process inventory as an attribute of the model.

2. *User-defined expressions.* The software should provide the same basic capabilities of any high-level programming language, such as Visual Basic or C++. This includes if-then logic, nested logic, looping (e.g., while-do statements), and mathematical and Boolean operators that can be combined in any way desired.
3. *Access to system state variables.* The software should be able to get or set (when appropriate) the current state or statistical values being gathered by the simulation software during the simulation. For example, the number of entities in a particular queue is a system variable that a modeler may use for modeling a balking situation in a call center process model, when a caller comes into the system, then decides not to wait. The model needs to have access to that state variable and write a simple expression for correct modeling of the behavior.
4. *Access to system methods.* The software should provide access to methods or commands that provide flexibility for modeling complex behaviors, reading data from and writing to external files, creating traces, etc.

Another very important question to ask regarding extendability is "Where and how can these flexible language elements be used?" The software should allow use or activation of these elements wherever needed. A user should be able to trigger a customized expression by any event or at any time during the simulation.

3. Simulation and Animation Functions

One of the greatest advantages of building a process model is that it provides a visual approach to defining a process, its workflow, and its resources. This approach is easy and intuitive and, when the model is finished, the graphical layout serves as the background animation.

Simulation models help you see what might happen.

The graphical representation of a model can be defined in terms of five components:

1. Static background objects
2. Static model objects
3. Dynamic model objects
4. Dynamically updated status
5. Dynamically updated statistical information

Static background objects include maps, layouts, and background text. Static model objects include process icons, connectors, and static resource icons. Since static background and static model objects do not possess motion characteristics, they are easily depicted. On the other hand, animation and status-updating requirements for dynami-

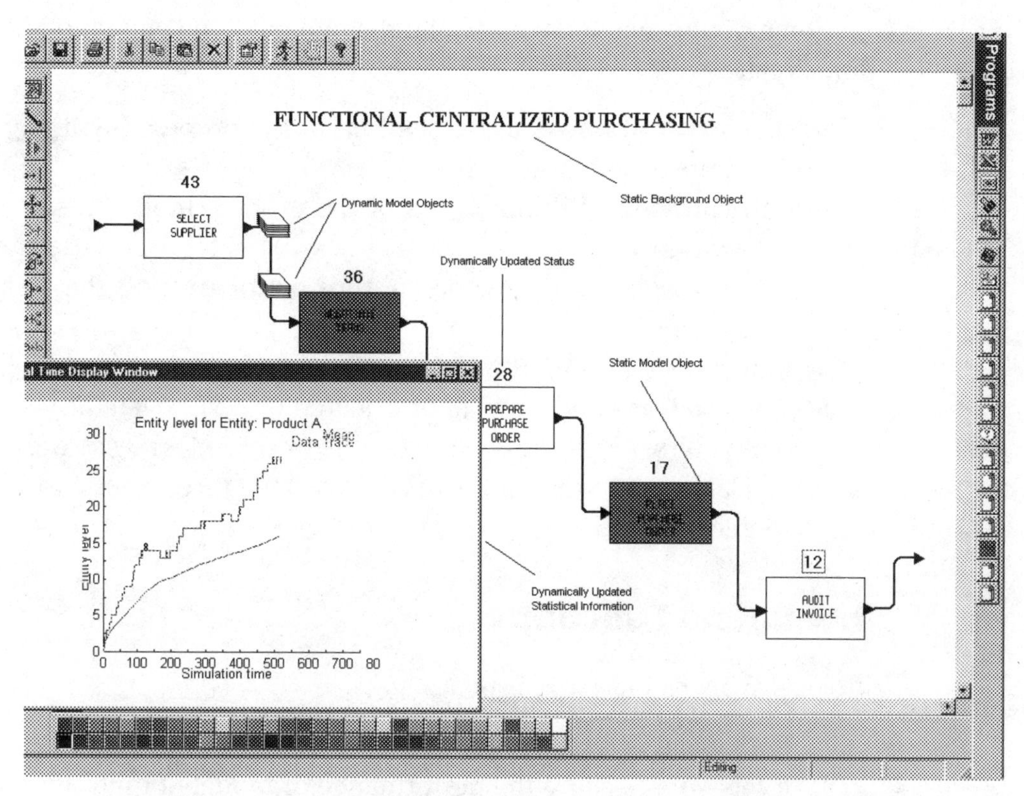

FIGURE 3-3. Five components of process animation

cally changing objects present a more difficult challenge. Dynamic objects include entities (documents, customers, etc.) and resources (transportation equipment, people, etc.). Dynamically updated objects include counters, gauges, plots, etc.

Animation can range from simple animated flow diagrams to detailed animation. Spending time developing detailed graphics should always be weighed against the need to spend time performing a complete simulation study. An impressive graphical representation can be justified for certain presentations, as long as the overall objectives of a simulation study are kept in perspective. One should question the benefits of being able to maintain symmetry along a curving link while animating the movement of a transportation resource if it provides no additional useful information.

Some of the questions to ask about simulation and animation functionality are:

- Can you drill down and ascend up in the process hierarchy as the simulation is running?
- Can you view multiple layers of the process model in side-by-side windows?
- Can you speed up, slow down, turn on, or turn off the animation?
- Can you single-step through the simulation?
- Can you trace and view all or selected types of events?
- Can you display (with colored icons or text messages) warning or alarm conditions for situations where rare events are presented?

4. Analysis Functions

Process analysis has two purposes:

1. It allows you to collect and analyze data for model input.
2. It lets you measure the performance of model output.

These two purposes, when combined, can facilitate increasing efficiency, effectiveness, and adaptability of a process and can reduce costs. Simulation tools come with widely varying input and output analysis functions. Although general-purpose simulation languages have excellent statistical capabilities, many business process simulation products lack important statistical analysis functions.

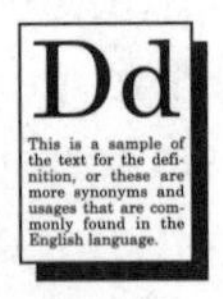

Process analysis—A statistical analysis of model input data, such as customer demand and resource capacity, and model output data, such as cycle time and process cost.

Effectiveness—The extent to which the output of a process or activity meets the needs and expectations of its customers. Effectiveness is having the right output at the right place, at the right time, and for the right price.

Efficiency—A measure of the resources (human, money, cycle time, etc.) that are used by a process in order to produce its output. A close synonym to efficiency is *productivity*.

Adaptability—The ability of a process or activity to handle the fluctuations in its input and still meet its effectiveness and efficiency requirements or objectives. It is a measure of the process's ability to handle future, changing customer expectations and today's individual, special customer requests.

Typical measurements are:

- percentage of special orders processed without management intervention
- allowable sigma of the input measurements

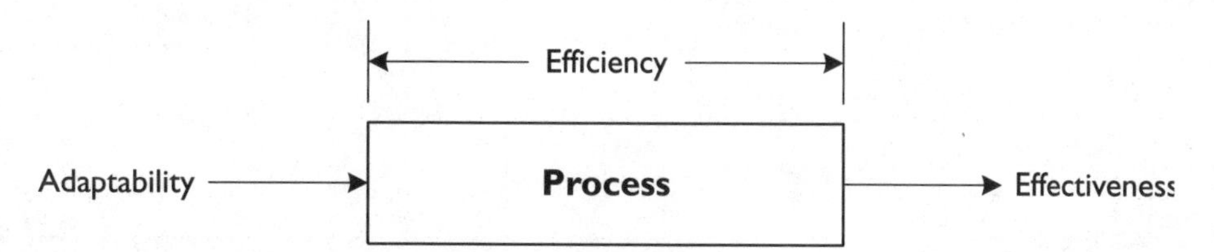

FIGURE 3-4. Types of process measurements

For model input analysis, a good tool should provide for defining activity times, arrival rates, and random failures in terms of statistical distributions. Some of these model inputs may require continuous distributions while others may require discrete distributions, so support for both types of distributions is useful. Some tools provide a visual display of these distributions, showing the probability density and cumulative distribution functions. This can be very helpful in analyzing model input data. Sometimes, input data may not fit a standard distribution. This requires a function to define the model input using an empirical or user-defined distribution. Some of the sophisticated process simulation tools provide built-in functions for analyzing input data, fitting data to statistical distributions, and assigning the distribution and its parameters to a model parameter—all seamlessly.

The software should also be able to define the critical path through the process and calculate cycle time and cost of that critical path. It should also be able to define the second and third critical paths.

For model output analysis functions, a good tool should provide both time-persistent and observation-based statistics for all types of model objects. For example, a tool should provide a total count of transactions processed (observation-based) as well as utilization of a server (time-persistent). For complete output analysis, a report for a given metric should include minimum, maximum, average, standard deviation, and final value at the end of simulation.

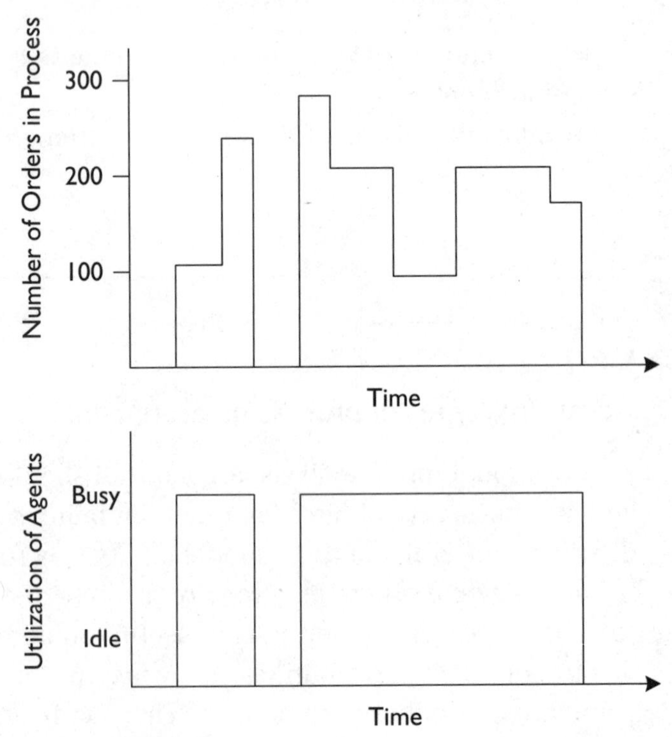

FIGURE 3-5. Model output

The tool should provide for steady-state performance analysis. This means the user should be able to define a warm-up period for discarding biased statistics prior to steady state. The tool should also provide for transient-state analysis by allowing definition of initial conditions at the beginning of a run.

Some of the considerations for analysis functions are:

- How many built-in distributions are supported? Are empirical or user-defined distributions supported?
- Does the program allow for multiple replications? Can selected seed values be automatically reset between replications?
- Does the software provide confidence intervals? Does the software provide other information that will help in statistical analysis of output reports?

A very important aspect of the process analysis functionality is *scenario analysis*. This is what allows the assessment of what-if scenarios. A good tool provides functionality for comparing metrics from multiple scenarios in a statistically sound way. For example, if the objective of a simulation study is to determine whether a centralized purchasing process reduces process costs and minimizes cycle time as compared with a decentralized purchasing process, then the output analysis should provide comparison of the metrics from multiple scenarios.

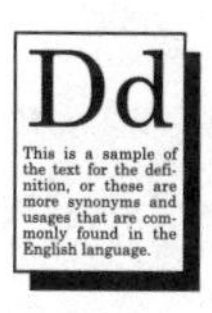

Scenario analysis—A statistical analysis of model output for a given performance measure under different sets of input data.

---

5. Input and Output Functions

When model input data are available in a database or application in a form suitable for a simulation model, it is much more efficient to input those data.

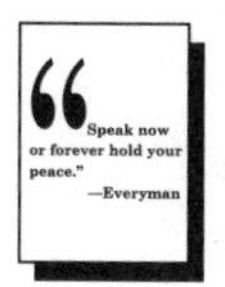

"Building and analyzing manufacturing processes requires a thorough understanding of both the process and the data associated with the process," says William Lilegdon of Pritsker Corporation, a major simulation vendor. "Fortunately, many systems—such as enterprise resource planning, CAD (Computer-Aided Drawing), and CAPP (Computer-Aided Process Planning)—produce critical data about manufacturing processes and store it in an accessible format. Simulation software can use this data to begin defining the process flow and operation times. While such data won't fully represent the process," Lilegdon admits, "it does reduce the time to build the model and increase its accuracy by eliminating erroneous data."

When model output data are needed by another application, it's also more efficient to output the data to a database or to interface the simulation application with another application.

It is sometimes desirable to interface with a program or subroutine outside of the simulation model. This might be a spreadsheet application or a subroutine written in Visual Basic or C++ that it would be helpful to have linked to the model logic. There are several import/export formats, including ASCII, Object Linking and Embedding (OLE), and Open Data Base Connectivity (ODBC). Linking may be through a dynamic link library (DLL).

Specific questions to ask regarding the interfacing capabilities of the software are:

- Does the software allow importing data from databases or other applications? If so, how is it done? ASCII files? OLE? ODBC? Active X?
- Does the software allow exporting data to a database or other applications? If so, how is it done? ASCII files? OLE? ODBC? Active X?
- Does the software allow linking with external applications or subroutines? If so, how is it done? DLLs? Object Broker?
- Can the model input or output be viewed or modified through a Web browser?

Usability

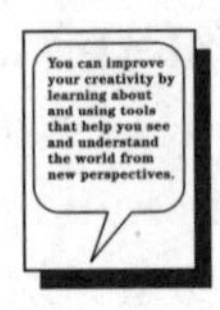

Many simulation software vendors advertise capability, but their software is so lacking in usability that it becomes extremely difficult to achieve any productivity with it. We have seen modeling tools with seven or eight dialogs deep. We have also seen tools with a blank window where the user is expected to type in expressions for modeling business rules. Sometimes users throw up their arms in despair, feeling that they will never be able to get a model built and running.

Other simulation software vendors have, unfortunately, misrepresented their products by claims that their software is easy to use. The question to ask those vendors is "Easy to use for whom and compared with what?" A simulation product may be easy to use for a computer scientist in the sense that it is easier to code the model than to write a model in a language such as C or C++. Ease of use should be gauged primarily by the time and effort required to learn and use the software. Specific features to look for that make simulation software easy to use include the following:

- Modeling constructs that are intuitive and descriptive.
- Model-building procedure that is simple and straightforward.
- Use of graphical input wherever possible.
- Input prompts that are clear and easy to follow.
- Context-sensitive help.
- Simplified data entry and modification.
- Automatic gathering of key performance measures.
- Automatic management of multiple experiments.
- Debugging and trace features.
- Output reports that are easy to read and understand.

If the modeling language is foreign and terminology is unnatural or unfamiliar, it's difficult to learn and retain the language. It helps to have a close correspondence between the modeling terminology and the language typically used in describing the problem domain.

Straightforwardness refers to how intuitive the interface is. Defining down times, for example, should be readily apparent from the modeling environment of the simulation software. Brooks (1975) makes a point of the fact that software can be simple, yet not necessarily straightforward, noting that both "simplicity and straightforwardness proceed from conceptual integrity." Conceptual integrity refers to the unity of the product interface in which methods and conventions are consistent and everything fits together, as one would expect. A simulation language may be very simple in the sense that it

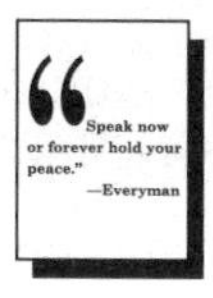

provides a basic set of elementary constructs from which models can be created. However, the convoluted and difficult way in which these constructs are combined may not be at all straightforward. Where certain items are, by nature, a bit complicated, there should be sufficient and easily accessed online help and documentation describing the feature in further detail.

Software that is easy to use will generally provide convenient facilities and mechanisms for defining models. Currently, the trend is toward graphical user interfaces, such as Windows, that provide easy "fill in the blank" approaches to model definition, reducing keyboard entries. Being able to define objects and relationships graphically is well as textually also makes products easier to use.

The simplification of data entry and data modification is a feature that is often not appreciated until one has been doing modeling for some time and finds that certain tasks, while straightforward and easy to perform, require an excessive amount of tedious effort to complete. A considerately designed product is one in which input requirements are kept to a minimum and model information is kept as efficient as possible. One way to minimize input effort is through the use of macros and subroutines that allow a segment of logic or a series of similar rescues to be defined only once.

The ease of using a particular simulation product can be best determined by conducting the following simple experiment.

1. Define two small, but representative problems of your own. (If you let the vendor define them, they will be tailor-made to fit his or her product.)
2. Invite someone in your company who knows nothing about simulation to participate (your trainee).
3. Ask your simulation vendor to build a model of the first sample while your trainee is watching how the model is built. Be sure to measure how long it takes, keeping in mind that the supplier is also training one of your people.
4. Let your trainee drive the software.
5. Let your trainee try to build a simulation model for the second problem while you watch.

6. Evaluate the degree of difficulty in building the second model.

This procedure has been used by one major corporation to score simulation products and it has proven to be very effective. Additional questions to ask pertaining to aids that make software easier to use include:

- Does the software have online help? Context-sensitive? Hypertext?
- Does the software have a built-in trainer or tutorial? Wizards?
- Does the software come with reference models for using its constructs?
- Does the software detect syntax errors?
- Does the software provide descriptive error messages and point you to the appropriate section of the model for making corrections?

Reliability

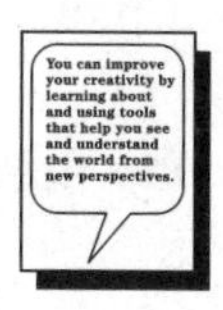

Reliability of process simulation software is perhaps the most difficult criterion to assess when evaluating process simulation products. In addition to normal software bugs that may be caused by GUI (graphical user interface), OS (operating system), or device drivers (e.g., graphics adapter or printer), process simulation tools may suffer from reliability problems that are unique to discrete-event simulation.

Even a simple dynamic process model contains a very large number of possible situations when it is executed. The challenge of scheduling and sequencing thousands of simultaneous events, coupled with the challenges of animating graphical representations of many objects and recording thousands of observations in a database, is extremely tedious. So, most powerful simulation products, unless they are obsolete, contain some bugs. The key to evaluating reliability is to understand the source of bugs and their severity, and to establish a certain level of confidence with a product.

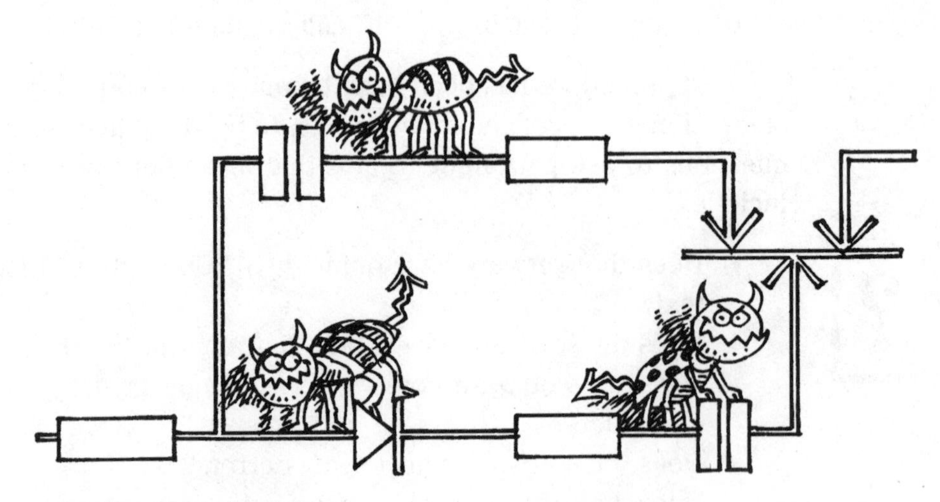

Watch out for bugs.

Unlike static models, graphical representations of dynamic simulation models present a tremendous testing challenge for simulation software vendors. For example, it is perfectly acceptable to build a static diagram where the output connector from a branch activity does not connect to a downstream activity object. However, a process model cannot be simulated unless such a connection is established both graphically and logically.

Some of the questions to consider when evaluating reliability are:

- How robust is the underlying technology used in the simulation software?
- What is the process for fixing bugs? How are the fixes provided to users?
- What testing procedures are in place to ensure that no new bugs are introduced in the fixing process?
- Is the vendor ISO 9000-certified?
- Are the bugs related to GUI, OS, device drivers, or animation? Or are the bugs in the simulation engine or output reporting?

Maintainability

In thinking about maintainability, there are four aspects to consider:

1. Security
2. Documentation
3. Hardware and other software requirements
4. Upgrades and enhancements

1. Security

In order to protect their software from illegal duplication and use, simulation vendors use two types of security modes: software keys and hardware keys (sometimes called *dongles*). Once the simulation software is installed, these keys enable the user to launch the application. Otherwise, the software cannot be used. These security measures cause a certain inconvenience and annoyance; however, they are unavoidable.

In addition to security provided by the supplier, sometimes organizations like to establish model or data security to limit access to certain aspects of the modeling software. For example, a system administrator may provide access to certain functionality or certain data by user class, to maintain security in large models or multi-user projects.

2. Documentation

When evaluating software, documentation is perhaps the most overlooked criterion. Yet it's extremely important to document the software capabilities, troubleshooting, and guidance for modeling different situations. Before selecting software, carefully review both on-line documentation and printed manuals. The care and detail put into the documentation is often a reflection of the vendor's interest in providing quality software and services.

3. Hardware and Other Software Requirements

Many simulation products are developed to run on multiple hardware platforms. The advantage of this approach is that models can be portable across platforms. Sometimes, however, there is a loss of performance when software is not written to take advantage of a platform's specific features. With the rapid developments in hardware technology, it is important to make sure that the simulation product takes advantage of future technologies. Basic questions affecting the hardware configuration that will be required include:

- Does the software run under multiple operating systems?
- Does the software require special graphics cards or drivers?
- Can the software be used on a network?
- Can the software print or plot model layouts, model data files, output statistics, or graphs?
- Does the software require special compilers? If so, how much are they?
- How much memory (RAM) is needed to run the software?

4. Upgrades and Enhancements

Software is perhaps the most rapidly changing commodity on the market today. Many of the process simulation tools in use today will undergo significant improvements in just the next year. Some simulation tools may even be obsolete within the next year or two, simply because they are not being adequately updated. If a simulation vendor does not have an aggressive R&D program, its products will quickly become outdated. Specific questions to ask might be:

- How often does the vendor provide new releases?
- Is the software vendor up-to-date with the latest developments in software technology?
- Is the vendor involved in industry standards committees?
- Are the new releases compatible with the old ones?

Scalability

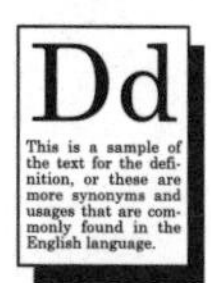

Scalability—The ability of process simulation software to allow use of a modeling tool at multiple levels by various skill levels.

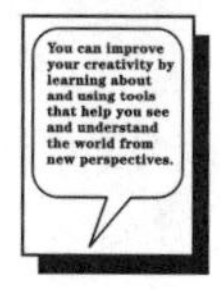

At high levels, the models are built with basic building blocks and using a graphical interface by process owners. At low levels, the models are refined with procedural language commands or expressions by simulation engineers, analysts, or consultants. As described in the "Modeling Functions" section earlier in this chapter, the basic building blocks provide simplicity while language functions provide flexibility. Ability to create and support run-time models is another dimension in scalable simulation software.

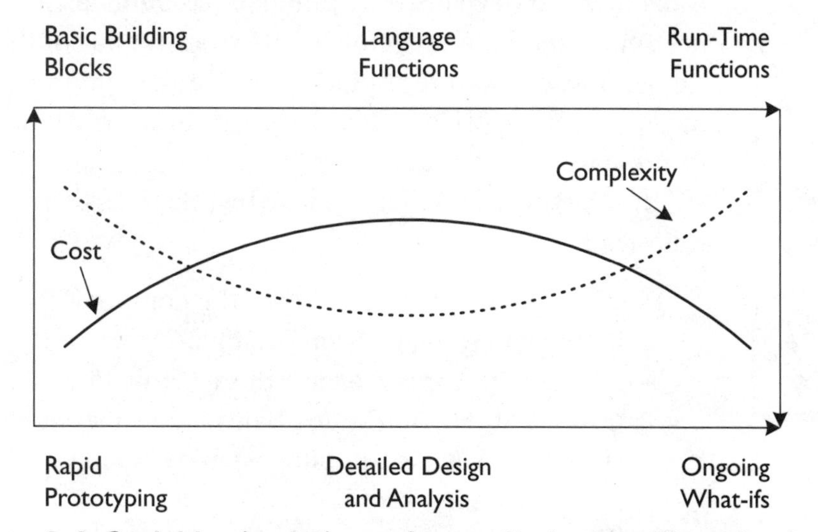

FIGURE 3-6. Scalable simulation software. During the lifecycle of a project, cost and complexity are highest in "detailed design/analysis," while "language functions" are being used.

Scalability makes it possible to use a process simulation tool cost-effectively throughout the life cycle of a project. In the rapid prototyping phase, the building block approach may be used. In the detailed design and analysis phases, the advanced modeling functions such as language expressions can be added. Finally, after the rollout phase, the run-time functions can be used by either process owners or customers. Assuming that the scalable products have scalable pricing, this evaluation criterion may become quite significant in selecting a tool.

Supplier Quality

The quality and reputation of the vendor may be just as important as the functionality or price of the process simulation software. It's very important to make sure that the tool that is evaluated is fully supported by the supplier. Some of the tools developed by consulting firms contain methodologies that are slanted toward creating professional services work rather than general purpose use by the customer. Other tools that are developed by graduate students as academic exercises are supported by a few individuals working out of their homes. Even though these software products may look good in demonstrations or have attractive prices, their support may be short-lived and their future may be uncertain.

In selecting a supplier, it's worthwhile to ask questions such as the following:

- What is the business focus of the company? What percentage of its revenues comes from products?
- How many employees are there? How does that number break down by R&D, Marketing/Sales, and Customer Services?
- How long has the supplier been in business? What is the company's installed user base?
- Who are the supplier's key reference accounts? How long have they been customers?
- What is the supplier's financial status?

Customer Services

Users of process simulation tools will need some level of customer service from the product vendor, regardless of the expertise of the modeler or the simplicity of the product. Therefore, timely and cost-effective customer service is an important criterion in selecting software. The services provided can be in terms of technical support, training and education, and consulting.

1. Technical Support

Technical support needs may be as simple as an installation problem and as complex as a software crash during a simulation run. In general, vendors provide adequate technical support for basic questions and problems. However, this is not necessarily true for questions requiring additional research or the attention of a developer. Whether the support requirement is very basic or very involved, users deserve timely and courteous support. On the other hand, users need to realize that they cannot expect vendors to offer modeling services under the pretense of "technical support."

The following questions should be helpful in assessing the quality of technical support:

- How does the vendor provide technical support (e.g., phone, bulletin board, user groups)?
- What percentage of the total staff is dedicated to customer services?
- Are the developers of the product willing to talk to the end users?
- How responsive is the vendor to user deadlines?
- How close is the nearest authorized representative? How competent is that representative?

2. Training

Effective training can help users new to simulation get off to a good start. Training may vary from standard product training to customized, on-site training. Some vendors offer a standard training course that assumes everyone is on the same level. Other vendors offer a variety of courses, including methodology training or application-specific training that is relevant to a particular industry. Questions to ask regarding training include:

- How frequent are the training courses? Where are the training locations?
- What levels of training are offered? Is industry-specific training available?
- Is on-site training available? If so, how much does it cost?
- Is customized training available? If so, how much does it cost?

Training is important.

3. Modeling Services

Some vendors have developed in-house modeling departments that provide modeling services to their customers. Others have developed consulting services. Modeling services should not be confused with consulting services. That is, a vendor may be very competent to build a model based on a specification, but may not have the expertise to make system design decisions. Modeling services performed by professional modelers can often save time and money over doing the work in-house. If, however, the modeling services are not performed professionally, the results can be disappointing. Often the representative who is responsible for selling modeling services may be very competent, but then once the project is purchased, someone with lesser credentials is assigned to perform the project.

Questions to ask regarding the modeling services provided by a vendor include the following:

?

- Who will be working on the project?
- What are his or her credentials?
- Can the model be used after the consultant is finished with the project?
- What deliverables (e.g., model, report, video, etc.) will you get at the end?

4. Other Services

In addition to normal customer services that should be expected, there are other vendor services that may be of interest. These services are typically available from vendors that are very customer service-oriented. Specifically, you might want to ask:

?

- Is there an Internet news group where users can exchange ideas?
- Does the vendor provide a newsletter? How often is published? What is the content?
- Does the vendor provide case studies? How useful are they?

- Does the company have user group meetings? Where and when are they held?

Cost of Ownership

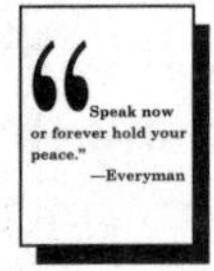

"The price of simulation software varies from $1,000 to $80,000. It is ill-advised to buy software on the basis of price. Productivity is more important."

— *JERRY BANKS, PROFESSOR OF INDUSTRIAL AND SYSTEMS ENGINEERING AT GEORGIA TECH UNIVERSITY AND SIMULATION CONSULTANT*

The cost associated with selecting a particular simulation product involves more than the purchase price of the software license. While a simulation license may cost $10,000, the labor cost for doing a single simulation project can easily end up being two to three times that amount if the product is limited and difficult to use. When evaluating costs, therefore, consider the entire cost of doing simulation projects, not just the cost of the product itself. More expensive products are typically designed to minimize both the learning time and the time to model and analyze systems. Don't be misled, however, into thinking that a higher price tag necessarily means less difficulty.

Another important consideration in software costs is the way in which pricing is based. Some vendors price their products in modules. Therefore, you should understand what those modules are and the costs associated with each module before selecting a software product. Other products come as a complete package with everything included. Questions to ask regarding product pricing should include:

- What does the software purchase price include?
- If software comes in modules, do you need all of the modules?
- How much are the annual maintenance, support, and upgrade costs?
- How much is standard training? How much is on-site or custom training?

- What types of discounts are offered for multiple purchases, site licenses, etc.?

A Weighted-Criteria Approach to Software Selection

After you have defined the criteria for selecting a process simulation software, you need to establish a means of applying those criteria. The best method for evaluating alternative products against the criteria is using a weighted-score selection method. The steps involved in the procedure are essentially as follows:

1. List the criteria to be used for making the product selection.
2. Weight each criterion in terms of its relative importance.
3. Define a scale for scoring each product against each criterion (e.g., 1 = nice to have, 2 = desired, 3 = needed, 4 = must have).
4. Obtain product information relative to your criteria. If necessary, go back to step one to refine the criteria, scoring method, and weight factors.
5. Score the features of each software package and supplier using the scale and weight factor.
6. Conduct a sensitivity analysis on the results of the software evaluation.
7. Select the software with the highest weighted score.

An alternative scoring method when comparing only two or three products is a *relative ranking* approach. First, the best product for each category is identified. The chosen product for each category is then multiplied by the weight factor, so that for some categories the winning product may get counted two or three times. The entries for each product are then added up; the one with the most entries wins.

In the previous section, we provided you with the typical criteria for evaluating simulation software. Figure 3-7 shows an example of an evaluation matrix using the weighted-criteria method. The matrix in Figure 3-7 evaluates two simulation products (A and B) based on the criteria defined previously. For a more extensive evaluation, each of the evaluation criteria can be further subdivided.

To each criterion a weight is assigned. Here's an easy way to assign weights. First, identify the least important criterion and assign it a weight of 1. In our example, if scalability is considered least important, it would have a weight of 1. Second, identify the most important criterion and assign it a value relative to the least important criterion. For example, if functionality is considered the most important criterion and if it is felt to be five times more important than scalability, then it would have a weight of 5. Using these two extremes as a measuring stick, it becomes relatively easy to assign weights to all of the remaining criteria.

		Product A		Product B	
Criteria	**Wt.**	**Raw Score**	**Wt. Score**	**Raw Score**	**Wt. Score**
Functionality	5	3	15	4	20
Usability	4	2	8	3	12
Reliability	4	2	8	2	8
Maintainability	3	2	6	2	6
Scalability	1	4	4	3	3
Supplier Quality	5	2	10	3	15
Supplier Services	3	2	6	3	9
Cost of Ownership	4	4	16	3	12
Total			73		85

FIGURE 3-7. Example of an evaluation matrix

In scoring products A and B against each criterion, a raw score is first assigned, based on a scale from 1 to 4 (1 = poor, 2 = fair, 3 = good, 4 = excellent). A weighted score is then computed by multiplying each raw score by the weight for that criterion. Finally, all of the weighted scores for each product are added to arrive at a total score for that product. The total scores are 73 for product A and 85 for product B, which would indicate that product B is the preferable selection.

In order to eliminate bias in an evaluation, it may be beneficial to have two or more people score each product. Another way to eliminate bias is by giving the same evaluation matrix to the vendor as well as to a reference customer. It is also fair to assume that software vendors are developing new products and providing additional features, so the state of the art will change and the answers to your questions will most likely be different in a year. We have seen software evaluations that included future development plans of the vendor as an evaluation criterion with a high weight factor.

Summary

Software selection is one of the most critical success factors for process simulation. When evaluating process simulation software, one should consider such unique criteria as functionality, scalability, and cost of ownership in addition to general software evaluation criteria such as usability, reliability, and customer service. Although a particular tool may score high for multiple criteria, it does not mean that it's the most suitable. A weighted-criteria approach provides an effective evaluation of alternative products by assigning weights to the criteria and comparing alternatives on the basis of their weighted scores.

Just remember that the impact of a process simulation tool in a business depends not only on the overall quality of the tool and its supplier, but also on the capability of the end users, the project management life cycle, and, most important, the suitability for the application.

"The only thing more important than the software is the people who use it."

References

Banks, Jerry, and Randall Gibson, "Simulation Modeling: Some Programming Required," *IIE Solutions*, February 1997, pp. 26-31.

Brooks, Frederick P., Jr., *The Mythical Man-Month* (Reading, MA: Addison-Wesley, 1975).

Hansen, Gregory A., *Automating Business Process Reengineering: Breaking the TQM Barrier* (Englewood Cliffs, NJ: Prentice-Hall, 1994).

Harrell, Charles, and Kerim Tumay, *Simulation Made Easy: A Manager's Guide* (Norcross, GA: Industrial Engineering and Management Press, 1995).

Lilegdon, William, "Stand Alone No More," *Manufacturing Systems*, August 1997, p. 56.

Sellers, Gordon, "BPR Tools: Bridging the Gap Between Theory and Practice," *Proceedings of the National Business Process Reengineering Conference '96* (Washington, DC: Feldman Group, 1997), pp. 476-481.

CHAPTER 4

Phase II: Implementation

When the planning is done, the work has just begun.

Introduction

A simulation study is, by its very nature, a project or a major task inside a project. Like any project, there are tasks to be completed, resources to be assigned, and deadlines or budgets to be met. A simulation project should be implemented with an understanding of the requirements of each of the tasks involved and the resources required within a given time and budget.

In Chapter 2, we presented the resource, time, and budget considerations in a simulation project. This chapter describes in detail the steps involved in a successful implementation. Specifically, the following implementation steps are explained:

- Plan the simulation project.
- Collect and analyze data.
- Build a useful model.
- Verify and validate the model.

- Conduct experiments.
- Analyze, document, and present the results.

One Final Check

Enough background information should have been obtained about the nature of the problem to determine whether simulation is a suitable solution. If the project is conducted by individuals within the company, there may already be a basic knowledge of the process and the problem. For consultants or those unfamiliar with the process, a brief process walk-through and current process performance review are needed. This brief review serves a final check before takeoff. And sometimes, this final check may result in identifying and resolving issues that could lead to failures.

Also as part of developing a business case, we have identified specific projects that would benefit from the use of simulation modeling weapons. We are now ready to apply the simulation-modeling tool to the projects approved by management. After this stage, management approves its use on a pilot project before it is rolled out throughout the organization.

Many simulation projects are doomed to failure from the outset due to poor planning. Undefined objectives, unrealistic expectations, and a general lack of understanding of requirements may result in frustration and disappointment. If a simulation project is to be successful, a plan must be developed that is realistic, communicated clearly, and followed closely.

Implementation Steps

Once a suitable application or project has been confirmed, the implementation steps can resume. There are no strict rules on how to perform a simulation study. Typical implementation steps are listed below. Each step need not be completed in its entirety before moving on to the next step. The procedure for doing a simulation is iterative: activities are refined and sometimes redefined with each iteration.

Step 1. Plan the simulation project.
Step 2. Collect and analyze the data.
Step 3. Build the model.
Step 4. Verify and validate the model.
Step 5. Conduct experiments.
Step 6. Analyze, document, and present the results.

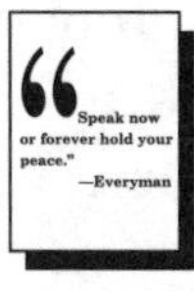

Describing this iterative process, Pritsker and Pegden (1979) observe, "The stages of simulation are rarely performed in a structured sequence beginning with problem definition and ending with documentation. A simulation project may involve false starts, erroneous assumptions that must later be abandoned, reformulation of the problem objectives, and repeated evaluation and redesign of the model. If properly done, however, this iterative process should result in a simulation model which properly assesses alternatives and enhances the decision making process."

Obviously, the time to perform a simulation project will vary depending on the size and difficulty of the project. If data are not readily available, it may be necessary to add several weeks to the project. A small project can take two to four weeks; large projects can take two to four months. A simulation schedule should be based on realistic projections of the time requirements, keeping in mind the following:

- Defining the system to be modeled can take up to 50% of the overall project time.
- Model building usually takes the least amount of time (10% to 20%).
- Once a base model is built, it can take several weeks to conduct all of the desired experiments, especially if alternative designs are being compared.

Step 1. Plan the Simulation Project

This step is made up of three tasks:

Task 1. Define objectives.
Task 2. Define constraints.
Task 3. Define scope.

Task 1. Define Objectives

Defining an objective does not necessarily mean that there's a problem to be solved. A perfectly valid objective may be to see if there are, in fact, any unforeseen problems. Common types of objectives for a simulation study include the following:

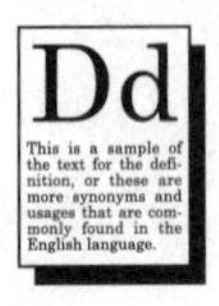

Performance analysis—How well does the process perform under a given set of circumstances in all measures of significance (utilization, throughput, waiting times, etc.)?

Capacity analysis—What is the maximum processing capacity?

Capability analysis—Is the process capable of meeting specific performance requirements (throughput, waiting times, etc.) and, if not, what changes (added resources, improved methods, etc.) are recommended for making it capable?

Comparison study—How well does one process design alternative perform compared with another?

Sensitivity analysis—Which decision variables are the most influential on one or more process performance measures, and how influential are they?

Optimization study—What combination of feasible values for a given set of decision variables best achieves desired performance objectives?

Decision/response analysis—What are the relationships between the values of one or more decision variables and the system response to those changes?

Constraint analysis—Where are the constraints or bottlenecks in the process and what are workable solutions for either reducing or eliminating the constraints?

Visualization—How can we visualize the dynamic behavior of the process so that process owners, customers, and stakeholders can communicate better?

Defining the objectives should take into account the ultimate intended use of the model. Some models are built as "throwaway" models, to be used only once and then discarded. Other models are built for use on an ongoing basis for continued "what-if" analysis. Some models need only provide a quantitative answer. Others require realistic animation to convince a skeptical customer. Some models are intended for use only by analysts. Other models are intended for use by managers with little simulation background and so must be easy to use. Some models are used to make decisions of minor consequence. Other models are relied upon to make major financial decisions.

Realizing that the objectives of a simulation should consider both the purpose and the intended use of the model, the following questions should be asked when defining the objectives of the study:

- Why is the simulation being performed?
- Who will be using the model?
- To whom will the results of the simulation be presented?
- What information is expected from the model?
- Is this a "throwaway" model? Is it a "reusable template"?
- How important is the decision being made? What are the projected savings or revenues?

"Simulation projects can easily get out of hand, especially if the rate of change in the scope of the project exceeds the rate at which the results are available to the owners of the process."
—ONUR ULGEN, PRESIDENT, PRODUCTION MODELING CORPORATION

Task 2. Define Constraints

Equally as important as defining objectives is identifying the constraints. It does little good if simulation solves a problem if the time to do the simulation extends beyond the deadline for applying the solution or if the cost to find the solution exceeds the benefit that is derived. Objectives need to be tempered by the constraints under which the project must be performed.

Constraints should not always be viewed as impediments. If no deadlines or constraints are established, there is a danger of getting too involved and detailed in the simulation study and run the risk of "paralysis from analysis." The scope of any project has a tendency to shrink or expand to fill the time allotted.

In identifying constraints, consider anything that could have a limiting effect on achieving the desired objectives. Specific questions to ask when identifying constraints for a simulation study include the following:

- What is the budget for doing the study?
- What is the deadline for making the decision?
- How accessible are the input data?
- What are the risks associated with making a bad decision?

Task 3. Define Scope

The scope is what helps you achieve the project objectives while staying within the given constraints. If, while developing the scope, you discover that the objectives are not being adequately met or that the constraints are violated, a decision must be made to reduce the expectations of the study and/or relax constraints where possible.

The most important reason for defining the scope is that it guides the implementation and helps set expectations by clarifying to others exactly what the simulation will include or exclude. Defining a clear scope is especially important if an outside consultant is performing the simulation, so that both parties have the same guidelines and expectations. Aspects of the simulation project that should be included in the scope include the following:

- Model extent
- Level of detail
- Degree of accuracy
- Type of experimentation
- Content and form of results

Each of these specification criteria will be discussed below.

Define Model Boundaries

There are four boundaries that need to be defined:

- Beginning (start) boundary
- Ending boundary
- Upper boundary
- Lower boundary

Defining these four boundaries is called "boxing in" the process to be simulated. Figure 4-1 is an example of a steak BBQ process that is boxed in.

The *beginning* boundary defines where the process starts. It should be related to an input that sets the process in motion. In the example, the guest arriving at the home starts the process.

The *ending* boundary defines the last activity or task that will be included in the simulation model. It is usually associated with an output that goes to an internal or external customer.

The *upper* boundary defines where inputs enter the process at points within the process being modeled, but not at the beginning of the process.

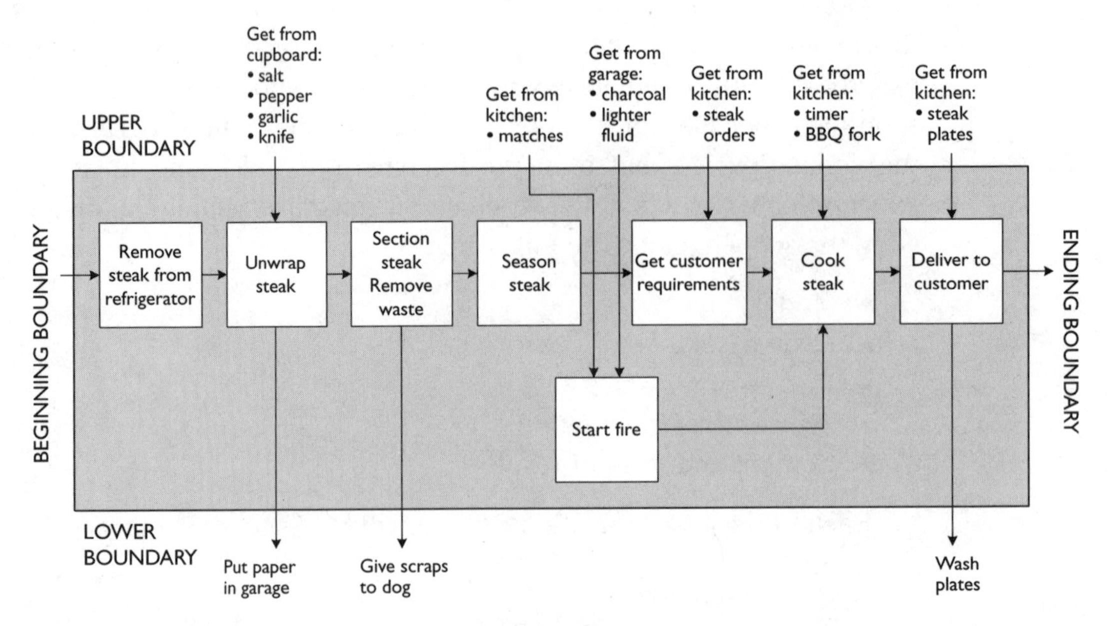

FIGURE 4-1. Boxing in the steak BBQ process

The *lower* boundary defines what leaves the process from points within the process, but not at the end of the process being modeled.

The boundaries of the model should be determined according to the impact of a particular activity on achieving the objectives of the simulation. A common tendency is to model as much as possible, even when the problem area and all relevant variables are isolated within a subprocess. However, if the objective is to identify the process cycle time in production, for example, it is not necessary to model the distribution process that follows production.

Define Level of Detail

The level of detail defines the depth or resolution of the model. At one extreme, a customer service process can be modeled as a single "black box" process with a random processing time. At the other extreme, every task requiring a resource is modeled explicitly.

Unlike the model boundaries, which affect only the size of the model, the level of detail affects model complexity as well as model size.

Determining the appropriate level of detail is an important decision. Too much detail makes it difficult and time-consuming to develop a valid model. Too little detail may make the model too unrealistic by excluding critical variables. Figure 4-2 illustrates how the time to develop a model is affected by the level of detail. It also highlights the importance of including only enough detail to meet the objectives of the study.

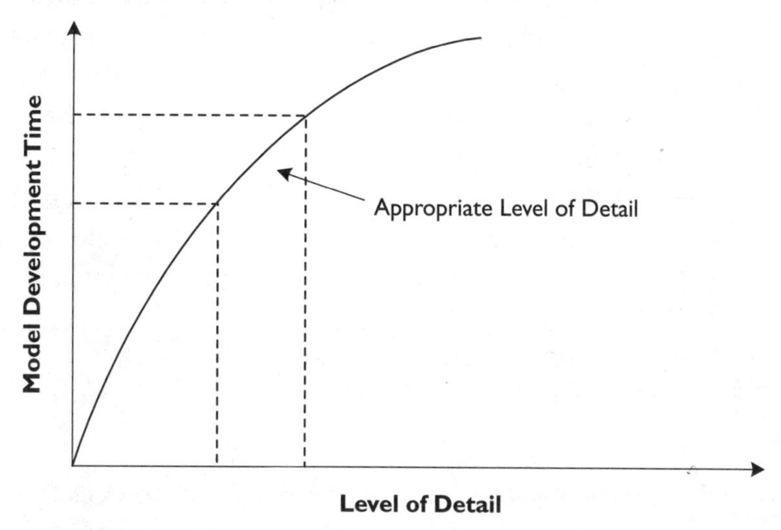

FIGURE 4-2. Effect of level of detail on model development time

The level of detail is determined largely by the degree of precision required in the output. For example, if we are modeling a supply chain process for strategic planning, it may be sufficient to model inventory updates on a weekly basis and analyze inventory costs on a weekly basis. However, if we are modeling a supply chain for tactical planning during the holiday season, it may be necessary to model inventory updates on a daily basis.

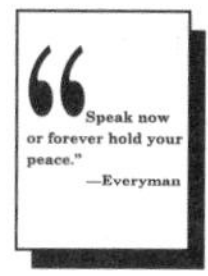

"There is a tendency to spend a great deal of effort modeling, in unnecessary detail, those portions of the system that are well understood while glossing over poorly defined portions that may be more important. This approach creates the illusion that great

progress is being made, until it comes time to produce valid, usable results."

—*Edward C. Russell*, Building Simulation Models with SIMSCRIPT II.5

Define Degree of Accuracy

The degree of accuracy pertains to the correctness of the data being used. Data gathered for a simulation are of two types: logic and numeric. *Logic* data identify the model objects, their behaviors and relationships, and business rules. Included in logic data would be routing sequences, assignment of resources, prioritization of tasks, etc. *Numeric* data identify quantitative information about the system, such as how much, how many, and how long. Numeric data include cycle times, move times, batch sizes, arrival frequencies, etc.

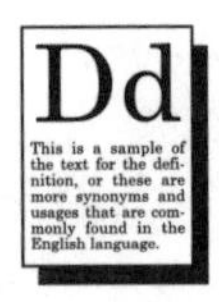

Logic data—Data that define the workflow, model objects, their behaviors and relationships, and business rules such as routing sequences, resources assignments, priorities, etc.

Numeric data—Quantitative information related to the item being modeled (e.g., cycle times, cost, batch size, etc.).

The information need not be as accurate or exact for some models or for certain activities as for others. The required degree of accuracy is determined by the objectives of the study. If the decision is important or a comparison is close, greater accuracy may be required. Accuracy sometimes has to be sacrificed if reliable information is simply unavailable, such as when modeling a completely new system.

The required degree of accuracy can have a significant impact on the time and effort required to gather data. It often has little impact, however, on the model-building time, since a model can be built with estimated values that can later be replaced with more accurate values. Output precision is often governed by the degree of accuracy of the model.

Define Type of Experimentation

The number and nature of the alternative solutions to be evaluated should be planned from the outset in order to ensure that adequate time is allotted. Often this decision is influenced by the deadline constraints of the study. Where the alternatives to be evaluated differ only slightly, a base model can be developed that requires only minor modification to model each alternative. If alternative configurations are significantly different, it may require nearly as much effort to model each configuration as to develop the initial model.

For studies considering improvements to an existing process, it is often helpful and effective to model the current process as well as the proposed process. The basic premise is that you are not ready to make improvements to a process until you understand how the current process operates. Information on the current process is easier to obtain than information on areas of change. Once a model of the current process is built, it is often easier to visualize what changes need to be made for the modified process. During the final presentation of the results, showing both "as-is" and "to-be" versions of the process design effectively demonstrates the impact that the changes can have on performance.

Define Content and Form of Results

The content of the results can vary from basic statistics of a performance measure to detailed statistics of that same measure. For example, a basic activity cycle time metric contains a single value, whereas detailed statistics for that activity may include minimum and maximum values and standard deviation. Another example is an aggregate activity time value versus a detailed activity time broken down by transaction type. If the detailed content is required, then more time should be allocated for the analysis of results. It is important to remember that an organization usually loses customers over the extremes of its processes, not the average performance value. (For example, the average cycle time may be three days, but 10% of the time it takes 15 days or more.)

The form in which the results are to be presented can significantly affect the time and effort involved in the simulation study. If detailed animation or an extensive report is expected, the project can easily stretch on for several weeks after the experimental phase has been completed.

Step 2. Collect and Analyze Data

Never gather data without a purpose. Data gathering should be goal-oriented, focused on information that will achieve the objectives of the study. There are several guidelines to keep in mind when gathering data:

- Identify cause-and-effect relationships.
- Look for key impact factors.
- Distinguish between *time*-dependent, *resource*-dependent, and *condition*-dependent activities.
- Focus on *essence* rather than *substance.*
- Separate *input* variables from *response* variables.
- Determine data requirements.
- Use appropriate data sources.
- Make assumptions when data are not available.
- Convert data into a useful form.
- Document and approve the data.
- How large or complex should the model be to be useful?
- What happens to the model after it is used?

Identify Cause-and-Effect Relationships

Cause-and-effect diagrams have long been useful tools for defining the relationships between an effect and its causes. The use of these diagrams not only reduces the time to collect the proper model input data, but also helps reduce the time to analyze the model output data by focusing on the things that really matter.

Let's consider the effect of capital-intensive process equipment being down. It is helpful to distinguish causes such as down time due to random equipment failure, planned down time for maintenance or tool change, or down time because stock is unavailable (as in Figure 4-3). If the causes are established and analyzed, process simulation can help evaluate the time-dependent behavior of these cause-and-effect relationships.

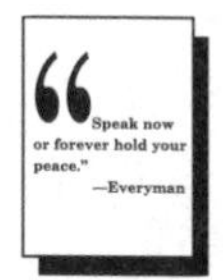

"In complex systems, cause and effect are not close in time and space."

—*Peter Senge*

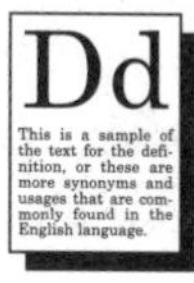

Cause-and-effect diagram—Diagram that organizes the thinking process and facilitates group dynamics during brainstorming sessions.

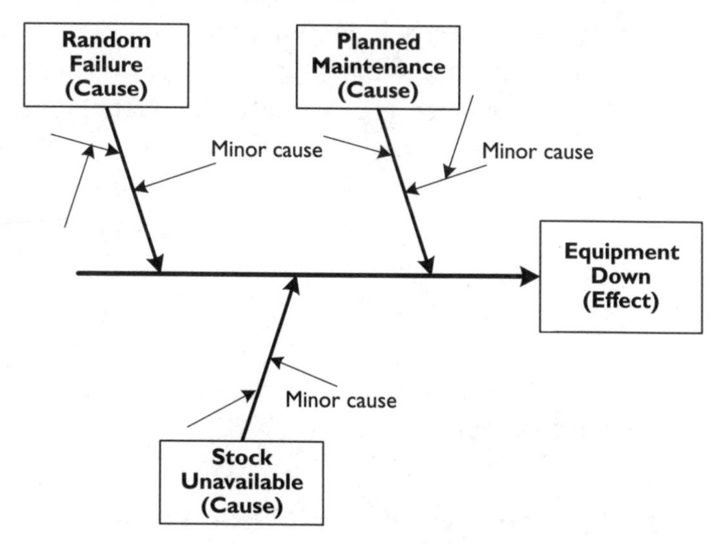

FIGURE 4-3. Sample cause-and-effect diagram

Look for Key Impact Factors

Discriminate when gathering data, to avoid wasting time examining factors that have little or no impact on process performance. For instance, it's of no value to collect data for an activity that takes a fraction of a minute while most other activities in the process are measured in fractions of an hour. Likewise, extremely rare events or activities that are outside the boundaries of the model may be safely ignored.

Distinguish Between Time-Dependent, Resource-Dependent, and Condition-Dependent Activities

Time-dependent activities are those that do not require a resource or a condition. An example would be a cool-down activity for a curing process. *Resource*-dependent activities cannot begin without the required resource or resources. An example would be a transportation activity that requires a truck. *Condition*-dependent activities can be completed only when certain defined conditions within the system are satisfied. Because condition-dependent activities are uncontrollable, they are unpredictable. An example might be filling a customer order or performing an assembly operation that requires component parts.

Some activities are partially time-dependent, partially resource-dependent, and partially condition-dependent. When gathering data on these activities, it is important to distinguish between the time required to actually perform the activity and the time spent waiting for resources to become available or other conditions to be met before the activity can be performed. For example, if historical data are used to determine repair times, the time spent doing the actual repair work should be used, without including the time spent waiting for a repair person to become available.

Focus on Essence Rather than Substance

A system definition for modeling purposes should capture the key cause-and-effect relationships and ignore incidental details. Using this "black box" approach to system definition, we are not concerned about the nature of the activity being performed, but only the impact that the activity has on the use of resources and the delay of entity flow. For example, the actual operation performed on a machine is not important, but only how long the operation takes and what resources if any are tied up during the operation. It is important for the modeler to be constantly thinking abstractly about the system operation in order to avoid getting too caught up in the incidental details.

Separate Input Variables from Response Variables

Input variables to a model define how the system works (e.g., activity times and routing sequences). *Response* variables describe how the system responds to a given set of input variables (e.g., work-in-process, idle times, and resource utilization). Input variables should be the focus of data gathering since they are used to define the model. Response variables, on the other hand, are the output of a simulation. Consequently, response variables should be gathered only to later help validate the model once it is built and run.

Collecting data and analyzing them so that they become useful information for the model is not a trivial task. The following steps are recommended to facilitate data collection and analysis:

- Determine data requirements.
- Use appropriate data sources.
- Make assumptions where necessary.
- Convert data into a useful form.
- Document and approve the data.

Determine Data Requirements

The first step in gathering process data is to determine what data are required for building the model. This should be dictated primarily by the model boundaries and level of detail required to achieve the model objectives as described earlier. It is best to go from general to specific in gathering data. As mentioned earlier, data consist of both logic data and numeric data. It is best to focus initially on gathering logic data and then determine the numeric values required.

In gathering logic data, it is best to start with the overall process flow. This approach not only provides an orderly approach to data gathering, but also enables the model-building process to get started.

Often, missing data become more apparent as the process model is being built.

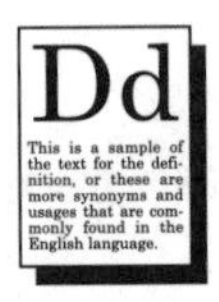

Flow diagram—A kind of drawing that visually defines the activities or tasks that make up a process, using symbols to depict the different types of activities (e.g., a big circle defines an inspection activity and a diamond defines a decision point).

In defining the workflow, a flow diagram is useful as a way of documenting and visualizing the process. Once a flow diagram is built, a structured walk-through can be conducted with those familiar with the process, to ensure that the workflow is correct and that nothing has been overlooked. If you need a better understanding of process flow diagrams, we suggest that you read Chapter 4 of *Business Process Improvement* by H. James Harrington.

The next step might be to define the detail of what happens in each activity and what resources are used for performing that activity. At this point it is appropriate to identify numeric values for the model, such as activity times and probabilities for branching activities. Some of the common measurements are:

- Cycle time per item
- Processing time per item
- Cost per item
- Percent of total process through this branch
- Percent defective
- Waste time
- Scheduled repair time
- Total down time
- Percent reworked
- Percent scrapped

To direct data-gathering efforts and ensure that meetings with others on whom you depend for model information are productive, it may be useful to prepare a list of questions that identify the data needed. Here are a few recommendations:

1. What are the various types of activities that give behavior to the process? Simple value-added activities or complex rule-based activities? What are their inputs and outputs? What are their durations?
2. What are the types of transactions or flow objects that are processed? What attributes, if any, distinguish the way in which entities of the same type are processed or routed?
3. What types of resources (agents, servers, equipment) are used by the process and how many units are there of each type?
4. What is the schedule of availability for resources (define in terms of shift or break schedules)?
5. What interruptions are planned for resources (holidays, scheduled maintenance, setup)?
6. What are the costs associated with resources (define in terms of usage or by hourly or annual rates)?
7. What is the workflow for each transaction type in the process and what decision criteria are used when choosing among alternative flows (e.g., probabilistic, deterministic, or conditional)?
8. What triggers the activities in the process (e.g., available capacity at the next activity, a request from the downstream activity, an external condition)?
9. Where, when, and in what quantities do entities enter the process? (Define the schedule, inter-arrival time, cyclic arrival pattern, or condition that initiates each arrival.)

Appendix B illustrates how data are gathered using a checklist. Depending on the purpose of the simulation and level of detail needed, some of these questions may not apply. For very detailed models, additional questions may be needed. Answers to these questions should provide nearly all of the information necessary to build a model.

Use Appropriate Data Sources

Some processes are inherently data-rich. Others are not. For example, a customer service process involving a call center is extremely data-rich. On the other hand, a customer service process involving an auto body shop is not. When the process under study is data-rich, the source of data is usually an automated system. When the process is data-poor, the only way to obtain data is by reviewing reports, conducting personal interviews, and personal observation.

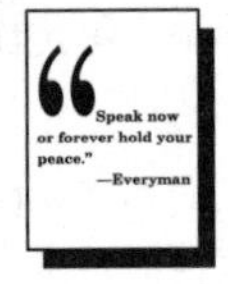

“It has been my experience,” notes Carson (1986), “that for large-scale real systems, there is seldom any one individual who understands how the system works in sufficient detail to build an accurate simulation model. The modeler must be willing to be a bit of a detective to ferret out the necessary knowledge.”

Typical sources of data for a process simulation study are:

- Process plans
- Time studies
- Flowcharts
- Sales forecasts
- Maintenance reports
- Equipment manufacturers
- Process walk-throughs
- Benchmarking

In deciding whether to use a particular source of data, it is important to consider the relevancy, reliability, and accessibility of the source. If the information that a particular source can provide is irrelevant for the model being defined, then that source should not be consulted. What good is a maintenance report if it has already been decided that the model will not include down times? Reliability of the source will determine the validity of the model. A manager's perception, for example, may not be as reliable as production logs.

Make Assumptions When Necessary

It doesn't take long after data gathering has started to realize that certain information is unavailable or perhaps unreliable. It's rarely possible to get complete, accurate, and up-to-date data for all of the information needs, especially when modeling a proposed process about which very little is known. Then it's necessary to make assumptions. There's nothing wrong with assumptions as long as the people involved can agree on them and recognize that they are only assumptions. Any design effort must use assumptions where complete or accurate information is lacking.

Many assumptions are only temporary until correct information can be obtained or until it is determined that more accurate information is necessary. A common technique in making assumptions is to run three scenarios—a "best case" using the most optimistic value, a "worst case" using the most pessimistic value, and a "most likely case" using a best-estimate value. This will help determine the amount of risk you want to take in assuming a particular value. The simulation team should keep a list of all the assumptions used in building the model.

Convert Data into a Useful Form

Data are rarely in a form ready for use in a simulation model. Usually, some analysis and conversion need to be performed for data to be useful as an input parameter to the simulation. Random phenomena must either be fit to some standard theoretical distribution, such as a normal or exponential distribution (see Law and Kelton, 1991), or be input as a frequency distribution. Activities may need to be grouped to simplify the description of the process. We will briefly discuss two common techniques for converting data into a useful form for simulation purposes.

1. Distribution Fitting

To define a distribution using a *theoretical* distribution requires that the data, if available, be fit to an appropriate distribution that best describes the variable (commonly used theoretical distributions in simulation are given in Appendix D). Several distribution-fitting packages (e.g., BestFit, ExpertFit, StatFit) are available to assist in fitting sample data to a suitable theoretical distribution. The alternative to using a standard theoretical distribution is to summarize the data in the form of a *frequency* distribution that can be used directly in the model. A frequency distribution is sometimes called an *empirical* or a *user-defined* distribution.

Whether fitting data to a theoretical distribution or using an empirical distribution, it's often useful to organize the data into a frequency distribution table. To define a frequency distribution, group the data into intervals and then state the frequency of occurrence for each interval. To illustrate how this is done, Figure 4-4 tabulates the number or frequency of repairs for an expensive piece of process equipment.

Repair Time (Minutes)	Number of Observations	Percentage	Cumulative Percentage
0 - 1	25	16.5	16.5
1 - 2	33	21.7	38.2
2 - 3	30	19.7	57.9
3 - 4	22	14.5	72.4
4 - 5	14	9.2	81.6
5 - 6	10	6.6	88.2
6 - 7	7	4.6	92.8
7 - 8	5	3.3	96.1
8 - 9	4	2.6	98.7
9 - 10	2	1.3	100.0

FIGURE 4-4. Frequency distributions of repair times

Although rules have been proposed for determining the interval or cell size, the best approach is to make sure that enough cells are defined to show a gradual transition in values, yet not so many cells that groupings become obscured. Note in the last column of the table that the percentage for each interval may be expressed optionally as a cumulative percentage. This helps verify that all 100% of the possibilities are included.

When gathering samples from a static population, one can apply descriptive statistics and draw reasonable inferences about the population. When gathering data from a dynamic and possibly time-varying system, however, one must be sensitive to trends, patterns, and cycles that may occur with time. The samples drawn may not actually be homogeneous samples and, therefore, unsuitable for applying simple descriptive techniques.

2. Activity Grouping

Another consideration in converting data into a useful form is the way in which activities are grouped for modeling purposes. Often it is helpful to group activities, so long as important detail is not sacrificed. This makes models easier to define and more manageable to analyze. In grouping multiple activities into a single activity time for simplification, consider whether activities are performed in parallel or in series.

If activities are done in parallel or with any overlap, the time during which overlapping occurs should not be additive. If, for example, a part is loaded onto a machine at the same time a finished part is unloaded from the machine, only the longer of the two times needs to be included.

Serial activities are always additive. For example, if a series of activities are performed sequentially, rather than specifying the time for each activity, it may be possible to sum activity times and enter a single time or time distribution.

Document and Approve the Data

When it is felt that all of the relevant information has been gathered and organized into a usable form, it is advisable to document the information in the form of data tables, flow diagrams, cause-and-effect diagrams, and assumption lists. Sources of data should also be noted. This document should then be reviewed by others who are in a position to evaluate the validity of the data and approve the assumptions made. This document will be helpful later if you need to make modifications to the model or look at why the actual process ends up working differently than what was modeled.

Validating system data can be a time-consuming and difficult task, especially when so many assumptions are made. In practice, data validation ends up being more of a consensus or agreement that the information is good enough for the purposes of the model. While this approved data document provides the basis for building the model, it often changes as model building and experimentation get under way.

Step 3. Build the Model

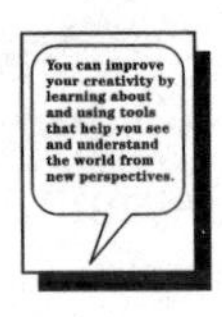

It's never too early to start building a model of the process. Getting the model started before all of the data are gathered may even help identify missing data needed to proceed. Waiting until the information is completely gathered and validated may unnecessarily postpone the building of the model. A model is neither true nor false, but rather useful or not useful. A useful model is one that is valid and provides the needed information to meet the objectives of the simulation.

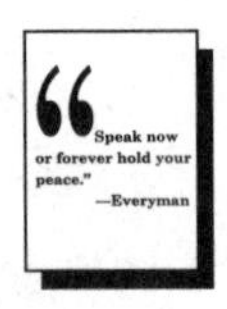

"All models are wrong; some models are useful."
—*George Box, "Robustness in the Strategy of Scientific Model Building"*

How Large or Complex Should a Model Be to Be Useful?

One nice feature of simulation is that models do not have to include all of the final detail before they will run. This allows a progressive refinement strategy to be used in which detail is added to the model in stages rather than all at once. Not only do models get built and running more quickly this way, but it also makes models easier to debug. In the initial stages of a model, for example, fancy graphics are not very useful and shouldn't be added until later, when preparing for the final model presentation, since they are likely to be changed anyway.

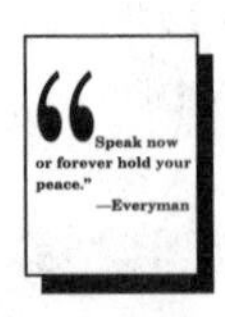

"Simulation modeling is a challenging intellectual task. It requires a combination of competence, ingenuity and experience that is neither intuitively obvious nor trivially learned."
—*Richard Conway,* User's Guide to XCELL Factory Modeling System *(Analysis Chapter)*

Never underestimate the complexity of model building. It's always better to begin simple and add complexity rather than to create an entire complex model at once. It's also easier to add detail to a model than to remove it. Building a model in stages makes it easier to identify and correct bugs.

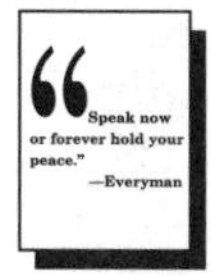

Law and Kelton (1991) have advised, "Although there are few firm rules on how one should go about the modeling process, one point on which most authors agree is that it is always a good idea to start with a simple model which can later be made more sophisticated if necessary. A model should contain only enough detail to capture the essence of the system for the purposes for which the model is intended: it is not necessary to have a one-to-one correspondence between elements of the model and elements of the system. A model with excessive detail may be too expensive to program and to execute."

For unusually large models, it may be useful to identify definable boundaries within a model to permit model partitioning. Model partitioning is the process of dividing a model into two or more modules that represent physically separate sections of the process. The purpose of model partitioning is to allow model sections to be built and debugged, possibly even by several individuals working independently of each other. Once sections are finished, they can be merged to create the overall model. This "divide and conquer" method of model building can greatly reduce the time and difficulty in building and debugging large models.

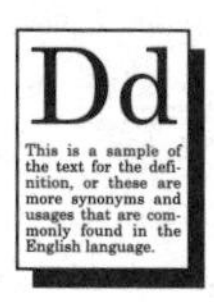

Model partitioning—The process of dividing a model into two or more smaller modules that represent physically separate sections of the process.

What Happens to the Model After It Is Used?

In the past, process simulation models were viewed as throwaway models that outgrew their usefulness once the decisions for which they were developed were made. This is no longer true. With the invention of object technology that provides reusability, the availability of scalable simulation tools, and the increased integration of related methods such as flowcharting, workflow management, and scheduling, simulation models can be used repeatedly.

For example, simulation may be used to help make strategic decisions as alternative goals and overall approaches are being established, such as determining the feasibility of alternative production levels or inventory strategies. As the design phase begins, alternative system configurations can be modeled. Once a configuration has been selected, the model can be further used at the operational level to find the best control or decision logic for managing the process. The algorithms used can even provide a basis for developing the actual control and information systems specification.

In some applications, the simulation model is put to use on a day-to-day basis for production scheduling. In many organizations today, the simulation model is being connected to the process data system so that individual transactions are being tracked on a real-time basis. This allows developing bottlenecks to be identified before they become problems and keep an individual transaction from being delayed. Another benefit from the model may come later when design changes are made. Since the base model already exists, model changes can be quickly evaluated.

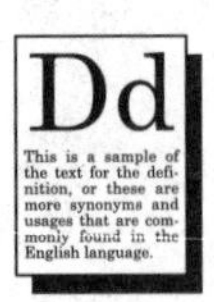

Event-trace—A software feature that enables the user to look inside the simulation to describe what the model is doing. An event-trace usually includes a time stamp, a transaction, an activity or a resource name, and a description of the event.

Step 4. Verify and Validate the Model

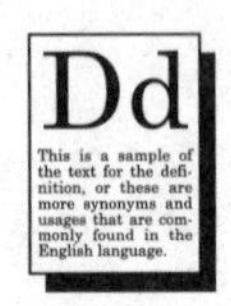

Verification—The act of demonstrating that a simulation model is working as intended.

Once a model is defined using a selected software tool, the model must generally be debugged to ensure that it works correctly. The process of demonstrating that a model works as intended is called *model verification.* It's much easier to debug a model built in stages and with minimal detail than to debug a model that is large and complex. Eliminating bugs in a program model can take considerable time, especially if a general-purpose language is used in which frequent coding errors occur. Most process simulation tools provide an event-trace capability in the form of screen messages or graphic animation or some combination of these two. A trace enables the user to look inside the simulation to see if the simulation is performing as it should. Good simulation products provide interactive debugging capability that further facilitates debugging. A thorough walk-through of the model input is always advisable.

Sim Time	Part Name	Part ID	Activity	Location
0.00	001563	120	Init Inventory	Regional DC West
0.00	001324	122	Init Inventory	Regional DC East
0.00	001228	124	Init Inventory	Central DC
0.00	001397	121	Init Inventory	Central DC
0.00	001228	124	Build Aircraft	SW Factory
1.23	001563	120	Build Aircraft	SE Factory
2.93	001324	122	Transport Part	MW Factory

FIGURE 4-5. A sample trace output

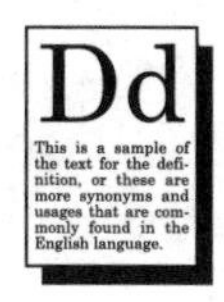

Validation—The act of determining the degree to which the model corresponds to the real process.

Face validity—Quality of a model that appears, from all outward indications, to be an accurate representation of the process.

During the process of model building, the modeler must be constantly concerned with how closely the model reflects the actual or proposed process. The process of determining the degree to which the model corresponds to the real world is called *model validation.* It's impossible to prove absolute validity. As Neelamkavil (1987) explains, "True validation is a philosophical impossibility and all we can do is either invalidate or 'fail to invalidate.'" For this reason, what we seek to establish is actually a high degree of face validity. Face validity means that, from all outward indications, the model appears to represent the process accurately.

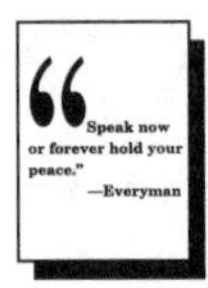

There is no simple test to establish the validity of a model. Validation is an inductive process in which the modeler draws conclusions about the accuracy of the model based on the evidence available. Gathering evidence to determine model validity is largely accomplished by examining the model structure (i.e., the algorithms and relationships) to see how closely it corresponds to the actual process definition. For models having complex logic, animation can be used effectively as a validation tool. Finally, the output results should be analyzed to see if they appear reasonable (Figure 4-6).

If it's possible to monitor the actual process, the model results may be compared with process performance results. If these procedures are performed without encountering any discrepancy between the real-world process and the model, the process model is said to have face validity.

Step 5. Conduct Experiments

The fifth implementation activity is to conduct experiments or run "what-if" scenarios with the model. Simulation is basically an application of the scientific method. We begin with a theory of why certain design rules or management strategies are better than others. Based on these theories, the designer develops a hypothesis, which he or she then tests through simulation. Based on the results of the simulation, the designer draws conclusions about the validity of that hypothesis. In a simulation experiment, there are input variables defining the model that are independent and may be manipulated or varied. The effects of this manipulation on dependent or response variables are measured and correlated.

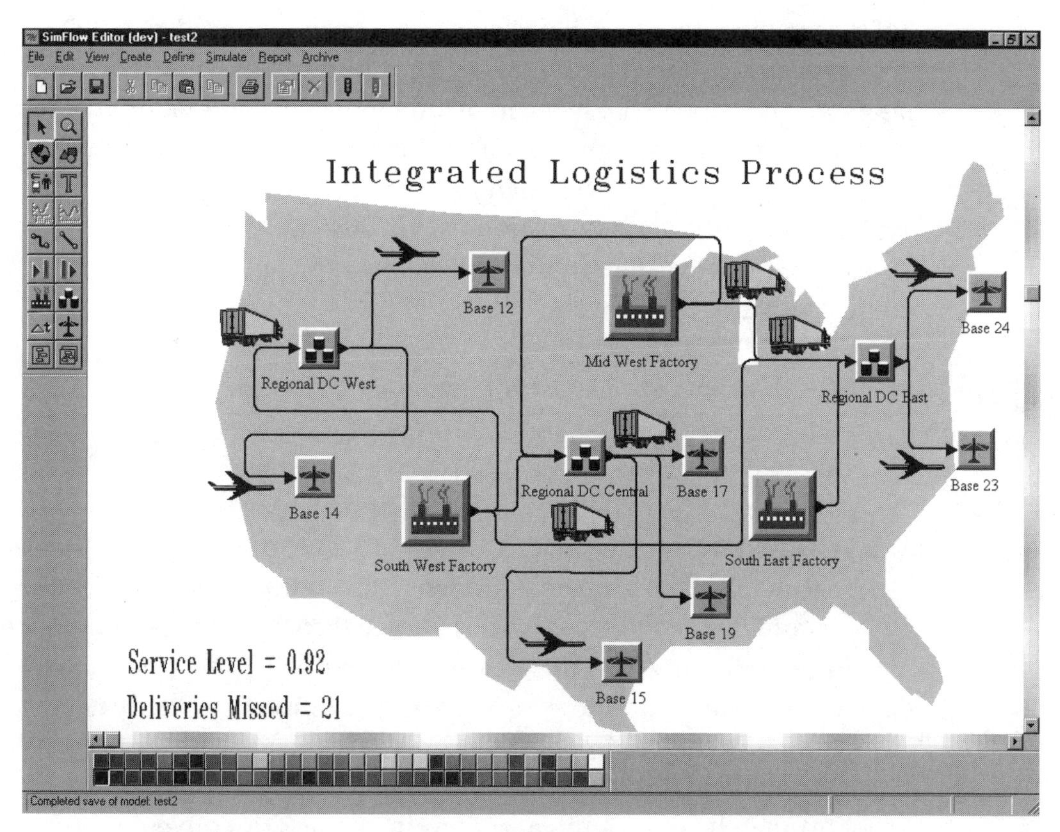

FIGURE 4-6. An animation screen

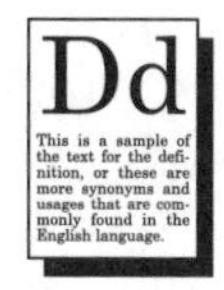

Replication—One cycle through a process simulation model. The number of replications affects the width of the confidence interval: the width of the confidence interval decreases as the number of replications rises.

Confidence interval—A basic component of output analysis. It is a numerical range with which we can analyze the output data for a given performance measure, a range within which we can have a certain confidence that the true mean falls.

As with any experiment involving systems dynamics and randomness, the results of the simulation will be random. The results of a single simulation run represent only one of several possible outcomes. This means that multiple replications must be run to test the reproducibility of the results. Otherwise, a decision might be made based on a fluke outcome or at least an outcome that is not representative of what would normally be expected. Since simulation uses a pseudo-random number generator, running the simulation multiple times simply reproduces the same sample. In order to get an independent sample, the starting seed value for each random stream must be different for each replication, thus ensuring that the random numbers generated from replication to replication are independent.

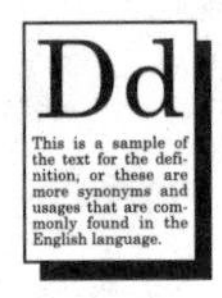

Seed—A value provided for the random number generator.

Depending on the degree of precision required in the output, it might be desirable to determine a confidence interval for the output, a range within which we can have a certain level of confidence that the true mean falls. For a given confidence level or probability, say .90 or 90%, a confidence interval for the average throughput rate of a system might be determined to be between 45.5 and 50.8 units per hour. We could then say that there is a .90 probability that the true mean throughput of the model (not of the actual process!) lies between 45.5 and 50.8 units per hour.

Fortunately, most simulation products make it convenient to conduct experiments, run multiple replications, and calculate confidence intervals. However, the modeler must still decide which types of experimentation are appropriate. When conducting simulation experiments, the following questions should be asked:

- Am I interested in the steady-state behavior of the system or a specific period of operation?
- How can I eliminate start-up bias or get the right initial condition for the model?
- What is the best method for obtaining sample observations that may be used to estimate the true expected behavior of the model?
- What is an appropriate run length for the simulation?
- How many replications should be made?
- How many different random streams should be used?

- How should initial seed values be controlled from replication to replication?

Answers to the above questions will be determined largely by the following three factors:

1. The nature of the simulation (terminating or non-terminating)
2. The objective of the simulation (capacity analysis, alternative comparisons, etc.)
3. The precision required (rough estimate versus confidence interval estimates)

We explain in Chapter 6 how these factors are taken into account when conducting simulation experiments.

Step 6. Analyze, Document, and Present the Results

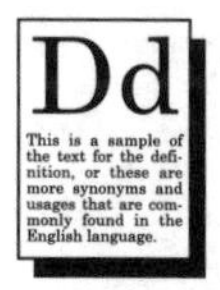

Output analysis—A way of using simulation output to develop inferences about the actual process or system.

Output analysis deals with drawing inferences about the actual system based on the simulation output. When conducting simulation experiments, use extreme caution in interpreting the results. Since the results of a simulation experiment are random (given the probabilistic nature of the inputs), an accurate measurement of the statistical significance of the output is necessary.

People doing simulation in academia are often accused of working with contrived and often oversimplified assumptions, yet are extremely careful about ensuring the statistical significance of the model results. Simulation practitioners in industry, on the other hand, are usually careful to obtain valid model data, yet tend to ignore the statistical issues associated with simulation output. To achieve useful results, it's important to maintain a proper balance between establishing model validation and establishing the statistical significance of simulation output.

The most valuable benefit from simulation is to gain insight, not necessarily to find absolute answers. The goal of conducting experiments is not just to find out how well a particular process operates, but to gain enough insight to be able to improve the process. Unfortunately, simulation output only reports the symptomatic behavior of problems, but rarely identifies causes of problems. Bottleneck activities, for example, are usually identified by analyzing queue time and resource utilization statistics. Detecting the source of the bottleneck is sometimes a bit trickier than identifying the bottleneck. Bottlenecks may be caused by excessive activity times, prolonged delays due to the unavailability of resources, or an inordinate amount of down time. The ability to draw correct inferences from the results is essential to making process improvements.

The results of the process simulation analysis should be supported with good documentation and a well-rehearsed presentation so that an informed decision can be made. Documentation of the data and assumptions, the model(s) developed, and the experiments performed should all be included in a final simulation report. Modern simulation tools facilitate this activity by providing hypertext markup language (HTML) versions of the model input and output, a format that allows the documentation to be viewed using a Web browser.

A simulation has failed if it has produced evidence to support a particular change and then that change is not implemented, especially if it is economically justified. The process of selling simulation results is largely a process of establishing the credibility of the model. It isn't enough for the model to be valid; the customer or management must also be convinced of its validity if it is to be used in making decisions. Finally, the results must be presented in terms that are easy to understand and evaluate. Relating the value of results in terms of bottom-line impact always produces a compelling case for recommendations.

It's best to present results in terms of alternative solutions and their implications, without suggesting one alternative over another. For example, a proposed process alternative that yields the lowest process costs may result in headcount reduction. In such a case, it is best to caution the decision makers that your simulation study looks only at the quantitative aspects of the process and that it does not take into account the qualitative aspects that may result in long-term employee loyalty.

Animation and output charts are extremely useful for communicating the results of a simulation study. This usually requires some touch-up work to create the right effect in visualizing the process status. In preparing the results, it is often necessary to add a few touch-ups to the model (like a full dress rehearsal) so that the presentation effectively and convincingly presents the results of the simulation study.

The dress rehearsal

After the presentation is finished and there is no further analysis to be conducted (the final presentation seems to always elicit suggestions for trying this or that with the model), the model recommendations, if approved, are ready for implementation. If the simulation has been adequately documented, it should provide a good functional specification for process implementation or change management purposes.

In the following chapter, we will get into the details of building a simulation model and provide examples of the data that are necessary to build a simulation model.

Why Simulation Projects Fail

If you follow the implementation activities outlined in this chapter, your simulation project is very likely to be successful. Typical reasons why simulation projects fail include the following:

- Failure to state realistic objectives, constraints, and scope at the outset
- Failure to involve individuals affected by outcome
- Overrunning budget and time constraints
- Failure to obtain data and to properly convert them into a useful form
- Including more detail than is needed or too much detail too soon
- Failure to verify and validate the model
- Basing decisions on a single-run observation or not running multiple experiments
- Basing decisions on average statistics when the output is cyclical
- Not preparing meaningful reports or not preparing and rehearsing the presentation

Summary

A simulation project has distinct steps that must be understood and followed in order to be successful. Steps for implementing a simulation study include planning the project, collecting and analyzing data, building a model, verifying and validating the model, conducting experiments, analyzing the output, and presenting the results. Following these steps in an iterative fashion will ensure successful simulation.

Just remember that ongoing communication with owners, stakeholders, and customers during a simulation study is also vital, to

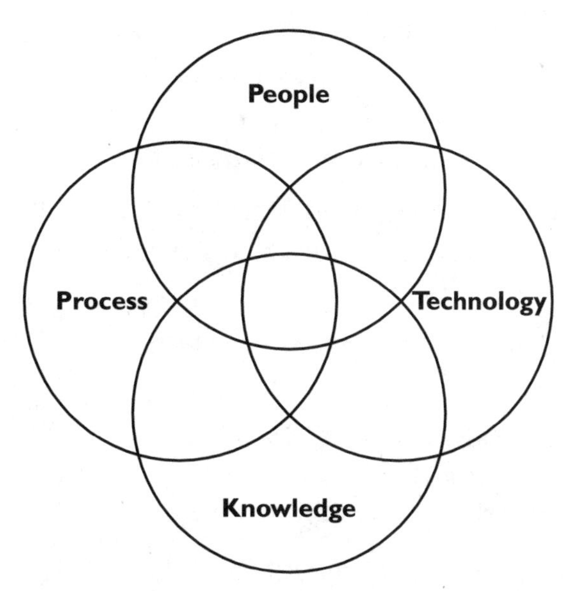

FIGURE 4-7. Four essentials of any project

ensure that the model suits the intended purposes and that everyone understands the objectives, assumptions, and results of the study.

"During installation of any project, four things must be managed:

Process
Technology
People
Knowledge

Most projects fail because all four are not managed equally well."

References

Box, George, "Robustness in the Strategy of Scientific Model Building," *Robustness in Statistics: Proceedings of a Workshop*, eds. Robert L. Launer and Graham N. Wilkerson (New York: Academic Press, 1979), pp. 201-236.

Bresnahan, Jennifer, "Success: Data Modeling," *CIO*, March 1997, pp. 57-66.

Carson, John S., "Convincing Users of Model's Validity Is Challenging Aspect of Modeler's Job," *Industrial Engineering*, June 1986, p. 77.

Conway, Richard, William L. Maxwell, and Steven L. Worona, *User's Guide to XCELL Factory Modeling System* (Palo Alto, CA: The Scientific Press, 1986), pp. 65-66.

Gordon, Geoffrey, *System Simulation*, 2nd edition (Englewood Cliffs, NJ: Prentice-Hall, 1978).

Harrington, H. James, *Business Process Improvement: The Breakthrough Strategy for Total Quality, Productivity, and Competitiveness* (New York: McGraw-Hill, 1991).

Hoover, Stewart V., and Ronald F. Perry, *Simulation: A Problem-Solving Approach* (Reading, MA: Addison-Wesley, 1990).

Knepell, Peter L., and Deborah C. Arangno, *Simulation Validation: A Confidence Assessment Methodology* (Los Alamitos, CA: IEEE Computer Society Press, 1993).

Law, Averill M., and W. David Kelton, *Simulation Modeling and Analysis* (New York: McGraw-Hill, 1991).

Neelamkavil, Francis, *Computer Simulation and Modelling* (New York: John Wiley & Sons, 1987).

Pritsker, Alan B., and Claude Dennis Pegden, *Introduction to Simulation and SLAM* (New York: John Wiley & Sons, 1979).

Russell, Edward C., *Building Simulation Models with SIMSCRIPT II.5* (La Jolla, CA: CACI Products Co., 1983).

Schlesinger, Stewart, "Terminology for Model Credibility," *Simulation*, 32 (3), March 1979, pp. 103-104.

Shannon, Robert E., *Systems Simulation: The Art and Science* (Englewood Cliffs, NJ: Prentice-Hall, 1975).

Thesen, Arne, and Laurel E. Travis, *Simulation for Decision Making* (Eagan, MN: West Publishing, 1992).

CHAPTER 5

Modeling Dynamic Behaviors

A static flowchart falls far short of defining dynamic processes.

Introduction

A process model consists of three major types of objects:

- activities
- resources
- transactions (products or services).

There are fundamental differences between modeling the dynamic behaviors of these objects and static process modeling. This chapter describes these three major modeling objects, their dynamic behaviors, and how they can be used in process simulation. We present various dynamic modeling objects and illustrate their use for process improvement. Some of these concepts may be confusing at first, due to the difficulty of describing dynamic and random behavior on paper. We suggest running the simulation examples on the CD-ROM before reading the section here on activity modeling.

This chapter also describes advanced modeling functions for process simulation. These functions include user-defined attributes, system-state variables, and user-defined expressions. Advanced modeling functions are needed to accurately model the dynamic behavior of real-world processes.

What Is the Difference Between a Process and an Activity?

Processes use an organization's resources to provide definitive results. *Activities* are things that go on within all processes. An activity may consist of one task or many.

In process modeling, a process object allows you to represent several subprocesses and activities in multiple levels of detail. The ability to decompose a process into layers is called *hierarchical process modeling.* For example, purchasing or product development can be modeled as hierarchical processes, with the actual process behaviors defined at lower levels.

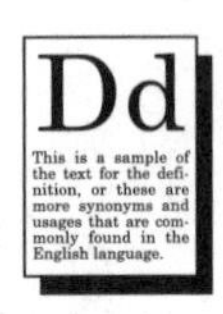

Hierarchical process modeling—The ability to decompose a process into layers.

Transaction—Any entity that flows through a process simulation model. Transactions represent physical objects, such as orders or other paperwork, or informational objects, such as triggers, signals, or flags.

Activity object—Symbol used for modeling unique dynamic behaviors of a process. Examples of activity objects would be BATCH and DELAY.

Batch—An activity object that holds a specified number of transactions until a batch is formed and then releases the batch to the next activity.

Delay—An activity object that holds a transaction for a specified period of time before releasing it to the next activity.

In process simulation, we use activity objects to model the unique behavior or behaviors of a process. Activities are nondecomposable. A DELAY activity is the most commonly used activity type in process modeling. It has at least an activity time and sometimes a resource requirement. For example, processing a claim or delivering a shipment can be modeled as DELAY activities.

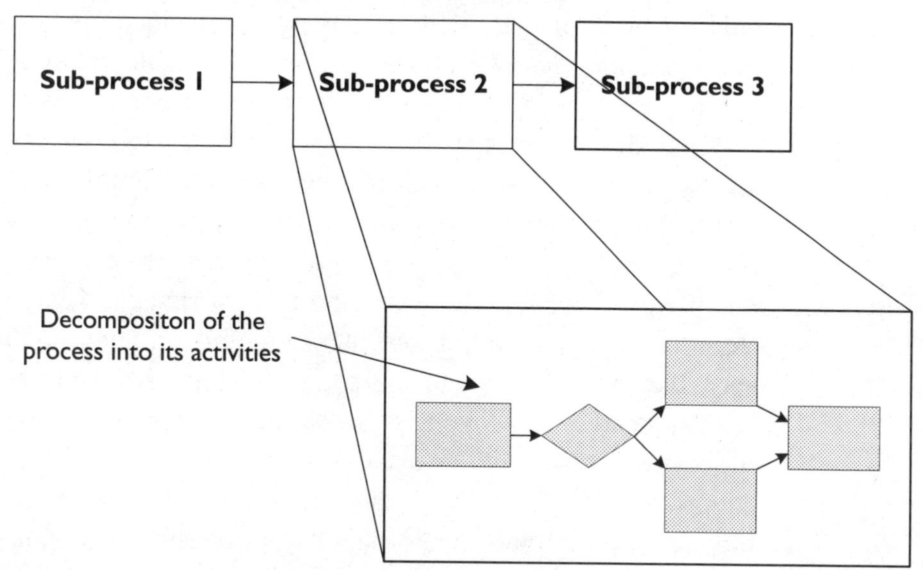

FIGURE 5-1. A hierarchical process

In a process, there may be several activities—such as BRANCH, BATCH, ASSEMBLE, or TRANSFORMATION—that accept an input and produce an output. For example, triggering of an order by a customer or final testing of the developed product is modeled using unique activity objects.

Branch—An activity object that holds a transaction for a specified period of time before releasing it to the next activity.

Assemble—An activity object that puts components together.

Transformation—An activity object that accepts an input and produces a different output.

Top-Down and Bottom-Up Process Modeling

There are two approaches to developing hierarchical process models. Each approach has its advantages and drawbacks.

In the *top-down* approach, the major process is decomposed into its subprocesses. Then, each subprocess is further decomposed into subprocesses or activities. This progressive decomposition approach continues until a sufficient level of detail is achieved in describing the behavior of a process, meaning no further decomposition is needed.

The advantages of the top-down approach are consistency and simplicity. These advantages can reduce model development time and maximize communication. One drawback of the top-down approach is to leave out activities that are general, assuming that they will be modeled in another process or subprocess. Another drawback is to stop drilling into the process too soon without incorporating sufficient detail. Generally speaking, executive management likes the top-down approach.

The second approach is the *bottom-up* approach, in which all of the lowest-level activities are defined first. They are then grouped into subprocesses. Once all of the subprocesses have been established, they are grouped into higher-level subprocesses or major processes.

This approach has the advantage of being complete. However, the price you pay is the number of iterations for fine-tuning the process model. This approach is more time-consuming than the top-down approach and may result in too much detail too soon. Usually, analysts like the bottom-up approach.

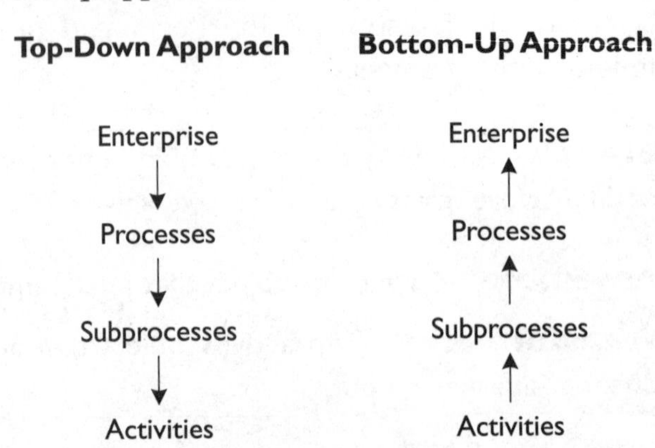

FIGURE 5-2. Top-down and bottom-up process modeling

Based on our experience, we recommend the top-down approach, because incorporating too much detail too soon is one of the pitfalls of process simulation. By establishing some guidelines up front for the top-down approach and following them, you will progressively refine the level of necessary detail. We recommend that a process not have any more than five to seven subprocesses and that a subprocess have no more than five to seven activities. These guidelines ensure that the top-down approach is consistent.

Static Versus Dynamic Activity Modeling

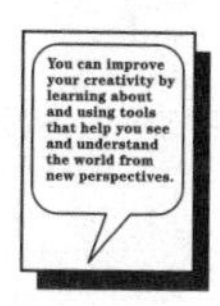

Activity modeling for process simulation is somewhat different than it is for static process modeling and analysis. In static modeling, the user simply defines the effects—activity cycle time and activity cost. On the other hand, in process simulation, the user defines the causes of delays (e.g., random arrivals, random activity times, resource unavailability, random equipment failures) and analyzes the effects of these factors on cycle time and activity cost.

For static process modeling and analysis purposes, activities can be classified into three categories:

- Real-value-added (RVA) activities
- Business-value-added (BVA) activities
- No-value-added (NVA) activities

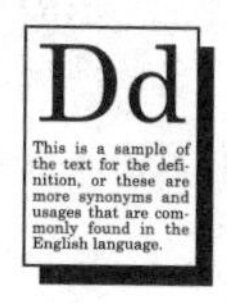

Real-value-added (RVA) activities—Activities that, when viewed by the external customer, are required to provide the output that the customer is expecting.

Business-value-added (BVA) activities—Activities that add no value from the customer's point of view, but are essential for the business.

No-value-added (NVA) activities—Activities that are not required by either the customers or the business.

There is a huge hidden office in most organizations that is made up of the no-value-added and business-value-added activities. No-value-added costs plus business-value-added costs are called *non-value-added* costs. Typically, real-value-added activities account for less than 20% of the total overhead costs (see Figure 5-3).

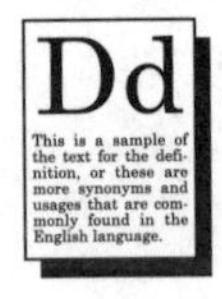

Non-value-added costs—No-value-added costs plus business-value-added costs.

RVA BVA & NVA

FIGURE 5-3. The "Hidden Office"

Examples of RVA activities are answering a customer service call or machining a raw material. Examples of BVA activities are checking the credit rating of a potential buyer or processing payroll. Examples of NVA activities are moving paperwork, waiting for something to happen, or approval activities.

Even though this classification of activities is sufficient for purposes of static modeling and analysis purposes, it is not sufficient for purposes of simulation modeling, because it does not reveal the hidden waste associated with no-value-added activities.

Let's take as our example the NVA activity of moving paperwork. In a static model, this activity is modeled as a DELAY that takes 10 minutes and uses a resource, say a clerk. This approach ignores two elements of dynamic modeling: variability and resource interdependence.

In a process simulation model, moving paperwork activity would also be modeled as a DELAY, but with a random duration and a resource requirement. The duration of the activity may vary between five and 15 minutes, with a most likely time being 10 minutes. During this time, the clerk may be assigned to perform another activity, such as "check incoming mail."

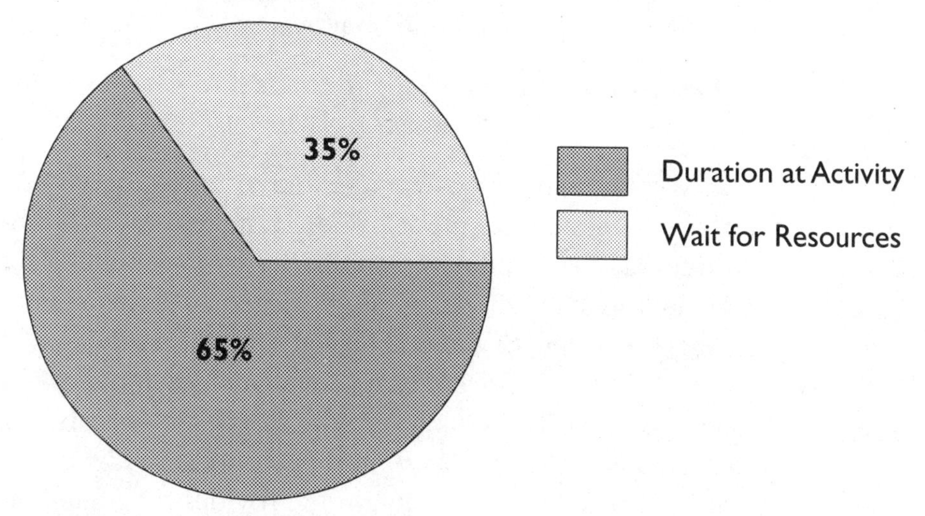

FIGURE 5-4. A pie chart of a non-value-added activity

During the simulation, when work arrives at the clerk's desk and the clerk is busy, the model places the paperwork in queue—just as it happens in the real world. Then it keeps track of the time that paperwork has to wait before being moved and reports the average and maximum waiting times. For an NVA activity such as "move paperwork," analysis of the process simulation results can reveal hidden elements of the delays, such as waiting time for a clerk and waiting time for an approval. Thus, random behaviors and resource interdependencies are two realistic aspects of process simulation modeling not included in static process modeling.

Why Is Variability Important? How Do You Model It?

Some simulations use fixed, non-random values as input and generate fixed, deterministic values as output. If the process you are modeling is really static and deterministic (no variability), this approach works like a charm. No matter how many times you simulate such a model, you will always get the same numbers.

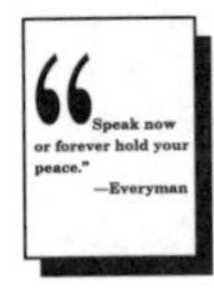

"A simulation is a model, but a model is not a simulation."
— GREG HANSEN, "SIMULATION 101—WHAT ARE MODELING AND SIMULATION?"

Most processes involve some kind of uncertainty or randomness, so realistic simulation models should include random input. In fact, ignoring random input can result in the wrong simulation output. For example, the average values of performance measures such as cycle time or queue length depend directly on the variance of the activity time distributions. So ignoring variability for input will most likely result in getting the wrong output. Of course, variable *input* into a model yields variable *output*. In this section, we discuss the variability associated with *input*. Chapter 6 provides a detailed discussion of analysis and interpretation of variability with model *output*.

Modeling variability is achieved using probabilities and probability distributions. For example, the variability associated with the outcome of an approval activity can be modeled using a probability. If the probability that an application is approved is 0.80 and that it is rejected is 0.20, then the outcome of this activity will be based on a random probability of selecting one condition out of five possible conditions each time an application is processed.

Imagine that we have a box that holds 100 marbles, 20 white and 80 black. The marbles are constantly being stirred, evenly mixing the marbles. If we reach into the box without looking and take out a marble at random, the probabilities would be 0.20 for a white marble and 0.80 for a black marble. With a simulation model, we can show these probabilities electronically, without a box and marbles.

Modeling variability associated with activity times, inter-arrival times, or time-to-failure and time-to-repair values is achieved using probability distributions. These distributions are models of actual data representing the mean and variance of random variables. Probability distributions have parameters that describe the shape and a range of values.

For example, the variability associated with the approval activity time may be modeled using a triangular distribution that is a continuous type of a distribution. The triangular distribution has three parameters, namely minimum, mode, and maximum values. Let's assume that the approval activity takes at least 10 minutes, at most 30 minutes, and generally 15 minutes. So you would use a triangular distribution with those three parameters (Figure 5-5).

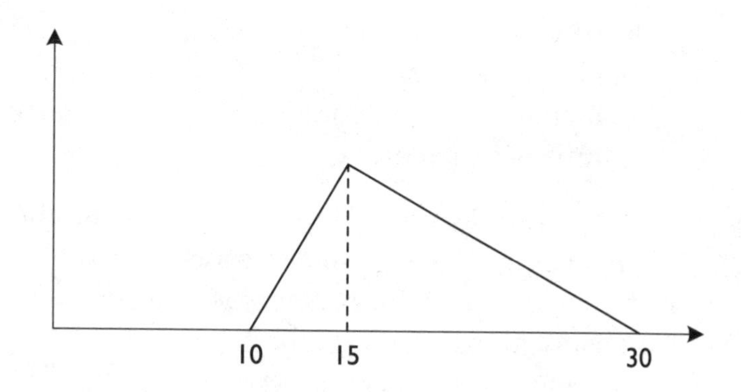

FIGURE 5-5. A triangular distribution

When you simulate the process, the simulation software generates a random number from the triangular distribution each time an application enters the approval activity. The activity time yields a different approval time for each transaction—just as it happens in the real world. For example, if we simulate the process, we may get activity times of 14, 17, 11, 21, 27, 16, and 12 for seven transactions.

Most of the proven methods used in simulation products for describing probability distributions and generating random numbers can be found in Law and Kelton (1991). Fortunately, the techniques for modeling distributions are provided in data analysis tools that are often integrated with simulation software. So you need not be concerned about which distribution or what parameters to use if you have actual data. You can simply feed your data into these tools and they provide recommendations for the best-fit distribution.

Even though you can obtain recommendations for the best distribution to use, we recommend that you familiarize yourself with the shapes and parameters of continuous distributions that are commonly used in simulation models. See Appendix D for shapes and parameters of commonly used statistical distributions. Below are some of the commonly used distributions and practical guidelines as to how they are used in process simulation models.

- gamma, exponential—for modeling time between arrivals of transactions
- triangular, beta, lognormal, Erlang, gamma, Weibull—for modeling activity times
- lognormal, exponential, Weibull—for time between random failures or down times

Figure 5-6 illustrates the danger of using the wrong distribution. Given an activity with a single resource and a single queue and exponential inter-arrival times, actual service time data were collected for 200 observations. Then the data were fit to four statistical distributions, using distribution-fitting software. When the queuing model was simulated using the four distributions for 100,000 transactions, each delay was recorded and the percent error was calculated. The example clearly shows that the Weibull distribution was the best fit and the other three distributions were way off. (This example is developed by Averill Law, an international authority in the area of simulation modeling and analysis.)

It is worth knowing that the normal distribution (bell-shaped curve) is not a very good distribution to use for simulation model input data (see Figure 5-6). The reason for this is that the tails of the normal distribution extend beyond a range of minimum and maximum values. There is also a chance of getting negative values (depending on the standard deviation), which may be invalid.

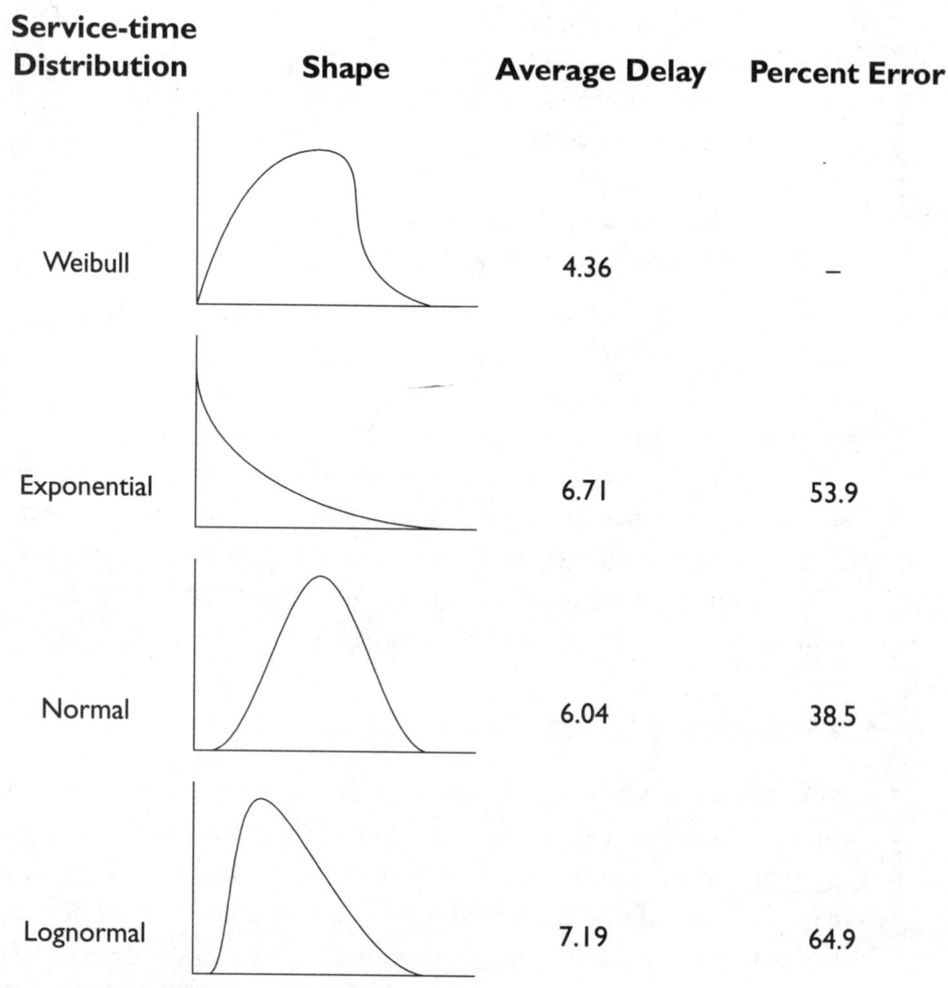

FIGURE 5-6. Finding the best distribution

Activity Modeling

It has been proven that applying common process improvement principles results in reduced cycle time, reduced cost, and increased process quality. Some of the common process improvement principles are:

- Combine duplicate activities.
- Eliminate multiple reviews and approvals.
- Automate repetitive tasks.

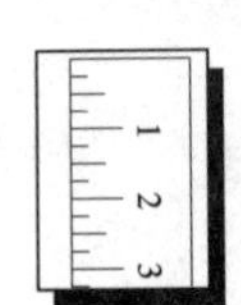

- Simplify complex activities.
- Reduce batch sizes.
- Reduce amount of handling.
- Process in parallel.
- Error-proof activities.
- Implement demand pull (build to orders).
- Outsource inefficient activities.

In order to model and accurately analyze the impact of these process improvement principles on process performance, we have to model and simulate the behavior of activities. Activity modeling objects contain the functionality for modeling the unique behaviors of processes.

Using the activity modeling objects, we can model the current state of a process and validate the model. Then we can create and simulate future-state alternatives for process improvement. In this section, we illustrate how activity modeling can be used to model dynamic behaviors of some common processes.

A Proposal Review Process

Simulation modeling and analysis of the current process can validate the real costs and delays associated with the review and approval process. Visualization of the animated review loops and queuing can help understand the impact on total process time. The proposed solution may be to redesign the proposal development process or to automate it using groupware, to minimize or eliminate the delays. A process simulation model usually is helpful for visualizing and accurately measuring the cycle time and activity costs associated with the future-state process.

In a typical proposal review process, there are very few real-value-added activities. They are the creation, review, and approval of the proposal. Some of the no-value-added activities are obvious, such as the updating and second or third review activities. However, the waiting times associated with resource constraints are often invisible.

Combining the preparation (a value-added activity) and no-value-added activities such as review and update is often an effective way to detect and correct errors at their source. This not only eliminates the no-value-added activities such as rework, but also eliminates no-value-added time associated with waiting for resources.

Activity Number	Activity	Activity Type	Resource
1	Prepare draft proposal	DELAY, Wait for Reviewer	Creator
2-3	Review draft	DELAY + BRANCH, Wait for Creator	Reviewer
4	Update proposal	DELAY, Wait for Reviewer	Creator
5-6	Review updated proposal	DELAY + BRANCH, Wait for Creator	Reviewer
7	Finalize proposal	DELAY, Wait for Reviewer	Creator
8	Approve final proposal	DELAY	Reviewer

FIGURE 5-7. Activities of a proposal review process

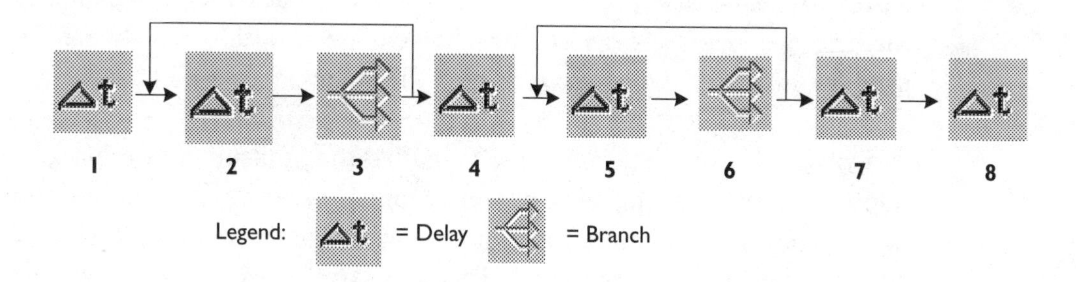

FIGURE 5-8. Process map of the proposal review process

A Mortgage Application Process

Workflow automation is an ideal tool for automating repetitive activities. In a mortgage application process, most of the no-value-added time is attributable to paperwork delays and information searches. With the use of database, workflow, and imaging technologies, parallel mortgage processing activities can be sped up significantly. This results in minimizing the queue time where paperwork must be held until all of the mortgage conditions are met.

A typical mortgage application process starts with the creation of an application form. Copies of the application form initiate various parallel activities, such as credit check and employment verification. When all parallel activities are completed, the corresponding documents are joined and the mortgage is submitted for approval. Two unique activity constructs needed for modeling a mortgage application process are SPLIT and JOIN. A SPLIT activity takes an incoming transaction and creates clones of that transaction. A JOIN activity takes the clones and original transaction that were split up and matches them to produce the single transaction that represents a customer's loan file.

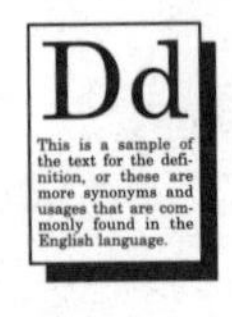

Split— Activity that takes an incoming entity and creates clones of that entity as well as providing an output of the original entity. For example, clones of a purchase order may be created with a SPLIT activity and sent to accounts payable and shipping.

Join—Activity that takes the clones and original entity and matches them to produce the original entity. For example, a JOIN activity may be used for matching the paperwork with the shipment.

Although flow diagrams help visualize the splitting and joining of paperwork flow in a process like mortgage processing, only animation of an event-driven simulation can help visualize the queuing associated with delay and join activities. Usually, parallel activities following a split activity are not completed at the same time; therefore, there is a waiting time associated with combining all of the documents in a file for the loan approval activity.

Activity Number	Activity	Activity Type	Resource
1	Review application for completeness	DELAY, split	Mortgage Specialist
2	Send copies to credit specialist and appraiser	SPLIT	
3	Perform credit check	DELAY, Wait for CS	Credit Specialist
4	Perform employment verification	DELAY, Wait for MS	Mortgage Specialist
5	Perform property assessment	DELAY, Wait for Appraiser	Appraiser
6	Gather all documents in a single file	JOIN, Wait for MS and Documents	Mortgage Specialist
7	Review and approve mortgage	DELAY, Wait for Loan Manager	Loan Manager

FIGURE 5-9. Activities of a mortgage application process

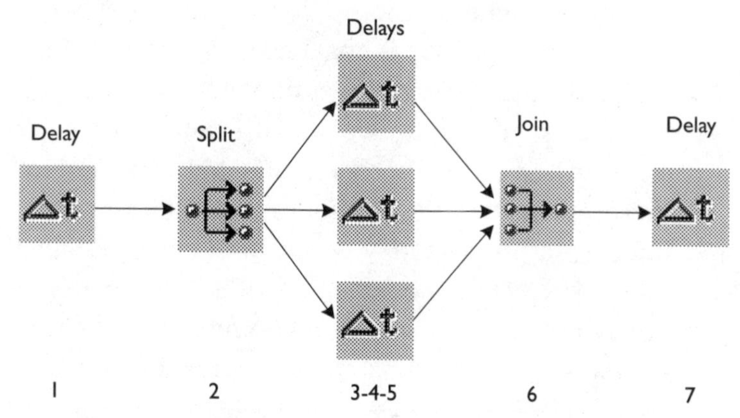

FIGURE 5-10. Process map of the mortgage application process

A Receiving/Shipping Process

Reducing batch size minimizes the queue time associated with holding up transactions until a batch is formed. This process improvement principle naturally reduces the time to batch; however, it results in increased number of batches. Often in logistics or customer service processes, delivery frequency is a competitive weapon. Federal

Express has proven this concept by building an international business based on "overnight delivery."

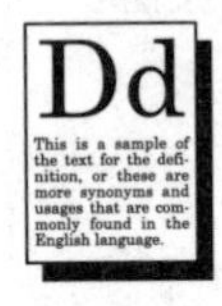

Batch—Activity that combines a given quantity of entities into a single batch. For example, mail may be accumulated for delivery using a BATCH activity.

Unbatch—Activity that splits a batch into individual entities. For example, unloading a truck that results in multiple loads may be modeled with an UNBATCH activity.

All receiving and shipping activities contain UNBATCH and BATCH activities. An UNBATCH activity splits a single transaction into multiple transactions. For example, unloading of a truck that results in multiple loads may be modeled with an UNBATCH activity construct. A BATCH activity combines a given quantity of transactions into a single batch.

The queuing of transactions until either a desired batch quantity (container capacity) is reached or a desired time (departure time) is reached causes the greatest no-value-added time in a BATCH activity. Waiting for resources is also a no-value-added activity.

There are definite trade-offs between reducing batch sizes and increasing deliveries or increasing setups. Reducing batch size to improve a process may result in excessive delivery or setup time or costs. Therefore, the dynamics of upstream processes to batching and downstream processes to unbatching must be simulated and analyzed so that the optimum batch size can be achieved.

Activity Number	Activity	Activity Type	Resource
1	Prepare each load for shipment	DELAY	Shipper
2	Accumulate loads for shipment	BATCH, Wait for batch	
3	Load truck	DELAY, Wait for driver	Driver
4	Move loads with truck	DELAY, Wait for dock	Driver, Truck
5	Unload truck	UNBATCH	Driver

FIGURE 5-11. Activities for receiving and shipping processes

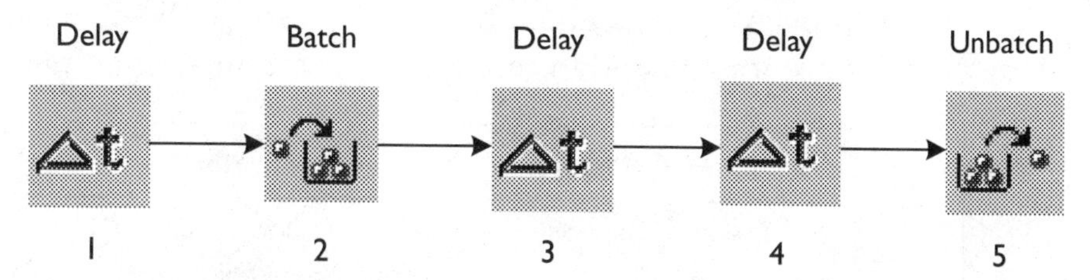

FIGURE 5-12. Process map of the receiving and shipping processes

An Assembly Process

An assembly process involves coordinating and combining multiple input entities (components) into a single output. An assembly process may be performed in one of two ways:

1. Each component is held up until all components are available; then they are assembled.
2. Components are assembled as they become available.

An assembly process consists of a value-added state and two no-value-added states. The no-value-added steps are queuing for the arrival of components and queuing for the resource.

Minimizing the queue time for the individual components of the assembly is the key to improving an assembly process. A common process improvement solution to this problem is outsourcing. By outsourcing, an enterprise can avoid capital investments while improving customer service. However, outsourcing can be expensive, unreliable, or impossible for proprietary reasons.

Alternatives such as multiple sources or internal production supplemented by outsourcing may be viable solutions for improving an assembly process. Another viable option may involve the redesign of the product so that assembly can be performed as components become available. This is called *just-in-time* production and requires that the setup time at each activity be minimized. Batch size is often determined based upon how long it takes to set up an activity, to start, and to process the inputs. For example, it often takes longer to set up the fixtures and ensure that they are working correctly than to process one item after the setup is complete. Modeling and simulating the process will highlight the actual causes of the no-value-added time, whether it is related to resources, constraints, or components.

Activity Number	Activity	Activity Type	Resource
1	Produce Component A	DELAY, Wait for other components, Wait for subassembly	Subassembler
2	Produce Component B	DELAY, Wait for other components, Wait for subassembly	Subassembler
3	Produce Component C	DELAY, Wait for other components, Wait for subassembly	Subassembler
4	Assemble end product	ASSEMBLY, Wait for final assembler	Final Assembler
5	Send to storage	DELAY	Transporter

FIGURE 5-13. Activities of an assembly process

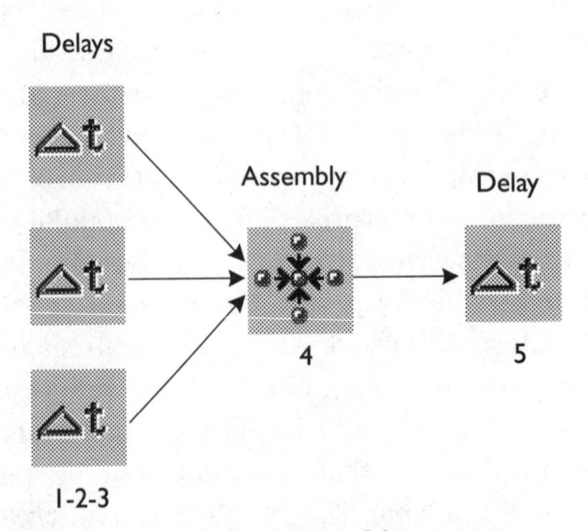

FIGURE 5-14. Process map of the assembly process

Resource Modeling

Resources are the agents that are required to perform an activity. The performance of a dynamic process is usually constrained by the limited availability of resources or by resource interdependencies, which result in queuing for transactions. Process simulation allows you to model capacity, cost, schedule, and allocation for resources. During the simulation, the model automatically keeps track of the utilization of resources, the queuing delays, and the costs incurred by activities and transactions using the resources.

Typical examples of resources are:

- customer representative
- engineer
- supervisor
- department
- equipment
- money
- materials

Human resources are typically defined in terms of full-time equivalents (FTEs). Other resources may be defined in terms of capacity or number of units. An FTE may be an individual resource as well as part of a work group. Work groups may consist of a group of resources that may be required to perform a specific activity, a department, or a group of resources that share the same job function. A resource may belong to multiple work groups.

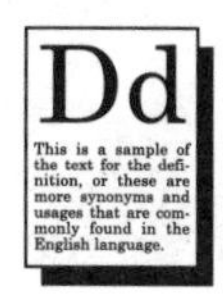

Full-time equivalent (FTE)—The number of hours that an individual would work in a given time period (without overtime), typically 1920 hours/year or 40.0 hours/ week. For example, activity A consumes 200 hours/week, which equates to 5 FTEs (200 hours ÷ 40 hours).

Another important attribute of a resource is its cost. Activity-based costing (ABC) is an ideal source for obtaining cost information. An activity-based process costing study can provide a resource costing

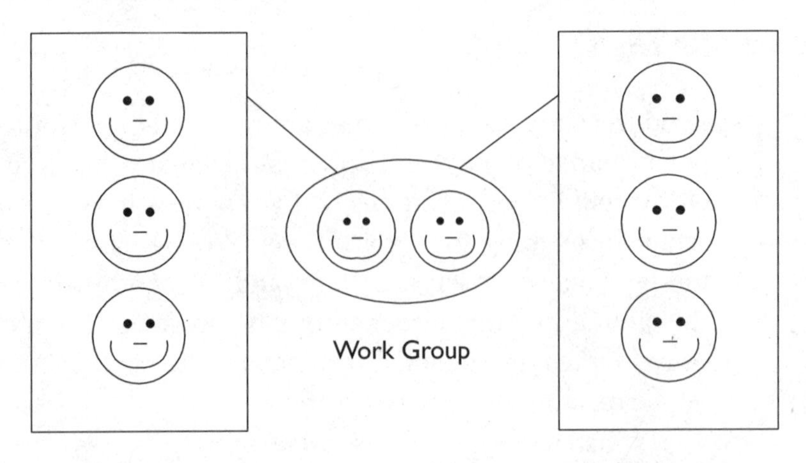

FIGURE 5-15. Graphical depiction of departments, work groups, and resources

rate, which can be used in a process simulation model. If headcount is the basis for assigning cost to activities in the ABC study and the number of people engaged in each of the activities is known, then the resource costing rate is a pretty accurate measure of the annual cost for an FTE. This approach works well for long-range simulations with a planning horizon of months or years.

For modeling resources in short-range simulations, it's more meaningful to define hourly rates. For example, a customer service process that is simulated over a 40- or 80-hour span would be a good candidate for using hourly rates. For consumable resources such as money, computer facilities, and fuel, the most important element of cost is the usage cost per resource unit.

Resource Schedules and Interruptions

Resources generally have scheduled off times, such as shifts, breaks, or holidays, during which they are unavailable to perform activities. Resources also experience random interruptions, such as absenteeism or equipment failures. Because the unavailability of a resource causes queuing, modeling resource schedules and interruptions is essential to developing a realistic process simulation model. When modeling these resource behaviors, you need to address the following considerations:

- Off time or down time
- Interval
- Basis for down time

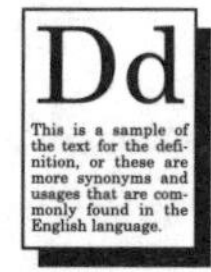

Off time or down time—A period of time when the resources are not available.

Off time or down time may be scheduled or unscheduled. For scheduled shifts and breaks, resources are unavailable for a fixed period of time. In this case, you need to define the starting time and ending time of the unavailability. For random interruptions, the duration of the interruption is a random variable and it can be modeled as a statistical or empirical distribution. In this case, you will need to model the starting time of the interruption which itself can be random.

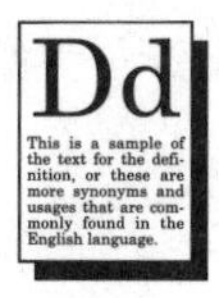

Interval—The time between recurring periods when resources are unavailable.

If the shift schedule or random interruption is recurrent, the interval between unavailability periods must be specified. For scheduled shifts, this is usually a fixed interval; for unplanned interruptions, it is a random variable.

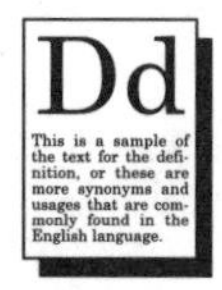

Basis for down time—The period between scheduled or unscheduled down times.

The basis for down time is a consideration more applicable to modeling random equipment failures than scheduled off times. The issue here is whether to base the down time interval or MTBF (mean time between failures) on clock time or usage time. Usually, equipment failures occur based on usage rather than clock time.

An example would be a tool that wears out after 200 hours of use. If this behavior were modeled on the basis of clock time, meaning the tool is unavailable after 200 hours of simulated time, it would not reflect reality. Thus, it is inaccurate to model such a down time on the basis of clock time. Powerful process simulation tools provide a built-in facility for modeling down times based on usage to ensure correct modeling of this behavior.

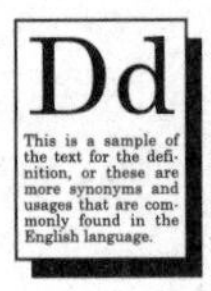

Off units—Units of resources that are unavailable.

Resources are sometimes modeled as a group with multiple units without differentiating among individual units. In such cases, shift schedules need to include the quantity of units that are unavailable during the off time or interruption. For example, five customer service reps in a call center who each have exactly the same capability could be modeled as a resource with five units. In a call center where customer service continues around the clock with a minimum staff level of two reps, you need to model the unavailability of three units of the resource during the off time.

Simulations only take you so far.

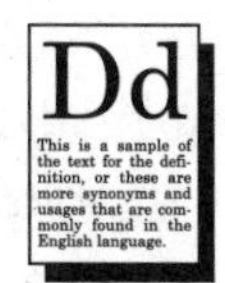

Dormant period—Time when no activities are going on in a process.

If no activity is going on in the process during the off shift time, it is a dormant period. If the entire process is suspended for a period when the resources are scheduled to be off shift, it is not necessary to model the shift. For example, if you are modeling a purchasing process and the whole purchasing process is dormant between 5:00 p.m. Friday and 8:00 a.m. Monday, this period does not need to be modeled.

Resource Setups and Wrap-Ups

Some activities involve a setup task or a wrap-up task. Often, the same resource assigned to that activity performs this task. For example, a customer representative in a call center has to perform a wrap-up activity during which he or she logs the problem and the resolution into a database. This means that the customer representative is still busy, therefore unavailable to service the next customer, even though the previous customer has left the activity.

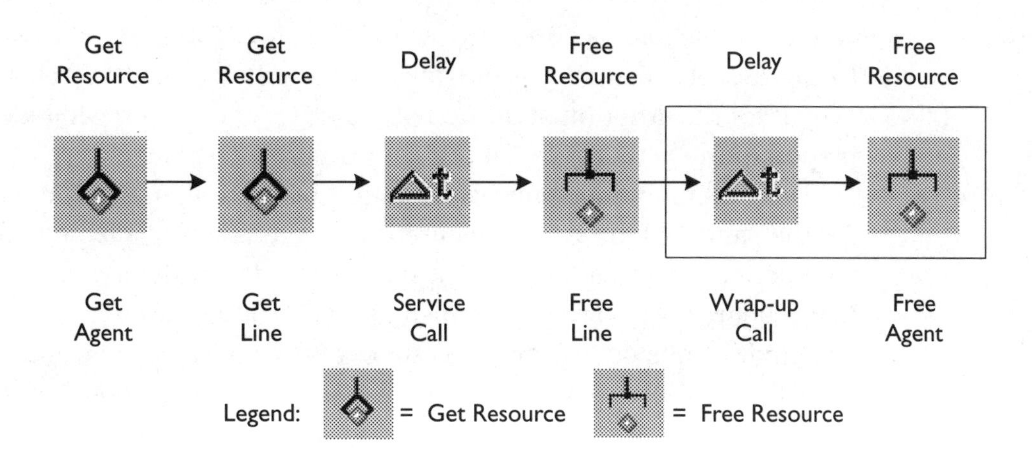

FIGURE 5-16. Setup activity in a call center

The primary reason for modeling resource setups and wrap-ups explicitly is to study their effect on the queuing time element of the total process time. The duration of the setup or wrap-up may depend on the type of transaction. For example, in a job shop production process, there may be minor and major setups. A minor setup may take a short time if the next job type is similar to the previous job type. A major setup may take longer if the next job type is significantly different from the previous job type. By modeling the setups and wrap-ups explicitly, you can evaluate the feasibility of designating a special setup or wrap-up resource.

Resource Assignment and Allocation

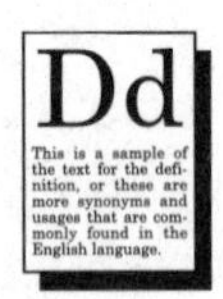

Resource assignment—Ensuring that the right resources are together at the correct time to execute the activity.

Once resources are defined, they need to be assigned to the activities where they are required to perform a task. In the modeling process, this is called *resource assignment.* If an activity requires a single resource, this task is straightforward. You simply assign the resource to the activity, meaning each transaction will capture the resource, keep it for the duration of the activity, and free the resource upon completion of the activity so that the next transaction can get it.

During simulation, many transactions may simultaneously contend for the same resource. If a required resource is not available when a transaction arrives at an activity, the transaction waits in a queue for that resource. This state is defined as "wait for resource" state. Once an activity gains control of a resource, that resource is unavailable to any other activity that requests it. The activity retains control of the resource until it finishes processing the transaction unless the resource is preempted by a higher priority transaction.

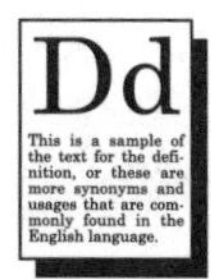

Wait for resource—The status of a transaction when it is ready to be processed but not all of the resources are available to process the transaction.

Sometimes an activity requires more than one resource. For example, a resolution activity in an insurance claim adjustment process may require an expert and a service representative working together. Or two nurses may be necessary to service an emergency patient. When assigning resources to such activities, you need flexibility to define the rules for *resource allocation.*

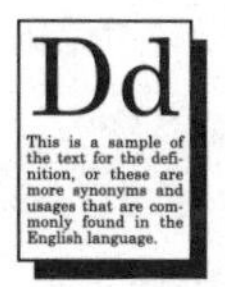

Resource allocation—A system of priorities that defines how resources are assigned if there are multiple assignments for the same resource.

If an activity requires two resources and only one is available, the process simulation model may or may not obtain the resource that is available, depending on the rules you've defined for your model. For example, if you model a test activity that requires a test engineer and a design engineer, then the test activity can start only when both resources are available. Otherwise, the transaction representing work will wait until the resource requirement is met.

During the simulation, all attempts to satisfy resource requirements are made in the order of the priority of transactions queued for the resource. Priority is a transaction attribute assigned when the transaction is defined. All transactions with the same priority are treated on a first-come, first-served basis.

Transaction Modeling

Transactions are the entities that flow through a process simulation model. Transactions can be used to represent physical objects, such as orders or other paperwork, or informational objects, such as triggers, signals, and flags. They may be assigned attributes to define such characteristics as order size, customer type, and priority.

Typical examples of transactions are:

- Customer
- Order
- Message
- Service
- Project

For static process modeling purposes, products and services produced by each activity are defined as *outputs* of that activity and *inputs* into the next activity. In fact, definition of inputs and outputs is an integrated step within an activity modeling session. However, for dynamic process modeling purposes this approach needs to be enhanced, because it does not take into account two very important dynamic transaction modeling concepts.

The activity time of a transaction may be dependent on the *type* of the transaction. For example, a credit check activity may take longer for a customer with a long credit history than for a recent college graduate with little credit history. The activity time of a transaction may also be dependent on the *state* of the transaction, that is, it may vary according to circumstances. For example, an investment transaction may take longer while trading is heavy.

Thus, for process simulation modeling purposes, the inputs and outputs of the activities need to be defined in terms of types of transactions. A general guideline for classifying transactions is to analyze all of the types of transactions and group them into three classes, say A, B, and C. These classifications are based on a criterion that is significant in terms of the nature of the business.

For example, this technique has been used for inventory-analysis purposes for many decades. A very large number of inventory items can be grouped into three types:

- Type A: high-turnover items
- Type B: medium-turnover items
- Type C: low-turnover items

Transaction classification—A way of grouping transactions based upon a significant criterion.

How Are Transactions Generated?

Once the types of transactions that trigger the process are identified, then the trigger mechanism for each type of transaction needs to be established. This is also referred to as the *scheduling* or *arrival* mechanism for generating instances of the transactions in the process model.

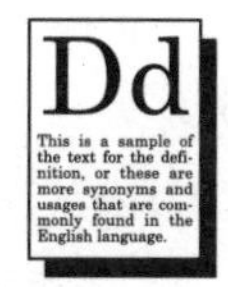

Trigger—The input that starts a transaction through a process or activity.

A GENERATE or START activity triggers the arrival of transactions, customers, or jobs in the process model. Examples of this type of an activity are the arrival of patients in a clinic, the placement of orders by a customer, or the schedule of jobs for production. Arrivals or schedules may be random, deterministic, or conditional. A GENERATE activity may have attributes for arrival time for each transaction, quantity that arrives at that time, frequency, and number of occurrences of that arrival.

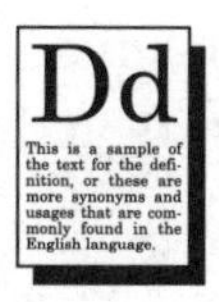

Deterministic arrivals—When things arrive regularly. For example the mail arrives at 12:00 every day, Monday through Friday.

Conditional arrivals—When things arrive based on a condition. For example, if customer inventory drops below 50 units, a supply of 1,000 units arrives.

Transaction generation may be modeled using four types of techniques:

1. periodic arrivals
2. cyclical arrivals
3. calendar-based or scheduled arrivals
4. state-dependent arrivals

Periodic arrivals occur at regular or random intervals. The number of transactions that arrive each time may be a random variable. Also, the time between arrivals (inter-arrival time) may be a random variable. Examples of periodic arrivals are:

- Invoices arriving in an accounts payable department
- Checks arriving in a check-processing department

Cyclical arrivals occur periodically; however, the patterns of arrivals vary by cycles. A cycle is a window during which the arrival patterns or inter-arrival time for each cycle is unique and recurring. Examples of cyclical arrivals are:

- Phone calls arriving at a call center
- Patients arriving in an emergency department

Calendar-based or scheduled arrivals are transactions that arrive at an established time. A scheduled arrival occurs once. It may contain multiple instances of the transaction type. Scheduled arrivals are usually generated by a scheduling system. Examples of scheduled arrivals are:

- Scheduled production jobs arriving at a machine
- Scheduled patients arriving for surgery

State-dependent or conditional arrivals occur when certain conditions exist. These conditions might involve inventory levels, as in the example above.

As mentioned earlier, the boundaries of a simulation model are defined by a GENERATE activity and a DISPOSE activity. A GENERATE activity creates a transaction to be processed. A DISPOSE activity removes the transaction from the process when it has been completely processed. A DISPOSE activity can be used for collecting customized statistics for throughput or total process time. Unless you dispose of transactions, they will continue to use memory during the simulation, degrading simulation performance and ultimately freezing your computer.

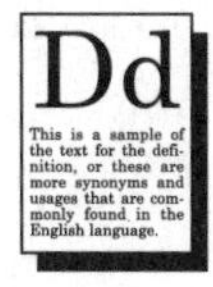

Generate—Activity that creates a transaction to be processed.

Dispose—Activity that removes a transaction after it has been processed.

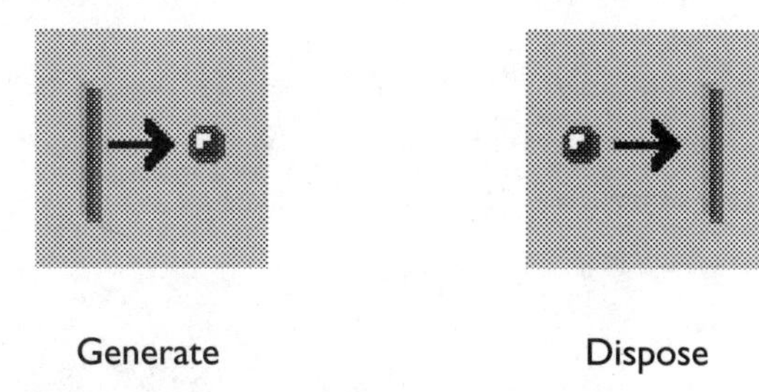

FIGURE 5-17. Generate (A) and Dispose (B) activities

Connectors and Connection Objects

In addition to the three major process modeling objects (activities, resources, and transactions), there are two types of objects that are critical for process simulation—*connectors* and *connection objects*. These objects not only help to graphically define workflow during model building but also make it easier to visualize the process dynamics during the simulation.

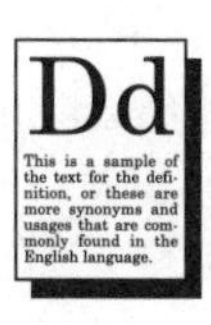

Connector—An object used to define workflow between activities and subprocesses.

Connectors

Connectors are the links or arcs among activities, subprocesses, or processes. They are used for defining the workflow. Connectors are modeling objects in their own right, with characteristics depending on the activity they are emanating from. There are three types of connectors:

1. OR connectors
2. AND connectors
3. Logical connections

OR connectors represent probabilistic or conditional outcomes: the transaction emanating from the upstream activity takes only one of the connectors. For example, a BRANCH activity representing an inspection may have three OR connectors emanating from it:

1. for transactions that pass
2. for transactions that need rework
3. for transactions that are scrapped

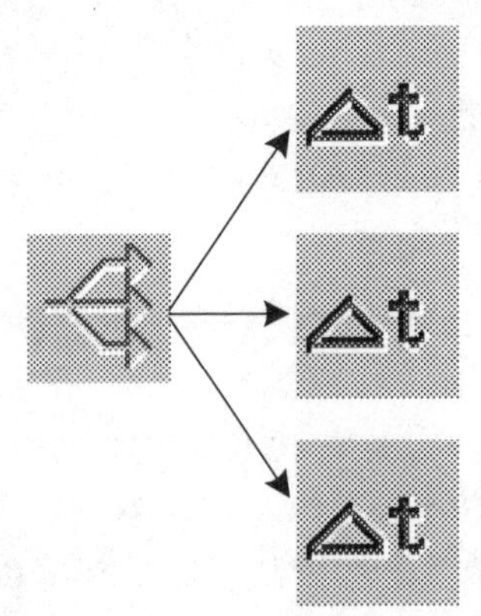

FIGURE 5-18. BRANCH activity with three OR connectors

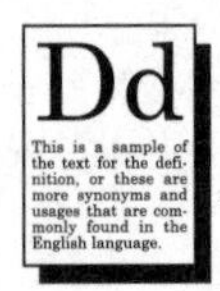

OR connector—Object used when the output for an activity may be directed to different activities based upon preset conditions or probabilities.

AND connectors represent deterministic outcomes where a copy or clone of the transaction emanates on each connector from the upstream activity. For example, a COPY activity representing a duplication task may have two AND connectors emanating from it:

1. for the original transaction
2. for the duplicate transaction

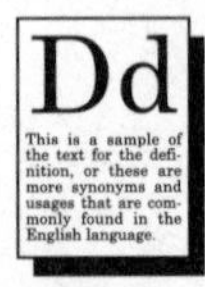

AND connector—Object used when one or more copies or clones of the transaction need to come together before they can continue through the process.

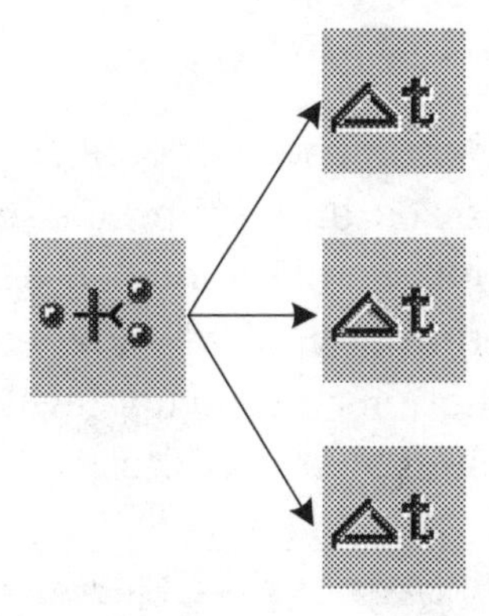

FIGURE 5-19. COPY activity with three AND connectors

Logical connectors represent logical connections for modeling information flow, messages, or triggers. For example, a DEMAND activity representing a customer may have a logical connector emanating from it and going into a SUPPLY activity. This connection represents the signal that triggers a physical transaction flow from the supplier to the manufacturer.

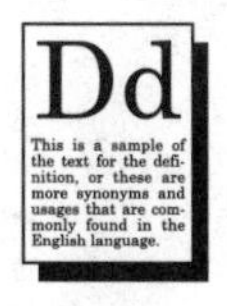

Logical connector—Connectors representing a logical relation.

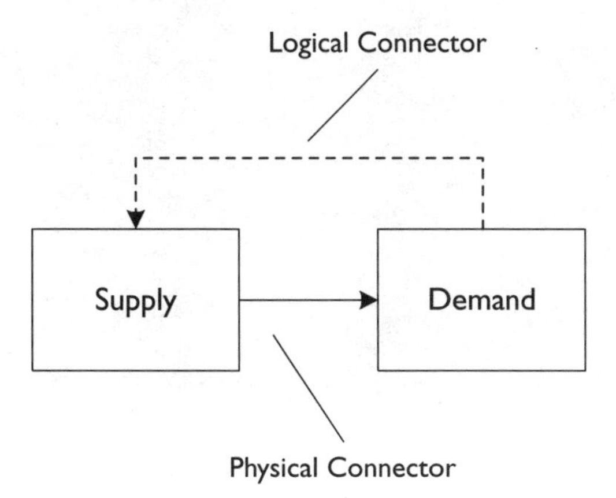

FIGURE 5-20. DEMAND and SUPPLY activities connected by a logical connector

Connection Objects

One of the common uses of connection objects is in hierarchical modeling of processes and subprocesses. A process that has multiple inputs or outputs can be modeled using multiple connection objects. These connection points, when labeled, can be very useful in following the connections of higher-level subprocesses with lower-level activities within that subprocess.

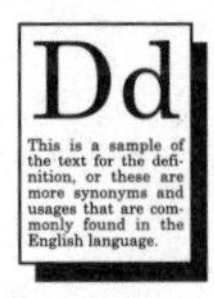

Connection objects—Object used to connect the inputs and outputs of different hierarchical processes or levels of simulation models.

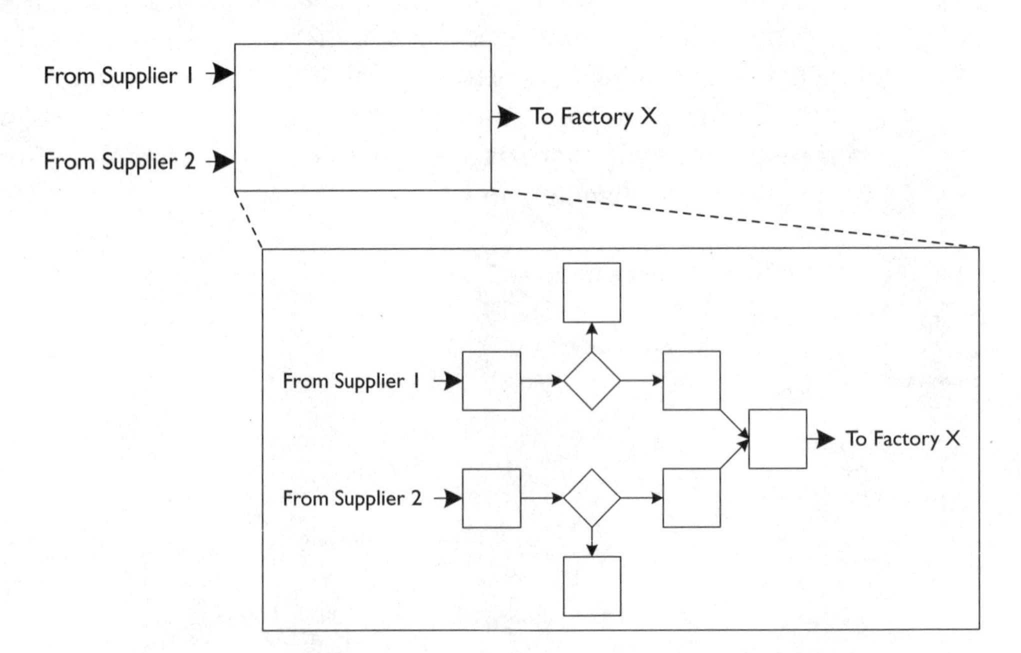

FIGURE 5-21. Connection objects for a hierarchical process

Another use of connection objects is in modeling activities with multiple input and output capabilities. A GATE activity for modeling demand-pull is a good example. In a GATE activity, there are two input connection objects. The first connection object is for the transactions that are entering this activity from the upstream activity. The second connection object is for the trigger transaction that signals the opening of the gate for pull demand.

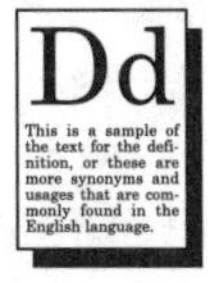

Gate activity—An activity where two or more things must come together before the transaction can be processed.

A SPLIT activity for modeling parallel flow is also a good example for the use of connection points. In a SPLIT activity, there are two output connection points. The first one is for emanating the original transaction whereas the second one is for emanating cloned transactions for the parallel flow.

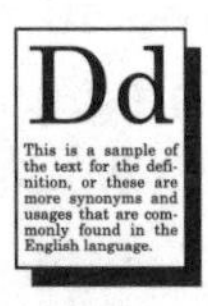

Split activity—A connection point where the original transaction and its clone are separated and sent to different activities.

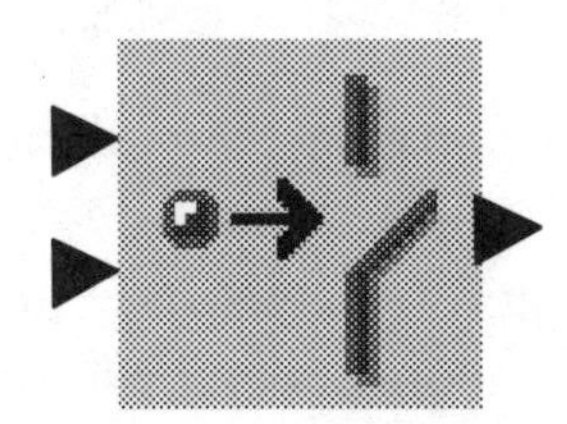

A **GATE activity** holds entities in a queue until a signal is received. For example, a GATE activity would be used to model orders held in inventory until a signal is received from the distributor to fulfill the demand.

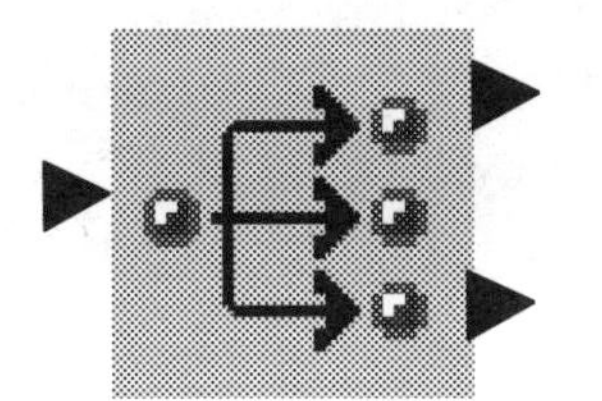

A **SPLIT activity** takes an incoming entity and creates clones of that entity as well as providing an output of the original entity. For example, clones of a purchase order may be created with a SPLIT activity and sent to accounts payable and shipping.

FIGURE 5-22. GATE activity (A) and SPLIT activity with multiple connection objects (B)

Advanced Modeling Functions

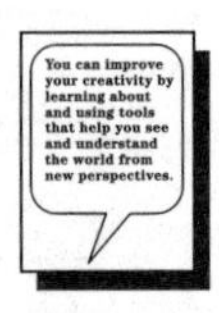

Let's suppose you need to model a process in which the customer service time depends on the type of the customer. How would you model this situation with basic modeling elements? Or let's suppose that service level is one of the key performance measures for the customer service process, where service level is defined as a function of on-time delivery of full shipments and some partial deliveries. How would you customize the results of the process simulation to include service level statistics?

These types of real-world process behaviors can be modeled only with user-defined attributes, system-state variables, and user-defined expressions. Advanced modeling functions combined with programming capabilities provide the power and flexibility to accurately analyze the dynamic behavior of real-world business problems. The following presents how these types of behaviors would be approached.

User-Defined Attributes

User-defined attributes allow you to customize the characteristics of modeling objects. For transaction objects, attributes serve as "tags" that travel through the model with each transaction. Such attributes can be used for conditional branching, sequencing, or decision making in user-defined expressions or logic. For example, order quantity may depend on which customer placed the order and order-processing time may depend on the size of each order. By defining an attribute named "order quantity" and defining an expression that multiplies "order quantity" by "process time per order," you can accurately model the order-processing DELAY activity in your model.

System-State Variables

These variables keep track of the states of model elements so that expressions or logic can be written to deal with complex situations. For example, the number of customers waiting in queue for a service representative is a system-state variable that changes during the simulation. In a typical service process, the number of servers is adjusted based on the number of customers in line. This situation can be modeled by defining a user-defined expression that monitors the system variable "customers in queue" and allocates resources accordingly.

User-Defined Expressions

When modeling dynamic processes, you will inevitably come across situations that will require modeling flexibility. Examples of such situations are:

- IF "customer on hold" > 2 minutes, THEN ...
- IF "inventory level" < 200, THEN ...
- IF "patient type" = "urgent," THEN ...

You may also need to customize performance measures. User-defined expressions provide you the flexibility to achieve those objectives. For example, service level may be an important performance measure for a business that is trying to fulfill orders within 48 hours from the time each order is placed. Using user-defined attributes, system-state variables, and user-defined expressions, you can compare the cycle time for each order with the 48-hour target and calculate the service level of the process. Then, you can write the recorded values to a file for analysis purposes.

Summary

Three main building blocks of a process simulation model are activities, resources, and transactions. When modeling these objects, you need to define variability and dynamic behaviors such as resource interdependencies so that your simulation model mimics the real-world process as closely as possible. A process consists of subprocesses and activities. Hierarchical process modeling provides top-down and bottom-up approaches for grouping activities into subprocesses and major processes. Resource contention is one of the primary sources for queuing. Transactions are used for modeling products or services. They are induced into the model with a GENERATE activity and removed with a DISPOSE activity.

Activities are linked with connectors to model the workflow. In order to create a realistic process simulation model, the dynamic behavior of activities must be modeled. Activity modeling objects such as BRANCH, SPLIT, JOIN, and ASSEMBLE facilitate the modeling of such behaviors. Advanced modeling functions combined with programming capabilities provide the power and flexibility to accurately model the dynamic behavior of real-world processes.

"A static process is a lot like defining the average human being. They're so unusual, you might find one only in a carnival sideshow."

References

Hansen, Gregory A., *Automating Business Process Reengineering: Breaking the TQM Barrier* (Englewood Cliffs, NJ: Prentice Hall, 1994).

Hansen, Gregory A., "Simulation 101—What Are Modeling and Simulation?" *Enterprise Reengineering*, August 1996, pp. 14-15.

Harrell, Charles, and Kerim Tumay, *Simulation Made Easy: A Manager's Guide* (Norcross, GA: Industrial Engineering and Management Press, 1995).

Harrington, H. James, and James S. Harrington, *Total Improvement Management: The Next Generation in Performance Improvement* (New York: McGraw-Hill, 1995).

Law, Averill M., and W. David Kelton, *Simulation Modeling and Analysis* (New York: McGraw-Hill, 1991).

Pritsker, Alan B., and Claude Dennis Pegden, *Introduction to Simulation and SLAM* (New York: John Wiley & Sons, 1979).

Schriber, Thomas J., and Daniel T. Brunner, "Inside Simulation Software: How It Works and Why It Matters," *Proceedings of the 1996 Winter Simulation Conference*, eds. John M. Charnes, Douglas M. Morrice, Daniel T. Brunner, and James J. Swain (Piscataway, NJ: Institute of Electrical and Electronics Engineers, 1997), pp. 23-30.

Tumay, Kerim, "Business Process Simulation," *Proceedings of the 1995 Winter Simulation Conference*, eds. Christos Alexopoulos, Keebom Kang, William R. Lilegdon, and David Goldsman (Piscataway, NJ: Institute of Electrical and Electronics Engineers, 1996), pp. 55-60.

CHAPTER 6

Process Simulation Analysis

Because variable input produces variable output, process simulation results should be analyzed with proven statistical output analysis techniques.

Introduction

Building a good process simulation model can be a lot of work. But you could underutilize or even waste all of that effort by running the model once or twice, watching the animation, taking a few numbers you like out of output reports, and making process improvement recommendations based on those numbers. Instead, we recommend that you use proper statistical techniques and effectively analyze the model performance measures. You will gain tremendous benefits from the experimental power of simulation with this approach. First of all, you will greatly enhance the credibility of your simulation activity. Second, you will minimize the risk of making erroneous recommendations.

This chapter presents you with typical process performance measurements generated by simulation. It describes how simulation generates statistics for these measures and what techniques to use for statistical output analysis. Then, it presents techniques for designing simulation experiments and evaluating the outcome of these experiments. The chapter ends with guidelines for selecting the best-value future-state solution for process improvement.

Model Performance Measurements

Measurements are the key. If you cannot measure it, you cannot control it. If you cannot control it, you cannot manage it. If you cannot manage it, you cannot improve it. It's as simple as that. Measurements may be focused on finances, quality, resources, or investors. Process simulation aids in the improvement of quality-driven measurements, such as service level and waiting time, and resource-driven measurements, such as cycle time and activity cost.

In order to improve a process, you need to develop critical effectiveness, efficiency, and adaptability measurements and targets for the process. Process *effectiveness* is how well the process meets the requirements of its end customers. Process *efficiency* is the output per unit of input. It is a measure of how many resources the process uses to provide the output. Efficiency is for the benefit of the process owner whereas effectiveness is for the benefit of the customer. Process *adaptability* is the flexibility of the process to handle future, changing customer expectations and today's special customer requests. Although process simulation focuses on analysis and improvement of *efficiency* measurements, it also provides indirect benefits for process *effectiveness* and *adaptability* measurements. It's very important to realize that if you consider only efficiency in your future-state solution, it often will result in negative impacts on both effectiveness and adaptability, so that the new process will be less acceptable and valuable than the old process. It's a lot like putting on a clean shirt and a new tie to go to a formal dinner, but going unshaved, unwashed, and in a suit that's old, dirty, ripped, and wrinkled.

Specifically, process simulation provides key performance measurements such as:

You have to be both efficient and effective.

- cycle time
- activity cost
- transaction throughput
- resource utilization
- wait time
- inventory level

Most process simulation tools automatically provide statistics on these performance measures. However, some performance measurements need to be customized. For example, service level is a custom performance measure because its definition varies by industry or by organization. Measurement of service level for a call center is different than measurement of service level for a supply chain. As described in the previous chapter, only the powerful process simulation tools provide the flexibility to define custom performance measurements, collect statistics, and provide output analysis with custom performance measures.

Cycle Time

Cycle time is the total time a transaction spends traversing a process. This means cycle time includes value-added process time, waiting time for resources, and waiting time for conditions. Reducing total cycle time is a key issue in almost all critical business processes. Reducing total cycle time may reduce cost and improve the quality of the output; it can even increase sales. For example, if you cut product development cycle time, you will probably gain market share because you get your product to your potential customer earlier. If you reduce production cycle time, you can reduce inventory. If you reduce billing time, you will definitely improve cash flow.

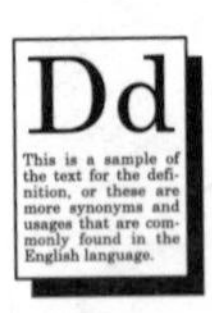

Cycle time—The time that elapses between when input enters a process or activity and when it is delivered to the next activity or process.

One of the most valuable outputs of process simulation is the automatic tracking and calculation of cycle time. Every time a transaction enters the model through a GENERATE activity, the model logs in the entry time. When that transaction exits the model through a DISPOSE activity, the model logs in the exit time. The difference between the exit time and the entry time is the calculated cycle time for that instance of that transaction type. Armed with these data, a process simulation tool provides valuable statistics for average, standard deviation, and minimum and maximum cycle time measurement.

Transaction Count

Transaction count measurement provides throughput information. Throughput is the number of transactions that traversed the process. At the end of the simulation period, some transactions may still be in process; they are not counted as throughput. Each time a transaction departs the model through a DISPOSE activity, the throughput count is incremented.

Throughput—The number of transactions that traverse the process.

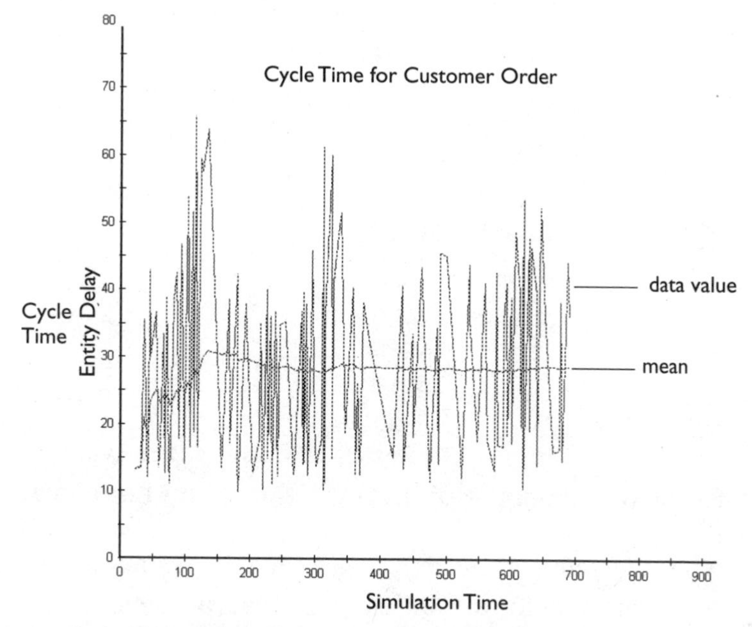

FIGURE 6-1. Example of a cycle-time graph

Transaction No.	Entry Time	Exit Time	Cycle Time
1	0.00	1.42	1.42
2	0.45	1.90	1.45
3	0.75	2.25	1.50

FIGURE 6-2. How cycle time is calculated

Activity Cost

When we define a *resource* in a process model, we define it in terms of the number of available units, usage costs, setup costs, and fixed costs.

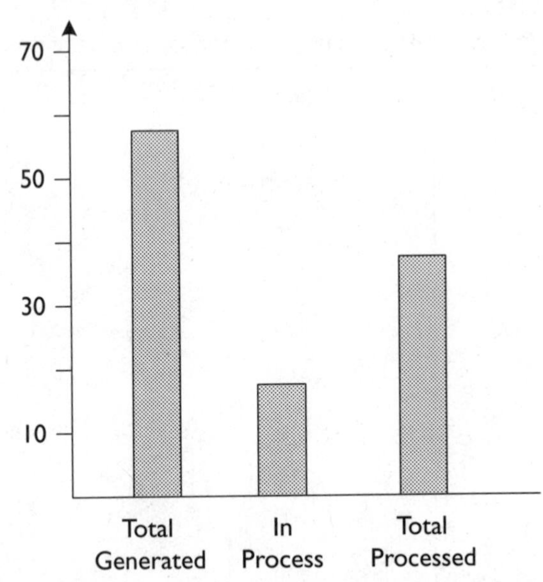

FIGURE 6-3. Example of a transaction count bar chart

When we define an *activity*, we assign the resources required to perform it, the duration for the activity, and the transactions that it processes.

During the simulation, the model automatically keeps track of the time each transaction spends in an activity and the time each resource is assigned to that activity. Activity cost calculations provide a realistic way for measuring and analyzing the costs of activities. Object-oriented process simulation tools allow detail breakdown of activity costs by resource or transaction type in addition to providing aggregated process costs.

Resource Utilization

Resource utilization statistics are time-persistent statistics. During a simulation, resources change states from busy to idle, from unavailable to reserved. Resource utilization defines the percentage of time that a resource spends in each state. The availability and assignment of resources dictate the allocation of resources to activities in a model. So, the resource utilization results provide useful statistics in measuring and analyzing underutilization or overutilization of resources.

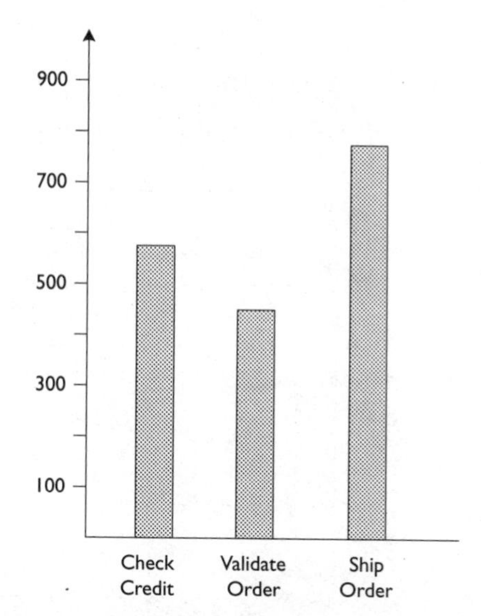

FIGURE 6-4. Example of an activity cost graph

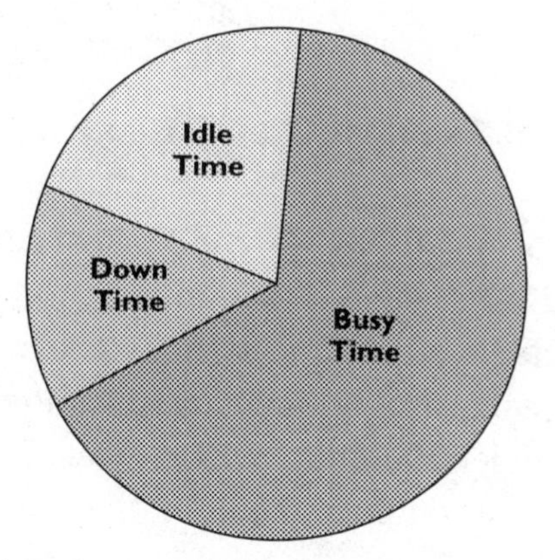

FIGURE 6-5. Example of a resource utilization pie chart

Wait Time

This is perhaps one of the most valuable performance measurements provided by process simulation. When designing a process or improving a process, reducing wait time should be given the utmost priority because it always reduces total cycle time and increases customer satisfaction. Wait time can be attributed to understaffing, unreliable equipment, or large fluctuations in demand. In any case, analysis of the wait time measurements can pinpoint the causes and evaluate alternative ways to minimize wait time.

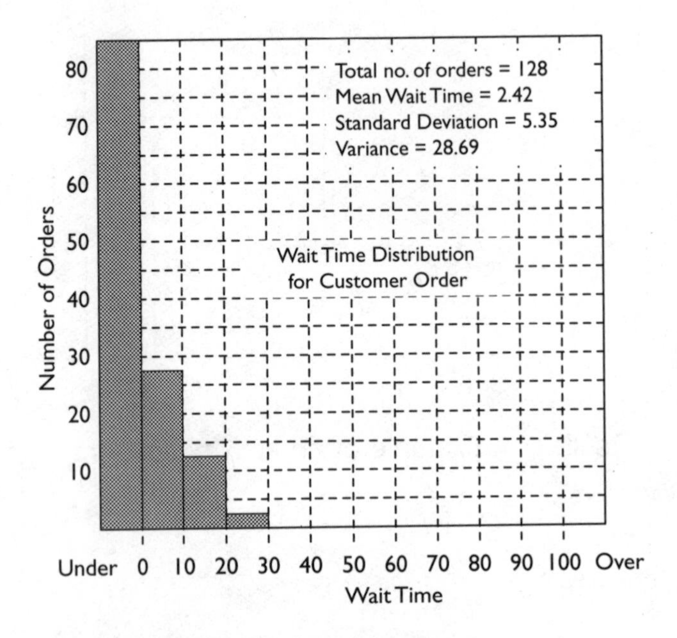

FIGURE 6-6. Example of a wait-time histogram

A process simulation model keeps track of how long each transaction waited in each queue in the model. Then, it provides minimum, maximum, average, and standard deviation statistics for each activity with a queue. The above example shows that 85 of the 128 customers waited under 10 minutes for service. However, three of the customers waited between 20 and 30 minutes.

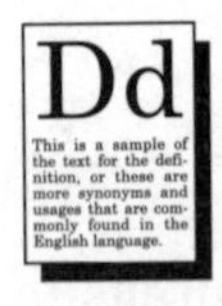

Queue—The status of a transaction when it has completed one activity and cannot continue because the next activity cannot start processing it for some reason (e.g., all the resources are busy, all the parts are not ready to be assembled, or the equipment is being prepared).

Queue Length

This measurement is also a very useful performance indicator because it helps you to identify the location of bottleneck resources in the process. For production processes, queue length represents inventory levels. For a service process, queue length represents customers waiting for service.

Every time a transaction is queued up for processing, its queue length statistic is incremented and that time is marked. When that transaction is removed from the queue for processing, the queue statistic is decremented and that time is also marked. Upon completion of the simulation, the model produces minimum, maximum, average, and standard deviation statistics for queue length measurement, based on the technique described for time-weighted statistics.

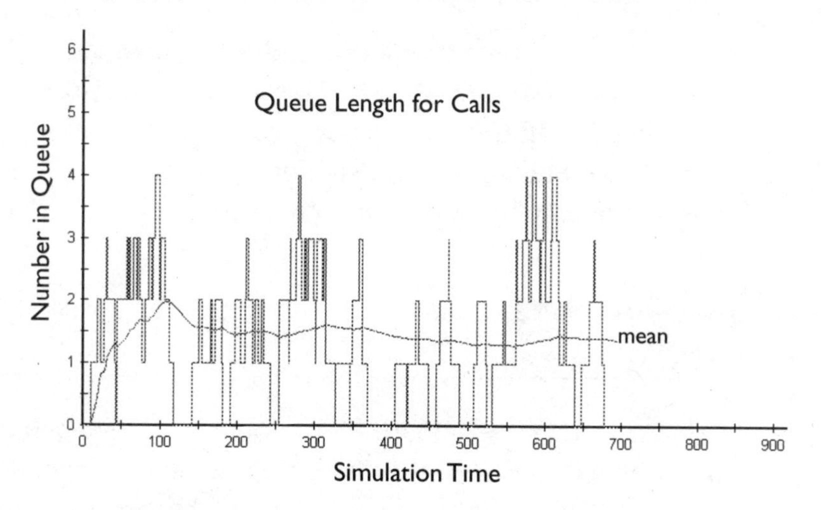

FIGURE 6-7. Example of a queue length real-time graph

Types of Statistical Model Output

Some of the statistics generated by process simulation are time-*independent* while others are time-*dependent*. It is important to understand the difference between these two types before describing key performance measures in detail.

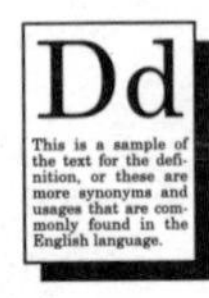

Time-independent Statistics—Observation-based statistics that arise from independent observations.

The mean and standard deviation can be calculated for these types of statistics. Cycle time or transaction count statistics are examples of time-dependent statistics.

For a time-independent statistic, the model collects data on:

- the sum of each observed piece of data,
- the sum of each piece of data squared,
- the number of observations,
- the maximum value observed.

For example, if the simulation were collecting time-independent statistics for cycle time, the values in the output report would include:

- total cycle time for all transactions processed
- (total cycle time for all transactions processed) * (total cycle time for all transactions processed)
- total number of all transactions processed
- the maximum cycle time observed

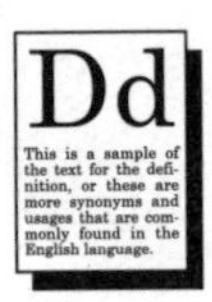

Time-dependent statistics—Statistics that are sensitive to changes over time.

The mean and standard deviation for time-dependent statistics cannot be calculated in the same way as time-independent statistics. The mean and standard deviation must be based on time-weighted data. An example of a time-dependent statistic is a waiting line.

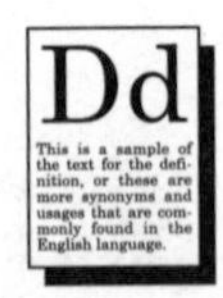

Time-weighted average—A statistic for process performance measures that changes values over time.

If a queue (a waiting line) has 10 customers in it for 20 minutes and one customer for one minute, the average number of customers would be 5.5 or (10+1)/2 if we were using time-independent statistical calculations. This could be interpreted as being that there were, on average, 5.5 customers in the queue over a 21-minute period. However, this would not be accurate. The time-dependent statistic would be calculated as follows: [(time 10 customers waiting in queue ÷ total simulation time) * 10 customers] + [(time 1 customer spent in queue ÷ total simulation time) * 1 customer]

$$= [(20 \div 21) * 10] + [(1 \div 21) * 1] = 9.57.$$

This would be the accurate time-dependent mean for the number of customers in the waiting line over a 21-minute period.

Thus, for a time-dependent statistic, the model collects data on:

- the product of the observed value multiplied by the period over which it retained that value
- the product of the observed value squared multiplied by the period over which it retained that value
- the maximum observed value
- the total period of observation

Fortunately, you need not worry about performing all of these calculations, because the process simulation tools and your computer takes care of them. Now, let's take a look at some of the key performance measures for process analysis.

A Few Words of Expert Advice on Analysis of Simulation Output

David Kelton, a co-author of the popular textbook, *Simulation Modeling and Analysis*, says, "Even in simple queuing models, which form the basis of basic building blocks for many simulations, the averages (expected values) of model output performance measures like queue length and waiting time depend directly on variance of the service time distributions. So, ignoring randomness gets you the wrong answer."

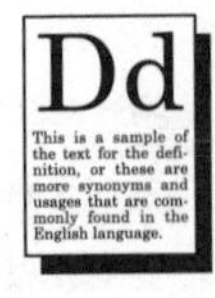

RIRO (random in, random out)—Term used to describe the nature of the relationship between random model input data and model output data.

Kelton explains, "The simulation proceeds by drawing realizations from the input probability distributions and transforms them into an observation on each of the output distributions. All you get from one run of a stochastic simulation [RIRO simulation] is a single observation on the output distribution (see Figure 6-8). Thus, you have to do the right kinds of analysis on the output data generated from the simulation."

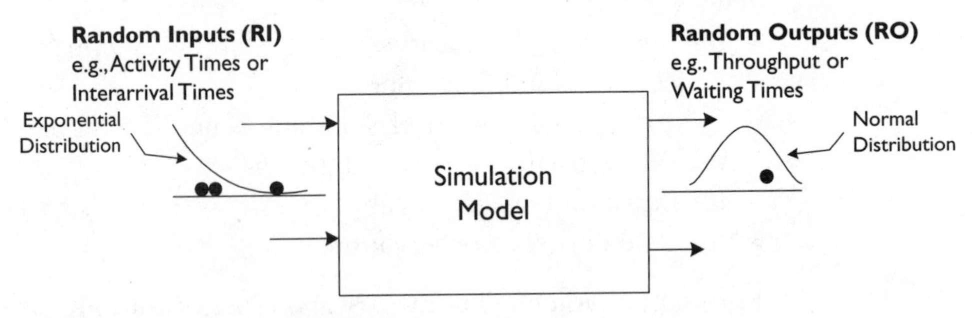

FIGURE 6-8. RIRO simulation

A Refresher on Basic Statistical Concepts

To correctly interpret statistical values from simulation model output, you need to have an understanding of basic statistics. Even if you have some background in statistics, it's always worthwhile to review the fundamentals.

We use special terminology and symbols to distinguish between the properties of data sets and probability distribution. Properties of data are called *sample* properties, while properties of the probability distribution are called *population* properties. We use the Greek letters μ (mu) for the *population* mean and σ (lowercase sigma) for the *population* standard deviation. We use the Roman symbols $\overline{X}$ (X bar) for the *sample* means and s for the *sample* standard deviation.

Let's review the definitions.

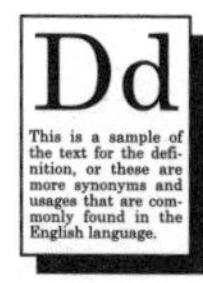

Population—The entire set of possible outcomes (e.g., all possible rolls of a die).

Sample—One, single unbiased observation of the population (e.g., a single roll of a die that results in a six).

Sample size—The number of samples you are working with (e.g., four rolls of a die that result in a six, a five, a two, and another six).

Our purpose in running a simulation is to obtain a sufficient number of samples (observations) so that we can correctly interpret the model output of a performance measure such as cycle time or waiting time (meaning that we draw a conclusion about the population). In order to obtain valid and useful inferences about the population, you need to gather a large enough sample size while keeping the time and cost of gathering the sample at a minimum. What this really means is that you need to run your process simulation model long enough so that when you recommend that the average cycle time for a particular transaction be 14.7 minutes (for a proposed future-state solution), you have based that number on more than 10 transaction counts. After all, you would not want to argue that a die is fake based on only four rolls, would you?

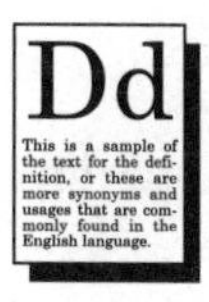

Replication—One cycle through a process simulation model.

To conduct an experiment with your process simulation model, you can run it once. That's one replication. The outcome of a replication represents a single sample and is not sufficient to draw conclusions about the population. To obtain a sample size n, you need to run n replications of that experiment.

You must also account for random variations. Random numbers are the nuts and bolts of simulation. One of the most valuable characteristics of process simulation is to reproduce and randomize replication of a model. This is accomplished using a random number generator. Most process simulation tools use proven random number generators that generate a sequence of random variables that are assumed to be inde-

You've got to roll the dice enough times to determine whether they're loaded or not.

pendent of each other. These random numbers are then used to simulate random variables from different probability distributions.

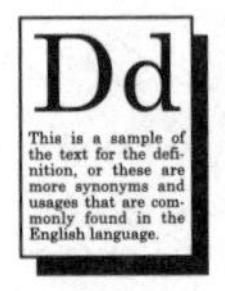

Random number generator—A program that generates a sequence of unique random numbers that are independent of each other and uniformly distributed between 0 and 1.

Mean value—The sum of the sample values divided by the number of samples.

Let's suppose that you want to determine the average time a customer waits in line for a service representative. Let's use m to denote the true mean wait time of the population and $\overline{X}$ (X-bar) as the expected wait time. If you run n replications of the simulation (changing only the initial random seed), you would have n sample wait time observations ($x_1, x_2, \ldots, x_n$). You could then calculate the average wait time value as follows:

$$\overline{X} = \frac{\sum_{i=1}^{n} X_i}{n}$$

FIGURE 6-9. Formula for calculating mean value

Let's say that you've made five replications of the simulation and obtained five values. For example, the wait times from the five replications were 44, 36, 38, 47, and 39 minutes. Using the formula above, you can compute the expected wait time in line for a customer to be 40.8 minutes. The more samples you took, the more accurate estimate you would have.

n = number of replications
$\overline{X}$ = expected wait time
X_n = sample wait time observations
$X_1 = 44$, $X_2 = 36$, $X_3 = 38$, $X_4 = 47$, and $X_5 = 39$
$n = 5$
$X * \overline{X} *$ (expected weight time for 5 replications) =

$$\frac{44 + 36 + 38 + 47 + 39 \text{ (sum of 5 sample weight times)}}{5 \text{ (number of replications)}} = 40.8$$

(In this section, we're using the terms *sample mean*, *average*, and *expected value* to refer to the same thing.)

Besides knowing the average wait time, we would also like to describe the spread (the range of the wait times). For example, if the wait time for each sample were 40.5 minutes, the spread would be zero.

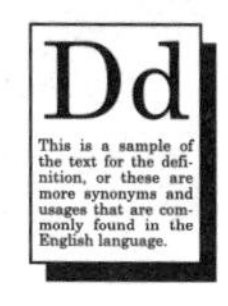

Standard deviation—A measure of spread of sample values around the mean value.

Standard deviation is denoted with *s* and computed using the formula:

$$s = \sqrt{\frac{\sum_{i=1}^{n}\left[X_i - \overline{X}\right]^2}{n - 1}}$$

$$\sqrt{\frac{(44 - 40.5)^2 + (36-40.5)^2 + (38 - 40.5)^2 + (47 - 40.5)^2 + 39-40.5)^2}{5-1}}$$

$$= \sqrt{\frac{12.25 + 20.25 + 6.25 + 42.25 + 2.25}{4}}$$

S = 4.55 (S = Square Root)

FIGURE 6-10. Formula for calculating standard deviation

Using the formula above, you can compute the standard deviation to be 4.55 for the five samples with a mean value of 40.8. These mean and standard deviation values are the estimated statistics for the average wait time for a sample size of five. Once again, note that the estimated statistics will be better estimates of the true mean wait time if you use a larger sample size.

According to the Central Limit Theorem, if you take random samples of size n from a population of mean m and standard deviation s, then as n gets larger, $\overline{X}$ approaches the normal distribution.

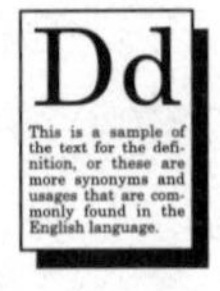

Central limit theorem—The theory that the distribution of multiple sample averages tends to be normally distributed regardless of the shape of the original distribution (the distribution from the first sample).

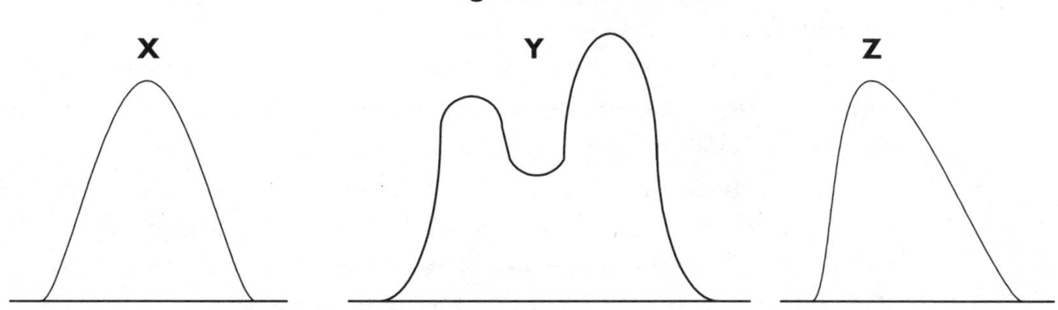

The three distributions above all have the same mean and standard deviation. X, Y, and Z represent *original* distributions. Despite the differences in the shapes of these three original distributions, when sample size is large, say n = 20, the *sampling* distributions (see below; as opposed to *original* distributions) of the mean, $\overline{X}$, are nearly identical.

Sampling Distributions

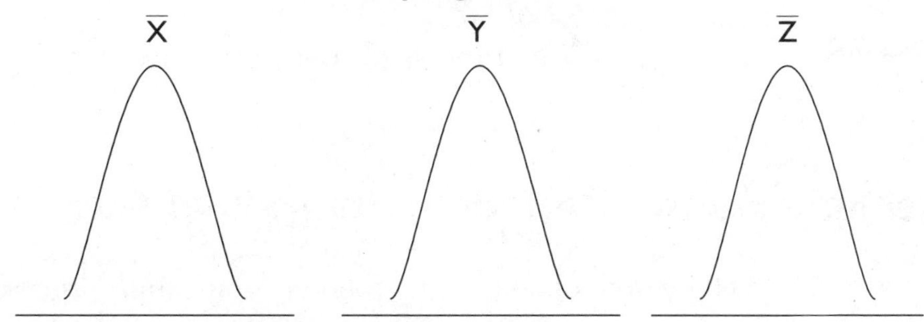

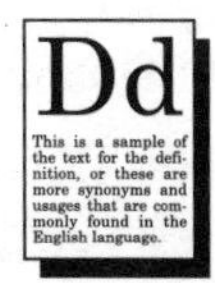

Confidence interval—A numerical range with which we can analyze the output data for a given performance measure, a range within which we can have a certain confidence that the true mean falls.

Probability—A number between 0 and 1.

Confidence level—A percentage between 0% and 100%.

For a given confidence probability, say 0.90, or confidence level, say 90%, a confidence interval is calculated by using X-bar as the midpoint and computing an interval half-width (*hw*), which is the portion of the interval that lies between ($\overline{X}$ – hw) and ($\overline{X}$ + hw). (See Harrell and Tumay, *Simulation Made Easy: A Manager's Guide*, Appendix C, for calculating confidence intervals.)

Using the values from the example above, you can calculate a 90% confidence interval for the wait-time statistic where the lower limit ($\overline{X}$ – hw) is 34.48 minutes and the upper limit ($\overline{X}$ + hw) is 47.12 minutes. The interpretation is that you are 90% confident that the true mean (μ) falls between 34.48 and 47.12 minutes. Naturally, if want to be 95% confident, the range would be greater. And, if you can settle for 85% confidence, the range would be tighter.

Gonick and Smith's book, *The Cartoon Guide to Statistics*, and Harrington, Hoffherr, and Reid's book, *Statistical Analysis Simplified*, are very entertaining and complete references on statistics. We highly recommend them if you need to polish up on your statistics.

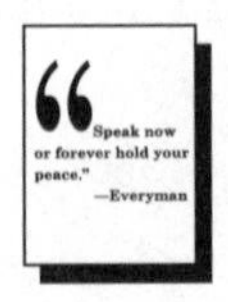

"Nothing in life is certain. But for most of human history, probability, the formal study of the laws of chance, was used for only one thing: Gambling!"

— *Larry Gonick*, The Cartoon Guide to Statistics

Techniques for Statistical Analysis of Output

Whether you obtain useful output from your process simulation depends on the design of the simulation runs. This means deciding how long to run the simulation (one day, one week, or one year) and how many times to replicate the simulation. To obtain useful output and make meaningful recommendations, you could run a number of independent replications, each short, or you could use a single replication with a very long run.

Traditional statistical techniques that work well for analyzing input data are not adequate for analyzing simulation output data. So, how do you perform output analysis of your process simulation model? Well, this is a very involved topic and there are many excellent books written on it. Rather than diving into great detail on this topic, we will briefly describe the concepts and commonly practiced techniques and provide you with references for additional reading on the topic.

Terminating Simulations

Terminating simulations have a definitive time or state for beginning and a definitive time or state for ending. For example, if you are interested in modeling the front-office processes in a bank, the start and end times for the simulation may be 9:00 a.m. to 4:00 p.m. Or, if you are interested in modeling the front-office processes during peak hours, the start and end times may be 11:30 a.m. and 1:30 p.m.

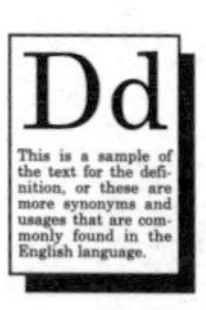

Terminating simulation—A simulation activity that has a definitive time or state for beginning and a definitive time or state for ending.

Terminating simulations repeat a cycle of starting empty, becoming busy for a while, and finally emptying again. For terminating simulations, deciding on simulation run length is easy: it's the period during which you wish to analyze the process. As for the number of replications (or sample size), the following formula works well for establishing a statistically valid number of replications.

$$n = \frac{Z^2_{\alpha/2}\sigma^2}{d^2}$$

α = alpha σ = sigma

FIGURE 6-11. Formula for replications

In this formula, n is the number of desired replications, d is the accuracy expressed in the same units as those of the performance measurement (e.g., within two minutes), z is the critical value from the standard normal table (found in Law and Kelton, *Simulation Modeling and Analysis*) at a given confidence interval, $1 - \alpha$, (e.g., 95% confidence leads to an $\alpha = 0.05$), and σ is the standard deviation desired.

Just remember that n is the minimum number of replications (not simulation runs).

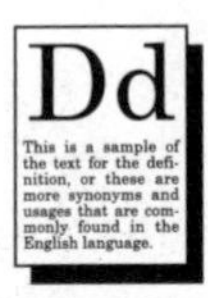

Run—What happens between the time you click on the "run" option in the process simulation tool and the time the model finishes writing output statistics to disk and comes back to the main menu. A run may consist of multiple replications.

As we've mentioned, a replication is one cycle through a process simulation model, what happens from the simulation start time to the simulation end time. Even though the simulation output from replication to replication is different, the simulation output from run to run would be the same.

Nonterminating Simulations

Nonterminating or steady-state simulations do not have a specific start or end time. These simulations can go on and on forever without affecting the outcome of the performance measures. There are two techniques for analyzing the output from nonterminating simulations:

1. multiple replications
2. batch means

1. Multiple-Replication Technique

This technique is essentially the same technique as used for analyzing terminating simulation output. So, what's wrong with making a very long run and running multiple replications for nonterminating simulations? The problem is that the initial conditions you use to start the simulation (if you start with no transactions in the process) are probably not representative of steady-state performance of the process. Such conditions, of course, introduce *biases* into the simulation output.

One approach for eliminating bias for nonterminating simulations is to define a *warm-up* period and remove the statistics collected during that period from the simulation output for analysis. In fact, most process simulation tools provide a way to do this. Those simulation tools that provide real-time graphing features make it easier to determine how long the warm-up period should be. All you need to do is run the simulation while observing a model performance measure on the real-time plot. When the graph levels out, indicating that the simulation is at steady state, that's a good indication of the tick mark for the warm-up period, meaning that statistics collected after the warm-up will have little or no bias.

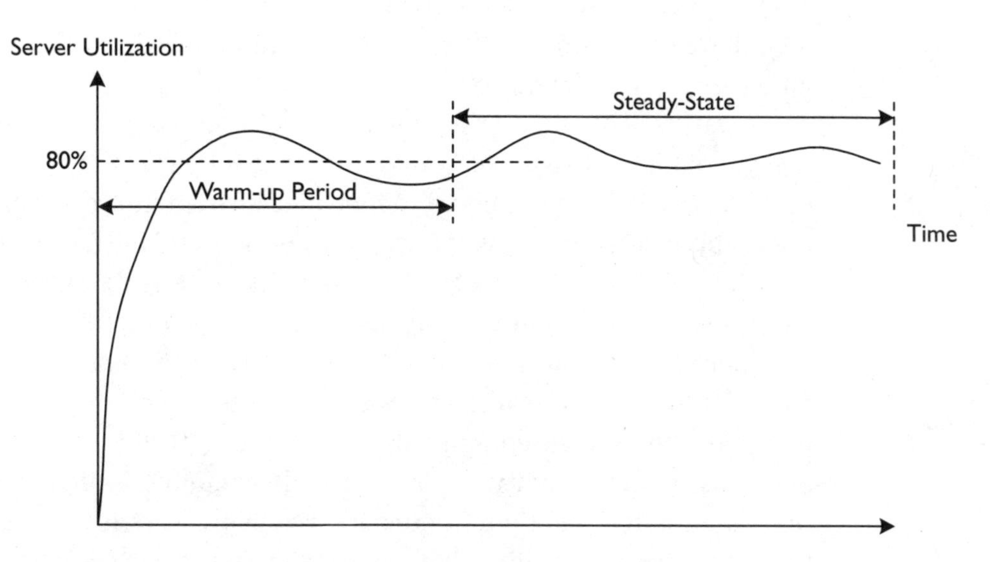

FIGURE 6-12. A real-time graph with warm-up period

Since you cannot simulate a model forever (it would take forever!), another consideration for nonterminating simulations is determining when to stop. This can be tricky. If you run the model too long, then you are wasting time. But if you run the model too short, then you may not obtain sufficient observations for the performance measure for proper output analysis.

2. Batch-Means Technique

An alternative technique to the multiple-replication technique is the batch-means technique. Since the ideal situation is to get as close to steady state as possible, you can make one very long simulation run. This gives you only one replication, so you can't really estimate variances or do statistical analysis. The batch-means technique allows you to slice the simulation into batches of observations and treat the means of these batches as independent and unbiased observations of steady-state performance. Because the simulation run is very long, the initial bias is not as severe as with the multiple-replication technique.

The batch-means technique is proven to be a robust technique for analyzing nonterminating simulations. The key with the batch-means technique is determining the size of the batch or slice. Of course, the larger the batch, the more reliable the estimates.

Regardless of whether a simulation is terminating or nonterminating, you should always perform confidence interval analysis to obtain correct statistics for the performance measures of interest. This builds credibility and robustness into the output analysis of the results. Law and Kelton's *Simulation Modeling and Analysis* is an excellent textbook for proper statistical analysis of simulation output.

There is absolutely no correlation between the statistical significance of the model results and the validity of the model. Only ensuring that the model data accurately represent the actual process enhances model validity. In other words, running sufficient replications to produce a 90% confidence interval with a 10% error means that there's a 90% probability that the replication results are within the range (between 34.48 and 47.12 minutes for the average wait-time statistic in our example) of the estimated model output. This does not mean that the model produced results with 90% accuracy for the wait-time performance measure.

Designing Simulation Experiments

Today, design of experiments (DOE) is used extensively in industrial process optimization, medicine, and social sciences. Design of experiments involves three basic principles:

1.replication
2.randomization
3.control

We have already described *replication* and *randomization* principles in simulation. *Control* refers to systematically varying the independent variables or inputs used in the simulation model.

When you defined the objectives of your process simulation activity and determined the performance measures of interest, you took the first steps toward designing simulation experiments. Unfortunately, we have seen many simulation projects in which users get too busy with the model-building tasks and do not follow through with the design of simulation experiments. Rather, these users simulate a few scenarios and move on to recommendations. We recommend that you go the extra mile and use design of experiments in your process simulation projects. It is well worth it and eliminates potential risks with erroneous results.

Designing an Experiment

The design of the experiment is the specification of different input configurations of interest and the statistics used to measure their effect on performance. This specification depends on the type of statistical analysis desired, which in turn depends on the objective of the experiment.

There are two elements in a designed experiment:

1. factors
2. levels

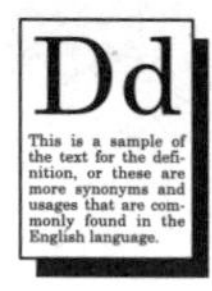

Factor—A decision variable whose value may or may not affect the performance of a model output variable.

Factors

Any process behavior that affects the statistical output of a simulation is a candidate for a factor. In a process simulation model, activities, transactions, and resources are modeling elements that all affect statistical performance of the model. Activities, transactions, and resources, while elementary from the perspective of modeling the logical interactions of a system, may have multiple behaviors from the DOE point of view, each of which can affect the statistical output of a simulation. Each behavior of a modeling element is a potential factor for experimentation. Each factor has a domain that is appropriate for the modeled behavior. Factors that model random processes have a sample domain that can be a constant or a statistical distribution.

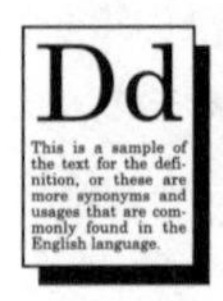

Domain—The value or values that a factor may take during the simulation experiment.

Model Element	Factor	Domain
Generate Activity	Inter-arrival Time	Statistical Distribution
Delay Activity	Duration	Statistical Distribution
Resource	FTEs	Constant
Batch Activity	Batch Quantity	Constant

FIGURE 6-13. Examples of factors

Levels

These are the different input values you want to assign to the factors within an experiment. For example, you may want to design an experiment in which you wish to change the FTE factor for a resource from two to three and analyze the impact on process time.

Creating a Scenario

Experiments are designed to determine the effects of changing the input configuration on one or more output statistics. A scenario is a specification of the input configuration (i.e., the input values used for a single simulation run). Let's consider an experiment in which we are interested in evaluating the effects of changing activity time and resource units on total process time. Let's assume that each scenario will be simulated five replications.

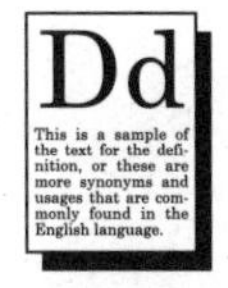

Scenario—A specification of the input configuration.

Experiment Input	Case 1	Case 2	Case 3
Factor	Level 1	Level 2	Level 3
Activity Duration	Triangular (5,10,15)	Triangular (3,6,9)	Triangular (4,8,12)
Number of FTEs	3	2	
Scenarios	Factor 1 (Duration)	Factor 2 (FTEs)	# of Replications
Current State	Triangular (5,10,15)	3	5
Future State-Alternative 1	Triangular (3,6,9)	2	5
Future State-Alternative 2	Triangular (4,8,12)	3	5

FIGURE 6-14. Multiple scenarios

This particular experiment has two factors: the activity duration factor has three levels and the FTE count has two levels. In this experiment, we defined only three scenarios and did not consider all possible combination of scenarios. In DOE terms, we set up a partial experiment design rather than a complete experiment design.

Consider an experiment with three factors and five levels of each factor. There would be 5∗5∗5 or 125 possible scenarios if you want to set up a complete design. An experiment with four factors and five levels would have 5*5*5*5 or 625 possible scenarios! Increasing the number of factors and/or the number of levels rapidly increases the number of permutations necessary to conduct an experiment with a complete design.

Obviously, a full-factorial design requires an astronomically large number of factor combinations. Fortunately, there are several factor-screening designs to help separate which factors matter and which ones don't. The statistics literature includes screening designs such as random designs, supersaturated designs, group screening designs, and so on (Kleijnen, 1987).

Running the Scenario

Some of the powerful process simulation tools include DOE functionality making your job easy. All that you need to do is define the factors and levels for the model elements, define the performance measures of interest, define the number of replications, and press the Run button.

A process simulation tool with DOE functionality uses the expected value of a performance measure (i.e., the mean value) obtained from each replication to estimate the expected value of the performance measure. These estimates assume that the observations obtained from each are identically, independently distributed. In the case of terminating simulations, the DOE module assumes that the warm-up period is long enough so that any bias is removed from the resulting observations. In the case of nonterminating simulations, it is assumed that the replication lengths are of sufficient size to remove significant correlation from the observations.

Analyzing Single- and Multiple-Scenario Output

Once you have run an experiment and obtained statistical output for the performance measures of interest, you are ready to analyze the data and draw conclusions to achieve your simulation objectives. There are various techniques that facilitate this task. If your simulation objective is "to predict the process time for a future-state scenario," then you can use the confidence interval technique.

Analyzing Single-Scenario Output

Figure 6-15 shows a sample replication summary table for the "total processing time" performance measures in the current-state scenario.

Replication No.	Minimum	Mean	Std. Deviation	Maximum	Count
1	9.8	21.5	3.1	33.1	121
2	10.1	20.2	2.6	30.0	118
3	10.7	21.3	3.2	33.2	115
4	9.4	19.6	2.8	29.4	124
5	11.6	20.3	3.6	35.1	114

FIGURE 6-15. Current-state scenario output for performance measure "total processing time"

Using the statistical techniques presented earlier, the DOE module of your process simulation tool adds up the mean values from each replication and averages out the performance measure for this scenario. Furthermore, standard deviation and confidence interval calculations are automatically provided so that you can make a statistically correct conclusion about the results of the simulation.

Analyzing Multiple-Scenario Output

Most of the time, you will be evaluating multiple scenarios. Sometimes, the difference between the scenarios may simply be changes to factor levels. Other times, the differences may be structural model changes, such as a new process design. Figure 6-16 illustrates a three-scenario experiment in which each scenario was simulated five replications.

When evaluating the output from multiple scenarios, you can apply several selection and ranking techniques. Box plots and confidence intervals are useful techniques with graphical and visual comparison tools.

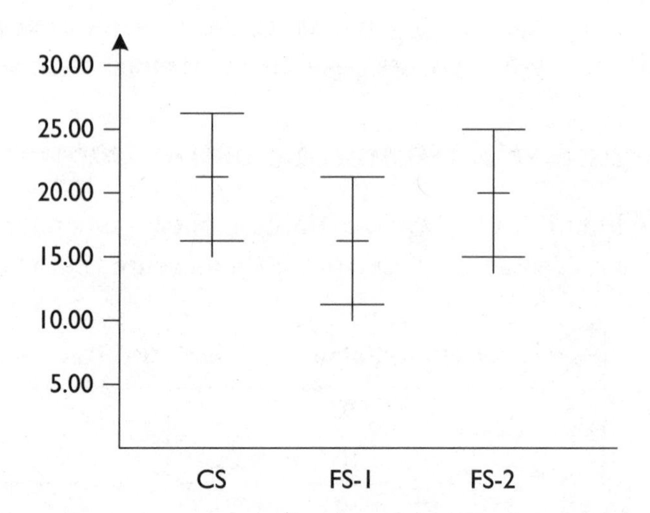

FIGURE 6-16. 95% confidence interval for processing time

Scenario	Average	Std. Deviation	No. of Reps
Current State	20.58	2.1	5
Future State - A1	14.23	3.2	5
Future State - A2	18.57	1.3	5

FIGURE 6-17. Multiple-scenario analysis of the total processing time measure

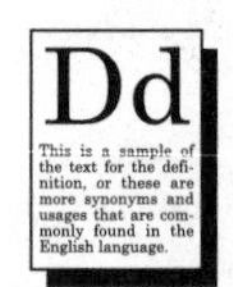

Box plot—A graphical technique for comparing multiple alternatives.

Selecting the Best-Value Future-State Solution

As we mentioned in the beginning of this chapter, process simulation focuses on analysis and improvement of process efficiency measurements as well as some effectiveness and adaptability measures. To decide on which process is the correct one for the organization, an improvement, cost, and risk analysis of each alternative is needed.

This analysis consists of two steps:

1. Performance estimates of each future-state alternative
2. Implementation estimates, including cost, time, probability of success, and major implementation problems (e.g., Is the solution in line with the organization's culture?)

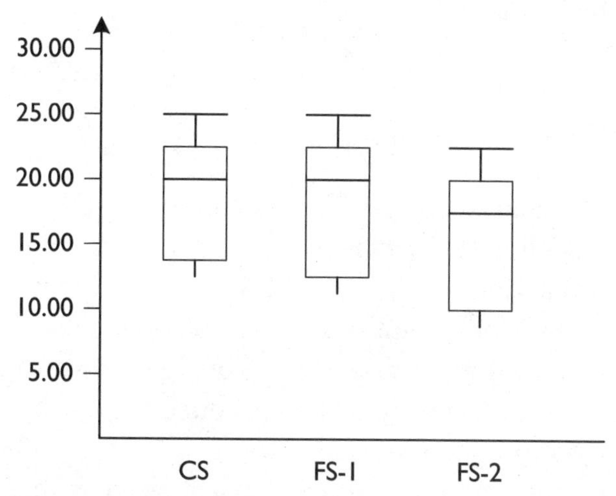

FIGURE 6-18. Box plot comparisons of "total processing time"

Figure 6-19 illustrates a sample improvement, cost, and risk analysis summary. This analysis shows that, although the performance esti-

Measurements	Original Performance	Future-State Solutions		
		1	2	3
Cycle Time (days)	35.0	16.2	19.5	17.5
Processing Time (hours)	10.0	6.5	8.3	7.5
Errors/1000	25.1	12.3	9.2	3.0
Cost/Cycle	$950	$631	$789	$712
Service Response Time (hours)	120	65	30	8
Implementation				
Cost in $1000		$1000	$100	$423.50
Cycle Time (months)		29	8	16
Risk		35%	10%	12%

FIGURE 6-19. Benefits, cost, and risk analysis chart for three alternative future-state solutions

mates of the new process design alternative are most desirable, implementation estimates make the process redesign alternative the best future-state solution.

For more detail on how to select best-value future-state solutions, read Appendix E.

Summary

The analysis of process simulation results is just as important as the modeling of the process. Process performance measures produced by simulation aid in validating a current state or estimating proposed future-state solutions. Such performance measures as cycle time, waiting time, transaction throughput, resource utilization, and activity costs are automatically produced by simulation. Because variable input produces variable output, statistics generated for model performance measures should be analyzed with proven statistical output analysis techniques. Multiple replication and confidence interval analysis are two useful techniques for analyzing model output.

Whether you obtain useful output from your simulation model depends on the design of the simulation runs. The design of simulation runs involves two considerations:

1. how long the model is simulated
2. how many replications are run

Output analysis techniques may vary depending on whether a simulation is terminating or nonterminating. While multiple-replication analysis is appropriate for terminating simulations, the batch-means technique is more appropriate for nonterminating simulations.

Design of experiments is also a very useful technique for analyzing simulation results. Methodically designing simulation experiments, creating and running scenarios, and analyzing scenario results provides a complete and scientific approach to evaluating alternatives. Sound process simulation analysis produces valuable process efficiency measures. However, implementation estimates such as cost,

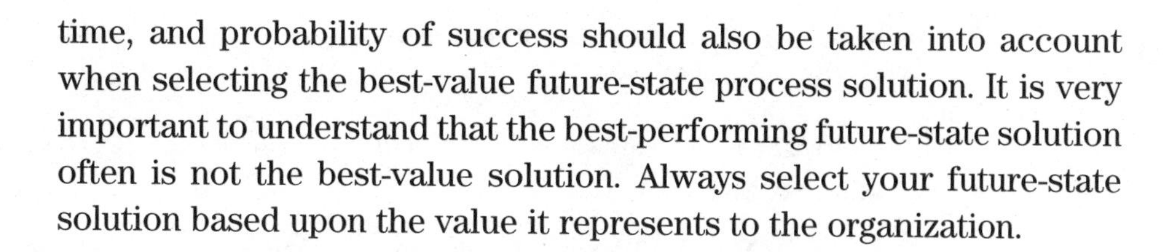

time, and probability of success should also be taken into account when selecting the best-value future-state process solution. It is very important to understand that the best-performing future-state solution often is not the best-value solution. Always select your future-state solution based upon the value it represents to the organization.

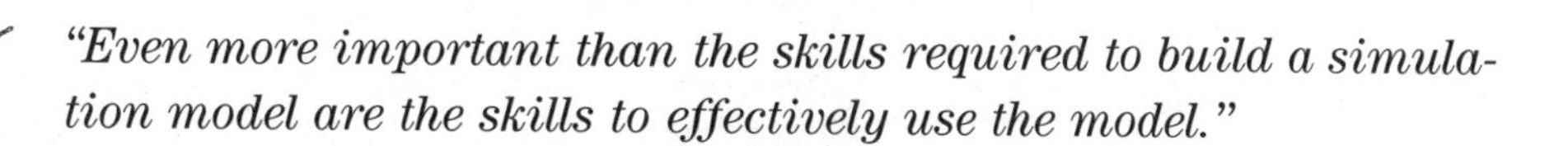

"Even more important than the skills required to build a simulation model are the skills to effectively use the model."

References

Banks, Jerry, ed., *Handbook of Simulation* (New York: John Wiley & Sons, 1998).

Centeno, A. Martha, "An Introduction to Simulation Modeling," *Proceedings of the 1996 Winter Simulation Conference*, eds. John M. Charnes, Douglas J. Morrice, Daniel T. Brunner, and James J. Swain (Piscataway NJ: Institute of Electrical and Electronics Engineers, 1997), pp. 15-22.

Gonick, Larry, and Woollcott Smith, *The Cartoon Guide to Statistics* (New York: HarperPerennial, 1993).

Harrell, Charles H., and Kerim Tumay, *Simulation Made Easy: A Manager's Guide* (Norcross GA: Industrial Engineering and Management Press, 1995).

Harrington, H. James, *Business Process Improvement: The Breakthrough Strategy for Total Quality, Productivity, and Competitiveness* (New York: McGraw-Hill, 1991).

Harrington, H. James, *The Complete Benchmarking Implementation Guide: Total Benchmarking Management* (New York: McGraw-Hill, 1996).

Harrington, H. James, Glen D. Hoffherr, and Robert P. Reid, Jr., *Statistical Analysis Simplified—The Easy-to-Understand Guide to SPC and Data Analysis* (New York: McGraw-Hill, 1998).

Kelton, W. David, "Statistical Issues in Simulation," *Proceedings of the 1996 Winter Simulation Conference*, eds. John M. Charnes, Douglas J.

Morrice, Daniel T. Brunner, and James J. Swain (Piscataway NJ: Institute of Electrical and Electronics Engineers, 1997), pp. 47-54.

Kleijnen, Jack P.C., *Statistical Tools for Simulation Practitioners* (New York: Marcel Dekker, 1987).

Law, Averill M., and W. David Kelton, *Simulation Modeling and Analysis* (New York: McGraw-Hill, 1991).

Seila, Andrew F., "Introduction to Simulation," *Proceedings of the 1995 Winter Simulation Conference.* Ed. C. Alexopoulos, K. Kang, W.R. Lilegdon, and D. Goldsman, pp. 7-15.

CHAPTER 7

Phase III: Measurement and Phase IV: Continuous Improvement

No improvement activities should be undertaken until you have measured the current state.

Introduction

There is no doubt that the lack of measurements is a major obstacle to improvement. Understanding measurements, establishing a measurement system, reporting, feedback, rewards, and recognition are keys to continuous improvement. So, every process simulation implementation must have measurements and rewards.

Once process simulation is implemented successfully in your organization, you can build on that. The only way to do so is by continuous improvement. As the simulation technology changes and the human resource skills change, you must keep up with the changing environment. This chapter presents measurement and continuous improvement activities associated with process simulation implementations.

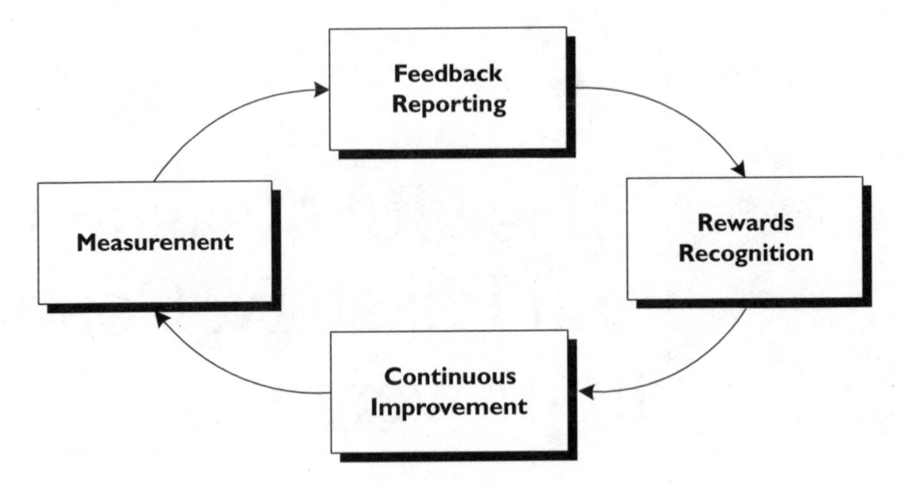

FIGURE 7-1. Measurement and continuous improvement

Phase III: Measurement

The following are the 9 W's of measurement:

- Why,
- When,
- What, and
- The six Who's

In the following sections, we'll briefly explain these 9 W's.

Why Should You Measure?

Good performers want to be measured. Only the poor performers do not want to be measured. But everyone needs to be measured. Without measurement, you deprive those involved in process simulation activities of feeling a sense of accomplishment. Measurements and rewards motivate the analysts, modelers, software developers, and consultants in the simulation project. They also stimulate the team to make a special effort next time around. The only people who don't like measurement are the poor performers—and you don't want them on your process simulation team anyway.

Just like people, processes beg for measurement. Without measurement, a process cannot be improved. Measuring the simulation process allows you to understand how long it takes for each task, see where the out-of-control conditions are, and determine how to set priorities. Another very important reason for measuring the simulation process is to develop realistic budgets for future projects.

When Should You Measure?

One major problem with process measurements is that performance is measured only at the end. This is very much like testing a complex electronic product after assembly without testing its components and subassemblies along the way. Unfortunately, waiting till the end provides no feedback about individual process simulation activities or, when it does, it's too late. It also often leads to missed schedules and cost overruns.

The process simulation team should establish measurement points close to each activity so that corrective actions can be taken and proper expectations can be set before it is too late. For example, if the data collection and analysis activities are estimated to take two weeks and they are not yet completed after two weeks, then the measurement process should signal a warning indicating an out-of-control point.

What Should You Measure?

Like any other process measurement, the performance of process simulation must include effectiveness, efficiency, and adaptability. For example, typical measurements might be:

- dollars saved versus dollars spent
- time saved versus time spent
- risk avoided by simulating
- number of end users for the process model
- reusability of templates for other applications

- number of proposals won using process simulation
- percentage of simulation results that are implemented

Who Should Be Measured?

Everyone involved in the process should be measured. Members of the process simulation team, software supplier, consultants, and managers all play a role in achieving success and reaching performance targets.

Start by identifying those activities that significantly impact total process efficiency and effectiveness. Give highest priority to measuring the resources involved in those activities.

Ask the customers what's important to them. Ask the CEO, CFO, and CIO what's most important to them. If it's the cost of the modeling and analysis activities, then measure that. If it's the ability to leverage the process simulation team in another business unit, then measure that.

Who Should Do the Measuring?

Whoever is performing the activity is the best person to measure it. For example, the person who built the process model is the best person to measure the time it takes to build the model. The person who evaluated software products is the best person to measure the time it takes to evaluate software.

It takes almost as much time or longer to evaluate the output of a process as it does to perform the activities. For example, if you are tasked with measuring the simulation model verification process and you have not built the model, it would take you twice as long to measure it as it would take the person who built the model. So, it makes most sense for the doer to do the measuring.

Remember: make sure that the measurement time is built into each activity in the planning process.

Who Should Provide Feedback?

Feedback should always start with the customer. Of course, the customer of each activity may not be the same. For example, the customer of the data collection activity is the modeler. On the other hand, the customer of the simulation model output is the analyst. The customer of each activity should provide feedback about the time, cost, and quality of the output he or she receives. For example, if the time it took to obtain data is too long or the quality of the data is poor, then it should be fed back to the analyst. Whatever the reason may be for the delay or poor quality, the person receiving the feedback should not take it as criticism but as communication for continuous improvement.

Who Should Audit?

Although it is difficult to audit a process simulation study, it is possible. Only those studies that have high visibility and lots of dollars at stake are audited. There are no specific rules or procedures for auditing. However, independent consultants with subject matter knowledge, statistics, software engineering, and simulation modeling typically perform audits. Even though it may be cost-prohibitive to do audits each time, you should consider it if your organization wants to maximize its benefits from process simulation. If the project has an assigned project manager, he or she should audit the process to be sure that the committed objectives are being met.

Who Should Set Simulation Process Targets?

How effective do you need to be? And how efficient do you have to be? These are the simulation process targets you should establish and use for comparison against actual performance. These targets are the basis for reporting and establishing rewards.

The customer should set effectiveness targets. Being effective with process simulation means completing the project on time and within budget, providing accurate and meaningful results. Customers who are not knowledgeable about the simulation process may set unrealistic targets. It may be necessary to educate the customers on the simulation process in order for them to set targets that are realistic.

The process controls efficiency. Inherent to each process is waste and inefficiency. Much of the waste in process simulation studies can be traced to poor project management, unnecessary details, untrained personnel, or inappropriate software. Thus, the project manager is the best person to set the efficiency targets and manage the process carefully. If the organization is going to use simulation modeling extensively, it should benchmark one project to the others. External benchmarking is also a useful way to set realistic targets.

Who Should Set Challenge Targets?

Challenge targets are set for the purpose of delighting the customer. They need to be set higher than the simulation process targets. Achieving challenge targets requires outstanding performance and a strong desire for continuous improvement. The members of the process simulation team should set these targets. If challenge targets are achieved, rewards and recognition are inevitable.

Feedback and Reporting

As important as measurement is, by itself it is worthless. Unless an effective system exists for feedback and reporting, measurement is a waste of time, effort, and money.

Feedback

Feedback enables continuous improvement. Specific feedback provides the means for correcting errors, justifying additional training, and setting proper objectives and realistic schedules.

Process animation is the most powerful tool for generating instant feedback. Anyone who sees the animated model starts thinking about his or her areas of interest. For example, if the process modeling activity is at a high level, the feedback from the process owners may be to drill down and add more detail. If the analysis activity is based on old data, the feedback from the analysts may be to collect new data.

Another important area for feedback is modeling assumptions. In order to make realistic abstractions of the cause-effect relationships, modelers always need to make some assumptions. These assumptions need to be validated through the feedback process. For example, if the business process is assumed to run 16 hours a day for five days a week and that assumption is built into the process model, you should not allow someone to question the validity of the model results in the final presentation because it does not consider a scenario for 24 hours a day seven days a week. So, make sure that those who need to provide feedback on modeling assumptions speak up in the early going.

Reporting

Reporting provides opportunity for review and feedback. Without reporting there will be no feedback. Reporting progress in a process simulation study is extremely important for ensuring feedback and continuous improvement.

It's also important to report the results of each simulation project so that customers and management get the opportunity to provide feedback. Users of simulation in major corporations such as Ford Motor Company have established intranets that provide a common place for process simulation users to report their applications. Reporting can be in the form of a written success story or a presentation of the model. The next chapter, which presents five success stories, provides a template for reporting the outcome of simulation projects to management. The report consists of the following sections:

- Problem background
- Objectives, scope, and resources
- How process simulation was used
- Results
- Lessons learned

Rewards and Recognition

If a process simulation effort saves the organization millions of dollars, the project team and its members deserve financial rewards and recognition. Rewards are what motivate people to act in a desired way. Three factors affect the degree to which the desired behavior is reinforced:

- type of reward,
- elapsed time between when the desired behavior occurred and when the reward is given,
- extent to which the behavior meets or exceeds the performance standard.

In today's business environment, an organization needs to reward not only individuals but also teams. Since process simulation is a team effort, its members must be encouraged to work together to be effective, efficient, and adaptable. If you reward only the individuals, you run the risk of developing an organization of prima donnas who are interested only in doing things that make them look good. For example, rewarding the analyst who prepares impressive charts and graphs while ignoring the modeler who spends hours building models is not good practice.

Types of Rewards

Rewards can be direct and tangible, such as compensation and awards. Or, they can be humanistic stimulation, often called recognition, either public or private. Whenever possible, direct and humanistic stimulation should be combined. Typical rewards and recognition that can be offered to successful process simulation teams and members are:

- financial compensation
- monetary awards
- group/team rewards
- public personal recognition
- private personal recognition

- peer rewards
- customer rewards
- organization rewards

Let's take a look at some the rewards that can be used to motivate outstanding performances in process simulation.

Compensation

Compensation can be in the form of salary increase, team bonus, or stock options. The amount of a compensation reward must be somewhat proportional to the savings or revenues. And, the reward must immediately follow a contribution that is unusual or far exceeds expectation. A major information technology services firm recently rewarded its process simulation team with a team bonus. The team played a major role in winning a contract worth $5 million. It was presented with a $5,000 bonus soon after the announcement was made.

Awards

Awards can be in the form of patent awards and special awards for individuals or organizational awards for a business unit. These awards may include monetary value, plaques and trophies, published communication, and special privileges. Usually, awards require an application and approval process and the recipients are selected from among multiple candidates.

For example, the Board of Directors of Consolidated Freightways awarded Dr. Mani Manivannan with the "1996 Ray O'Brien Award of Excellence" for his outstanding contributions using simulation. He was the project leader for building a series of simulation models to improve and redesign the Emery Worldwide Dayton Hub and the pioneer of CNF transportation simulation software, SIMTRAN 2000.

Recognition

Recognition may come in the form of public or private acknowledgment of excellence of an individual or a team. Team recognition may include three P's:

1. presentation to the executives
2. plaques to hang on the wall
3. pats on the back

A very effective team recognition method is to encourage members of the process simulation team to publish a technical paper and finance their trip to a conference. DuPont, Ford Motor Company, Boeing, and IBM use this recognition method year after year by encouraging their members to publish at the Winter Simulation Conferences.

The military makes excellent use of recognition to bring out superior performance. While a medal may consist of a 3¢ piece of cloth and a $5 piece of metal, it symbolizes and tells others this soldier was ready to or did sacrifice life and limb for his country.

Recognition produces great benefits.

The Measurement Process

A typical measurement process for the simulation process might include the following activities:

- Review important goals.
- Review measurement principles.
- Conduct a brainstorming session.
- Discuss and debate.
- Develop a scorecard.
- Develop a baseline.
- Establish reporting and feedback procedures.
- Reward and recognize outstanding performances.

Phase IV: Continuous Improvement

Organizations that have demonstrated an uncommon capacity for continuous improvement establish a lessons-learned methodology with respect to every improvement effort. This is no less true with respect to best practices of process simulation. Take the time to discuss, capture, and share information and insights that will improve your process simulation capability by asking questions like the following:

- What worked well? What didn't?
- How was sponsor commitment obtained and sustained?
- What obstacles were most difficult to overcome?
- How can you leverage the knowledge obtained from previous implementation?
- How can you leverage the people, software tools, and models in other parts of the organization?
- What would you do differently next time, on the next process?

When these questions become part of the measurement and continuous improvement process, that means that your organization is on track to unleash the power of simulation.

The Continuous Improvement Process

A typical continuous improvement process for the simulation process might include the following activities:

- ▸ Assess today's process simulation capability.
- ▸ Establish environmental vision statements.
- ▸ Set performance improvement goals.
- ▸ Define desired behavior and habit patterns.
- ▸ Develop a three-year plan.
- ▸ Develop a rolling 90-day implementation plan.
- ▸ Implement the continuous improvement process.

For a detailed explanation of the continuous improvement process, see Harrington and Harrington, *Total Improvement Management*, Chapter 3.

Summary

As organizations become virtual and transitional in the 21st century, knowledge will become their greatest asset. This is how we like to describe the meaning of measurement: "To measure is to understand, to understand is to gain knowledge, to have knowledge is power." Process simulation can become a powerful weapon only if it has measurements. Those involved in the measurement process must have a well-defined feedback system with rewards and recognition for outstanding performance.

In today's turbulent environment of mergers, acquisitions, downsizing, and outsourcing, demands for change are continually accelerating. The fact remains that there will be losers, survivors, and winners. Your organization's ability to manage and implement change will eventually determine its place among losers, survivors, and winners. If your organization is using or planning to use process simulation as a weapon for managing change, it must integrate a continuous improvement process for its process simulation capability.

"Most organizations waste their most valuable knowledge source because they do not share what they learned on the last project and apply it to the next."

References

Harrington, H. James, and James S. Harrington, *High Performance Benchmarking: 20 Steps to Success* (New York: McGraw-Hill, 1996).

Harrington, H. James, and James S. Harrington, *Total Improvement Management: The Next Generation in Performance Improvement* (New York: McGraw-Hill, 1995).

Harrington, H. James, and Dwayne D. Mathers, *ISO 9000 and Beyond: From Compliance to Performance Improvement* (New York: McGraw-Hill, 1997).

Musselman, Kenneth J., "Guidelines for Simulation Project Success," *Proceedings of the 1994 Winter Simulation Conference*, eds. Jeffrey D. Tew, Mani S. Manivannan, Deborah A. Sodowski, and Andrew F. Seila (Piscataway, NJ: Institute of Electrical and Electronics Engineers, 1995) pp. 88-95.

CHAPTER 8

Success Stories

Success is an attitude.

Introduction

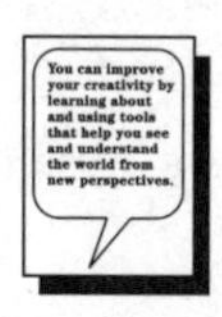

This chapter contains various success stories about process simulation. It's probably the most interesting chapter of the book because it demonstrates how organizations have saved millions of dollars and avoided major risks using process simulation.

Each success story starts with a background describing the company or division and its situation prior to deployment of process simulation. Then, project objectives, scope, and resources are summarized. The section titled "How Simulation Was Used" includes data collection activities, assumptions, model input and outputs, and scenario analysis. The "Results" section explains the quantitative and qualitative results of the simulation project. Each success story ends with lessons learned from the project.

Within each success story, we introduce the analysts, engineers, and managers who "made it happen" with process simulation in their companies. Their success could not have been realized without the support and leadership of the simulation sponsors and champions in their organizations. We hope that the success stories in this chapter will motivate many future sponsors and champions who will support their analysts, engineers, and managers.

IBM PC Company Saves $40M per Year in Distribution Costs

One of IBM's largest personal computer manufacturing plants is in Greenock, Scotland. The plant produced about 1.2 million units in 1992 and supplied the bulk of IBM's personal computers to Europe, the Middle East, and Africa.

In early 1993, IBM PC Company in Europe faced a number of challenges that were eroding its market share, such as frequent price cuts, rapid customer order response times, and a steady arrival of new products and features by increasingly agile and aggressive competitors. Also, poor forecasting caused critical shortages of popular products and excess supplies of others. At that time, Louis Gerstner, IBM's new CEO, reacted to record corporate losses and emphasized the necessity of reducing operational costs and inventory throughout the company.

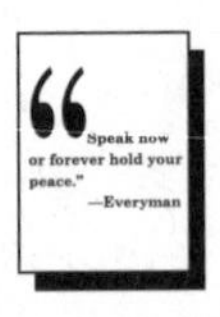

"Breakthrough improvements in the supply chain requires that all constituents, including suppliers, freight forwarders, transportation service providers, third party logistics, and customers, view the entire supply chain as interrelated processes. Synchronizing the delivery quantity of the product from an upstream constituent to a downstream constituent provides a seamless flow through the supply chain. The key for achieving this result is 'timing,' which can be achieved when there is minimum uncertainty within the supply chain."

—JACK CHEN, "ACHIEVING MAXIMUM SUPPLY CHAIN EFFICIENCY"

Objectives, Scope, and Resources

IBM PC Company management formed a team of operations research analysts and management science experts from IBM Research Center to help identify, analyze, and recommend the most cost-effective changes for the manufacturing and distribution operations in Greenock. First, the team developed a detailed understanding of the current demand and supply planning, manufacturing, and distribution processes. Then, the team identified those key subprocesses and activities that had a major impact on operational costs and customer responsiveness.

The purposes of the process simulation study were to:

- evaluate different manufacturing execution strategies,
- examine the effect of different planning and forecasting methods,
- identify lower-cost distribution policies.

How Simulation Was Used

The analysts at IBM Research developed a supply chain simulation model that allowed detailed modeling of various business processes of a manufacturing and distribution supply chain. The team defined the supply chain in terms of seven major process objects:

- Customer
- Manufacturing
- Product Distribution
- Transportation
- Inventory Planning (including Order Management and Part Supply)
- Demand Planning
- Supply Planning

Creating a model of the European PC operations was then a matter of integrating these objects into a network that represented all the relevant business processes and their interactions. The next step was to collect appropriate data that would drive the simulation. Once the model was validated, a number of experiments were performed to evaluate alternatives under different market scenarios.

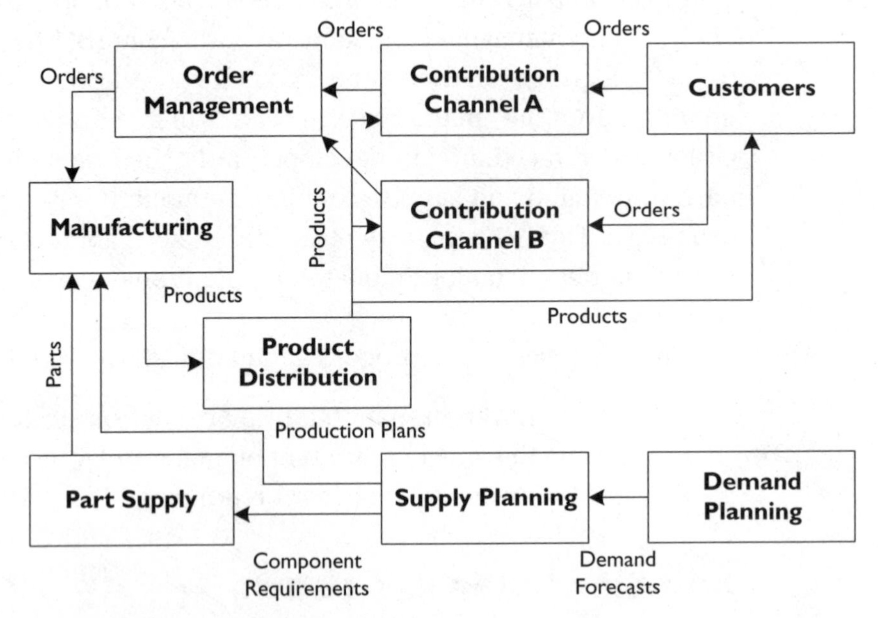

FIGURE 8-1. Processes of the supply chain model

To analyze the output of the simulation model, statistics were collected on the following performance measures:

- Cycle time
- Serviceability
- Shipments
- Inventory
- Fill rate
- Stockout rate
- Resource costs and utilization

Results

Ultimately, the simulation analysis led to significant changes in both manufacturing and distribution, including the following:

- Adoption of a build-to-order (BTO) manufacturing strategy
- Direct-ship distribution process that bypassed costly country distribution centers
- Rejection of a popular idea that proved to be cost-inefficient, the introduction of a new late-customization (LC) assembly plant on the European continent.
- The analysis of the demand and supply planning alternatives indicated that the flex planning method for safety stock planning required less inventory compared with the existing MRP-based method. The analysis of alternative manufacturing strategies revealed that, in the business environment at that time, the BTO strategy achieved the same level of service with significantly less inventory in the supply chain than either LC or build-to-plan (BTP) strategies.
- The analysis of alternative distribution policies showed that by avoiding the country distribution centers and effectively pooling inventory in one location, IBM would improve its customer service levels and, at the same time, decrease finished goods inventory. The estimated savings in distribution costs for IBM PC Company would total approximately $40 million per year.

Lessons Learned

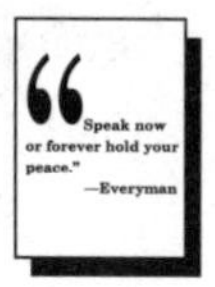

Dr. Stephen Buckley, a member of the modeling team, observed that the integration of process mapping, simulation, optimization, and activity-based costing in a single tool was enormously valuable in helping reengineering teams make the best decisions. Buckley then added, "By providing an objective means to quantitatively assess the impact of different decisions, this simulation study helped IBM avoid harmful, but politically easy decisions, and make good, but less popular decisions."

Siemens Solar Group Saves $7.5 Million per Year

SSI, a member of the Siemens Solar Group, is the world's largest-volume maker of solar electric products. Everything from power supplies for telecommunications systems to utility-scale solar electric plants uses its cells and modules. The company also produces solar panels and solar-powered outdoor lighting.

SSI decided to introduce clean-room contamination-control technology into its photocell fabrication. Clean rooms are standard practice for semiconductor manufacturers; however, the solar industry had never used them before SSI decided to take the plunge. There was a lot at stake. And there were high hopes. "This new facility would enable Siemens to attain higher levels of quality in the cell-fabrication process," says Mike Fahner, the SSI project manager responsible for improving information accuracy and implementing logistics systems to enhance supply-chain performance. "This was also an opportunity to improve productivity by redesigning the facility layout and material flows to increase throughput, decrease the work-in-process levels, and reduce cycle times."

Objectives, Scope, and Resources

According to Fahner, SSI's primary goals were to model the proposed production process, concentrating on the wafer-diffusion, oxidation, and plasma-etch processes for the new cell-fabrication room. The company also wanted to identify and remove system constraints and evaluate alternative scheduling, delivery rules, and material flow with respect to queue levels, throughput, cycle time, machine utilization, and work-in-progress levels.

The project began in 1994 with a partnership between SSI and the Industrial Engineering Department at Cal Poly San Luis Obispo. This collaboration resulted in a win-win situation for SSI and Dr. Sema Alptekin's engineering students. First, Alptekin visited SSI to tour the plant and discuss the project's objectives. Then, Fahner visited Cal Poly twice during the 10-week project, defining project objectives for the students, providing data, and answering questions whenever industrial expertise was needed.

How Simulation Was Used

The students developed a baseline that defined the model's scope and objectives based on real data. The production process was modeled as a series of six steps. The boundaries between the steps were determined by the capacity of the transport vehicles.

The model elements included the process equipment, their capacities, and the probability distribution functions of their stochastic service times and inter-arrival rates of incoming parts. Some of the resources in this model were chemical etching baths, spin-rinse dryers, wafer-transfer stations, diffusion tubes, oxidation tubes, and plasma-etch ovens.

Also, the students defined the routings used for producing wafers. There were two product lines in the model, plus a sequence of operations, batch sizes, and logical rules that determined which machines could be used under specific conditions.

SSI and the students developed and evaluated alternative scenarios. Many involved the problems of producing two different models of solar cells that called for different machine setups and process times. The students considered adding extra spin-rinse dryers, diffusion and oxidation tubes, and/or plasma-etch ovens to the system; modifying machine-setup times; and using a type of dryer that required no setup or changeover. Other potential changes included a variety of scheduling options for both production and parts arrival, modifying batch sizes according to cell model, and changing the distribution of diffusion and oxidation tubes within the facility.

Results

In February 1997, SSI's Cell Fab I clean room commenced operations. Approximately 50,000 wafers per day can be processed through the new $1 million clean-room facility. The improved capabilities of the new facility, fine-tuned by simulation, have enabled SSI to realize significant production improvements. Because it can clear up production bottlenecks in advance, the new clean room is saving the cell-fabrication department roughly $7.5 million annually.

Product yield has improved from a baseline of 83% to its current level of nearly 98%. The reduction in scrap loss is primarily the result of better material flow and contamination control in the process. In addition, process variability has been reduced. As the variation in surface resistivity decreases, the fabrication process becomes more repeatable and yields more consistent electrical properties.

As a result of this project, SSI was able to make significant changes that improved the efficiency of the clean-room facility and plan for further changes that would allow even more productivity. For example, SSI's solar-cell line includes two types of photocells, called the M-line (which accounts for 62% of production) and the PC-line (38%), that require different machine setups and production times. The facility's four spin dryers were initially set up so that three handled M-line cells and one handled PC-line cells. Simulation showed that changing the setup to two machines for each model would improve throughput and cut queuing times.

Another change that grew out of the spin-dryer study involved scheduling dedicated shifts for each model type. By running M-line product for 13 consecutive eight-hour shifts and then changing over to PC-line product for eight consecutive shifts, SSI could significantly increase throughput, reduce waiting times, and minimize time devoted to equipment setup and changeover.

Lessons Learned

While SSI's new fabrication process operates effectively, thanks in part to the simulations that went into the planning, there's still room for improvement. In particular, Fahner says that if SSI were to do the simulation project all over again, he would make some important changes.

First, he would involve manufacturing personnel to a greater degree during the what-if discussions when deciding which options and alternatives to explore. Second, he would work harder to develop a stronger in-house simulation capability. This would allow SSI to take better advantage of the model and to use it as a tool for continuing improvement. Finally, he would develop run-time models so that those who are not familiar with programming could still run the simulations and explore new alternatives with new data.

Although simulation languages and software applications are improving at an accelerated rate, Fahner acknowledged that simulating a complex process still requires highly skilled engineers, a clear focus, and dedicated time for modeling.

How Tropicana Makes Million-Dollar Logistics Decisions

Tropicana Products Inc. is the leading juice producer and marketer in the U.S. and Canada. With over 4,000 employees, the company is No. 1 in orange and grapefruit juice sales. In 1970, Tropicana launched the "Tropicana Train," which now carries 2.26 million 64-ounce cartons of juice to the Northeast three times a week from its facility in Bradenton, Florida.

Growth in consumer demand dictated additional rail traffic to Tropicana's new distribution center in the Midwest. This meant 250 rail car deliveries every week. Maintaining and monitoring the system became a logistics nightmare while making it difficult to achieve superior levels of customer service. Product demand fluctuations resulted in frequent scheduling and transportation changes.

Several spreadsheet models had been developed to assist schedulers in the task of locating, queuing, loading, and moving the appropriate rail cars. However, these models were not able to capture the system dynamics and resource interdependencies.

Objectives, Scope, and Resources

The complexity of the process and system interaction required a dynamic simulation model of the logistics processes. The purpose of the simulation model was to allow management to analyze and understand future capital expenditures to support product growth and delivery. Howard Way, a senior project manager with Tropicana Products Inc., and Michael Carr, a simulation consultant with Computer Companion Inc., conducted the simulation study.

The model scope included the entire rail operation in Bradenton and two distribution facilities—starting with loading rail cars, following transport to and from the distribution centers, and completing the cycle at either the maintenance facility or the originating rail yard in Bradenton (see Figure 8-2).

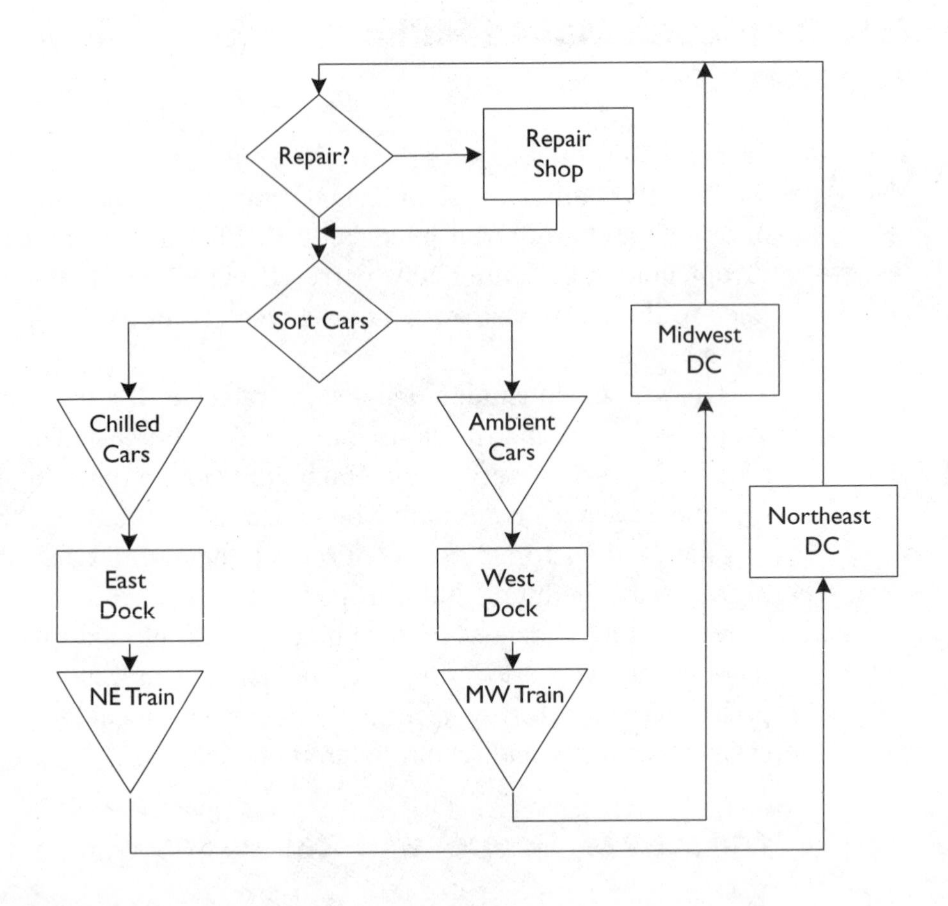

FIGURE 8-2. Tropicana's rail operations flowchart

How Simulation Was Used

The model consisted of two major sections: one modeled the overall system and the other modeled the detailed operations of the loading dock in Bradenton. Because the number of rail cars available to Tropicana is fixed, the model was designed as a closed system: once the model generated a total of 415 cars (the entire available Tropicana fleet), they remained in the model for the duration of the simulation.

Various statistics were collected from the rail simulation model:

- Distribution of the number of chilled and ambient cars available in the yard
- Crew utilization at the Bradenton docks, the Northeast DC, and the Midwest DC
- Dock utilization
- CSX train switching needs
- Cycle time of cars through various points in the system

The model was initially validated with the Northeast distribution center only, because that DC had been in operation for many years and historical data were readily available. The model was run with existing train schedules, crew and car availability, and warehouse unloading times. These results were presented to the traffic/scheduling personnel within the rail department. The model performance data closely matched the actual data.

Once the model was validated, several scenarios were run to determine the impact of rail car cycle times between Bradenton and the DCs on rail car utilization. To evaluate crew loading, 12 different scenarios were run. The model indicated that additional crews would be needed to satisfy the Midwest demand. To determine the optimum crew assignments, the number of discharge points from the warehouse was held at the current level and the number of rail spots was also kept constant. The highest crew utilization and system throughput occurred for crews utilized over two shifts. Unloading times had been entered into the model based on historical data from each distribution center. These times were varied to determined overall system impact.

Results

The model allowed Tropicana to evaluate many loading and delivery schedules and understand their impact before implementation. Tropicana senior project manager Way explains, "As a result of the study, it was determined that we did not need to add more rail cars to the fleet in order to meet increased demand in Midwest. We avoided a capital investment of over $4M."

Lessons Learned

The simulation team for the Tropicana study learned how processor- and memory-intensive simulation applications can become. The computer had to be upgraded during the project to speed up the simulation runs. Another valuable experience was the tradeoffs between ease-of-use and flexibility of process simulation tools. Even though the team was easily able to come up to speed with the simulation tool and developed models quickly, it experienced some challenges in modeling complexities of the flow control and resource scheduling.

Hallmark Cards Cuts Cycle Time from 80 Days to Eight Days

Hallmark Cards is the leading producer of greeting cards and related personal expression products, with 1996 worldwide sales totaling $3.6 billion. In addition to greeting cards, Hallmark also produces gift-wrap products for many occasions.

In the past, gift-wrap production at Hallmark was a lengthy and expensive process. The production of gift-wrap from the initial artist's design to the final printing was cumbersome, involving eight departments with diverse physical locations. Individual functions were isolated from one another. Poor communication among departments and a lack of understanding of other people's responsibilities resulted in an unacceptably high level of costly remakes. The process cycle time was over 80 days.

Objectives, Scope, and Resources

Hallmark formed a process improvement team with a representative from each of the eight departments and established a set of objectives to significantly reduce cycle time, reduce remakes, and lower overall job cost for the gift-wrap production process. The simulation study was lead by Jim Moore, a senior industrial engineer with Hallmark Cards.

The purpose of the simulation study was to evaluate two alternatives. The first involved integrating new digital engraving technology into the existing workflow, which would decrease costs within the 80-day cycle. The second approach considered was to reengineer the whole process and create a work team in order to reduce cycle time as well as cost.

How Simulation Was Used

The first activity of the process improvement team was to document the current process, which consisted of eight major activities. Gift-wrap designs could loop through this cycle many times before going into final production. Moreover, even if the engineer realized that the image needed a different color even before cylinder engraving, it would take two months for the design to make its way back to the scanner responsible for color, so the design was no longer fresh in the scanner's mind. Even with the many proofings before cylindrical etching, a full 20% of all designs that reached the final stage had to be remade.

Once the current process was documented, the team developed a baseline simulation model. The model showed that the capacities were not balanced between the departments and the remakes were excessive. This validated the model and increased confidence among the team members for simulation output.

Departments	Tasks
Artist	Conceives the design according to timing and season
Scanner	Scans the artist's images and converts them to four-color film
Color Proofer	Looks at many proofs with different color layouts
Engineer	Approves and oversees the color
Finisher	Resizes the image through cropping and nesting
Step Operator	"Steps" to proper cyclinder size for printing
Cylinder Maker	Photo etches and engraves image onto cylinder
Engineer	Proofs color and checks mechanics

FIGURE 8-3. Departments and tasks for as-is current gift-wrap production process

Next, a "to-be" model was developed to evaluate the proposed alternatives. In the new model, three proposed changes to the process were incorporated:

1. A dedicated work team was created, consisting of members from each department, all located in one work area. This reduced the number of activities in the process from 13 to three. The first and the last steps—the artist's design and the actual printing—were still done in separate areas, but the heart of the process was carried out in one area with a multidisciplinary team. The model input for the individual task times were reduced to represent the effect of the restructuring.
2. A new philosophy of "make it right the first time" was built into the model, meaning that no work was passed on until it was correct and approved.
3. Etching designs on cylinders was a tricky process: too much heat for too much time would etch the design too deeply, while too little heat or too little time would result in the opposite problem. To increase precision and eliminate the guesswork, the team proposed digital engraving, which gives an exact specified depth and is, for all practical purposes, error-free.

Results

The results of the simulation study showed three radical improvements:

- process cycle time of 80-plus days could be reduced to eight days,
- digital engraving, combined with the multidisciplinary work team, could cut remakes by 50%,
- overall production costs could be reduced by 10%, because the engravers were faster and more consistent.

The management approved the proposal and the new process was implemented over a four-month period. Initially, the team produced work in a consistent 11-day cycle. After several months, the process team was meeting all forecasted results.

Lessons Learned

"This simulation study showed how extraordinary improvements can be achieved through very ordinary means," says Moore. He further explains, "Using simulation, the team looked at what was happening, what could be happening and how they could make it happen. The primary objective was to illustrate the conventional versus the proposed process to management in relative and accurate terms. And, simulation helped us do that."

How Process Simulation Saves Patents for Thiokol

Thiokol Corporation is one of the nation's leaders in the development and production of high-technology solid rocket motors for aerospace, defense, and commercial launch applications. As an industry leader, Thiokol realizes the importance of intellectual property—particularly patents—to protect its products, lines of business, and income.

Patent rights can be lost easily. In the U.S., for example, if the invention has been disclosed without restrictions, publicly used, offered for sale, or sold more than one year prior to filing a patent application with the U.S. Patent and Trademark Office, all U.S. patent rights are lost. This is referred to as a "statutory bar" and could cost Thiokol millions of dollars in lost revenue. (It's worse outside the U.S. Most countries provide no grace period: the moment any of the above acts occurs, all foreign patent rights are lost.)

The old patent application process was quite lengthy. When a Thiokol propellant research chemist developed a more energetic polymer, he or she prepared an invention disclosure and submitted it to the management of the research laboratories. After approval, the disclosure moved on to the Thiokol patent board. If the patent board determined that the invention was valuable, the invention disclosure continued on to the intellectual property law department.

From there, a patentability search was conducted in the U.S. Patent and Trademark Office and an evaluation was made regarding whether or not the invention was patentable. If the patent board rejected the invention, the inventor had the opportunity to rebut the rejection and resubmit the invention disclosure to the patent board with comments and additional information. If the patent board approved the invention and determined that it was patentable, the intellectual property department instructed an outside patent attorney to prepare and file a patent application. Often, this process exceeded the one-year statutory bar limit.

The patent application process crossed so many organizational boundaries that certain unusual patent cases set up a chain of events that could exceed the statutory bar. Not being able to see the entire process interact made it difficult to spot potential problems. Since Thiokol's patent acquisition process involved several departments, many possible outcomes, and enormous variability, in 1996 the company decided to apply a process simulation tool.

Objectives, Scope, and Resources

The objective was to find a solution to minimize delays in processing inventions and acquiring patents in the intellectual property law department. With information in hand, Jim Ekstrom, a process engineer at Thiokol, constructed a process simulation model. This allowed

Thiokol to evaluate how implementing changes to the process would affect the system over time.

How Simulation Was Used

The model inputs included the following:

- Resource variables (number and types of people)
- Hourly rates
- Activity times for each operation
- Travel times for documents

The key performance measure was span time—the time between when a document enters the system and when it leaves the system. The model was used to play what-ifs with:

- how often the patent board meetings take place
- how quickly an invention disclosure is processed
- how quickly a patent search is conducted

First, the process was flowcharted. Then, simulation model input data were defined and entered into the model. When the model was simulated, everyone involved in the intellectual property process could see the documents flowing across the screen. This simulation and a review of model input and output data resulted in validation of the model. The process was simulated for one year (2,000 hours). Each time the model was run for what-if scenarios, span time statistics were analyzed and compared with the current-state performance.

Results

The simulation helped Thiokol's intellectual property law department identify process bottlenecks and staffing problems that resulted in statutory bars. Changes to the intellectual property process were evaluated to ensure that the new processes minimized the risk of statutory bars and lost patent rights.

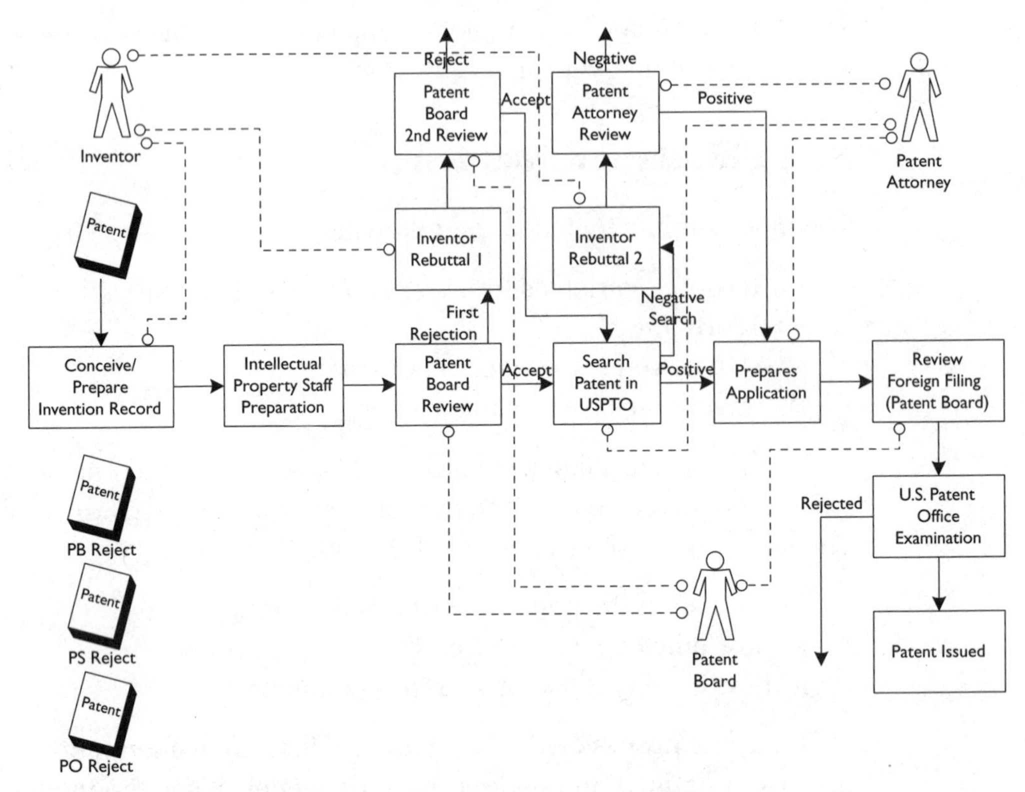

FIGURE 8-4. Intellectual property process flow diagram

As part of the solution, Thiokol increased the frequency of the patent board meetings and outsourced the patent searches and other time-consuming legal processes. This not only alleviated the amount of work placed on the in-house patent attorney and paralegal staff, but also shortened the time required to process each invention disclosure and patent application by an average of 30%. Of greater importance, the unusual process flows that could cause the company to lose a patent or invention were identified and corrected.

Lessons Learned

Although the flowcharting approach worked well, perhaps the greatest strength of the simulation model was its use of animation. Using graphics to represent invention disclosures, patent applications, patents, patent attorneys, paralegal personnel, and the patent board, the model successfully identified bottlenecks that delayed or interrupted the process. The visual capabilities of the model allowed the intellectual property department and management to easily see both the problems and the solutions.

Summary

The success stories presented in this chapter come from organizations that are determined to make the "best decisions" in the 21st century, rather than making just "good decisions." By asking what-if questions with simulation models, these organizations evaluate various alternatives before they decide on the "best alternative." Their success stories are proof of how your organization can take the risk (and stress) out of change.

"For every process there is a better way. Find it."

References

Carr, Michael, and Howard Way, "Million Dollar Logistics Decisions Using Simulation," *Proceedings of the 1997 Winter Simulation Conference*, eds. Sigrún Andradóttir, Kevin J. Healy, David H. Withers, and Barry L. Nelson (Piscataway NJ: Institute of Electrical and Electronics Engineers, 1998), pp. 1206-1209.

Chen, Jack, "Achieving Maximum Supply Chain Efficiency," *IIE Solutions*, June 1997, pp.30-35.

Feigin, Gerald, Chae An, Daniel Connors, and Ian Crawford, "Shape Up, Ship Out: How a Team of OR Analysts Redefined Manufacturing Strategy for the IBM PC Company in Europe," *OR/MS Today*, April 1996.

Larson, Elizabeth, "Getting the Most Out of Your Process," *Quality Digest*, May 1998.

Moore, Jim, "More Than a Hunch," *Manufacturing Systems*, August 1997, pp. 50-56.

Vacca, John R., "Faking It, Then Making It," *Byte Magazine*, November 1995.

CHAPTER 9

Using Simulation Modeling for Process Redesign Projects

A good simulation model takes much of the risks out of process reengineering and process redesign projects.

Introduction

So far, we have been presenting the processes that are used to develop simulation models. Now we will show you how to use the simulation models to facilitate organizational improvement. In actuality, simulation modeling is useful whenever you need to study, understand, or monitor a process. It's a natural for all TQM activities, because TQM is based upon controlling and improving processes to ensure meeting the customers' expectations.

This is particularly true with the five breakthrough business process improvement (BPI) technologies:

- process reengineering
- process redesign
- process benchmarking
- Fast Action Solution Technique (FAST)
- High-Impact Team (HIT)

These five business process improvement technologies can swiftly bring about changes that decrease cost, cycle time, and error rates from 30% to 90% while improving output quality (see Figure 9-1).

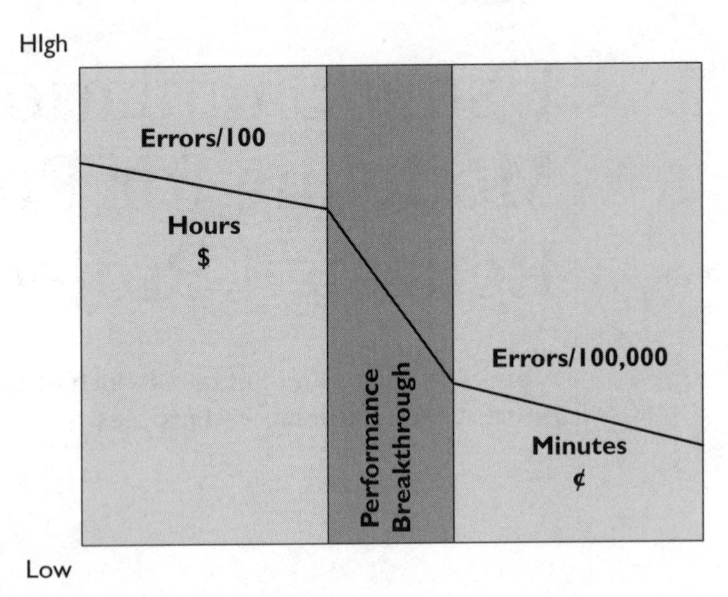

FIGURE 9-1. Performance breakthrough

These types of drastic improvements can be accomplished only when an organization drastically changes the way the employees interface with the process.

To provide you with a comprehensive understanding of how simulation modeling is used in the BPI methodologies, we will present an overview of the process redesign methodology and, at the end of each phase, we will discuss how simulation modeling should be used to analyze, evaluate, measure, or control the process under study.

When applying the BPI methodologies, four ingredients need to be considered:

1. process
2. technology
3. people
4. knowledge

Failure to understand and manage any one of these four factors can destroy what otherwise would have been a very effective improvement.

For a successful BPI project, you need the following:

- a reason for the organization to improve
- a process that would have a significant impact upon the organization if it were improved a minimum of 30%
- trained bpi technologists
- dedicated resources
- good simulation modeling tools
- effective organizational change management methodologies
- a good understanding of the process enablers
- upper management interest and support
- an effective implementation team
- a lot of momentum

Even more important, you need to have people ready and willing to accept and even embrace the new process. The lack of any one of these ingredients will cause the project to fail, or at least not produce the results that it should have produced.

It is not our intent to train you to do process redesign, but rather to use the process redesign technology as a mannequin on which we will hang the simulation modeling activities so that the undesirable bulges are eliminated.

Overview

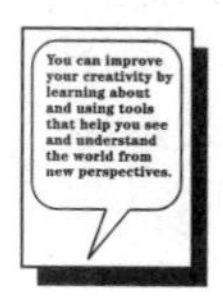

The purpose of this chapter is to take the simulation modeling activities discussed in this book and apply them to a process redesign project. This will allow you to see how the simulation modeling concepts can be effectively applied to a particular methodology. Understanding the simulation modeling concepts is an important first step, but the real payoff comes when you are able to apply these concepts to your job. This often is the most difficult part in the transformation that converts theories into practice. Taking a classroom concept and applying it to the maintenance shop or the development laboratory is the real challenge.

We will start by defining some common terms that need to be understood:

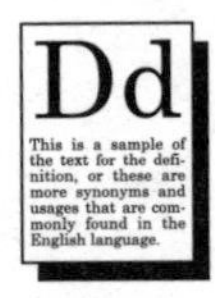

Business process improvement (BPI)—A methodology designed to bring about step-function improvements in administrative and support processes using approaches such as process benchmarking, process redesign, process reengineering, FAST, and HIT.

Process redesign—A methodology used to streamline a current process with the objective of reducing cost and cycle time by 30% to 60% while improving output quality from 20% to 200%.

Process reengineering—A methodology used to radically change the way a process is presently designed by developing an independent vision of how it should perform and using a group of enablers to prepare a new process design that is not hampered by current paradigms.

Enabler—A technical or organizational facility or resource that makes it possible to perform a task, an activity, or a process. Examples of *technical* enablers are personal computers, copying equipment, decentralized data processing, and voice response acceptance. Examples of *organizational* enablers are self-managed work teams, virtual departments, network organizations, and education systems.

Future-state solution (FSS)—A combination of corrective actions and changes that can be applied to an item (process) being studied to improve its performance and increase its value to the stakeholder.

Best-Value future-state solution (BFSS)—A solution that results in the most beneficial new item as viewed by the item's stakeholders. It is the best combination of implementation cost, implementation cycle time, risk, and performance results (e.g., return on investment, customer satisfaction, market share, risk, value-added per employee, time to implement, and cost to implement).

Process improvement team (PIT)—A group of individuals, usually from different functions, assigned to improve a specific process or subprocess. They design the best-value future-state solution using methodologies such as process redesign, process reengineering, and process benchmarking.

BPI Approaches

Three of the BPI approaches (process benchmarking, process redesign, and process reengineering) are covered in Harrington, *Business Process Improvement.* Fast Action Solution Technique (FAST) and High-Impact Team (HIT) are more recent concepts designed to identify and rapidly harvest the low-hanging fruit that has grown within our business processes.

Process Benchmarking

Process benchmarking is an old methodology that got new life when Xerox gave it primary credit for the company turnaround and winning the Malcolm Baldrige Award. This approach is very misunderstood today. Most people think they are benchmarking when they compare their process performance measurements with another organization's measurements. This is only an early step in the benchmarking process. This type of activity should correctly be called *comparative analysis.*

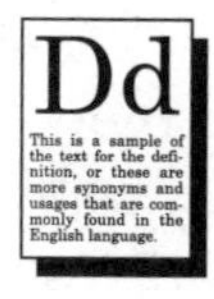

Benchmarking—A systematic way to identify, understand, and creatively evolve superior products, services, designs, equipment, processes, and practices to improve the organization's real performance by studying how other organizations are performing the same or similar operations.

Comparative analysis—The act of comparing a set of measurements with another set of similar measurements for a similar item.

Typically, the benchmarking process will reduce cost, cycle time, and error rates by 20% to 50%. A typical benchmarking project takes three to five months to design a best-value future-state solution (BFSS). Based on our experience, this is the correct approach to use on 5% to 20% of an organization's major processes.

Of course, there are many different types of benchmarking approaches. They include product, business process, production process, and equipment. Business process benchmarking is the approach that is relevant here.

In business process benchmarking, key processes are identified, understood, and compared with the best equivalent processes to define negative gaps. Typically, the analysis identifies a number of organizations that are performing better than the organization conducting the study, based on a comparative analysis. Then the benchmarking team evaluates the other organizations' processes to define why they are operating better than the processes of the organization that is conducting the study. The benchmarking team uses this information to design and implement an improved process that combines the best features of the other organizations' processes. This often creates a process that is better than any of the processes of the organizations that were being studied. This redesigned process is often called the best-value future-state solution. Frequently, the BFSS will not represent the very best practices available. For example, it may be a better business decision to get a 30% improvement in 90 days than a 40% improvement in 18 months.

Process Redesign (Focused Improvement)

The process redesign approach focuses the efforts of the process improvement team (PIT) on refining the present process. Process redesign is normally applied to processes that are working fairly well today. Typically, process redesign projects will reduce cost, cycle time, and error rates between 30% and 60%. With process redesign, it takes between 80 and 100 days to define the BFSS. This is the correct approach to use with approximately 70% to 90% of major business processes. This approach is used if improving the process performance by 30% to 60% would give the organization a competitive advantage.

In redesigning processes, the PIT constructs an as-is simulation model. Then, the following streamlining tools are used in conjunction with the simulation model to redesign the process:

- Bureaucracy elimination
- Value-added analysis
- Duplication elimination
- Simplification methods
- Cycle-time reduction
- Error proofing (current problem analysis)
- Process upgrading (organizational restructuring)
- Simple language
- Standardization
- Supplier partnerships
- Automation, mechanization, and information technology
- Organization restructuring

You will note that the information-technology enablers are applied after the activities in the present process have been optimized. Once the activities have been optimized, information technology and computerization best practices are used to support the optimum process. This truly puts IT in the role of process enabler rather than process driver. With the redesign concept, the process improvement team does not create new IT applications but takes advantage of the best practices that are already proven. Often, a process comparative analysis is conducted in parallel to the redesign activities, to ensure that the redesigned process will be equivalent to or better than today's best practices.

Process Reengineering (New Process Design or Process Innovation)

Process reengineering is the most radical of the five BPI approaches. It is sometimes called process *innovation* because its success relies heavily on the PIT's innovation and creative abilities. Process reengineering is also called *big picture analysis* or *new process design*. We prefer the term *new process design* because it uses the approach that an organization would use if it were designing the process for the first time.

Process reengineering, when applied correctly, reduces cost and cycle time between 60% and 90% and error rates between 40% and 70%. It is a very useful tool when the current-state process is so out-of-date that it is not worth salvaging or even influencing the BFSS. Process reengineering is the correct answer for 5% to 20% of the major processes within an organization. If you find it advantageous to use process reengineering in more than 20% of your major processes, the organization should be very concerned, as it may indicate a major problem with the way the organization is managed. This management problem should be addressed first, so that the PIT will not devote a great deal of effort to improving processes that will not be maintained.

The process reengineering approach to BPI allows the PIT to develop a process that is as close to ideal as possible. The PIT steps back and looks at the process with fresh eyes, asking how it would design this process if it had no restrictions. The approach takes advantage of the available process enablers, including the latest mechanization, automation, and information technology techniques, and improves upon them to come up with new IT products. Process reengineering challenges all of the paradigms that the present process is built upon. This process stimulates the PIT to come up with a radical new process design that is truly a major breakthrough.

The process reengineering approach provides the biggest improvement, but it is the most costly and time-consuming BPI approach. It also involves the highest degree of risk. Often, the process reengineering approach includes organizational restructuring, which can be very disruptive to the organization. Most organizations can effectively implement only one change of this magnitude at a time.

The process reengineering approach to developing a BFSS consists of four tasks:

1. Big Picture Analysis
2. Theory Of Ones
3. Future-State Solution Simulation
4. Future-State Solution Modeling

Task 1: Big Picture Analysis

In this task, the PIT is not constrained in developing a vision document that defines the ideal process. The only restriction is that the results of the process reengineering activities must be in line with the corporate mission and strategy. They should also reinforce the organization's core capabilities and competencies. All other paradigms can and should be challenged. Before the PIT starts to design the new process, it needs to understand where the organization is going, how the process being evaluated supports future business needs, and what changes would provide the organization with the most important competitive advantage.

Once this is understood, the PIT can develop a vision statement of what the best process would look like and how it would function. In developing the vision statement, the PIT needs to think outside the normal routine (think outside the box) and challenge all assumptions, challenge all constraints, question the obvious, identify the technologies and organizational structures that are limiting the process, and define how to improve them to create a process that's better than today's best. The vision statement defines only what must be done, not what is being done. Usually, the vision statement is between 10 and 30 pages and, in reality, is more like a new process specification. It will define all of the process, information technology, organizational, and people enablers that would be applied in designing the new process.

Task 2: Theory of Ones

Once the vision statement is complete, the PIT should define what must be done within the process from input to delivery to the customer. It needs to question why the process cannot be done using only one resource unit (person, time, money, space, etc.). The PIT should be miserly in adding activities and resources to the process (see Figure 9-2).

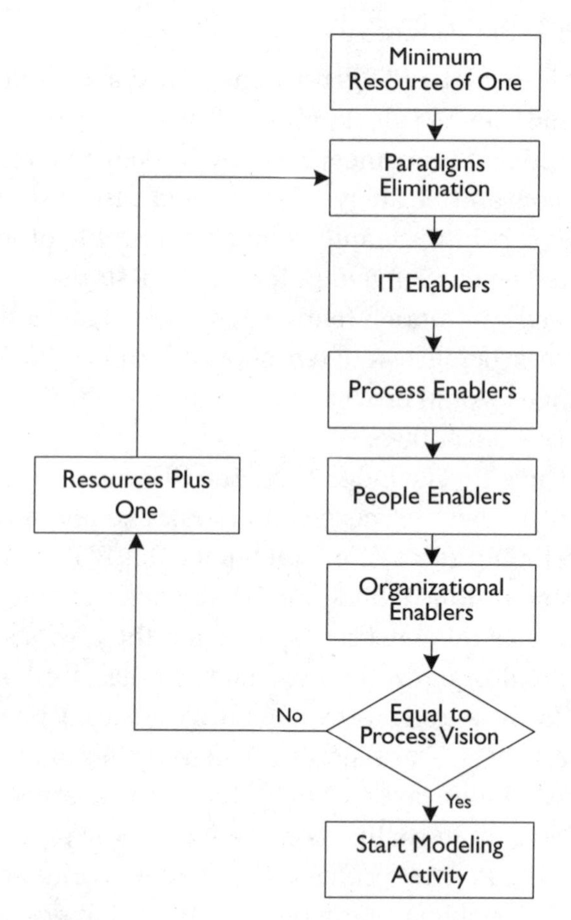

FIGURE 9-2. Theory of ones

To use the Theory of Ones, the PIT sets the minimum quantity of units that it is trying to optimize. For example, if the PIT is interested in optimizing cycle time and the current cycle time is five days, it might ask the question, "What if we had to do it in one second? What enablers would have to be used? What paradigms would have to be discarded?" Basically, the team considers four sets of enablers:

- Information technology enablers
- Process enablers
- People enablers
- Organizational enablers

After the PIT has looked at each of the enablers and challenged each paradigm, it defines a process design to accomplish the desired function. Then resulting process is then compared with the vision statement. If the PIT gets an acceptable answer, it goes forward. If not, it repeats the cycle with a new objective of doing the total process in one minute. At some point in time, the new process design and vision statement will be in harmony. As you can see, reengineering is very much an iterative process.

Task 3: Future-State Solution Simulation

When the new process design is theoretically in line with the objectives set forth in the vision statement, a simulation model is constructed. The simulation model is then exercised to evaluate how the new process design will function. If the simulation model proves to be unstable or produces unsatisfactory results compared with the requirements defined in the vision statement, the PIT should reinitiate the Theory of Ones activity, focusing on the inadequacies defined by the simulation model. When a new process is defined, the PIT prepares and exercises a new simulation model. This cycle is repeated until an acceptable simulation model is constructed.

Task 4: Future-State Solution Modeling

Once the simulation model indicates that the newly designed process will meet the vision statement, the theoretical model is physically modeled to prove the concepts. Typically, the new process design will be evaluated as follows:

- Conference room modeling (without the new computerization support) to verify the soundness of the new process design
- Pilot modeling in an individual location or small part of the total organization to prove the details of the concepts one at a time
- Pilot modeling of the entire process in a small part of the total organization

Impact of Different BPI Approaches

Figure 9-3 compares how typical process benchmarking, process redesign, and process reengineering methodologies improve cycle time in a process over time. It clearly shows the different levels of improvement that three of the BPI approaches, combined with continuous improvement, achieve in a typical process over a 36-month period.

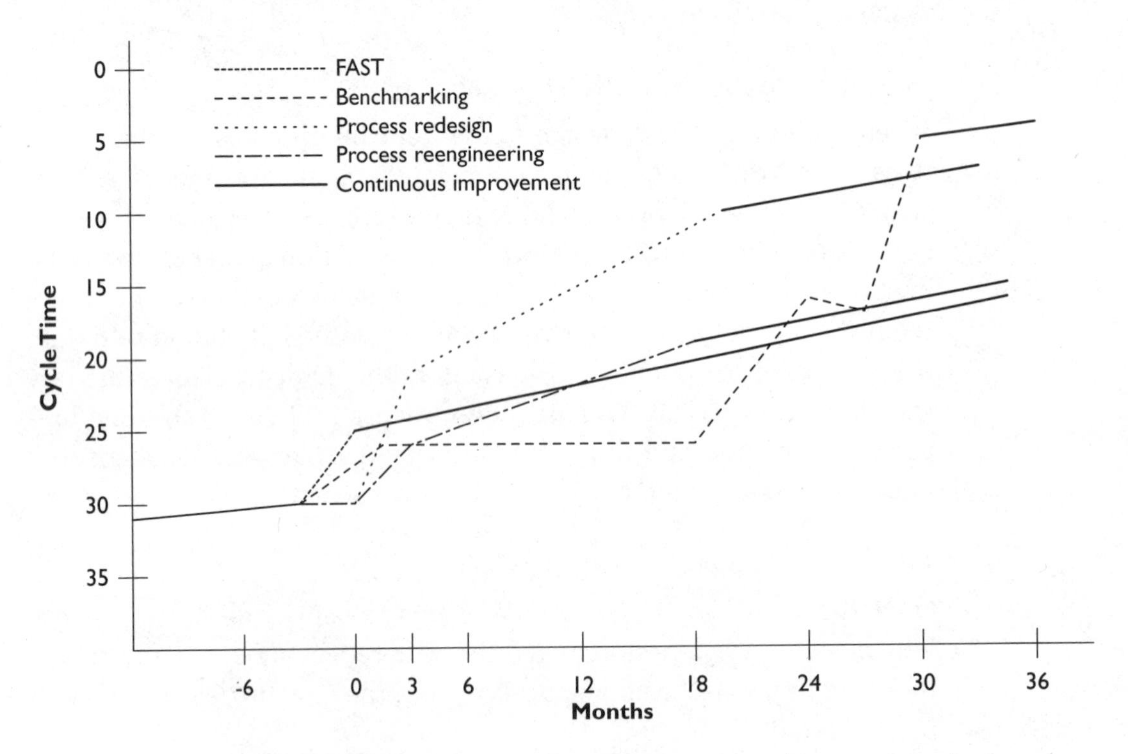

FIGURE 9-3. Comparison of three BPI approaches on a typical process's cycle time

FAST (Fast Action Solution Technique)

Fast Action Solution Technique is based on an improvement tool first used by International Business Machines Corporation in the mid-1980s. General Electric refined this approach in the 1990s and called it "Workout." Ford Motor Company further developed it under the title "RAPID." Today, Ernst & Young extensively uses this approach (which it calls "Express") with many clients around the world. It is also often used by other organizations throughout the Americas.

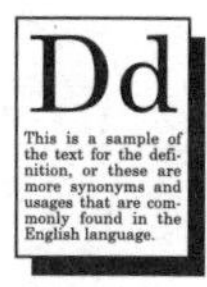

Fast Action Solution Technique (FAST)—A breakthrough approach that focuses a group's attention on a single process for a one- or two-day meeting to define how the group can improve the process over the next 90 days. Before the end of the meeting, management approves or rejects the proposed improvements.

FAST can be applied to any process level, from a major process down to and including the activity level. The FAST approach to BPI centers around a single one- or two-day meeting that identifies root causes of problems and/or no-value-added activities designed into a present process. Typical improvement results from the FAST approach are reduced cost, cycle time, and error rates between 5% and 15% in a three-month period. The potential improvements are identified and approved for implementation in one or two days, hence the term FAST for this approach.

The FAST approach evolves through the following eight phases:

1. A problem or process is identified as a candidate for FAST.
2. A high-level sponsor agrees to support the FAST initiative related to the problem or process that will be improved. (The process must be under the sponsor's span of control.)
3. The FAST team is assigned and a set of objectives is prepared and approved by the sponsor.
4. The FAST team meets for one or two days to develop a high-level process flowchart and define what actions could improve the process performance. All recommendations must be within the span of control of the team members and able to be completely implemented within a three-month time period. All other items are submitted to the sponsor for further consideration later.
5. A FAST team member must agree to be responsible for implementing each recommendation that will be submitted to the sponsor.
6. At the end of the one- or two-day meeting, the sponsor attends a meeting at which the FAST team presents its findings.

7. Before the end of the meeting, the sponsor either approves or rejects the recommendations. It is very important that the sponsor not delay deciding on the suggestions or the approach will soon become ineffective.
8. Approved solutions are implemented by the assigned FAST team member over the next three months.

High-Impact Team (HIT)

There are various definitions for a High-Impact Team (HIT). We won't go into detail here, but the HIT as an approach to BPI is usually created along the following lines.

A team charter is created that states the purpose, goals, and guidelines. The purpose requires that the members of the team work interdependently and there are mechanisms of team accountability to the organization. The team has a sponsor, someone to protect the team against bureaucratic realities and criticisms so that it can pursue its goals.

Team members are selected to combine diverse, yet complementary technical skills and knowledge. The team members must be competent, able to work with others, and committed to excellence in the area on which the team will be focusing.

BPI and Simulation Modeling

Simulation modeling concepts should be used in all five of the business process improvement methodologies—process reengineering, process redesign, process benchmarking, Fast Action Solution Technique, and High-Impact Team—each time they are applied. For our purposes here, we have decided to use process redesign as the example in this chapter.

The Five Phases of Process Redesign

The complexity of our business environment and the many organizations involved in the critical business processes make it necessary to develop a very formal approach to process redesign. This methodology is conveniently divided into five subprocesses called *phases* that consist of a total of 36 activities (see Figure 9-4).

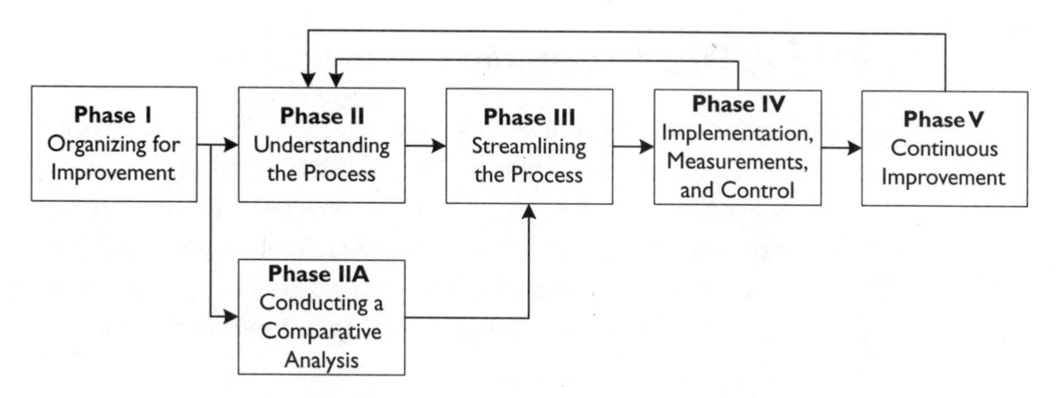

FIGURE 9-4. The five phases of process redesign

Phase I: Organizing for Improvement

An executive improvement team (EIT) is formed. A business process improvement (BPI) champion is assigned. Process owners and process improvement teams (PITs) are assigned, process boundaries are defined, total process measurements are developed, and initial business process improvement project plans are developed and approved. The outputs from Phase I are:

- The BPI champion educates the EIT in the process redesign methodology.
- The BPI champion starts employee communication processes.
- The EIT defines critical processes.
- The EIT assigns process improvement teams (PITs) and process owners.
- The PITs establish process boundaries.

- The PITs develop process measurements of effectiveness, efficiency, and adaptability and set goals.
- The BPI champion trains the PITs in team operating methods and the process redesign methodology.
- The PITs develop project change management plans and include them in the project plan.
- The PIT prepares project plans and the EIT approves them.

Phase II: Understanding the Process

This phase consists of six activities. During these six activities, the PIT flowcharts the process, develops the simulation model, conducts a process walk-through to understand the process, defines problems, and measures cycle time and cost. Additional studies are conducted to fill in any void in the database. The processes and procedures are aligned and quick-fix improvements are implemented.

Phase IIA: Conducting a Comparative Analysis

Often in parallel with Activities 1 through 6 of Phase II, a comparative analysis study is conducted to allow the matrix of the process under study to be compared to other similar processes. The comparative analysis study consists of the following steps:

Activity 7: Collect and analyze internal published information.
Activity 8: Select internal comparison sites.
Activity 9: Collect internal original research information.
Activity 10: Conduct internal interviews and surveys.
Activity 11: Collect external published information.
Activity 12: Collect external original research information.
Activity 13: Perform a gap/trend analysis.
Activity 14: Set more aggressive targets, if necessary.

The outputs from Phases II and IIA are:

- The PIT is trained in flowcharting, interviewing, measuring cycle time, estimating costs, walk-through methods, and simulation modeling.
- Processes are flowcharted.
- A process simulation model is developed.
- Process cycle time is calculated.
- Process cost estimate is calculated.
- Process problem list is developed.
- Quick-fix improvements are implemented and savings are documented.
- Processes are documented and are operating to the documentation.
- The organizational change management project plan is prepared and the PIT starts its implementation process.
- Project plans are updated.
- A comparative analysis is completed and the target performance levels are adjusted, if necessary.

Phase III: Streamlining the Process

The PIT now focuses its efforts on streamlining the process. The PIT will systematically work its way through the 12 streamlining steps to develop a group of future-state solutions; then it will select a best-value future-state solution. The outputs from Phase III are:

- The PIT is trained in the 12 streamlining steps and seven basic problem-solving tools.
- The PIT addresses the process problems.
- The PIT completes process improvement projections and implementation cost and cycle-time estimates for each option.
- The PIT analyzes the options and defines a preferred process (best-value future-state solution).
- The PIT prepares a preliminary implementation plan for the best-value future-state solution and the EIT approves it.
- The PIT updates project plans.
- The PIT is rewarded based on the projected process improvement.

Phase IV: Implementation, Measurements, and Control

Increased emphasis is placed on organizational change management during Phase IV. The best-value future-state solution is phased in with the appropriate number of trial runs that verify the magnitude and impact of each change. The simulation model is updated to reflect these changes. The outputs from Phase IV are:

- An implementation team (IT) is formed by the EIT and trained by the BPI champion.
- The EIT develops and approves a final improvement plan for the best-value future-state solution.
- The IT forms and trains department improvement teams (DITs) to help with the implementation.
- The IT implements the best-value future-state solution according to the implementation plan and measures the result of each change.
- The IT defines and puts in place internal process performance measurements and feedback systems.
- The IT implements management control systems.
- The IT implements and updates the organizational change management plan.
- The IT sets up the simulation model to track transactions through the new process.
- The IT is rewarded based upon how effectively it has implemented the new process.

Phase V: Continuous Improvement

The EIT reviews and approves the process improvement plans. The process evolves through a series of six qualification levels. Each time a change to the process is considered, the simulation model is used to check out the change and its impact on the total process. When a change to the process is implemented, the simulation model is updated to reflect the new process. The outputs from Phase V are:

- The DITs take over the responsibility of continuous improvement for their part of the process.
- The DITs implement process changes.
- The DITs measure process improvement results.
- The DITs update the process simulation model.

Simulation Modeling Applied to Process Redesign

To understand how simulation modeling is applied to process redesign, we will present what happens in each of the first four phases of the process redesign methodology, one at a time. At the end of each phase, we will explain how simulation modeling is applied during that phase.

Phase I: Organizing for Improvement

Phase I—Organizing for Improvement is divided into eight activities (see Figure 9-5):

1. Evaluate the applicability of BPI.
2. Define critical business processes.
3. Select process owners.
4. Define preliminary boundaries.
5. Form and train the process improvement team.
6. Box in the process.
7. Establish measurements and goals.
8. Develop project and change management plans.

FIGURE 9-5. The eight activities of Phase I

The process owner explains the process.

Applying Simulation Modeling to Phase I

Phase I is the phase that does not make extensive use of simulation modeling. Sometimes we do not start the simulation modeling activities until Phase II. But we recommend using a computer program that is part of simulation modeling during this phase and building upon it in Phase II.

The first opportunity to start the simulation model occurs during Activity 5, when the process owner block-diagrams the process flow from department to department between the beginning and ending boundaries. Then, as the process owner interviews each department manager, the managers' suggestions, process-related problems, and resource estimates are stored in the simulation model under the related box (see Figure 9-6).

Typical information that is recorded during the interview with the department manager and stored into the computer is:

- Department 160—Order Processing Department
- Manager—Bob Doright
- Estimated Resources
    - 36 employee months per year consumed by the process
    - $10,000 per month computer service costs
    - 400 square feet of space

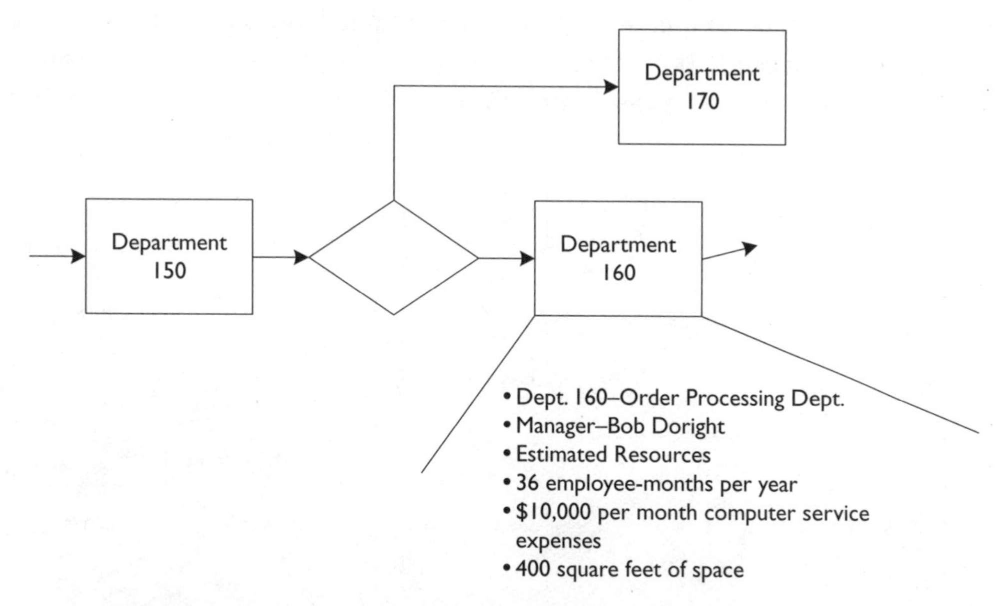

FIGURE 9-6. Data stored related to department 160 in the simulation model

- Problems
  - Orders not sent to Department 160 on time
  - Orders sent to Department 160 that should have been sent to Department 170
  - Sales personnel do not record the correct data
  - Sales personnel commit to delivery dates that cannot be met
  - Computer is too slow
  - The job is very monotonous and therefore my people are prone to make errors
  - There is a lot of distraction that causes errors
  - We have hot jobs, very hot jobs, extremely hot jobs, but no regular jobs
  - There is a big backlog—it takes us four days before we can get to a job
  - Some jobs get misplaced so the cycle time is very long on these jobs

The simulation model is expanded during Activity 6, when the process is boxed in. This allows all of the inputs and outputs to the process to be associated to the related departments (see Figure 9-7).

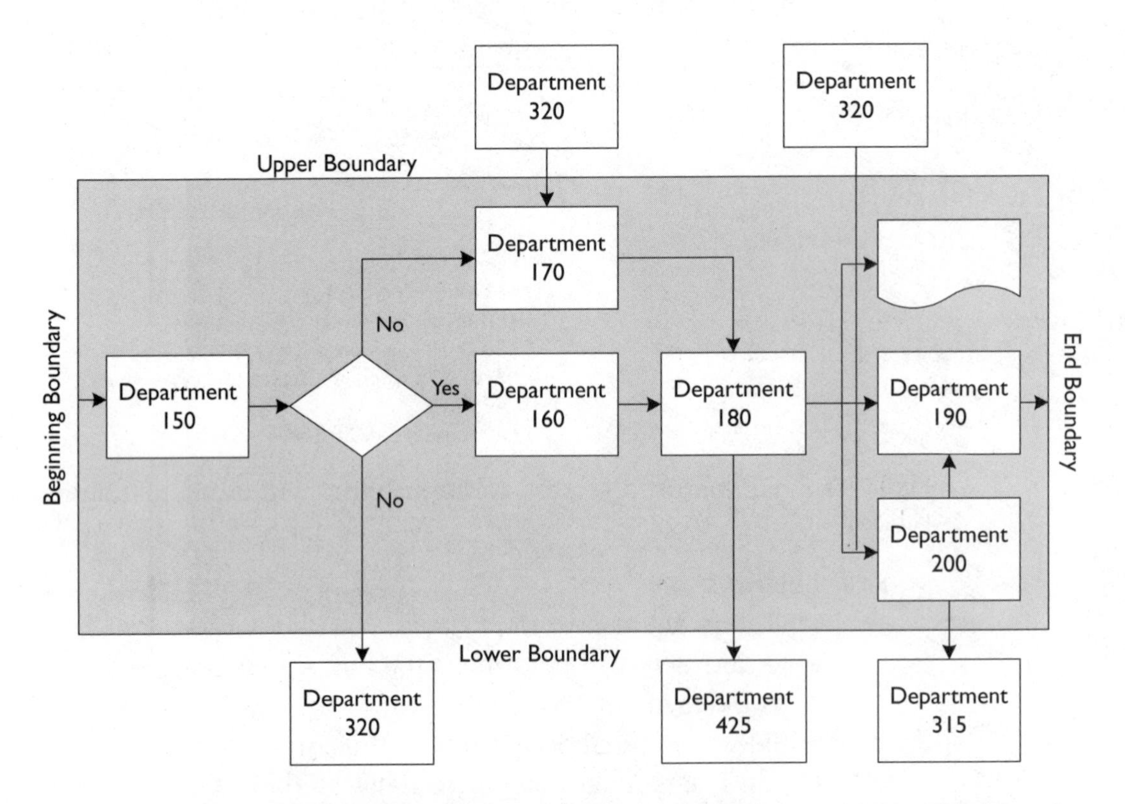

FIGURE 9-7. The simulation model expanded as a result of boxing in the process

At the end of Phase I, all of the departments involved in the process under study have been identified in the simulation model and all of the major inputs and outputs to the process have been defined in the simulation model.

Phase II: Understanding the Process

Unfortunately, most business processes are not documented and often, when they are, the procedures are not followed. During Phase II, the process improvement team (PIT) will draw an as-is picture of the present process; analyze compliance with the present procedures; collect cost, cycle-time, and error data; and align the day-to-day activities with the procedures (see Figure 9-8). The 14 major activities in this phase are:

1. Flowchart the process.
2. Prepare the simulation model.
3. Conduct a process walk-through.
4. Perform process cost and cycle-time analysis.
5. Implement quick fixes.
6. Align process and procedures.
7. Collect internal published information.
8. Select internal comparison sites.
9. Collect internal original research information.
10. Conduct internal interviews and surveys.
11. Collect external published information.
12. Collect external original research information.
13. Perform a gap/trend analysis.
14. Set new targets.

The purpose of Phase II is for the PIT to gain detailed knowledge of the processes and the matrices for cost, cycle time, processing time, error rates, etc. related to the process being studied. The flowchart and simulation model of the present process will be used as the primary working tools in defining the improvement activities.

Activity 1: Flowchart the Process

There are many types of flowcharts that can be used, including the following:

- Block diagram
- ANSI standard flowchart
- Geographic flowchart
- Functional flowchart
- Communications flowchart
- Timeline flowchart
- Data flowchart

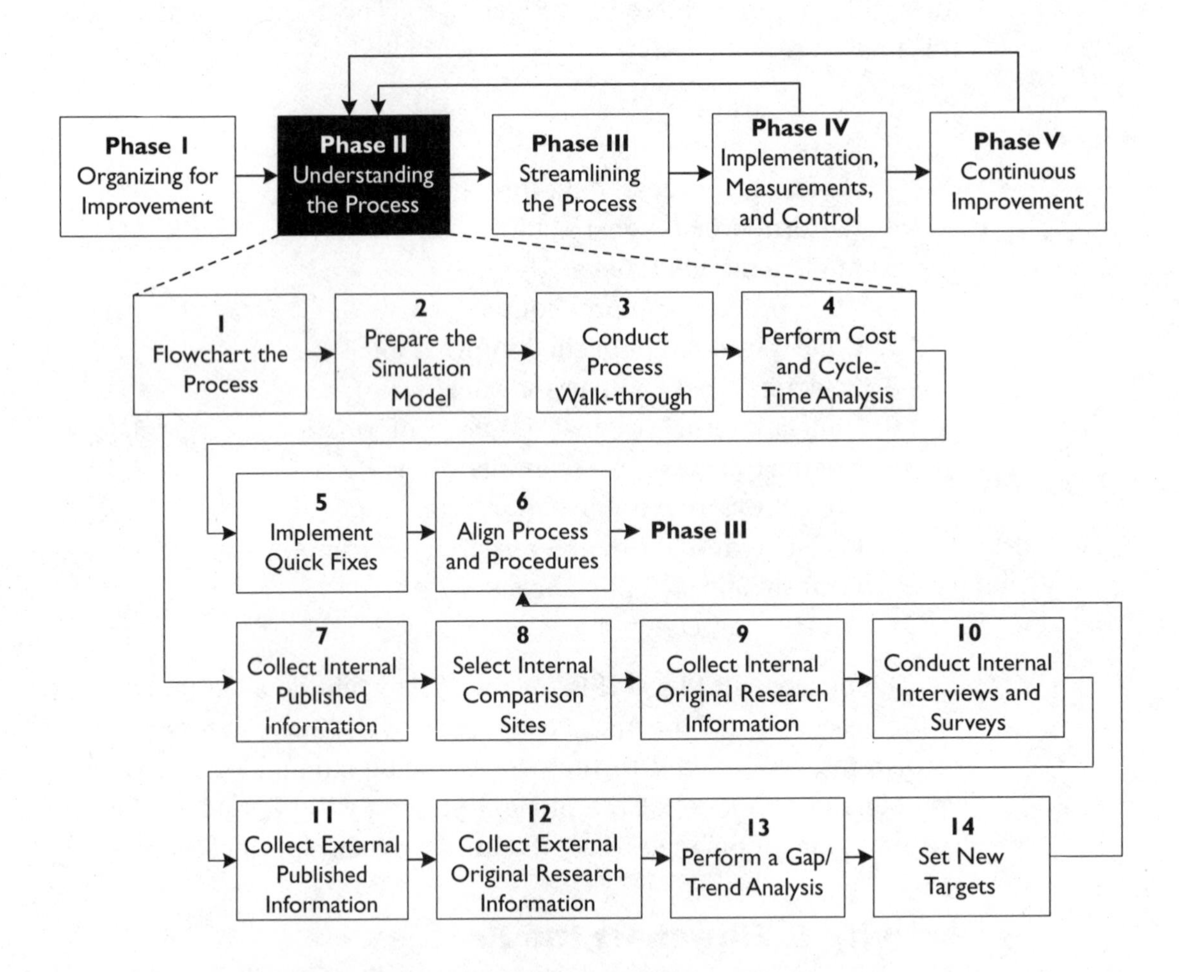

FIGURE 9-8. The 14 activities of Phases II and IIA

In most cases, two or more flowcharts will be used to understand and analyze a business process. Cycle time, processing time, and costs are also frequently recorded on the flowchart. Normally, flowcharts go down to the activity level only. Sometimes the important activities are flowcharted down to the task level.

Develop a process flowchart.

To prepare the flowchart, we like to start off with a wall covered with butcher paper or a flip chart, where each page represents a subprocess. We've found that an effective way to lay out the flowchart is to use sticky tabs, connected by strings. This allows easy movement of the activities as the process becomes better defined.

Typically, the flowcharting activity will start with a block diagram; then each activity on the block diagram will be subdivided into a detailed flowchart. The title of the activity can readily be recorded on the sticky tab. In addition, we recommend also recording on a sticky tab an estimate of the cycle time, processing time, and cost related to each activity. At this point, we should provide only estimates. These estimates are used to determine how detailed the flowchart should be. High costs or long delays for an activity often require that the activity be further broken down in the flowchart.

In many cases, the block diagram created in Phase I serves as a geographic flow diagram for the process, but sometimes a more

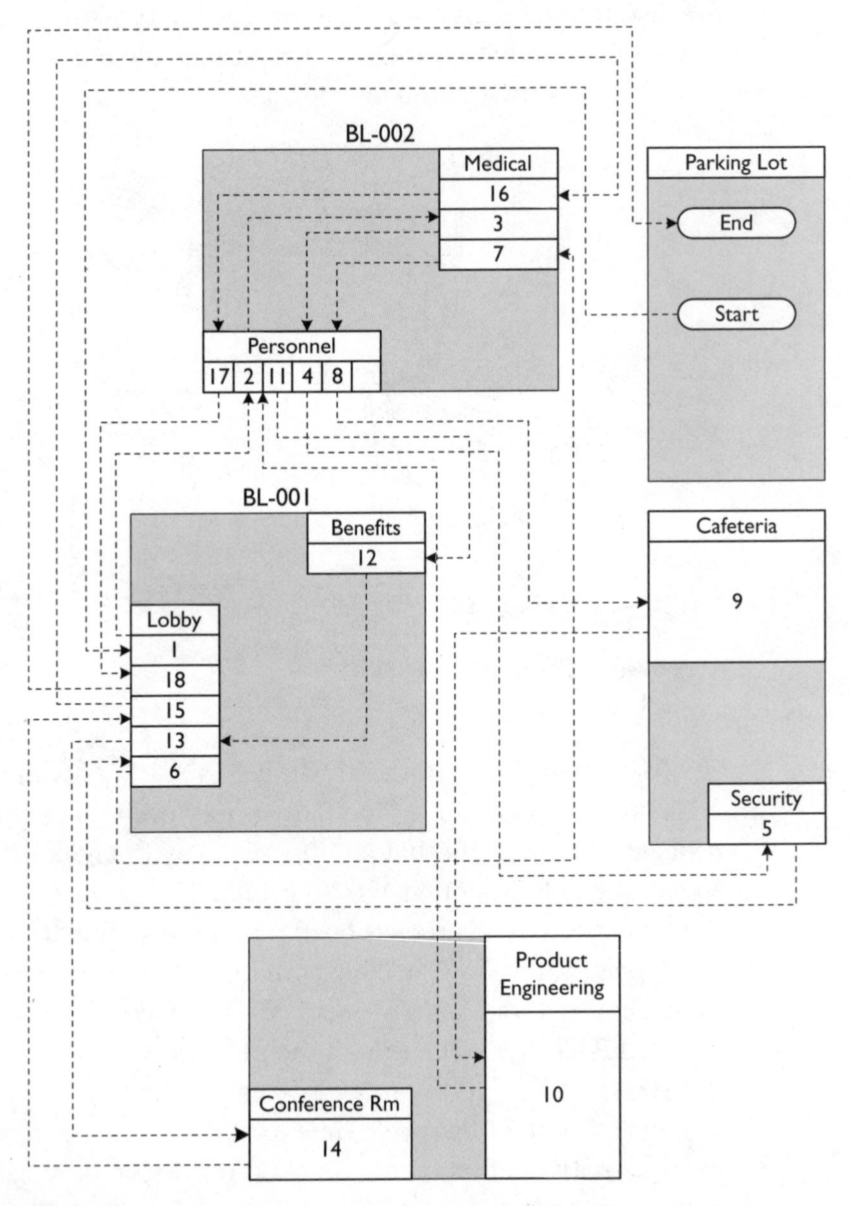

FIGURE 9-9. Geographic flowchart of a new employee's first day at HJH Company

detailed geographic flow diagram is needed to study process flow. Figure 9-9 shows an example of a geographic flowchart.

On occasions, in processes that depend heavily on information transfer, it is often necessary to construct an information flow diagram

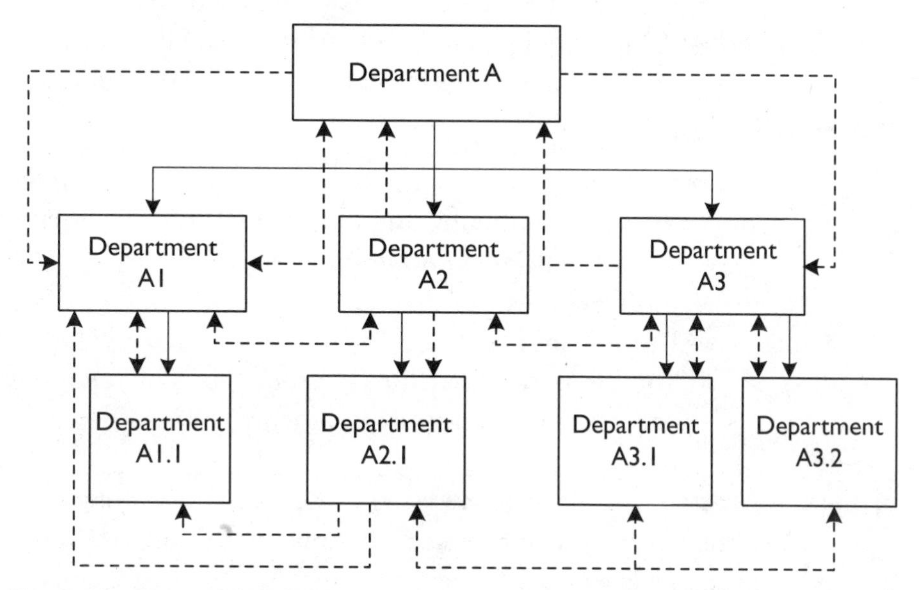

FIGURE 9-10. A block diagram with its communication system flow added with broken lines

to make it easier to analyze these processes. Figure 9-10 is a typical example.

Activity 2: Prepare the Simulation Model

The data collected during the flowchart activity are put into the computer along with the data that define how the activity is performed, cost, cycle time, processing time, and error rate estimates. The computer program will allow the data to be flowcharted in a number of ways. It will also be used to define the process's critical path. In processes where there are many decision points, it is almost impossible to calculate the average cost, cycle time, and processing time by hand. This problem can be handled by using the simulation model to perform a Monte Carlo analysis. The Monte Carlo analysis will also provide a distribution of minimum- and maximum-cost, cycle-time, and process-time calculations. It is important to know that the organization typically loses customers over worst-case conditions during worst-case output from the process, rather than from process averages.

As data are collected, they will be used to update the simulation model. This model will be used during Phase III to evaluate the impact of proposed changes on the total process. Typical outputs from the simulation model are:

- Average, minimum, and maximum total cycle time
- Average, minimum, and maximum total processing time
- Average and maximum total cost
- Various types of flowcharts
- Critical paths
- Total expenditures for different types of resources (e.g., storage, waiting, transportation, work)

Monte Carlo analysis—An approach to varying process variables over a broad range of reasonable options to simulate the variability in a process's key measurement.

In this type of simulation, a chance process generates occurrences in a system at a particular point in time. It is often used to reflect the structure of data and serve as the engine for driving a simulation. Monte Carlo simulations are generally static rather than dynamic: the passage of time plays no substantive role. The method starts with a forecast of three numbers for every item:

High: There's one chance in 10 of getting this result.
Mean: This is the most likely result.
Low: There's one chance in 10 of getting this result.

Activity 3: Conduct Process Walk-Through

The PIT is divided into two- or three-member teams. These walk-through teams personally observe each activity in the process and interview employees performing the activity. Prior to the interview, the walk-through teams become familiar with the tasks required to perform each activity. The teams fill out a detailed walk-through questionnaire that is used to collect process data. Typically, the process walk-through accomplishes the following:

- The tasks for each activity are defined.
- All of the inputs are defined.
- Training inadequacies are defined.
- In-process problems and inhibitors are listed.
- A list of improvement ideas is developed.
- Cycle time is determined.
- Variations between documentation and practice are identified.
- Non-value-added tasks are identified.
- The activities are flowcharted down to the task level.
- Processing time is defined.
- Processing costs are defined.
- The accuracy of the simulation input data is determined.
- Reject rates at the individual activities are defined.
- Repair activities are identified.

As the individual walk-through team completes its assessment of individual activities, this information is fed into the simulation model so that it is updated to reflect actual data in place of estimated data. Often, the walk-through team will collect both averages and extremes for measurements like cycle time, processing time and cost for each activity. At the completion of the process walk-through, the simulation model is populated with actual data and it will regenerate all the major measurements for the process.

Activity 4: Perform Process Cost and Cycle-Time Analysis

Data are collected to define processing time and cycle time during the process walk-through. The data are then used to define the cost and cycle time for each activity in the process. To supplement the data and to fill in any voids, designed experiments are conducted. Often, data are plotted alongside the flowchart to identify opportunities for improvement. A cost/cycle-time chart is useful in helping to identify and prioritize future improvement opportunities (see Figure 9-11). A

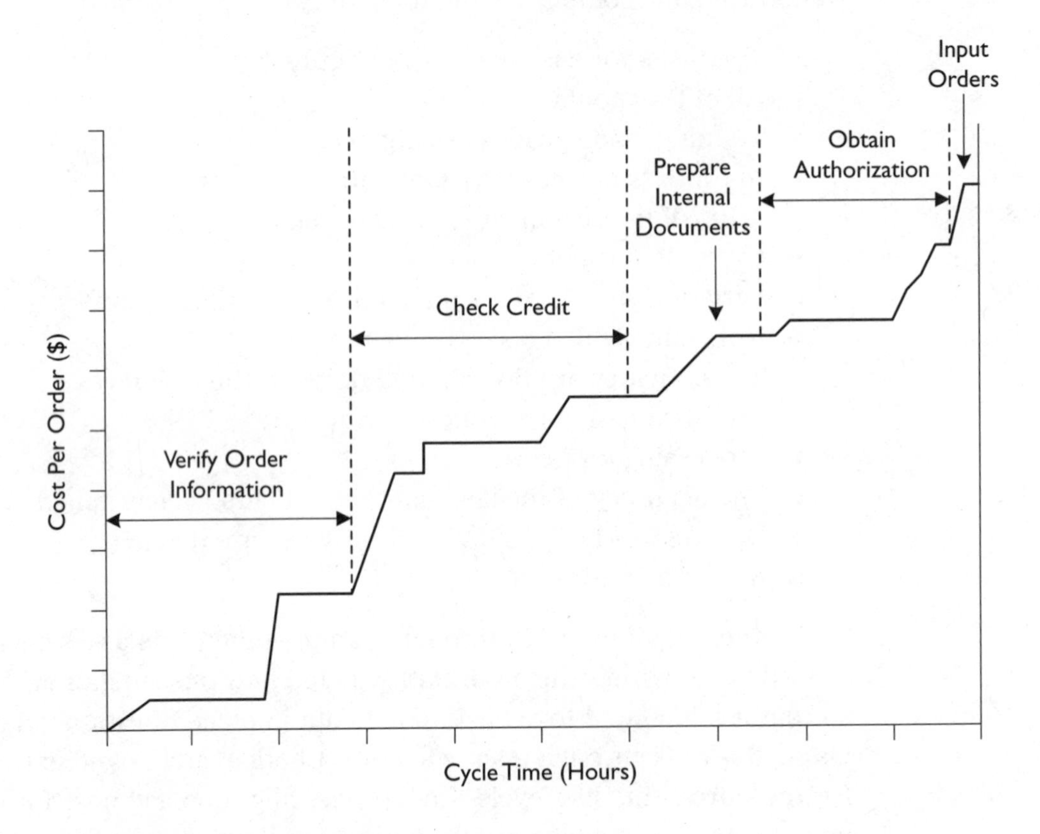

FIGURE 9-11. Cost/cycle-time chart

technique called activity-based costing is frequently used in collecting the required cost and cycle-time data.

Activity 5: Implement Quick Fixes

By now, the PIT should have identified many opportunities to improve the process. Many of them are things that can be done right away at little or no cost. These quick fixes can often save a lot of money and improve performance. As a rule of thumb, a change that has a three-month savings of three times the implementation cost should be implemented at this time. All potential changes are not implemented at this time because the activity in question may be eliminated during the streamlining process.

Activity 6: Align Process and Procedures

The process walk-through may reveal activities that are not being performed according to documentation. If the employees have identified a better way of performing the procedure, the documentation should be modified to reflect the current method. If the present procedure is correct, employees who are not following the procedure should be trained.

Comparative Analysis

In parallel with Activities 1 through 6, the PIT may conduct a comparative analysis (Activities 7 through 14). The comparative analysis allows the PIT to make a gap analysis that compares the as-is model with best practices. Based on this gap analysis, the PIT needs to reassess its improvement goals. For details related to performing a comparative analysis, read Harrington, *Benchmarking Workbook*, chapters 3 through 5.

Using Simulation Modeling During Phase II

Now let's go back and look at the first six activities in Phase II and determine how simulation modeling should be used during this part of the process redesign cycle. It is important to note that this phase will typically be completed in two to three weeks.

Simulation Modeling Applied to Activities 1 and 2 of Phase II

In Phase I the PIT recorded the boxed-in process in the computer. The PIT will now simply take each block in Figure 9-7 and explode it.

The best way to prepare the complete flow diagram is by projecting the computer screen on a large wall or screen so that all the members of the PIT can easily view it. The PIT can start the flowcharting process by characterizing the input to the first block in the diagram. Here are typical questions asked to characterize the major inputs:

- How is the input received? (telephone call, mail truck, email, etc.)
- How frequently is it received?
- How many are received per time period?
- What is the input?
- What data are included in the input?
- Where do the data come from?
- What is the cost of the input?

All inputs are not alike. In most cases, they vary greatly. Let's use order processing for an example.

One order can be for a standard part that the organization has in stock. The next order can be for a complex assembly that needs to be developed, reliability tested, and new manufacturing processes established before it can be produced. One order can be for a single part; another order can be for a hundred thousand parts. One order will need parts to be delivered within 24 hours; another order wants their parts delivered within 24 days. One order uses all standard parts; the next order requires a great deal of subcontracting and fixture manufacturing. Add to this the complexity of orders that are received at different rates depending upon the time of the month and the process has an extremely complex input that needs to be considered. The same type of variation occurs within the process itself. Resources vary at different times of the year (e.g., vacations) or at different times in the month (e.g., during the month-end closing, the financial resources are very limited).

It becomes very obvious that these many differing factors affect the process's performance. Variation in a single factor can have a drastic impact upon one activity and yet no impact upon another or it can impact the total process. This mean that input factors and resource factors need to be defined and quantified for each activity. Typical factors are:

- Number of people available to do work
- Number of work stations
- Monthly variation day by day
- Weekly variation day by day
- Daily variation hour by hour (e.g., lunch)
- Quantity to be processed
- Complexity of the item being processed

To account for these different factors, a number of statistical formulas are developed for individual or groups of activities. The PIT will generate a matrix that defines the requirements for data to be collected during the process walk-through in order to populate these statistical formulas. This type of characterization data is collected by the PIT and recorded in the simulation model, along with the electronic sample input form, if forms are used.

Next, the PIT will explode the first block in the block diagram. This is often called *drilling down* to the next level of detail. The simulation program allows the PIT to drill down from each block to an additional level that defines the activity flow that occurs during that block in the block diagram. To fill in the second-level information about the process, the PIT will define where the input goes and define what activities take place from the time the input enters the block being exploded to the point when it leaves the block being exploded (see Figure 9-12).

In Figure 9-12, the subprocesses or activities within Department 150 are shown as one block in the block diagram at level one. At level two, these activities are detailed into a flow diagram.

We like to use a whiteboard to construct each small subprocess. Once the PIT feels comfortable with the subprocesses, it takes this information and inputs it into the simulation model. PITs that are very familiar with flowcharting frequently will skip the step of using a whiteboard and construct the subprocess flowcharts entirely in the

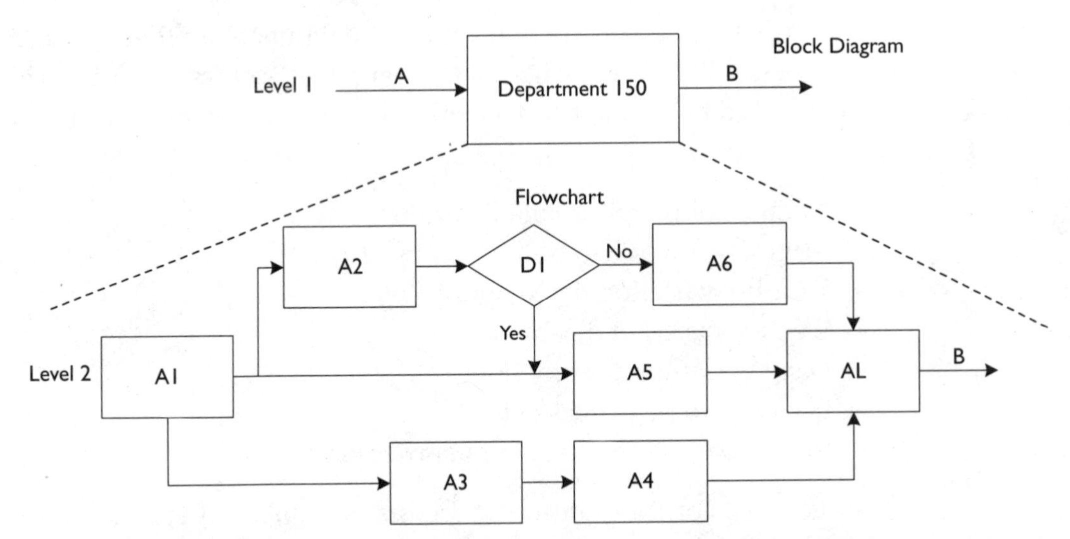

FIGURE 9-12. Department 150's block diagram exploded into its subprocesses

simulation model. Once the flowchart is input into the simulation model, each of the blocks in the second-level flowchart (Figure 9-13) will be characterized. Typical measurements that are used to characterize individual blocks in the simulation model are:

- Processing time
- Supporting cost (e.g., computer processing cost)
- Quality (percent reworked, percent first-time yield, errors per unit)
- Percent of total input/product process through the specific block
- Major problems
- Reject rates
- Outputs
- Activities that receive the outputs from outside of the block being exploded
- Sources for all inputs
- Output formats
- Problems related to the subprocess or activities

At this point in time, estimated values are good enough. It is important for key measurements such as cycle time, processing time, cost, and quality to include averages and extreme values in the estimates. Measurements such as cycle time are calculated by the simulation model and the data collected during the process walk-through are used for validation purposes. The extreme values are used to calculate worst-case conditions. We recommend using the 2-sigma value (which represents 95% of the total population for a normal frequency distribution) for worst-case analysis, but many organizations prefer to use the 3-sigma value (which represents 99.73% of the total population) to provide an even more realistic look at the process. (For more detailed information on histograms, frequency distributions, and process variation, read *Statistical Analysis Simplified.*)

The step of drilling down from the level-one block diagram into the level-two flow diagram is repeated for each block within the block diagram. When this is done, the PIT will review each subprocess or activity in the second-level flow diagram to identify subprocesses or activities that consume large amounts of resources. For these subprocesses or activities, the PIT will drill down a third-level flowchart of each second-level activity. This process can be repeated until the desired level of detail has been defined. We have seen simulation models with seven levels of detail when complex processes are being analyzed.

Once the simulation model is complete and each activity and task within the simulation model has been characterized, the simulation model can calculate the process's key measurements. Typical calculations would be:

- First-time yield
- Throughput yield
- Cycle time
- Processing time
- Cost per item processed
- Scrap cost
- Rework costs

For those measurements where worst-case conditions were defined, the simulation program will be used to run a Monte Carlo analysis to calculate worst-case process conditions. This type of calculation is usually required for any process that has a decision step in it at which part of the process flow goes through a different set of activities than the main stream of process activities. For example, it would take much longer to process an application to take a judo class for people under age 18 than for older people if one step in the process stated, "If the applicant is under 18 years of age, obtain an approval statement in writing from the parents before processing the application."

Understanding the extremes in the process is very important, but very difficult to do without the aid of a simulation model. Let's look at a very simple example of just three activities in series whose processing time takes a normal, bell-shaped distribution (see Figure 9-13).

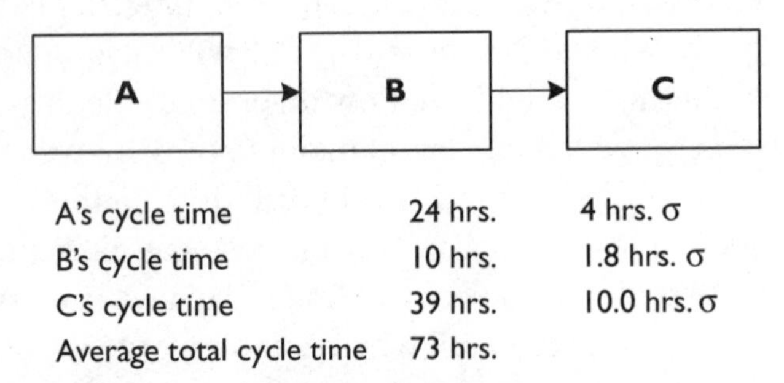

FIGURE 9-13. Data for three activities in a series

The following data relate to Figure 9-13:

- A's cycle time is 24 hours with a sigma of 4 hours.
- B's cycle time is 10 hours with a sigma of 1.8 hours.
- C's cycle time is 39 hours with a sigma of 10 hours.
- The average cycle time through A, B, and C is 73 hours (24 + 10 + 39 hours), but some of the items take much longer to go through these three activities. For example:
  - 2.5% (+2σ) of the items processed through A take more than 32 hours.
  - 2.5% (+2σ) of the items processed through B take more than 13.6 hours.

- 2.5% (+2σ) of the items processed through C take more than 59 hours.

In Figure 9.13, the average cycle time is 73 hours. But we all know that an average value indicates that 50% of the transactions take less time and 50% of the transactions take more time. It isn't the average that makes your customers unhappy. If your customers know you, they plan for the average so that their process can handle the average value. It's the extremes that make your customers unhappy and cause them to look for other suppliers.

Now let's make the simple three-activity flowchart in Figure 9-13 just a little more complex by adding a checkpoint that separates orders into customers with approved credit (70%) and customers without (30%). (See Figure 9-14.)

The cycle time through Activity D is 25 hours and its sigma is 10 hours. 70% of the orders go directly through B. 30% of the orders

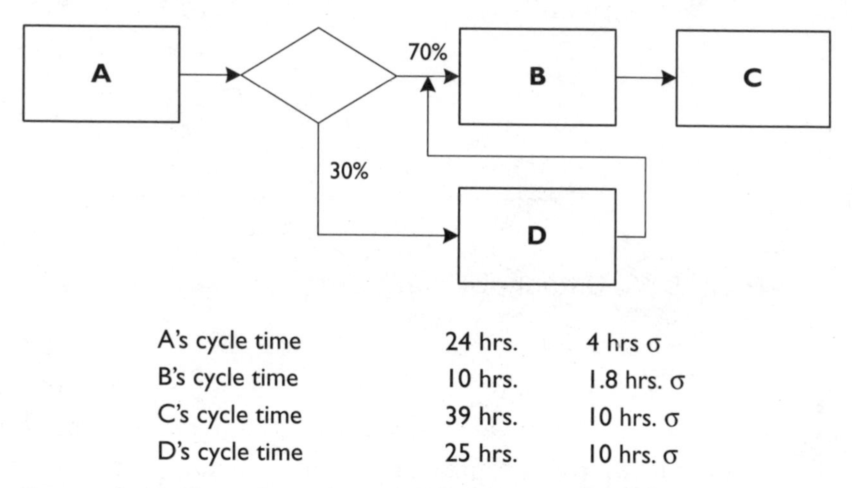

A's cycle time	24 hrs.	4 hrs σ
B's cycle time	10 hrs.	1.8 hrs. σ
C's cycle time	39 hrs.	10 hrs. σ
D's cycle time	25 hrs.	10 hrs. σ

FIGURE 9-14. Data for three activities in series and one in parallel

process through D, then go back through B. Of the orders processed through D, 2.5% (+2σ) take more than 45 hours, even though the average cycle time is 25 hours.

In the very simple example shown in Figure 9-14, it is extremely difficult for the PIT to calculate the average cycle time, let alone construct a distribution of the output from the process. Too often, organizations doing reengineering or redesign work use averages, which are extremely misleading. If they consider variation at all, they assume that the output from the process is a normal, bell-shaped curve. In our experience, this is rarely the case. Typical outputs from processes look more like Figure 9-15.

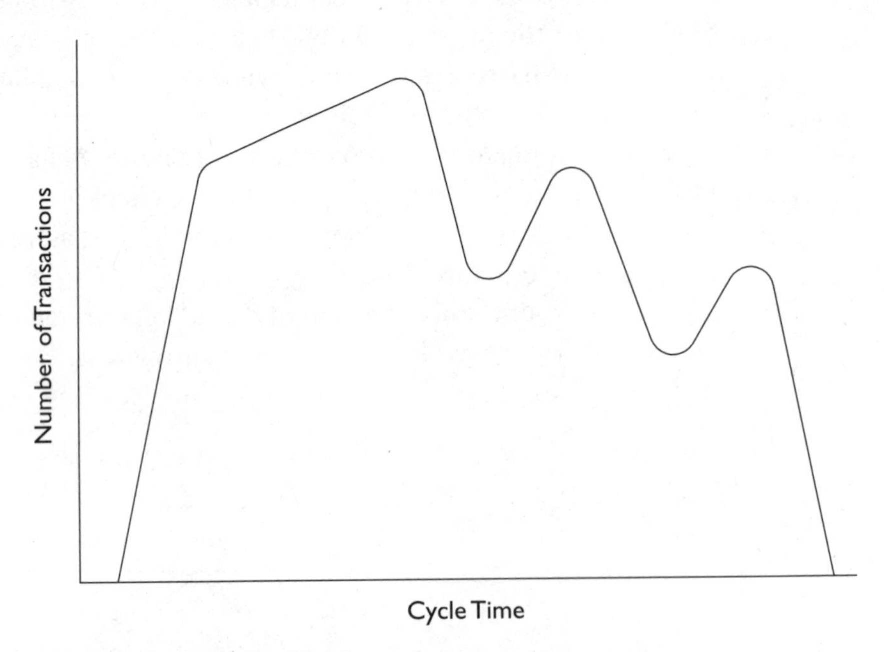

FIGURE 9-15. Output distribution of a complex process

These weird, misshapen distributions of output are caused because most business processes aren't single processes but are made up of many individual processes, each one having its own distribution. Almost every time there is a decision diamond in the flowchart, a new process is formed that has new metric characteristics. The single biggest mistake made in process redesign or reengineering work is to assume that the output takes the bell-shaped curve. The only practical way to truly understand the process that you are trying to redesign or reengineer is by using a simulation model that can run a Monte Carlo analysis to develop a histogram of your key output measurements

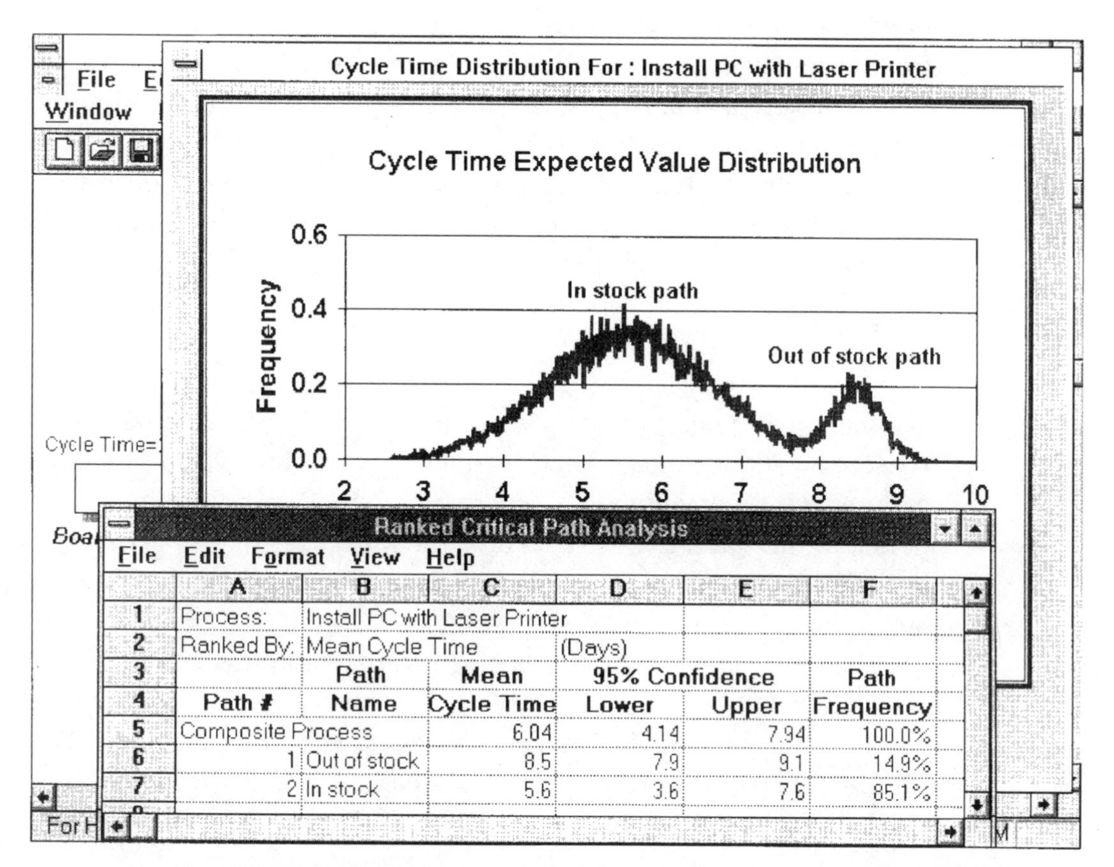

	A	B	C	D	E	F
1	Process:	Install PC with Laser Printer				
2	Ranked By:	Mean Cycle Time		(Days)		
3		Path	Mean	95% Confidence		Path
4	Path #	Name	Cycle Time	Lower	Upper	Frequency
5	Composite Process		6.04	4.14	7.94	100.0%
6	1	Out of stock	8.5	7.9	9.1	14.9%
7	2	In stock	5.6	3.6	7.6	85.1%

FIGURE 9-16. Output from a simulation model Monte Carlo analysis

based upon the variation within the process and the many different process routes that combine to produce a single output. Figure 9-16 is an example of an output cover that was generated by a simulation model for installing a PC with a laser printer.

When constructing the animation part of the simulation model, it is usually necessary to limit the model to the high-level graphic flow diagram, due to the complexity of the animation as viewed on the computer screen. On occasion, specific parts of the detailed simulation model will have an animation model constructed to enable the PIT to study a specific part of the total process.

In constructing your animation model, review the graphic flow diagram or the highest-level flow diagram to define which part of the flowcharts will be depicted by icons. Then select the appropriate icon for this activity (e.g., a truck to represent moving an item from one city to another or an employee sitting at a computer to represent inputting data into the computer). In the final animation model, you may want to show multiple items of the same activity that represent each work station. The details related to constructing an animation model have already been discussed in this book.

Data Dictionary

You may never need to use a data dictionary, if your flowcharts are reasonably uncomplicated and straightforward. However, if you cover a broad range of activities, you may need to go into considerable detail. In this case, the use of a data dictionary becomes necessary in order to be sure that all labels and definitions are clear and understood.

The most effective flowcharts use words and phrases that people will easily understand and only widely known, standard symbols. Often, it helps to provide an accompanying glossary of terms, which information-processing professionals call a *data dictionary*. Each entry in the dictionary refers to a label used in the flowcharts.

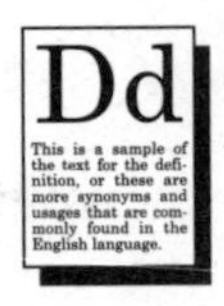

Data dictionary—A list of titles that are used to identify the individual symbols used in a flowchart, with a definition for each title.

A data dictionary serves a number of reference purposes. For example, it alerts you to database *homonyms*. A *database* is a collection of information inside an organization's files. (Often these files are computerized.) A *homonym* is when the same label refers to different items.

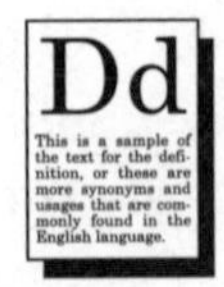

Homonym—A title that has more than one meaning.

Consider, for example, the label "Enter Employee ID." On one flowchart, this might mean "Record the employee's Social Security number on a form." On another flowchart it might mean "Type the employee's name into a computer system and wait for the system to verify the entry." Or take the title "Record cost." On one flowchart it might mean out-of-pocket cost, while on another "cost" could include overhead costs. Because of their multiple meanings, database homonyms can cause confusion in a set of flowcharts.

Homonyms occur because flowchart labels must be brief. You don't have space for a detailed explanation on the chart itself, but you can include the definition in the data dictionary. Checking the dictionary before selecting a label will tell you whether there are other ways in which your label is being used already. If so, you might select another label or take special measures to ensure that people using your flowchart know what you really mean.

You also can use the data dictionary for assistance with database *synonyms*—when different labels have identical definitions. For example, "receivables" might refer to the same thing as "sales collectible."

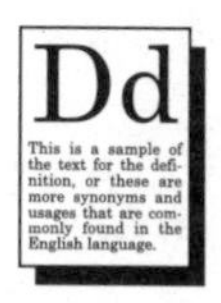

Synonym—One of two or more titles that mean the same thing.

As with homonyms, database synonyms may be necessary. People prefer to use familiar terms when constructing their flowcharts, and employees in different parts of the organization may have different words for an identical item. Recognizing the value of familiarity, information-processing professionals call database synonyms that are acceptable *aliases*.

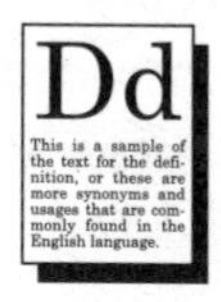

Alias—An additional or alternative name or title; an acceptable database synonym.

Synonyms must be identified. Otherwise, a team drawing an overview flowchart with activities from the accounting department and the sales department might include unnecessary duplication. That's where developing a data dictionary can help. When the accounting department is asked to define the sales collectible file, the team creating the flowchart will discover that the two files are the same.

In addition, a data dictionary can go beyond a definition, to include detailed information about the activity represented on the flowchart. In searching for ways to improve business activities, a team may be interested in how many records a certain file contains or how many items are processed each week through a certain activity. The team also may want to know on which flowcharts a given label appears to accurately evaluate the implications of a change. All these details can be stored in the data dictionary.

Data dictionaries can be maintained manually or on a computer system. With a computer system, you can more easily revise, arrange, and locate information. If you create your flowcharts with a computer, automating the data dictionary has even further advantages, since you can develop a system of automated cross references between the charts and the dictionary.

Simulation Modeling Applied to Activity 3 of Phase II

In Activity 3, the PIT performs a process walk-through using a process walk-through survey form. During the interviews, factual data are collected related to each activity and task defined in the simulation model. As data are collected, they replace the PIT's estimates that were stored in the simulation model and additional data are added. Typically, a list is developed of suggested improvements and problems related to each activity within the simulation model. Often, the flowcharts themselves will be revised as the PIT physically observes the process under study. At the end of the process walk-through, when all the real data have been input into the simulation model, the key measurements are rerun to obtain factual measurements of how the as-is process is performing.

The PIT and management are usually extremely surprised at the large amount of variation that is built into the present process. This frequently leads to a questioning of some of the basic data that were collected during the walk-through or there is a lack of reliable variation data related to some activities.

Simulation Modeling Applied to Activity 4 of Phase II

As a result, Activity 4 begins where design of experiments is run to quantify specific measurements, such as quantity in process, backlog, cycle time, and cost related to specific areas of the process. As the new data are collected, they are input into the simulation model to replace the data that were collected during the walk-through. Once again, all of the key measurements are recalculated using the simulation model.

Validation of the Simulation Model

The validation of the simulation model of the as-is process involves comparing the model's output with the actual process measurements and outputs. Typical measurements that could be compared are:

- input quantities and variation
- cycle time
- percent of items flowing through each path
- processing time
- supplier lead times
- personnel utilization
- equipment utilization
- critical paths
- output variation
- backlogs as specific activities

Now that the PIT has gathered all the data needed to populate the simulation model database, it's time to validate the accuracy of the model by comparing its operation with actual performance. This provides an easy way to ensure that all of the assumptions that were made related to the simulation model and the formulas used in it are correct. To accomplish this, load the model with the actual data that reflect the process being studied, at the beginning point of the validation run (e.g., at point A, there are three work stations and a backlog of 10 jobs). Then load the model with inputs that reflect the actual process inputs over a period of time. For example,

Working Day	Job Input into Process
1	4
2	3
3	5
4	6
5	4
6	2
7	1
8	5
9	6
10	3
11	3
12	4
13	5
14	3
15	3
16	9
17	10
18	11
19	17
20	16
21	16
22	10

Then run the model to simulate the comparative time period (in the above example, 22 working days), to compare the actual outputs from the process with the simulation model projected outputs. Figure 9-17 shows the daily job outputs from the process over a period of 22 working days for actual quantity process and calculated quantity process.

Figure 9-18 shows the daily job backlog at Activity Z over a 22-working-day period plotted of actual backlog versus calculated backlog.

Figure 9-19 shows a plot of the individual cycle time of the job's process over 22 working days based upon actual data and calculated data.

By studying these three figures, you will observe that the calculated data for Figures 9-17 and 9-18 are close to the actual data and thus

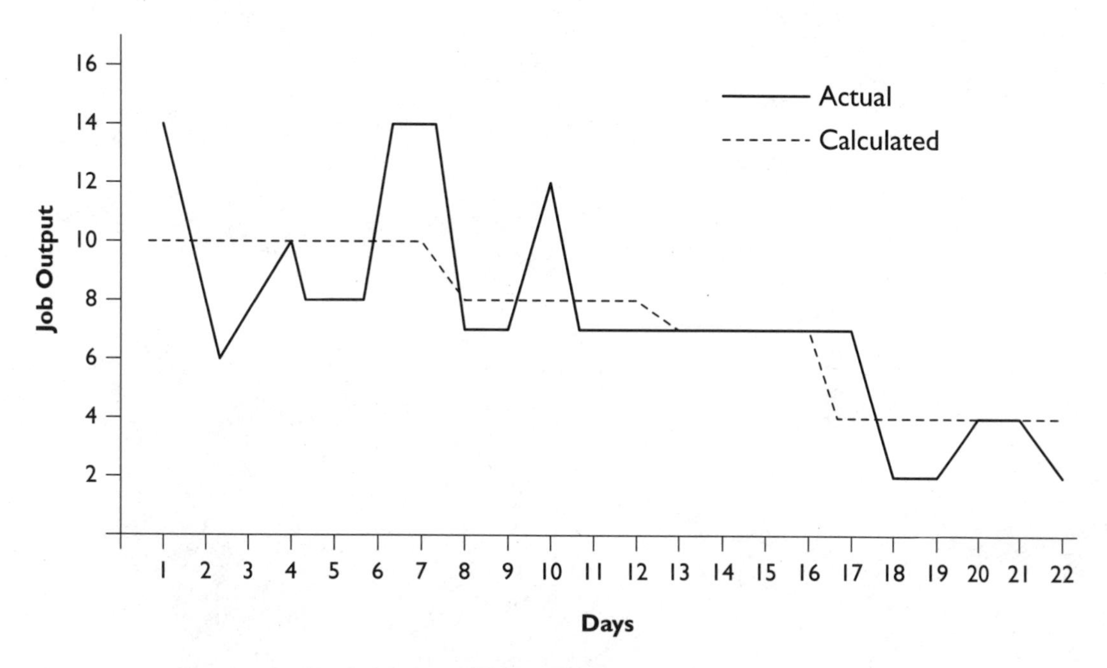

FIGURE 9-17. Jobs out of the process

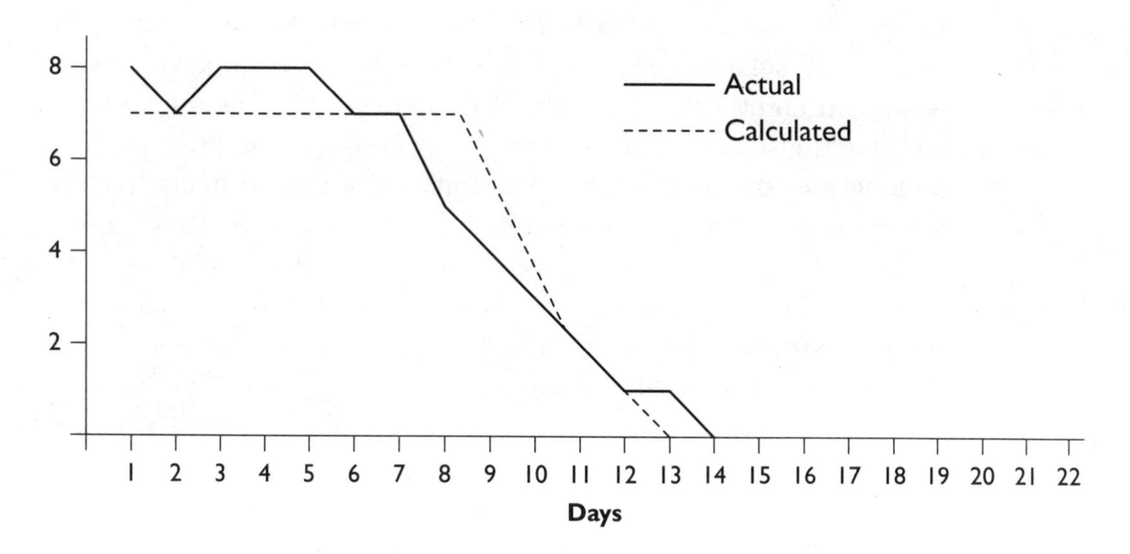

FIGURE 9-18. Jobs backlogged at Activity Z

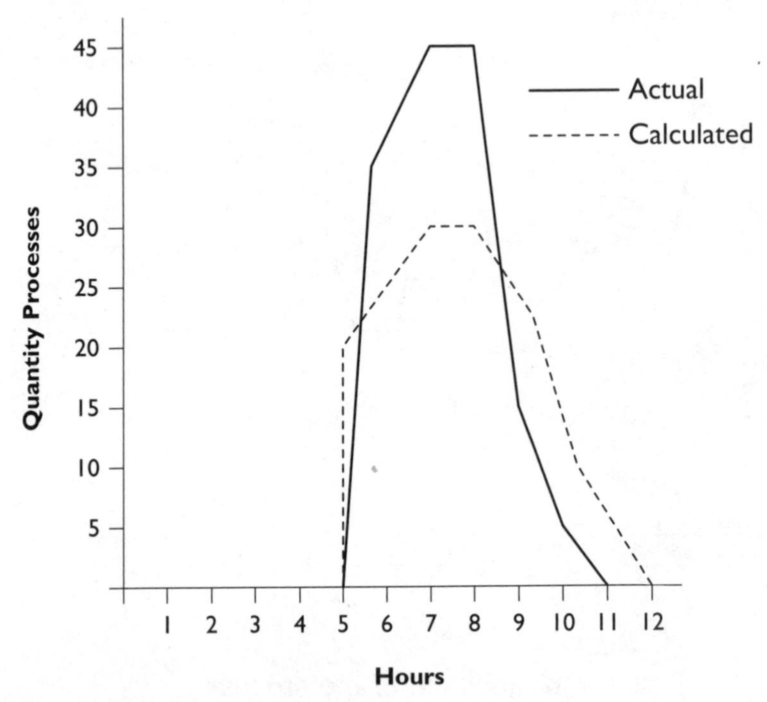

FIGURE 9-19. Cycle time per job

validate the assumptions used to define the calculation. But in Figure 9-19, the actual and calculated values for cycle time per job are significantly different. In this case, the PIT had made a bad assumption that all operations processed the items on a first-in, first-out basis. After looking into the problem, the PIT found that at two operations the selection of the next job was purely random. As a result, for these two operations a random number table was used in the simulation model to select which job would be processed next. When the simulation was rerun, the resulting curve was close enough to actual results to verify the validity of the simulation model.

At this point in time, embedded into a simulation model is a list of excellent ideas that can be implemented at relatively low cost that will have an extremely high return on investment. This leads us directly into Activity 5, where these quick fixes are implemented. As the quick fixes are implemented, the simulation model is revised and the key measurements are recalculated.

Summary of Simulation Modeling Applied to Phase II

As we complete Phase II, the PIT has an extremely accurate living model of the process that can be easily manipulated to determine what impact changes on the process will have on the process's key measurements. This will be a valuable tool as they move into Phase III, Streamlining.

Phase III: Streamlining the Process

During this phase of process redesign, the present process will be streamlined to reduce waste while reducing cycle time and making the process more effective. After the process is simplified, automation and information technology are applied to the new process to maximize effectiveness, efficiency, and adaptability measurements.

Phase III consists of five activities (see Figure 9-20):

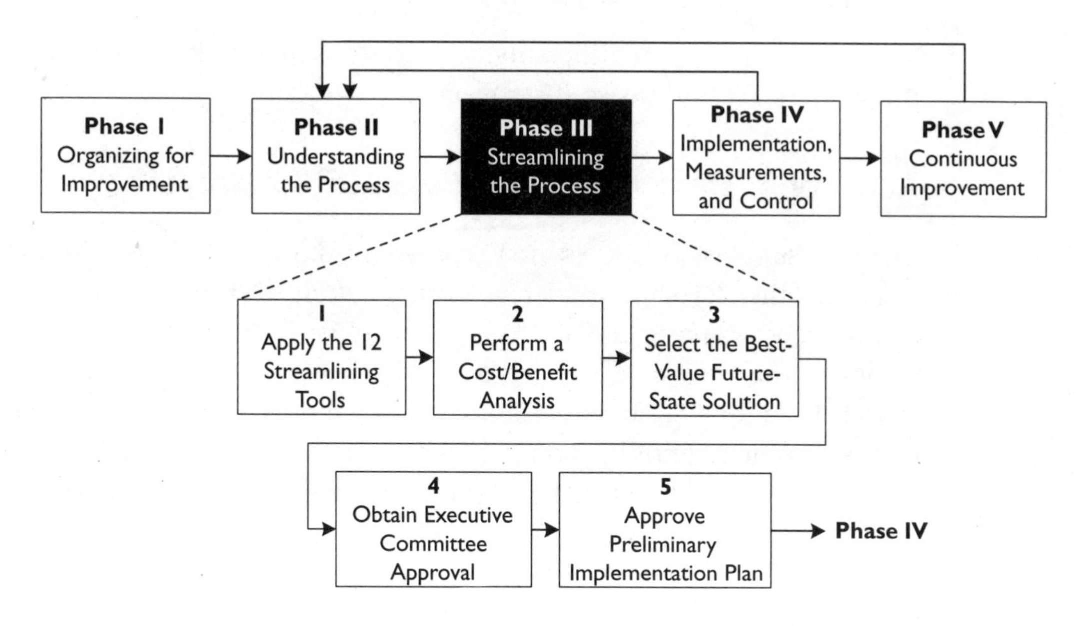

FIGURE 9-20. Phase III: Streamlining the process

Activity 1: Apply the 12 Streamlining Steps

During this activity, the PIT will use the simulation model as a framework for evaluating the impact on the process's total performance when the 12 streamlining steps are applied:

Step 1: Bureaucracy Elimination
Step 2: Value-Added Assessment
Step 3: Duplication Elimination
Step 4: Simplification Methods
Step 5: Cycle-Time Reduction
Step 6: Error Proofing
Step 7: Process Upgrading
Step 8: Simple Language
Step 9: Standardization
Step 10: Supplier Partnerships
Step 11: Automation, Mechanization, and Information Technology
Step 12: Organizational Restructuring

For detailed information about the 12 steps in Activity 1, read Harrington, *Business Process Improvement.*

Activity 2: Perform a Cost/Benefits Analysis

Once the simulation models are prepared for the potential future-state solutions, the PIT should analyze each solution to project its impact on the process's performance. This can be effectively done by defining the measurement parameters related to each activity in the simulation model. Then the PIT should prepare a preliminary estimate of the cost and cycle time required to convert the present process over to the proposed future-state solution. It should include training costs and decreased productivity impact during the learning cycle.

Another important factor that must be evaluated is the degree that the present workforce will need to be restructured in order to operate the new process effectively. Often, drastic changes that involve extensive use of information technology require that the skills and background of the employees be very different from those of the employees presently operating the process. This can create two major problems.

It is often hard to find employees with the required skills and it may not be practical to provide the present employees with the needed skills.

The organization is already faced with the problem of what to do with the employees whose jobs have been eliminated due to the process redesign (usually about 40% of the people employed in the old process). This situation makes the problem even more difficult to solve.

The PIT needs to evaluate the skill sets needed to operate the future-state solution and compare them with the skill sets of the current employees. The PIT should then prepare a *workforce restructuring index*. This index is usually expressed as a percentage of the current employees who do not have the skill set to operate the new process and cannot be trained at a reasonable cost to do the job.

The table in Figure 9-21 compares the results of the analysis of three potential future-state solutions.

Measurements	**Original Process**	**FSS-1**	**FSS-2**	**FSS-3**
Cycle time (days)	35.0	16.2	19.5	17.5
Processing time (yrs)	10.0	6.5	8.3	7.5
Errors/1000	25.1	12.3	9.2	3.0
Cost/Cycle	$950	$631	$789	$712
Service response time (hrs)	120	65	80	75
Cost in $1000		$1000	$100	$423.50
Cycle time (months)		29	6	16
Risk		35%	10%	20%
Workforce Restructuring Index		65%	5%	45%

FIGURE 9-21. Benefits, cost, and risk analysis chart for three alternative future-state solutions

The constraint placed on FSS-1 was to minimize cost per cycle. The constraint placed on FSS-2 was to develop a process that could be implemented in six months. The constraint that drove the design of FSS-3 was to improve the quality of the process as measured in errors/1000.

Activity 3: Select the Best-Value Future-State Solution

In making a final selection of the best-value future-state solution, the PIT has to consider many factors. Each factor will be weighted differently based on the customer's needs, the competitor's performance, the rate of change of the technology involved, the cost to implement the future-state solution, and the elapsed time before the results of the future-state solution will be realized. Typical questions that need to be asked are:

- If it costs more and takes longer to obtain better output quality, is it worth it?
- Is it more important to get fast results or to minimize cost?
- How much change will be accepted by the people involved in the process and is the change in line with the organization's culture?
- Can we sacrifice adaptability for efficiency?
- What is the long-term return on investment for each FSS?
- How much risk is there associated with each approach?
- How will we get people with the right skills to operate the process?

To add to the difficulty, the answers to these typical questions are very interactive with each other, having different priorities based on the individual circumstances. In the three future-state solutions analyzed in Figure 9-21, FSS-1 is obviously unacceptable, while the best-value future-state solution for one set of conditions will be FSS-2 and for another set of conditions it will be FSS-3.

Activity 4: Obtain Executive Committee Approval

The PIT should present its analysis of all the future-state solutions to executive management along with its recommendations. The executive committee must weigh the alternatives and make the final decision on how to invest the organization's resources. When the executive committee agrees on a best-value future-state solution, it should also authorize funding to implement it and assign an implementation team leader.

Activity 5: Approve Preliminary Implementation Plan

The PIT will now prepare a preliminary implementation plan and associated budget. This allows the PIT to document in greater detail the BFSS that it developed and explain what considerations it included in estimating the return on investment. The PIT should submit the preliminary implementation plan to the executive committee, along with recommendations related to who should be assigned to implement the new process and its accompanying measurement system. Once the executive committee has approved the plan and established a supporting budget, the members of the PIT should be rewarded for their work. Then the PIT is disbanded.

Applying Simulation Modeling to Phase III

Now let's look at how simulation modeling is used during Phase III. Typically, this phase will take approximately six to 10 weeks, depending on the complexity of the process being redesigned.

Using Process Simulation Modeling During Phase III

The PIT has expended a great deal of effort to prepare an accurate simulation model of the present process during Phase II. Now, during Phase III (Streamlining), this simulation model is dissected and rearranged to define different combinations that will provide the best possible results. It is during Phase III that the value of a simulation model is best understood. Through the effective use of a simulation model, the PIT can reduce the time required to streamline the process by almost 50% and improve the future-state solution's performance by an additional 20% to 40%. It is almost irresponsible to try to do Phase III without using a simulation model.

We strongly recommend that the PIT duplicate the simulation model that was created in Phase II and put the original aside, using the duplicate simulation model to experiment during Phase III. Often things that the PIT believed would be significant improvements turn out to be less effective than expected and sometimes even detrimental to the total process performance. By setting aside the original model, the PIT always has a reference to which it can return.

To start evaluating how simulation modeling is used during Phase III, let's focus upon the 12 steps in Activity 1.

Steps 1 and 2: Bureaucracy Elimination and Value-Added Assessment

The PIT will review each activity or task in the simulation model and classify it as:

- bureaucracy (blue)
- no-value-added (red)
- business-value-added (yellow)
- real-value-added (green)

As the PIT reviews and classifies each block in the simulation model, it should color the block as indicated above. This changes the model into what is known as a *rainbow* simulation model. In some cases, a single block is classified into more than one category (e.g., part of the block is classified as no-value-added and another part of the block is classified as business-value-added). There are three ways that the simulation model can handle this condition.

1. The block can be divided into two lower-level blocks, each of which has only one classification.
2. The percentage of the activity within the block for each classification can be recorded in the process's database (e.g., Activity K is 65% no-value-added, 35% business-value-added).
3. The percentage of the activity in each classification can be recorded in the process's database and the block is assigned the color that represents the predominant classification for the activity within the block.

Of the three alternatives, we prefer the first one because it presents a better visual picture of what's going on within the process.

When the processes have been classified, the simulation model will provide the PIT with answers to questions such as the following:

- How much money is lost doing bureaucracy and no-value-added activities?
- How much would the cycle time be reduced if all of the bureaucracy and no-value-added activities were removed?
- What is the real-value-added cost of the process?
- What is the difference between business-value-added processing time and cycle time?
- What percentage of the critical path through the process is real-value-added?
- List each bureaucracy activity and the name of the person or organization that is performing each activity, the measurement parameters related to each activity, and the savings that would result if each activity were eliminated.
- What would be the process improvement if all the activities classified as bureaucracy were eliminated?

Critical path–The sequence of activities that represents the longest total time to complete the process, such that a delay in any activity in the critical path causes a delay in completing the process.

Now the PIT is in an excellent position to go to the manager responsible for each of the activities classified as bureaucracy and ask him or her to cost-justify the operation. If the operation can be cost-justified, the PIT should then ask, "Why is the operation needed and what could be done to eliminate this activity?" Sometimes sampling is an acceptable way to decrease the cost and maintain some level of checks and balances for those bureaucracy steps that are cost-justified. Bureaucracy can usually be related to specific root causes, such as the following:

- lack of training
- lack of procedures
- lack of trust
- lack of information
- carelessness
- poor equipment

A basic root cause should be developed for each bureaucracy step that is not eliminated. This information is then used to update the simulation model and its database.

Now the PIT addresses the no-value-added activities. It looks at each no-value-added activity and performs a root-cause analysis to determine why that activity is in place. Here again, the PIT will find that most of the no-value-added activities fall into a series of specific root causes similar to the ones that cause bureaucracy in the process, with a few additional causes, such as the following:

- poor scheduling
- extreme variation in the processes feeding that activity
- need to move the item from one point to another

After determining the root causes, the PIT feeds this information into the simulation model's databases.

Next, the PIT focuses on the business-value-added activities of the process. Here again, the PIT looks at each block in the simulation model and asks the questions:

- Why is it necessary to do this job?
- What would happen if this job were not performed?
- Is the cost of performing the task less than the value added to the organization as a result of the task?
- If the customer who received the output from this block had to pay the expenses related to that block, would he or she consider this money well spent?
- Is this the best place and the best time to perform this particular task?

We are always amazed, when we perform this type of analysis of a data-reporting system, at how many reports are eliminated when the people who use them evaluate what those reports are worth to them.

The data collected and the decisions made related to the process during this activity are then used to update the simulation model and its database.

Now that the simulation database has been updated based upon the bureaucracy elimination studies, the simulation model has become greatly simplified, since blocks have been eliminated. Now the simulation model is used to group root causes and analyze which root causes have the biggest impact on the process under study. Once this is done, the PIT will look at the root causes to determine what impact the associated parts of the process would have on the organization's total process. Based upon this, priority is given to establishing corrective measures that will eliminate the root causes for the bureaucracy activities, no-value-added activities, and many of the business-value-added activities. Once the corrective action is defined, the PIT feeds this information into the simulation model and new performance characteristics are calculated.

Step 3: Duplication Elimination

The vast majority of the duplication activities occur related to data collection and analysis activities. Here again, the simulation model provides an excellent tool to automatically determine what data are being collected so that duplication of data collection, analysis, and reporting can be identified. If any duplication is identified, a corrective action program is put in place so that all the information can be collected and analyzed just once in a way that meets everyone's needs. Then, the revamped data collection scheme should be recorded in the simulation model and its impact upon the process's total performance recalculated.

Frequently, duplication elimination seems to have little impact upon the process if you don't look beyond the immediate impact. Many of the problems related to duplication elimination occur when you have two different databases, because no one is sure which database is correct and, as a result, actions are frequently put off.

Step 4: Simplification Methods

As a result of the first three steps, often 50% of the blocks in the simulation model have been eliminated. Often, the data collection requirements have also been reduced and movement of the product can be minimized. The simulation model provides a sound picture of how the process will function based upon the recommendations made in the previous steps. This allows the PIT to look at the newly created process in a different light and, as a result, the team is often able to combine operations to simplify and smooth workflow. Now the PIT will look at the process to determine if activities can be combined, if combinations of activities can be simplified, and if there are easier ways to do them. Each idea that the PIT comes up with is evaluated by changing the simulation model and calculating the impact on the total process measurements. The accepted changes that result from the simplification activity are also used to update the simulation model.

Step 5: Cycle-Time Reduction

Even with the greatly simplified process defined in the simulation model, there is still a need to focus on reducing cycle time. To accomplish this, the simulation model can be used to define the critical path through the new process. The analytical capabilities of the simulation model will define the activities that have the biggest impact on the critical path and cycle time. This allows the PIT to focus on the specific activities that it needs to improve. As changes are made to reduce the process' cycle time, they are input into the simulation model and new critical paths are calculated. This cycle is repeated until an acceptable cycle time is obtained or until no further refinements are possible.

Then the PIT will restart the cycle and this time look at specific paths. For example, 80% of the product may flow through one path and only 20% through another path. The PIT needs to analyze these two paths independently. Again, the simulation model is absolutely crucial in this analysis. Once this part of the cycle-time analysis has been completed, the simulation model should be used to run a Monte Carlo analysis using the variation data related to each activity. This will create a cycle-time distribution curve. The PIT should then focus on the entities within the processes that cause the cycle-time distribution to be as wide as it is. Minimizing cycle-time variation is absolutely critical in ensuring customer satisfaction. This is a place where the PIT should use a computer simulation model to provide the needed information. To accomplish this same task by hand would take weeks for each cycle.

Steps 6 and 7: Error Proofing and Process Upgrading

By accessing the simulation model database for individual activities, the PIT gets a detailed list of the problems related to each activity on the as-is simulation model as well as a list of recommendations for eliminating these problems. These inputs were provided by the individuals doing the work as well as by the PIT teams as they observed the operation. Ensuring that these problems do not exist in the new process is a very important part of ensuring the quality of the output from the new process design. Also included in this database are the suggestions that the employees made related to office layout, equipment needs, and ways of upgrading the work environment.

During these tasks, the PIT will develop a number of changes to reduce the errors made throughout the process. For each change, the project improvement related to the change will also be determined or estimated. These changes will be used to modify simulation models so that their impact on the total process can be calculated. Those changes that have a positive effect on the total process performance are left into the model.

Step 8: Simple Language

The simulation model database contains a complete list of all the documents pertinent to each block in the simulation model. This provides an easy way for the PIT to identify the documents that impact the process and perform the desired analysis. Once the analysis is complete, acceptable documents should be included in the simulation model database so that they are available for viewing once the process is rolled out.

Step 9: Standardization

The simulation model tends to standardize all activities because there is only one approach defined as being acceptable. If multiple approaches are used in practice, the PIT needs to analyze these approaches and determine which is the optimum approach and ensure that the simulation model reflects the optimum approach.

Step 10: Supplier Partnerships

The simulation model provides an excellent way for the PIT to identify all inputs to the process. It also effectively identifies what requirements should be placed upon these inputs in order for them to meet the process requirements. By analyzing the inputs and the activities they affect, the PIT can readily determine what the supplier specifications should look like and be able to eliminate those inputs that are not necessary. Here again, we like to ask the question, if the organization that is using the input had to pay for the input, would it consider the input value-added? The simulation model is used to define the cost of the input so that its worth can be analyzed. If it is not value-added, the input can probably be eliminated.

Step 11: Automation, Mechanization, and Information Technology

As the PIT worked through the previous 10 streamlining steps, it developed a list of potential IT enablers that might be applied to the process being studied. Now the software and automation potential refinements are applied to the simulation model, one at a time or in related groupings. Then the simulation model is exercised to define the impact of the proposed change on process performance. Typically, IT solutions are costly to implement and should be included in the final simulation model only if they have a significant positive impact on the key performance parameters.

Step 12: Organizational Restructuring

Organizational restructuring is always far more expensive than management realizes. Productivity usually drops off for a time; typically, a restructuring activity results in an average of 40 to 60 hours of lost for each person involved.

To evaluate the best organizational structure to support the redesigned process, the simulation model should be modified to reflect the different potential organizational structures. This will allow the process design to drive the organizational structure, rather than office politics. We were often surprised to find out that the expected benefits of reorganization were seldom realized when the new structures were not modeled before they were implemented. Don't reorganize unless it improves process performance by at least 5% in a way that can be reflected in the process design. We are past the point where an organization structure design is not modeled before it is implemented.

Final Process Design Analysis

On occasion, due to the extensive modifications that are made to the as-is simulation model during the streamlining tasks, and particularly when extensive use of information technology solutions is applied, the modified simulation model may be questionable. This may lead to creating a new simulation model based upon the final future-state solution design. When this occurs, the following steps are executed to prepare the new simulation model.

I. Identify model parameters.
- Outline model assumption.
- Determine process performance measurements.
- Establish model constraints.
- Prepare flow diagram.
- Arrange geographical layout.
- Document logic flow through model constraints.
- Refine model concepts.
- Redefine model assumptions.

II. Build and verify model.
- Build skeleton process simulation model.
- Establish quality assurance on model structure.
- Verify model logic.
- Apply complete data to the model.
- Verify model output.

III. Validate model.
- Establish credibility of the model and its assumptions.

IV. Experiment with model.
- Use design of experiments.
- Determine the number of replications.

Evaluate results.
Determine future test options.
Document analysis.
Compare performance matrix with targeted values.

Other Options

The 12 steps or portions of them are repeated two to four times to provide a series of future-state solutions based upon different assumptions (e.g.,: What can be done in six months? What is the best possible cycle time? What is the best quality at no increase in cycle time? What is the least cost with the same cycle time and quality level?). In each case, the simulation model performs a critical role in helping the PIT redesign the process and calculate its performance.

Activity 2: Cost/Benefits Analysis

The simulation model is used in this activity to automatically calculate the benefits for each of the future-state solutions based upon the input models and assumptions that were embedded into the model. This allows calculation not only of averages but also of extreme case conditions. Unfortunately, the simulation model can calculate only the benefits side of the formula. The PIT must calculate the actual cost of installation.

Phase IV: Implementation, Measurements, and Control

During this phase, the implementation team will implement the best-value future-state solution and establish the appropriate measurement and control system to support continuous monitoring of the BFSS. Phase IV consists of five activities (see Figure 9-22):

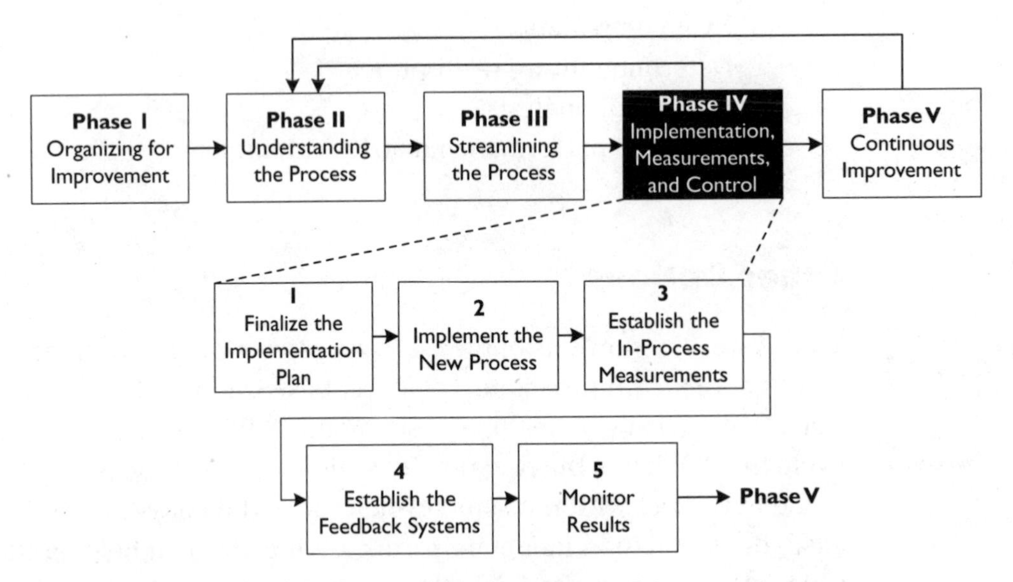

FIGURE 9-22. The five activities of Phase IV

Activity 1: Finalize the Implementation Plan

The executive improvement team now forms an implementation team to prepare a detailed implementation plan and install the changes. It may or may not include all the members of the PIT. Often, department improvement teams become part of the implementation plan, so that the people within the organization who will be affected by the change will be part of the group that plans and implements the change. Often, implementation teams are divided into subteams (e.g., information system team). The implementation plan is usually divided into three parts:

- Short-term changes—changes that can be made in 30 days.
- Mid-term changes—changes that can be made in 90 days.
- Long-term changes—changes that require more than 90 days to implement.

The final implementation plan for each change will include:

- schedule
- training requirements
- impact assessment plan

- modeling requirements
- data collection process
- documentation plan
- organizational change management plan
- resource requirements

Activity 2: Implement the New Process

The implementation plan and the change management plan are united at this point. The implementation team will maintain close control over each change to be sure that it is implemented correctly. Often, complex changes go through a series of modeling and/or prototyping to prove the concept and to ensure smooth implementation. After each change is installed, the team measures its impact to make sure that it has achieved its intended objective and has a positive impact on the total process. Each time a change is implemented, the simulation model is updated so that it always reflects the present process.

Activity 3: Establish the In-Process Measurements

As one employee puts it, "Management measures what they are interested in."

Before you can design a measurement system, you need to define requirements. Each activity in the best-value future-state simulation model should be analyzed to determine its customer requirements and how its effectiveness should be evaluated. A good measurement system is one in which the measurements are made as close to the activity as possible. Self-measurement is best because there is no delay in taking corrective action. Often, though, self-measurement is not practical and/or possible. Most business processes will use a mixture of attributes and variables data. Of course, variables data are always preferred.

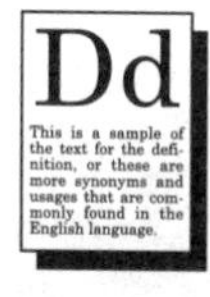

Attributes data—Data that are counted—yes/no, accept/reject, black/white, go/no-go, etc. These data are usually easy to collect, because it involves simply counting, but it often requires large samples.

Variables data—Data that are measured—in units such as inches, feet, volts, amps, ohms, and centimeters. These data provide detailed information of the system and samples are usually small and taken frequently.

It is often necessary to measure and track each transaction as it moves through the process because, more often than not, it is not the average cycle time that loses customers, but the exception. This will require that the online data collection system be tied into the simulation model so the actual cycle time of individual transactions is tracked independently. Automatic notices can be sent to the appropriate personnel when an individual transaction exceeds its normal cycle time. Typically, warnings are sent out when an individual transaction reaches the negative two-sigma limit of the activity's histogram.

Activity 4: Establish the Feedback Systems

Measurement without feedback to personnel performing the activity or task is just another no-value-added activity. Feedback always comes before improvement. In most organizations, too much data are collected and too few are used. Employees need ongoing positive and negative feedback about their output. Without it, it's like driving your car blindfolded. The feedback system should track averages and calculate control limits. The proper people should be notified whenever a point (transaction) falls outside the negative control limit and corrective action should be documented. Exception reporting is extremely important.

Activity 5: Monitor the Results

The installed measurement system should be used to measure the improvement results. The implementation team should report back to the executive committee the comparison of the projected performance improvement with actual results.

Applying Simulation Modeling to Phase IV: Implementation

During Phase IV, simulation modeling is put to its ultimate test. It is during this phase that the simulation model projections will be compared with actual performance as the future-state solution is implemented.

As the implementation team (IT) starts this phase, it has three key documents that will help it to implement the future-state solution:

- the as-is simulation model
- the best-value future-state solution simulation model
- the preliminary implementation plan

Simulation Modeling Applied to Activity 1 of Phase IV

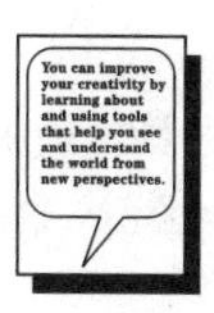

During Activity 1, finalizing the implementation plan for the best-value future-state solution, the simulation model plays a big role in doing capacity planning. First, the simulation model is upgraded to reflect the number of people or work stations required to meet the projected average throughput. To do this, the IT defines the average input rate for the process. The simulation model will then calculate the resources required to support that input for each step in the flowchart. Example: Activity A will require 108 processing hours per week.

The IT will then define the processing characteristics related to each activity. This information is input into the simulation database. Example: the people involved in Activity A have the following additional commitments:

- two hours per day for meetings
- one hour per day to answer the telephone
- one hour per day to review email
- one hour per day for personal time

Therefore, three hours per day are left to work on Activity A. The simulation model would recommend that 7.2 people (3 hours per day x 5 days per week divided into 108 hours) be assigned and that eight work stations be developed—not 2.7 people (40 hours per week divided into 108 hours) as might be the case if the processing characteristics were not considered.

Sometimes the IT will also input other key resource data, such as projected absentee rates, vacation impacts, maximum overtime allowed, and expected overtime for all employees. This provides a very realistic picture of the process resources and allows the simulation model to calculate actual requirements. For each activity in the simulation model, the IT will review the simulation model's calculated resource requirements. Using this as a starting point, the IT will input its plan for that activity.

Now the IT will develop a variable input projection that reflects the normal variation during the month and/or seasonal variation related to the specific process being upgraded. The model then simulates months of normal processing time in minutes. As the simulation model operates, bottlenecks in the process can be easily defined and cycle time distributions can be plotted. The IT can now adjust the capacity plan for each activity to optimize process performance. The backlog data that the simulation model generates are used to define the amount of storage required for each activity.

As the IT develops the work instructions and training procedure for each activity, it adds them to the database for that activity so that the future-state solution simulation model contains all the relevant information.

Simulation Modeling Applied to Activity 2 of Phase IV

A key part of the implementation phase is the pilot studies that verify the simulation model's projections. As the pilot programs are completed, the performance results and all refinements are input into the simulation model, to replace performance estimates with actual data.

As the process is rolled out, the simulation model is often brought online. This allows the people involved in the process to have at their fingertips their work instructions, training materials, and all relevant data related to the specific activity. It is also the time to install a transaction-tracking system that will allow accurate definition of cycle time, backlog, processing time, and percent of total product that flows through each process branch. As the in-process measurement and feedback systems are defined, the remaining key measurements data are fed into the simulation model, to replace estimates with actual performance data. This allows performance to be compared with the simulation model projections generated during Phase III.

Summary of Simulation Modeling in Phase IV: Implementation

The simulation model provides an excellent means of performing capacity analysis studies under the dynamic conditions of the real work environment. It also provides an excellent way to communicate training and performance requirements to employees. By the end of the implementation phase, the future-state solution simulation model has been updated to reflect the resources that are available within the process and real data have replaced estimates, which allows calculation of actual performance. The IT can then compare the FSS projections with the actual process performance.

Use of Simulation Modeling in Phase V: Continuous Improvement

If the simulation modeling program is put online, real data are continuously fed into the model and the data can be used to track individual items as they flow through the process. If this is done, the process distribution for cycle time and error rate can be calculated for each activity. Then, when an item exceeds preset limits, the appropriate person can be automatically notified.

For example, if Activity K has an average cycle time of 12 working hours and a sigma of three hours, then the person doing the activity is notified if an item is in his or her work area for more than +2 sigma or

18 hours (12 hours average plus 3 hours x 2) without being processed. This will allow the individual to find the item and to process it. If the item is in the area for +3 sigma (21 hours), the manager is automatically notified. This often happens when someone is out ill or on vacation or when the item has been misplaced. This is an extremely effective tool for reducing process variation.

In addition, the simulation model is used to test the impact of proposed changes to the process during the continuous improvement phase. Often, the total process impact is not obvious when an individual department in a process decides to improve its part of the process. Simply by modifying the simulation model to reflect all proposed changes, the impact of each change on the total process measurements can be assessed before the change is implemented.

Summary of Simulation Modeling in Phase V: Continuous Improvement

The simulation model is often used to track individual transactions as they move through the process. This helps keep all of the transactions moving and minimizes the process variations. It also provides a way to evaluate suggested improvements to ensure that each one has a positive impact on the total process and eliminates suboptimization.

Summary of Simulation Modeling in Process Redesign

Simulation modeling is to the process redesigner what the horse is to the cowboy. Although the cowboy can get along without a horse, the horse makes his job much easier. The same is true of the process redesigner: the simulation model is a key tool in designing and implementing the future-state solution. The model is also the legacy that the process redesigner leaves with the process that will help keep the process in control and serve as the basis for all future performance improvement activities.

In this chapter, we have discussed the process redesign methodology down to the activity level and sometimes even the task level. At the end of each of the five phases, we have discussed in detail the simulation modeling activities that took place during that phase. As a result of understanding this chapter, you should be able to apply the simulation modeling methodology to a process redesign assignment and have a good understanding of how to apply simulation modeling to any performance improvement opportunity or project.

"Simulation cuts redesign time and improves results by 30%."

References

Harrington, H. James, *Benchmarking Workbook* (New York: McGraw-Hill, 1998).

Harrington, H. James, *Business Process Improvement: The Breakthrough Strategy for Total Quality, Productivity, and Competitiveness* (New York: McGraw-Hill, 1991).

Harrington, H. James, Glen D. Hoffherr, and Robert P. Reid, *Statistical Analysis Simplified: The Easy-to-Understand Guide to SPC and Data Analysis* (New York: McGraw-Hill, 1998).

CHAPTER 10

Simulation Exercise

You can never really understand it until you do it.

Introduction

In this chapter, we illustrate the modeling and analysis concepts described in Chapters 5 and 6 through a real-world exercise. The purpose of this exercise is to build a model of an order-fulfillment process, simulate it for 24 hours, and analyze the performance measures of the process. Building the model involves three simple steps:

1. Map the process.
2. Define the activities and workflow.
3. Define the resources and their usage.

After you build the model, you define the length of the simulation period and start running the simulation. While the model is simulated, you can see an animated picture of the process flow.

After the simulation, you can analyze the performance measures of the process. In this exercise, the performance measures of interest are total order processing time, resource utilization, and activity costs.

This exercise is developed using SIMPROCESS, an object-oriented process simulation tool developed by CACI Products Company (www.modsim.com). A running demonstration of this exercise is included on the CD-ROM that comes with this book.

Model Description

Orders arrive at the mail order business via fax, phone, or mail. Customer orders arrive, on average, every six minutes. (Use an exponential distribution with a mean value of six minutes.)

A sales representative receives the orders and logs into the system. The original order goes to a supervisor for validation while a copy goes to a credit specialist for credit check. If an order is validated and credit is approved, an order entry clerk accepts the order and prepares it for shipment. If an order is rejected, the supervisor notifies the customer with a letter.

Figure 10-1 shows the activity times and resource requirements, Figure 10-2 shows the staffing and costs, and Figure 10-3 shows a flow diagram of the order-fulfillment process.

Activity	**Time (in minutes)**	**Resource**
Receive Order	Triangular (6,12,18)	Sales Rep
Check Credit	Normal (15,2.4)	Credit Specialist
Validate Order	3	Supervisor
Prepare Order	Normal (12,0.6)	Order Entry Clerk
Reject Order	3	Supervisor

FIGURE 10-1. Activity times and resource requirements

Resource	Capacity	Hourly Rate	Fixed Costs (weekly)
Sales Rep	2	$20.00	$1,500
Credit Specialist	3	$25.00	$1,000
Order Entry Clerk	2	$15.00	$1,000
Supervisor	1	$30.00	$1,500

FIGURE 10-2. Staffing and resource costs

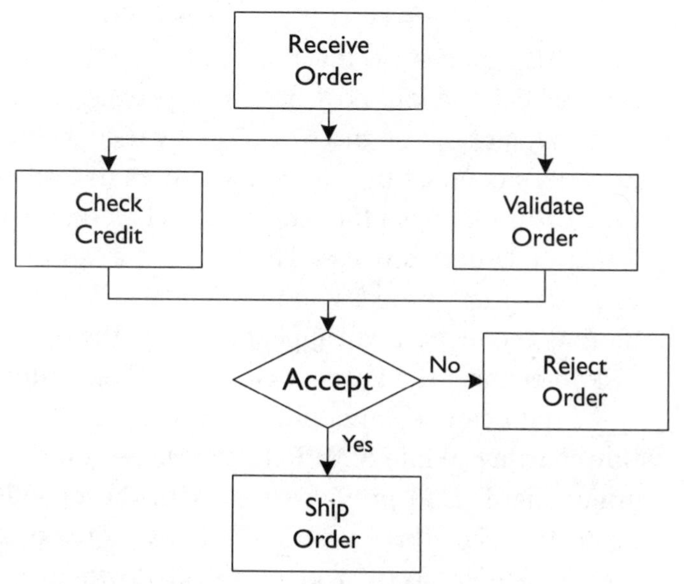

FIGURE 10-3. Flow diagram of order-fulfillment process

Building the Model

Step 1: Map the Process

Let's begin our exercise by mapping the order-fulfillment process. Let's first define three major processes—Generate Orders, Process Orders, and Ship Orders.

To define the first major process, simply click on the Hierarchical Process icon in the palette (the uppermost icon on the palette, next to the pointer), drag the mouse, and drop it on the layout. Notice that SIMPROCESS assigns a default name, Process1, for the object you placed on the layout. Let's define the name of this process as "Generate Orders." Also, notice that each process box has an input and an output connection object. These connection objects are referred to as *pads* in SIMPROCESS and they serve as the connection points between the processes.

To define the second process, click on the Hierarchical Process icon in the palette and drop the process to the right of the first process in the layout. Let's label this process "Process Orders." Finally, place the third process on the right side of the layout and label it "Ship Orders." Your layout now has three processes.

Next, let's define the workflow by connecting the three processes. First, let's connect the Generate Orders to Process Orders. Select the Connector tool from the palette and click on the right-hand side of the Generate Orders process. Then, drag the mouse to the left side of the Process Orders process and click again. When you release the mouse button, a connector will appear between the two processes. Repeat this task to connect the Process Orders to Ship Orders. (See Figure 10-4.)

As you can see, mapping your process is as quick and simple as flowcharting! While SIMPROCESS gives you the benefits of flow diagramming, it also provides you with the benefits of object-oriented simulation. The three processes that you just placed on the layout are *hierarchical objects*. You can drill down inside each process and define its subprocesses.

In this exercise, you will drill down one level within each process; however, there is no limit to the number of levels you can drill down. To practice drilling down, simply select a process and double-click on it. Notice that you have a new layout with an input pad on the left-hand side and output pad on the right-hand side of the layout. Also notice that SIMPROCESS keeps you informed as to where you are in the hierarchy by displaying (at the top of the window) the name of the parent process object for this current layer.

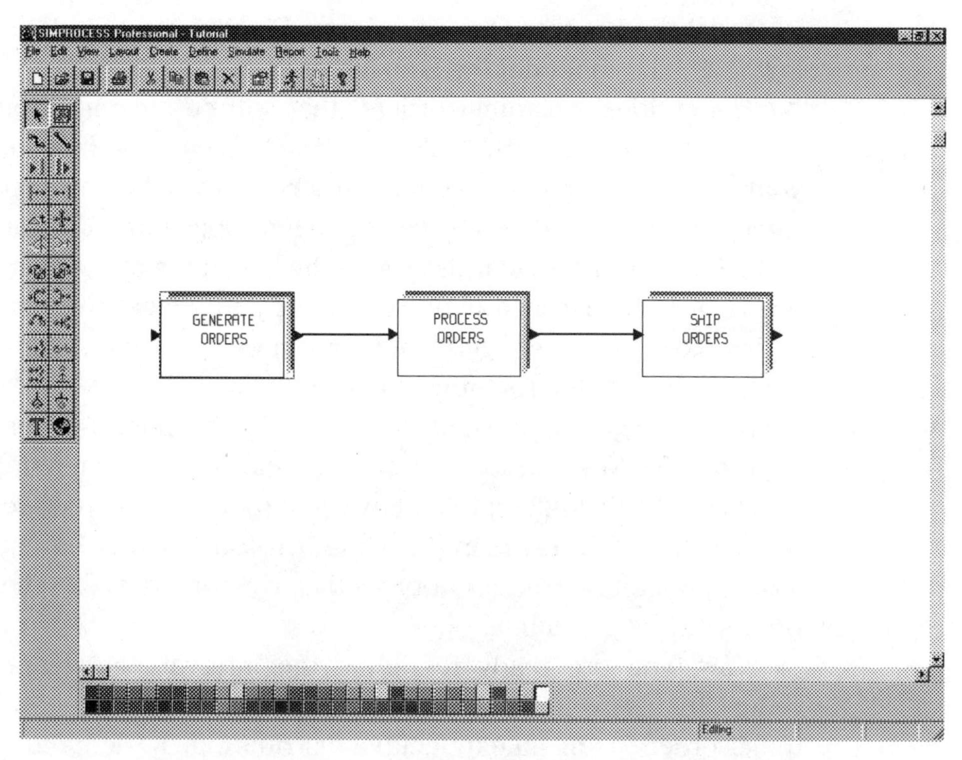

FIGURE 10-4. Process map of the order fulfillment process

To get back up, simply double-click any blank space on the layout or choose View/Ascend from the main menu bar. Now, you are ready to create a hierarchical simulation model of your process by using the activity-based modeling and resource modeling constructs.

Step 2: Define the Activities and Workflow

At the lowest level of each hierarchical process object are one or more activities that describe the behavior of that process. In Chapter 5, we described various dynamic behavior modeling concepts. In this exercise, you will use various SIMPROCESS activity objects. You will define a GENERATE activity to model the Generate Orders process. You will define SPLIT, JOIN, DELAY, BRANCH, and MERGE activities to model the Process Orders process. Finally, you will define a DISPOSE activity to model the Ship Orders process.

The entities (customer orders) that will be moving through your model are created with GENERATE activities. The first process in your model generates customer orders. Let's drill down inside the Generate Orders process by selecting that object and double-clicking on it. Since this particular process is the beginning of the exercise, you need not be concerned about the input pad. Select the GENERATE activity tool from the palette and place it on the layout. Then, double-click on the graphic to define its properties.

Let's change the name of this activity to "Generate Orders." Next, click on the New Entity button to define the customer order. This brings up the dialog box that allows you to define new entities. Select the Add option and type in the name "Customer Order." You can even assign an icon ($) to an entity so that you can visualize the flow of orders during the animation.

Now, you are ready to define the interval between customer orders. In this example model, we will represent the time between customer orders using an exponential distribution. To define the interval between customer orders, click on the down-arrow next to the Interval combo box for the list of available statistical distributions. Select the exponential distribution, Exp(10.0). Change the mean value for the interval to 6 and set the time units to minutes, meaning that an order is generated, on average, every six minutes.

For generation of orders, the default value in the Quantity field is 1, which is what you want for this model. The GENERATE activity is a very powerful object for modeling demand. You can use different generate activities for modeling orders via fax, phone, or mail. You can use a data file to generate the customer orders, instead of a statistical distribution, or you can create complex schedules and cyclical demand patterns.

At this point, you must do an important task to complete the description of the order-generation process: connect the output pad of the GENERATE activity to the output pad of the hierarchical process called Generate Orders (Figure 10-5). This concludes the definition of customer demand.

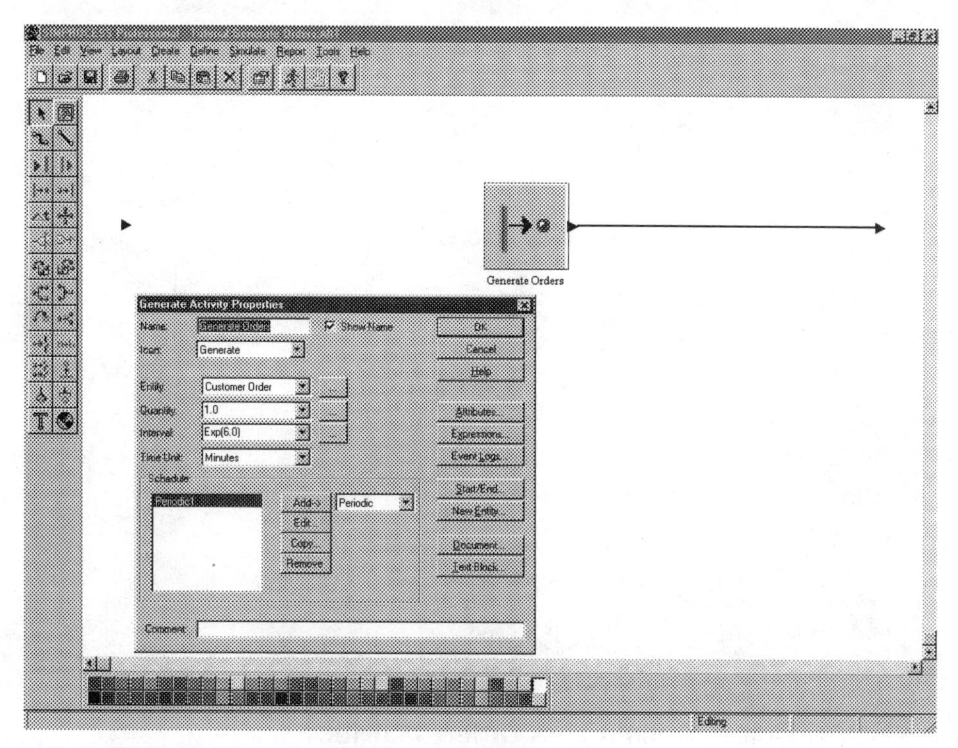

FIGURE 10-5. Generate Orders activity

Next, you will define the Process Orders process. When you drill into the hierarchical process, notice that SIMPROCESS gives you an input pad on the left-hand side, an output pad on the right-hand side, and a blank layout in the middle for placing the activities at this level. You will define SPLIT, JOIN, DELAY, BRANCH, and MERGE activities to model the Process Orders process.

The first value-added activity in the process is Receive Order. It will be modeled with a DELAY activity. From the palette, select a DELAY activity and place it to the right of the input pad. Then, select the connector tool and connect the input pad to this DELAY activity.

Next, double-click on the DELAY activity graphic to define its properties. Let's name this activity "Receive Order" and define the

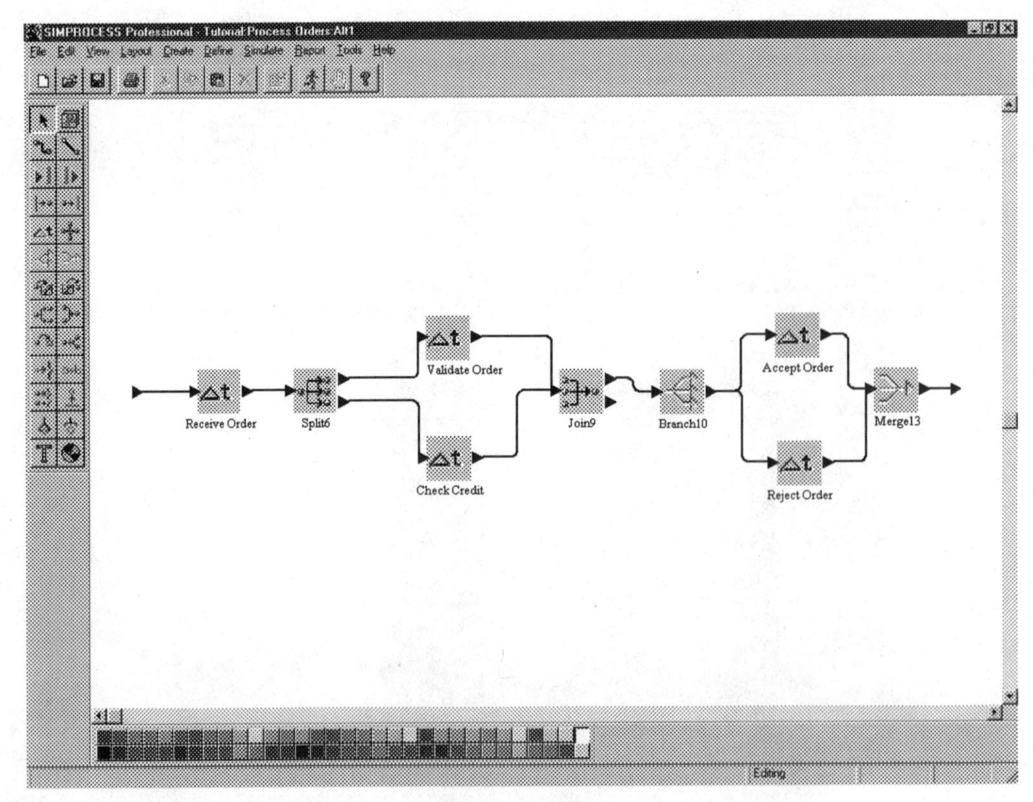

FIGURE 10-6. Process Orders activities

duration for receiving a customer order. The Duration field is a combo box much like the Interval field in the GENERATE activity. Select the Triangular distribution and define the parameters of the distribution (6 minutes for minimum, 12 minutes for mode, and 18 minutes for maximum). Notice that one of the buttons in the Delay Activity Properties dialog box is for defining resources required for this activity. You will do that after completing the workflow definition.

The SPLIT and JOIN activities are used for modeling parallel processing. In our exercise, after an order is received, two activities follow in parallel. So, select a SPLIT activity from the palette and drop it to the right of the Receive Order activity. Double-click on the SPLIT activity. Leave the name as default, but type "Order" in the Family Name field. You will later use this family name in the JOIN activity to

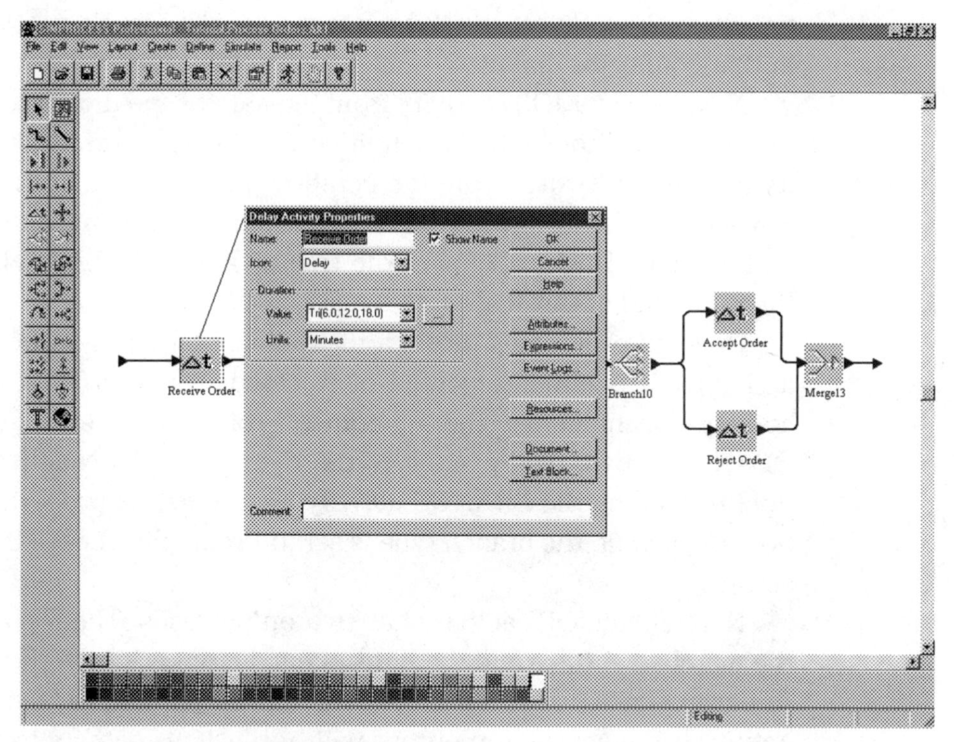

FIGURE 10-7. Receive Order activity

match the entities that will be joined. Click OK. Connect Receive Order to the SPLIT activity.

Next, you need to define two DELAY activities—Check Credit and Validate Order. As with the Receive Order activity, drop the DELAY activities in the layout, label them, and define activity times as specified in the problem description. Notice that the SPLIT activity preceding the two DELAY activities has two output pads. One of the pads is used for the original entity and the other is used for the clones. To connect the SPLIT activity to the DELAY activities properly, you need to do the following.

First, connect the bottom pad (original pad) of the SPLIT activity to the Validate Order activity. Next, connect the top pad (clones pad) of the SPLIT activity to the Check Credit activity. Then, double-click on the latest drawn connector. This brings up the Connector properties dialog box. Select the "Customer Orders" in the Entity Name field in that connector dialog.

Next, select a JOIN activity from the palette and drop it to the right of the two previous DELAY activities. Double-click on the JOIN activity and select "Order" from the combo box in the Family Name field. This ensures that SIMPROCESS matches the right copy with the original customer order. Connect the two upstream DELAY activities to the input pad of the JOIN activity.

Once an order goes through the Validate Order and Check Credit activities, it is either accepted or rejected. You will use a BRANCH activity for modeling the outcome. From the palette, select the BRANCH activity and place it to the right of the JOIN activity. Then, double-click on the BRANCH activity icon to get its properties dialog box. By default, the branch type is set to Probability. Leave the default setting.

Notice that JOIN activity has two output pads. The top one is for the matched entities and the bottom one is for entities with no match. In our exercise, we will use only the top output pad for the matched entities. Connect the top output pad of the JOIN activity to the input pad of the BRANCH activity.

If an order is validated and credit is approved, the order is accepted and prepared for shipment. If an order is rejected, the supervisor notifies the customer with a letter. You will use two DELAY activities to model the order acceptance and rejection activities. Place these DELAY activities to the right of the BRANCH activity and fill in the activity names and times as defined in the exercise description.

Next, connect the output pad of the BRANCH activity to the input pads of the Accept Order and Reject Order activities. To specify the probability of acceptance, double-click on the connector connecting the BRANCH to the Accept Order DELAY activity and type "0.90" in the Branch Probability field and click OK. Then, do the same for the connector connecting the BRANCH to the Reject Order DELAY activity. Type "0.10" in the Branch Probability field.

The last activity to model for the Process Orders process is MERGE. This activity is simply a junction for merging several connectors into a single activity. Drop a MERGE activity to the right of the most recently defined DELAY activities and connect them with the MERGE activity. To complete the description of the activities at this level, you need to connect the output pad of the MERGE activity with the output pad (for the hierarchical process) on the right-hand side of the layout. When you are done with those connections, you can get back to the major process level by double-clicking in any blank space in the layout.

The final task for completing the workflow is to describe the shipment of orders. Double-click on the hierarchical process named Ship Orders. The DISPOSE activity is used for disposing of the orders after they are fulfilled. That is why the DISPOSE activity has only an input pad. For now, you need not define any parameters for this activity. Just select the DISPOSE activity from the palette and drag and drop it in between the two pads. Then, using the Connector tool, connect the input pad of the hierarchical process to the left side of the DISPOSE.

When you are done making this connection, simply double-click in any blank space on the layout and go back up to the major process level. At this point, you are through defining your processes, activities, and workflow. You are now ready to define your resources and where they are required to perform work.

Step 3: Define the Resources and Their Usage

In this exercise, you will define the Order Fulfillment resources, their capacity (units available), hourly labor costs, and fixed costs. You will then assign them to the appropriate activities.

Resources are defined under the main menu option called Define. Select the Resources option to bring up the Resources list box. To define a new resource, click on the Add button. The Resource Properties dialog box will open. Type in the name "Sales Rep" and define Units as 2. To define the hourly labor rate, click on the Cost button and type "20" in the field called Hourly Cost per Unit. This means that each representative costs $20 an hour. Type "1,500" in the Fixed Costs per Unit field and set the period to Weekly in the combo box. This means that weekly fixed costs per sales rep are $1,500. During the simulation, the model will calculate the activity costs based on the actual usage of the sales representatives. Then, click on the OK button to complete defining the Sales Rep resources.

To define the other resources, click on the Add button of the Resources list box and repeat the same steps. When you are done defining the other resources, click on the Close button of the Resources list box to get back to the layout.

Now, you are ready to define how these resources are used in processing orders. This task is accomplished by going into the activities that use the resources. So, double-click on the hierarchical process named Process Orders and drill down to the lower level.

First, let's assign the Sales Reps to the Receive Orders activity by double-clicking on the activity. While in the Receive Orders activity dialog box, click on the Resources button. This brings up the dialog box for making the resource assignments.

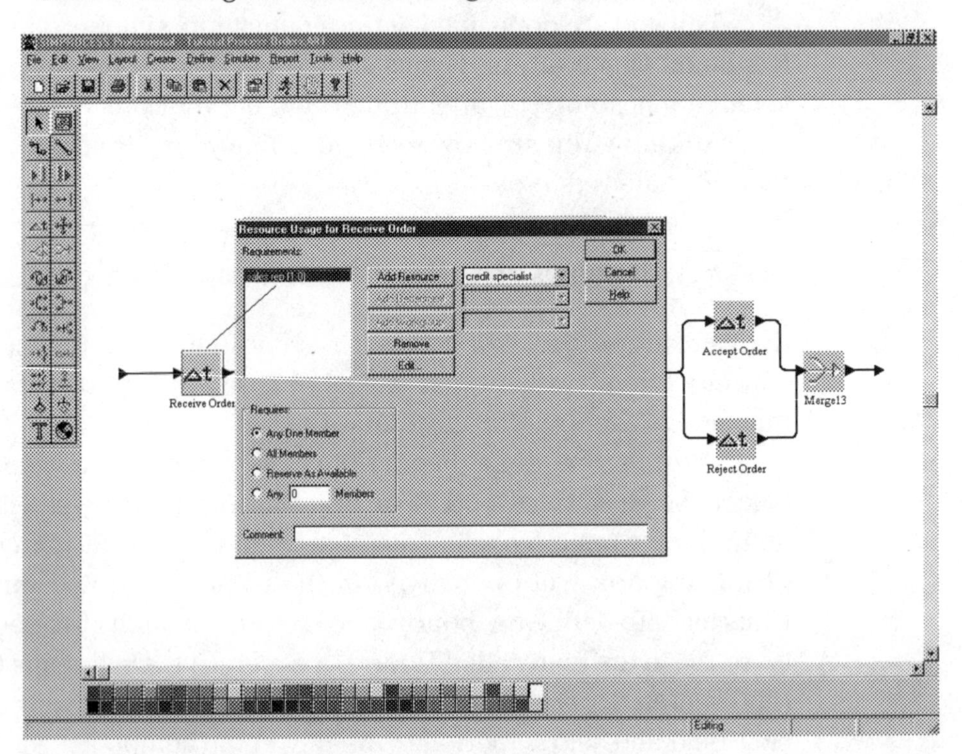

FIGURE 10-8. Assigning resources to activities

To define the resource requirements for this activity, first click on the combo box to see the list of the resources that you have defined. Select the Sales Rep resource and click on Add Resource, leaving 1 as the default for the Usage Rate. This means one sales representative is required to perform this activity every time an order comes in. During the simulation, when an order arrives, it will be serviced by one of the two sales representatives. If both are busy, then the order will wait in a queue until one of them becomes available. SIMPROCESS will automatically keep track of the number of orders in queue and how much time each order waits. Click on OK to close the dialog box.

To define the usage of the Supervisor, select the Validate Order activity and repeat the same steps to bring up the Resource Requirements dialog box. Select the Supervisor resource from the resource combo box and assign it to the activity.

When you are done assigning the resources to their corresponding activities, you are ready to simulate the process. But before running the simulation, let's save the model. Select the Save option under the File menu. Then, type in "tutorial" in the field next to File Name. Now, you are ready to simulate your process!

Simulating the Process

Once you have built your model, simulating the process involves two simple steps: defining the run settings and running the simulation.

Step 1: Define the Run Settings

Before running the simulation, we need to specify how long we want to simulate the process. To do this, select Simulate from the main menu and then the Run Settings option. This will bring up the Run Parameters dialog box. The default start date is "01/01/1996." For now, leave the start date as the default date and time. Change the end date to "01/02/1996." This means SIMPROCESS will simulate the model for one day (24 hours) and report statistics over that time. If you like, you can change the start and end dates to the current date. Click on OK to accept the inputs and close the dialog box.

Step 2: Run the Simulation

Now, you are ready to run the simulation. You can do this by clicking on the runner graphic on the tool bar or by selecting the Simulate/Run option from the main menu.

When the simulation starts running, SIMPROCESS gives an animated picture of the workflow. Animation is an extremely powerful tool for verifying your model and visualizing your process in motion. During the simulation, you will see the simulation clock in the lower right corner of your screen.

As the process is simulated, SIMPROCESS continuously updates the counters above the processes and activities. At the top level of your model is the animation of the three hierarchical processes. Let's double-click on the Generate Orders process to see the animation of its detail. The counter above the GENERATE activity displays the number of orders generated so far. Next, double-click on any blank space to back up to the top level. To watch the animation of the Process Orders process, drill down into the Process Orders object. The counters above these activities show the number of entities currently in process.

The counters above the DISPOSE activity display the number of entities processed so far in the simulation. In addition to these counters, you can display real-time graphs of cycle times, counts, and the number of orders waiting in queue. Figure 10-9 shows an example of a real-time graph.

Animation can be turned off anytime to speed up the simulation. To do this, select the Animation Off from the Simulation menu. While the simulation is in progress, notice that the status bar at the bottom of your screen displays "Trial: 1 of 1." When the simulation is over, the status bar will display the message "Editing." Once the process simulation is complete, you are ready to analyze the output reports.

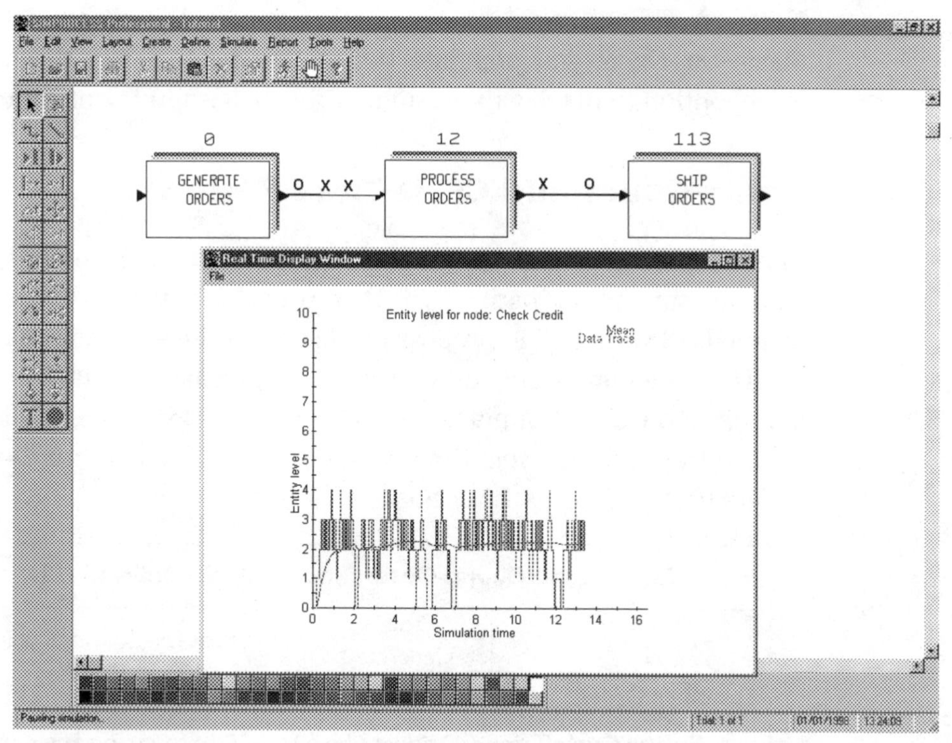

FIGURE 10-9. Animation screen of the order-processing activities

Analyzing the Performance Measures

To analyze the performance measures for this model, you will focus on:

- entity-count and cycle-time reports
- resource-utilization reports
- cost reports

Output reports can be displayed by selecting the Report options from the main menu. Standard reports include basic statistics on entity counts and cycle times. Activity-based costing reports include activity, entity, and resource cost statistics.

To bring up the standard reports, select the Report/Display Standard Reports option from the main menu. This brings up a dialog box with options to view the standard tabular report. The default option is text editor: this option loads Microsoft Notepad and brings up the report in

Notepad. The other option is spreadsheet-based: it allows you to load Microsoft Excel and populate the spreadsheet. Select the Microsoft Excel option to display the results of the order-fulfillment simulation.

Entity-Count and Cycle-Time Reports

The entity-count report shows that 227 orders were generated over the 24-hour simulation period. Of that total, 215 were processed and shipped; 12 were still in process at the end of the simulation period.

The cycle-time statistics are reported in terms of hours. On average, it took about 59.22 minutes (0.987 hours) to process an order. Even though the average cycle time was approximately an hour, one of the orders took as long as 1.527 hours.

Entity: Total Count–Observation Based: Replication 1			
	Total Generated	In Process	Total Shipped
Customer Order	227	12	215

Entity: Cycle Time (in hours) by State–Observation Based: Replication 1									
	# Shipped	Total Time in Process		Duration at Activity		Wait for Resources		Hold for Conditions	
		Avg.	Max.	Avg.	Max.	Avg.	Max.	Avg.	Max.
Customer Order	215	0.987	1.527	0.637	0.806	0.35	0.928	0	0

FIGURE 10-10. Entity-count and cycle-time statistics

A review of the cycle-time breakdown shows that a customer order *waited for resources* 21 minutes (0.35 hours), on average, and that one of the orders *waited for resources* as long as 55.68 minutes.

Resource-Utilization Reports

The resource state reports indicate the percentage of the time that the staff were busy (Figure 10-12). The sales reps were busy 92.43% of the

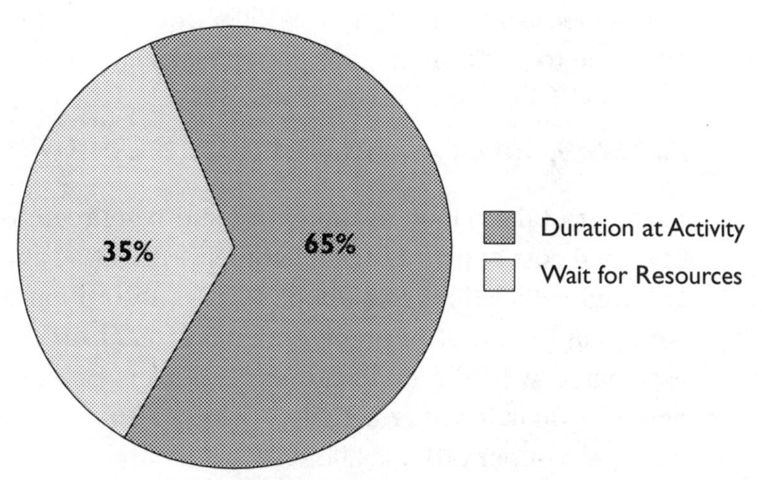

FIGURE 10-11. Cycle-time breakdown

time. This means that customer orders waited in queue for service. Credit specialists and order entry clerks were used 75.77% and 80.91%, respectively. This means that staffing of these positions was adequate.

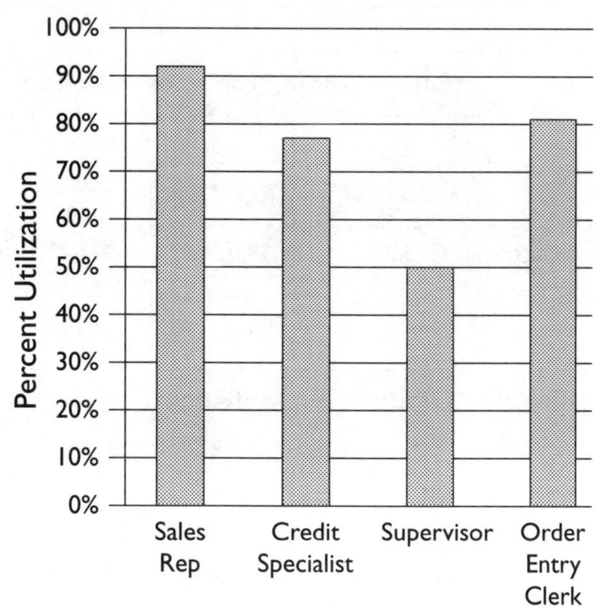

FIGURE 10-12. Resource-utilization graph

The supervisor utilization was 50%, meaning that the supervisor is available to perform administrative tasks.

Activity, Entity, and Resource Cost Reports

First, let's take a look at the entity and resource costs (Figure 10-13). The total cost of processing customer orders was about $4,250 (capacity-based calculation) and about $4,550 (absorption-based calculation). Note that total cost of processing a customer order includes the costs associated with the duplicate entity that is processed in the parallel activity (Validate Order activity). Since 215 orders were processed, the average cost per order is about $20.

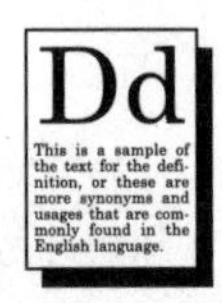

Capacity-based costing—Calculation that does not include fixed costs and one-time setup costs.

Absorption-based costing—Calculation that includes fixed costs and one-time setup costs.

Entity: Cost of Processing in Dollars: Replication 1				
	Capacity		Absorption	
	Total Cost	Avg. Cost Per Entity	Total Cost	Avg. Cost Per Entity
Customer Order	$3,824.52	$17.79	$4,024.39	$18.72
Duplicate	$426.27	$1.96	$524.85	$2.42
Total	$4,250.79	$19.75	$4,549.24	$21.14

FIGURE 10-13. Entity cost statistics

The report on the resource costs (Figure 10-14) shows the total resource costs and the cost per unit of resource. For example, the total cost for a sales rep was about $1,283 (capacity-based calculation). Since there were two sales representatives in the model, the cost per rep is about $641.

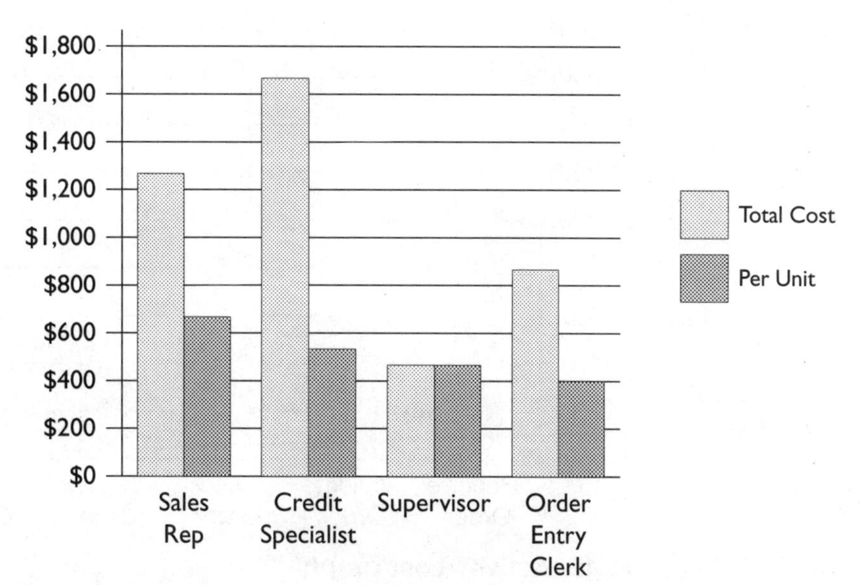

FIGURE 10-14. Resource cost graph

To bring up the Activity Cost reports, select the Display ABC Reports/Activities from the main menu. First, highlight the five activities where resources were used: Receive Order, Validate Order, Check Credit, Accept Order, and Reject Order. Then, click on the Detail option just below the Activity List box to display costs for each activity. Then click on the Quarter 1 under the Periods List box. Since you ran the simulation for only 24 hours, the costs were calculated for the 24-hour simulation run within the first quarter.

Finally, highlight all four of the resources in the Resources List box and click on the Detail button just below the list box. To bring up the Activity Cost Reports, click on the Display Reports button.

Let's review these statistics by maximizing this window. To see the exact values for activity costs, select Show Data from the Options menu. You will see that the activity costs (Figure 10-15) are $1283 for Receive Order, $426 for Validate Order, $1688 for Check Credit, $814 for Accept Order, and $39 for Reject Order. Activity costs for the order-fulfillment process for the 24-hour period add up to $4,250, which is consistent with the Entity Cost statistic.

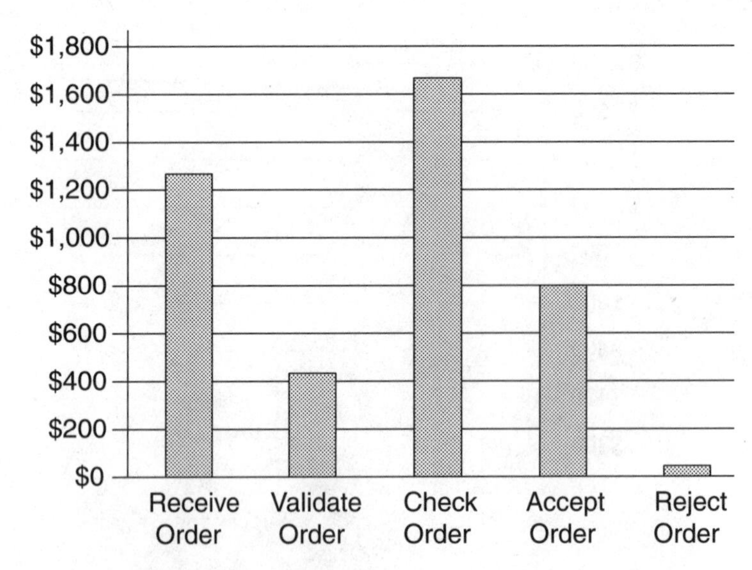

FIGURE 10-15. Activity cost graph

In addition to the standard reports, other reports can be generated for entity cycle times and counts, resources, and for activity cycle time and counts. This concludes our exercise.

Important note: This simple exercise is intended to provide you with an overview of SIMPROCESS and familiarize you with the mechanics of building, running, and analyzing a process simulation model. In a typical business process simulation project, you would need to build a more realistic model, run it for longer duration than 24 hours, and do multiple replications before making conclusions about the results. SIMPROCESS User's Manual explains the tools and techniques for conducting statistically valid simulation experiments.

The What-If Scenario

Based on the analysis of the cycle-time and resource-utilization reports, it is clear that the Receive Order activity is the bottleneck, because the sales staff is unable to meet demand. So, we can try a what-if scenario by adding a sales representative to see how that affects the performance measures.

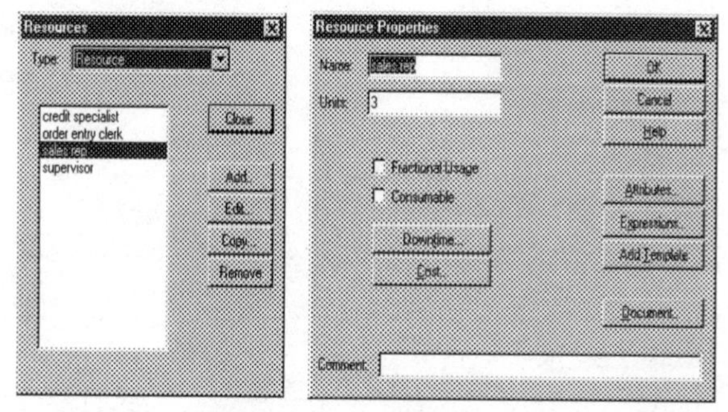

FIGURE 10-16. What-if scenario with three sales representatives

It is very simple to change the number of available sales representatives. Resources are defined under the main menu option called Define. Select the Resources option to bring up the Resources List box. Select the Sales Rep resource and edit its properties. Change the number of units from 2 to 3 and click on OK. Finally, save the model under a different name, such as "What if," and rerun the simulation.

After the simulation is completed, you can bring up the Standard Reports in Excel and look at the results. They can be summarized as follows:

- The total number of orders shipped was 222.
- On average, it took about 54.96 minutes (0.916 hours) to process an order.
- On average, a customer order waited 16.86 minutes (0.281 hours).
- Average utilization of the sales representatives was 64.44%.
- The average cost per order was about $22.
- The total process cost per day was $4419.

Comparing Results

You can now compare the results and see the potential process improvements and the cost associated with the what-if scenario (Figure 10-17). Adding a sales rep appears to have the potential to improve throughput by 3.3%, reduce cycle time by 7.2%, and reduce waiting time by 23.6%.

	Current State	What-If Scenario	% Change
Total number of orders shipped	215	222	+3.3
Average order processing time	59 minutes	55 minutes	-7.2
Average waiting time	21 minutes	17 minutes	-23.6
Resource utilization (sales reps)	92%	64%	-44
Average cost per order	$20	$22	+10
Total process cost per day	$4,250	$4,419	+4

FIGURE 10-17. Comparison of results

The cost of making these improvements is about $2 per order and an increase of 4% in daily process cost.

Summary

This process simulation modeling and analysis exercise demonstrates how fun and interesting it is to build a model, simulate your process, and visualize how it really works. It also shows the benefits of analyzing the process performance measures. When you have your model, you can simulate multiple what-if scenarios and future-state alternatives. Comparisons of results from those scenarios provide you with the information to make the best decisions.

"Simulation modeling is today's best error-prevention tool."

APPENDIX A

Glossary and Simulation Objects/Characters

Absorption-based costing—Calculation that includes fixed costs and one-time setup costs.

Activities—Things that go on within a process or subprocess. They are usually performed by units of one (one person or one department). The tasks that make up an activity are usually documented in an instruction, in terms of the tasks that make up the activity.

Activity-based costing (ABC)—A technique for accumulating cost for a given cost object (i.e., product, service, customer) that represents the total and true economic resources required or consumed by the object.

Activity object—Symbol used for modeling unique dynamic behaviors of a process. Examples of activity objects would be batch and delay.

Adaptability—The ability of a process or activity to handle the fluctuations in its input and still meet its effectiveness and efficiency requirements or objectives. It is a measure of the process's ability to handle future, changing customer expectations and today's individual, special customer requests. Typical measurements are the allowable sigma of the input measurements and the percentage of special orders processed without management intervention.

Alias—An additional or alternative name or title; an acceptable database synonym.

Analytical simulation models—The effects of process dynamics are pictured using queuing theory. The models consist of nodes that are connected with each other in a queuing network. Each node is analyzed as a GI/G/m queue, with an approximation for the mean waiting time based on the first two moments of the arrival and service time distributions.

AND connector—Object used when one or more copies or clones of the transaction need to come together before they can continue through the process.

Assemble—Activity that puts components together.

Attributes data—Data that are counted—yes/no, accept/reject, black/white, go/no-go, etc. These data are usually easy to collect, because it involves simply counting, but it often requires large samples.

Basis for down time—The period between scheduled or unscheduled down times.

Batch—Activity that combines a given quantity of entities into a single batch.

Batch activity—The combining of two or more transactions into one transaction.

Benchmarking—A systematic way to identify, understand, and creatively evolve superior products, services, designs, equipment, processes, and practices to improve the organization's real performance by studying how other organizations are performing the same or similar operations.

Best-value future-state solution (BFSS)—A solution that results in the most beneficial new item as viewed by the item's stakeholders. It is the best combination of implementation cost, implementation cycle time, risk, and performance results (e.g., return on investment, customer satisfaction, market share, risk, value-added per employee, time to implement, and cost to implement).

Block diagram—A pictorial method of showing activity flow through a process, using rectangles connected by a line with an arrow at the end of the line indicating direction of flow. A short phrase describing the activity is recorded in each rectangle.

Box plot—A graphical technique for comparing multiple alternatives.

Branch—Activity that holds a transaction for a specified period of time before releasing it to the next activity.

Business process improvement (BPI)—A methodology designed to bring about step-function improvements in administrative and support processes using approaches such as process benchmarking, process redesign, process reengineering, FAST, and HIT.

Business-value-added (BVA) activities—Activities that add no value from the customer's point of view, but are essential for the business.

Capacity analysis—What is the maximum processing capacity?

Capacity-based costing—Calculation that does not include fixed costs and one-time setup costs.

Capability analysis—Is the process capable of meeting specific performance requirements (throughput, waiting times, etc.) and, if not, what changes (added resources, improved methods, etc.) are recommended for making it capable?

Cause-and-effect diagram—Diagram that organizes the thinking process and facilitates group dynamics during brainstorming sessions.

Central Limit Theorem—The theory that the distribution of multiple sample averages tends to be normally distributed regardless of the shape of the original distribution (the distribution from the first sample).

Comparative analysis—The act of comparing a set of measurements with another set of similar measurements for a similar item.

Comparison study—How well does one process design alternative perform compared with another?

Conditional arrivals—When things arrive based on a condition. For example, if customer inventory drops below 50 units, a supply of 1,000 units arrives.

Confidence interval—A basic component of output analysis. It is a numerical range with which we can analyze the output data for a given performance measure, a range within which we can have a certain confidence that the true mean falls.

Confidence level—A percentage between 0% and 100%.

Connection object—Object used to relate output from different simulation models or levels of simulation models.

Connector—Object used to define workflow between activities and subprocesses.

Constraint analysis—Where are the constraints or bottlenecks in the process and what are workable solutions for either reducing or eliminating the constraints?

Continuous simulation models—An approach that involves the characterization of process behavior using differential equations to calculate the change in a state variable over time. In continuous models, the state variables (e.g., arrival rate of orders or processing rate of a resource) change continuously over time. Differential equations are usually used in small time-step increments to determine the values of state variables until they reach a threshold that triggers some action.

Critical path–The sequence of activities that represents the longest total time to complete the process, such that a delay in any activity in the critical path causes a delay in completing the process.

Cycle time—The time that elapses between when input enters a process or activity and when it is delivered to the next activity or process. It is usually based upon a 24-hour day (not eight hours) and a seven-day week (not five working days).

Data dictionary—A list of titles that are used to identify the individual symbols used in a flowchart, with a definition for each title.

Decision/response analysis—What are the relationships between the values of one or more decision variables and the system response to those changes?

Delay—A symbol that indicates an activity that holds a transaction for a specified period of time before releasing it to the next activity.

Demand-pull—Built to order that has been received.

Design of experiments (DOE)—A set of statistical methods for yielding the most information with the fewest possible number of experiments. An experimental design systematically and simultaneously changes input values to study the effects on the model's performance.

Deterministic arrivals—When things arrive regularly. For example the mail arrives at 12:00 every day, Monday through Friday.

Discrete-event simulation—In this type of simulation, the state of the model changes only at discrete (possibly random set of points) event times. Transactions (or entities) in discrete-event simulation flow from one point to another point (in time) while competing with each other for the use of scarce resources.

Dispose activity—Activity that removes a transaction after it has been processed.

Domain—The value or values that a factor may take during the simulation experiment.

Dormant period—Time when no activities are going on in a process.

Effectiveness—The extent to which the output of a process or activity meets the needs and expectations of its customers. Effectiveness is having the right output at the right place, at the right time, and for the right price.

Efficiency—A measure of the resources (human, money, cycle time, etc.) that are used by a process in order to produce its output. A close synonym to efficiency is productivity.

Enabler—A technical or organizational facility or resource that makes it possible to perform a task, an activity, or a process. Examples of technical enablers are personal computers, copying equipment, decentralized data processing, and voice response acceptance. Examples of organizational enablers are self-managed work teams, virtual departments, network organizations, and education systems.

Event-trace—A software feature that enables the user to look inside the simulation to describe what the model is doing. An event-trace usually includes a time stamp, a transaction, an activity or a resource name, and a description of the event.

Face validity—Quality of a model that appears, from all outward indications, to be an accurate representation of the process.

Factor—A decision variable whose value may or may not affect the performance of a model output variable.

Fast Action Solution Technique (FAST)—A breakthrough approach that focuses a group's attention on a single process for a one- or two-day meeting to define how the group can improve the process over the next 90 days. Before the end of the meeting, management approves or rejects the proposed improvements.

Flowchart—A method of graphically describing an existing process or a proposed new process by using simple symbols, lines, and words to pictorially display the process activities in sequence.

Flow diagram—A kind of drawing that visually defines the activities or tasks that make up a process, using symbols to depict the different types of activities (e.g., a big circle defines an inspection activity and a diamond defines a decision point).

Full-time equivalent (FTE)—The number of hours that an individual would work in a given time period (without overtime), typically 1800 hours/year or 34.6 hours/week.

Future-state solution (FSS)—A combination of corrective actions and changes that can be applied to an item (process) being studied to improve its performance and increase its value to the stakeholder.

Gate activity—A connection object in the process where two or more things must come together before the transaction can continue. A GATE activity holds entities in a queue until a signal is received.

Generate activity—Activity that creates a transaction to be processed.

Hierarchical modeling—The ability to decompose a process into layers.

Instance—A unique individual member of a product, an activity, or a resource class.

Interval—The time between recurring periods when resources are unavailable.

Join—Activity that takes the clones and original entity and matches them to produce the original entity.

Logical connection—An object used when the transaction cannot continue until something else happens.

Logic data—Data that define the workflow, model objects, their behaviors and relationships, and business rules such as routing sequences, resources assignments, priorities, etc.

Major process—A process that usually involves more than one function within the organizational structure and that has a significant impact on the way the organization functions. When a major process is too complex to be flowcharted at the activity level, it is often divided into subprocesses.

Mean value—The sum of the sample values divided by the number of samples.

Model partitioning—The process of subdividing a model into two or more smaller modules that physically represent separate sections of the process.

Monte Carlo analysis—An approach to varying process variables over a broad range of reasonable (and even unreasonable) options to simulate the variability in a process's key measurement.

No-value-added (NVA) activities—Activities that are not required by either the customers or the business.

Non-value-added costs—No-value-added costs plus business-value-added costs.

Numeric data—Quantitative information related to the item being modeled (e.g., cycle times, cost, batch size, etc.).

Object–oriented—A system that combines information and procedures in a single object.

Object-oriented simulation—This type of modeling views processes, products, services, and resources as objects. Object-oriented modeling can be applied to analytical, continuous, or discrete-event simulation. The purpose of object-oriented modeling and simulation is to enhance the modeler's ability to create complex models, to maximize the life cycle of the model, and to allow for integration with other models. The most visible aspects of object-oriented simulation are the graphical user interface and the process flow animation.

Off time or down time—A period of time when the resources are not available.

Off units—Units of resources that are unavailable.

Optimization study—What combination of feasible values for a given set of decision variables best achieves desired performance objectives?

OR connector—Object used when the output for an activity may be directed to different activities based upon preset conditions or probabilities.

Organization—Any group, company, corporation, division, department, plant, or sales office.

Output analysis—A way of using simulation output to develop inferences about the actual process or system.

Performance analysis—An analysis of how well the process performs under a given set of circumstances in all measures of significance (utilization, throughput, waiting times, etc.).

Polymorphism—Characteristic of a group of objects that share a common ancestry. They can also share a method, with each method implemented differently.

Population—The entire set of possible outcomes (e.g., all possible rolls of a die).

Probability—A number between 0 and 1.

Process—A logical, related, sequential (connected) set of activities that takes an input from a supplier, adds value to it, and produces an output for a customer.

Process analysis—A statistical analysis of model input data, such as customer demand and resource capacity, and model output data, such as cycle time and process cost.

Process flow animation—A process model that pictorially shows the movement of transactions within the process and how variability and dynamics affect process performance.

Process improvement team (PIT)—A group of individuals, usually from different functions, assigned to improve a specific process or subprocess. They design the best-value future-state solution using methodologies such as process redesign, process reengineering, and process benchmarking.

Process knowledge dictionary—A way of storing online the information related to a process that is organized according to each activity/task in the process.

Process mapping—Understanding what a business does and how it does it, which requires documenting inputs, processes, outputs, and resources. Process mapping combines the simplicity of flowcharting with the documentation features of word processing.

Process performance analysis—The collection of efficiency performance data at the activities or task level of a flowchart that are used to calculate the performance of the total process.

Process redesign—A methodology used to streamline a current process with the objective of reducing cost and cycle time by 30% to 60% while improving output quality from 20% to 200%.

Process reengineering—A methodology used to radically change the way a process is presently designed by developing an independent vision of how it should perform and using a group of enablers to prepare a new process design that is not hampered by current paradigms.

Process simulation—A technique that pictorially models or represents processes, resources, products, and services in a dynamic computer model.

Process variation analysis—A way of combining the variation that occurs in each task or activity in a process, in order to make a realistic prediction of the total variation for the entire process.

Queue—The status of a transaction when it has completed one activity and cannot continue because the next activity cannot accept it for some reason (e.g., all the people are busy, the competitor is running another job, or the equipment is being prepared).

Random number generator—A program that generates a sequence of unique random numbers that are independent of each other and uniformly distributed between 0 and 1.

Real-value-added (RVA) activities—Activities that, when viewed by the external customer, are required to provide the output that the customer is expecting.

Replication—One cycle through a process simulation model. The number of replications affects the width of the confidence interval: the width of the confidence interval decreases as the number of replications rises.

Resource allocation—A system of priorities that defines how resources are assigned if there are multiple assignments for the same resource.

Resource assignment—Ensuring that the right resources are together at the correct time to execute the activity.

RIRO (random in, random out)—Term used to describe the nature of the relationship between random model input data and model output data.

Run—What happens between the time when you click on the run option in the process simulation tool and the time when the model finishes writing output statistics to disk and comes back to the main menu. A run may consist of multiple replications.

Sample—One, single, unbiased observation of the population (e.g., a single roll of a die).

Sample size—The number of samples you are working with (e.g., four rolls of a die).

Scalability—The ability of process simulation software to allow use of a modeling tool at multiple levels by various skill levels.

Scenario—A specification of the input configuration.

Scenario analysis—A statistical analysis of model output for a given performance measure under different sets of input data.

Seed—A value provided for the random number generator.

Sensitivity analysis—Which decision variables are the most influential on one or more process performance measures, and how influential are they?

Sigma or σ—The symbol for standard deviation, the point when a normal histogram starts to go out at a greater rate than it goes down.

Split—Activity that takes an incoming entity and creates clones of that entity as well as providing an output of the original entity.

Split activity—A connection point where the original transaction and its clone are separated and sent to different activities. A SPLIT activity takes an incoming entity and creates clones of that entity as well as providing an output of the original entity.

Standard deviation—A measure of spread of sample values around the mean value.

Subprocess—A portion of a major process that achieves a specific objective in support of the major process.

Synonym—One of two or more titles that mean the same thing.

System—An assembly of components (hardware, software, procedures, human functions, and other resources) united by some form of regulated interaction to form an organized whole. It is a group of related processes that may or may not be connected.

Tasks—The individual elements and/or subsets of an activity. Normally, tasks relate to how a resource performs a specific assignment.

Terminating simulation—A simulation activity that has a definitive time or state for beginning and a definitive time or state for ending.

Throughput—The number of items that traverse the process.

Time-dependent statistics—Statistics that are sensitive to changes over time.

Time-independent statistics—Observation-based statistics that arise from independent observations.

Time-weighted average—A statistic for process performance measures that changes values over time.

Transaction—Any entity that flows through a process simulation model. Transactions represent physical objects, such as orders or other paperwork, or informational objects, such as triggers, signals, or flags.

Transaction classification—A way of grouping transactions based upon a significant criterion.

Transformation—Activity that accepts an input and produces a different output.

Trigger—The input that starts a transaction through a process or activity.

Unbatch—Activity that splits a batch into individual entities.

Validation—The act of determining the degree to which the model corresponds to the real process.

Variables data—Data that are measured—in units such as inches, feet, volts, amps, ohms, and centimeters. These data provide detailed information of the system and samples are usually small and taken frequently.

Verification—The act of demonstrating that a simulation model is working as intended.

Visualization—How can we visualize the dynamic behavior of the process so that process owners, customers, and stakeholders can communicate better?

Wait for resource—The status of a transaction when it is ready to be processed but not all of the resources are available to process the transaction.

Workflow automation—A tool set for the proactive analysis, compression, and automation of information-based tasks and activities.

Workflow monitoring—An online computer program that is used to track individual transactions as they move through the process, to minimize process variation.

Simulation Objects/Characters

Assemble—An *assemble* activity assembles multiple entities coming from multiple sources to create a single entity. For example, the development of a business proposal may contain three documents that are merged using an *assemble* activity.

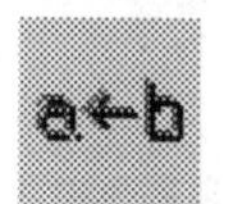

Assign—An **assign** activity provides a mechanism for defining or changing attribute values.

Batch—A *batch* activity combines a given quantity of entities into a single batch. An example of a batching activity is the accumulation of mail for delivery.

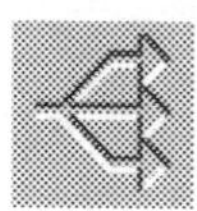

Branch—A *branch* activity allows for defining alternative routings for flow objects. Branching may be based on a probability or a condition. For example, the outcome of an inspection process may be modeled using probabilistic branching.

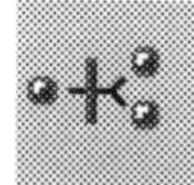

Copy—A *copy* activity makes multiple copies of the original entity. For example, if a document is being edited in a groupware software that results in multiple copies of a file, this activity may be modeled using a *copy* activity.

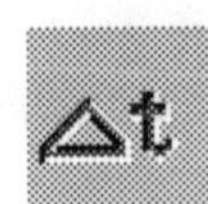

Delay—A *delay* activity defines value-added or non-value-added activity times. It is one of the most commonly used activities in *simprocess*. A *delay* activity with resource constraints provides queue statistics that can be used for analyzing wait times.

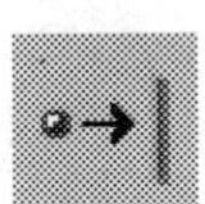

Dispose—A *dispose* activity disposes of the entities when they are finished with processing. A *dispose* activity can be used for collecting customized statistics for throughput or throughput time.

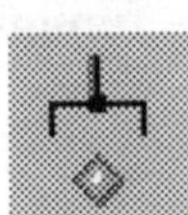

Free Resource—This activity provides a mechanism for releasing resources that were captured by a *get resource* activity.

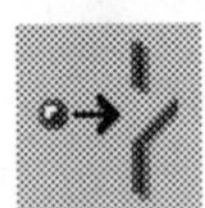

Gate—A *gate* activity holds entities in a queue until a signal is received. For example, a *gate* activity would be used to model orders held in inventory until a signal is received from the distributor to fulfill the demand.

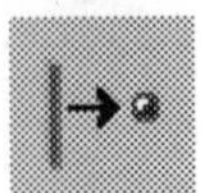

Generate—A **generate** activity generates the arrival of entities into the model. Arrivals may be random, deterministic, or conditional. An example of a *generate* activity is the arrival of patients in a clinic. A *generate* activity may have values for arrival time, quantity, frequency, and occurrences.

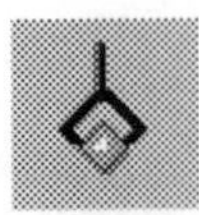

Get Resource—This activity provides a mechanism for capturing resources that may be used for a number of downstream activities.

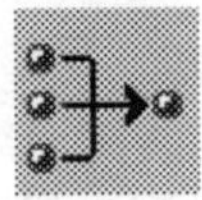

Join—A *join* activity takes the clones and the original entity that were split up and matches them to produce the original one. For example, a *join* activity may be used for matching the paperwork with the shipment.

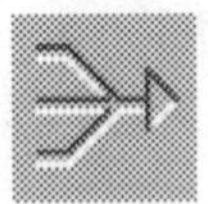

Merge—A *merge* activity provides a mechanism for merging a number of connectors into a single connector.

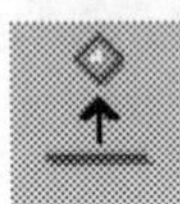

Replenish Resource—This activity allows for replenishment of consumable resources.

Split—A *split* activity takes an incoming entity and creates clones of that entity as well as providing an output of the original entity. For example, clones of a purchase order may be created with a *split* activity and sent to accounts payable and shipping.

Synchronize—A *sychronize* activity takes inputs that arrive at different times and outputs them in a synchronized fashion. For example, passengers and their baggage must be synchronized at a terminal.

Transform—A *transform* activity converts an incoming entity into another entity. For example, a prospective buyer is transformed into a customer when an order is placed. This activity can be modeled using the transformation construct.

Unbatch—An *unbatch* activity splits a previously batched entity into individual entities. For example, unloading of a truck that results in multiple loads may be modeled with an *unbatch* activity.

APPENDIX **B**

Software Evaluation Checklist

Software Characteristics

Functionality

1. **Process Mapping**
   - ▶ Hierarchical modeling (top-down and bottom-up modeling)
   - ▶ Ability to create templates
   - ▶ Drag-and-drop flow diagramming
   - ▶ Ability to define labels with variable font and size
   - ▶ Ability to customize icons for graphical objects
   - ▶ Ability to change the color, width, type of connectors
   - ▶ Methodology-independent process modeling
   - ▶ Tabular representation of model data

2. **Dynamic Behavior Modeling**
   - ▶ Transaction Modeling
     - Generation (periodic, cyclical, calendar-based, from trace file)
     - Disposal (time-based, count-based, conditional)
   - ▶ Activity Modeling
     - Branch (probabilistic, conditional)
     - Delay with or without a resource
     - Assemble
     - Copy
     - Batch/Unbatch
     - Gate for modeling a triggered activity
     - Split/Join for modeling parallel activities

- ▸ Resource Modeling
  - Resource assignment (single resource to multiple activities, multiple resources to a single activity, priorities)
  - Resource scheduling (shifts, planned and random interruptions)
  - Resource costing (hourly rate, fixed costs, one-time setup costs)
  - Consumable resources
- ▸ Advanced Modeling
  - User-defined attributes
  - User-defined expressions
  - System state variables
  - System methods

3. **Simulation and Animation**
   - ▸ Animation Development Components
     - Static background objects
     - Static model objects
     - Dynamic model objects
     - Dynamically updated status
     - Dynamically updated statistical information
   - ▸ Runtime Controls
     - View multiple layers of the process model in side-by-side windows
     - Animation controls (speed up, slow down, turn on, or turn off the animation)
     - Single-step through the simulation
     - Trace and view all or selected types of events
     - Ability to highlight warning or alarm conditions for rare events

4. **Analysis**
   - ▸ Input Data Analysis
     - Built-in statistical distributions
     - User-defined distributions
     - Tabular distributions
     - Distribution fitting

- Output Data Analysis
  - Time-persistent statistics
  - Observation-based statistics
  - Minimum, maximum, average, standard deviation values
  - Multiple replications
  - Confidence intervals
  - Gap analysis
- Output Reports
  - Entity reports (cycle time, count)
  - Resource reports (state, utilization)
  - Activity reports (cycle time, count)
  - Cost reports (entity, resource, activity)
  - Attribute reports
- Graphical Output
  - Bar charts
  - Pie charts
  - Histograms
  - Line graphs

5. **Model Import-Export Functions**
   - Ability to import data from databases or other applications
   - Ability to export data to databases or other applications
   - Ability to link with external applications or subroutines
   - Ability to view process model or its output via a Web browser
   - Ability to print the process model or its output

Usability

- Intuitive and descriptive modeling constructs
- Simple and straightforward modeling approach
- Maximum use of graphical input
- Input prompts that are clear and easy to follow
- Context-sensitive help
- Wizards
- Simplified data entry and modification

- Automatic gathering of key performance measures
- Automatic management of multiple experiments
- Debugging and trace features
- Output reports that are easy to read and understand

Reliability

- Robustness of underlying simulation technology used in process simulation tool
- Testing procedures used in software development
- Bug reporting and maintenance process
- Is the vendor ISO 9000-certified?
- Are there bugs related to GUI, OS, device drivers, or animation?
- Or are there bugs in the simulation engine or output reporting?

Maintainability

- Security
  - Software key
  - Hardware key
  - Model-specific password
- Documentation
  - Tutorial
  - Examples
  - User's guide
  - On-line documentation
- Hardware and Other Software Requirements
  - Operating system
  - Memory required (RAM)
  - Network support
- Updates and Enhancements
  - How often does the supplier provide new releases?
  - Is the software supplier up-to-date with the latest developments in software technology?

- Is the supplier involved in industry standards committees?
- Are the new releases compatible with the old ones?

Scalability

- ▸ Model size
- ▸ Model complexity
- ▸ Performance of large and complex models
- ▸ Growth path from simple to complex modeling requirements
- ▸ Ability to create and distribute run-time models

Supplier Characteristics

Supplier Quality

- ▸ What is the business focus of the supplier? What percentage of its revenues comes from products versus services?
- ▸ How many employees does the supplier have? How does it break down by R&D, Marketing/Sales, and Customer Services?
- ▸ How long has the supplier been in business? What is its installed user base?
- ▸ Who are the supplier's key reference accounts? How long have they been customers?
- ▸ What is the financial status of the supplier?

Supplier Services

1. **Technical Support**
   - ▸ How does the supplier provide technical support (e.g., phone, bulletin board, user groups)?
   - ▸ What percentage of the total staff is dedicated to customer services?
   - ▸ Are the developers of the product willing to talk to the end users?
   - ▸ How responsive is the supplier to deadlines of the user?

- How close is your nearest authorized representative? How competent is your nearest representative?

2. **Training**
   - How frequent are the training courses? Where are the training locations?
   - What levels of training are offered? Is industry-specific training available?
   - Is on-site training available? If so, how much does it cost?
   - Is customized training available? If so, how much does it cost?

3. **Modeling Services**
   - Who will be working on the project? What are his or her credentials?
   - Can the model be used after the consultant is finished with the project?
   - What are the deliverables?

4. **Other Services**
   - Is there an Internet news group where users can exchange ideas?
   - Does the supplier provide a newsletter? How often is published? What is the content?
   - Does the supplier provide case studies? How useful are they?
   - Does the company have user group meetings? Where and when?

5. **Cost of Ownership**
   - Software license cost
   - Training cost (standard, custom)
   - Annual maintenance and support cost
   - Optional modules
   - Discounts for multiple licenses, network licenses
   - Runtime version

Data Collection Checklist

1. **Process Model**
   - What is the purpose of the simulation modeling and analysis study?
   - What are the boundaries of the process to be modeled?
   - What are the inputs and outputs of the process?
   - How many layers are there in the process hierarchy?
   - What alternative process designs are being considered?
   - What is the planning horizon (simulation period)?
   - What are the sources of model input data?
   - When are the input data collected? How often are the data collected?
   - Who can validate the assumptions made in the model?
   - What are the key model performance measures?

2. **Entities**
   - What are the different types of entities that are processed?
   - How many of each type are processed during the simulation period?
   - How often do entities arrive in the process? What triggers their arrival?
   - Where do entities leave the process?
   - What are the key attributes of the entities?
   - What icons are available to represent the flow objects during the animation?
   - What statistics need to be collected for each entity type?

3. **Activities**
   - What is the sequence of activities in the process?
   - What happens to an entity at each activity? (This helps define the type of activity.)
   - What are the different types of activities in the process?
   - Are there parallel activities? If so, when do they come together?
   - Are there decision activities, such as branching? What are the criteria for making the decisions?
   - What are the key attributes of the activities?

- What resource or resources are required to perform each activity?
- How are the resources assigned to the activities? First-come, first-serve? Priority-based?
- What happens if a resource is not available? What is the maximum wait threshold?
- What icons are available to represent the activities in the process map?
- What statistics need to be collected for each activity?

4. **Resources**
   - What are the different types of resources used to perform the process?
   - What are the key attributes of the resources?
   - How many of each resource type are available?
   - If there are multiple skill sets, how is work assigned to the resources?
   - What is the availability schedule or shifts for the resources?
   - Are the resources subject to planned or unplanned interruptions?
   - If a resource is interrupted, what is the time between interruptions?
   - When a resource is interrupted, how long does it stay in that state?
   - What happens to an entity if its resource is interrupted in the middle of an activity?
   - What are the hourly rates, salaries, and fixed costs for resources?
   - What icons are available to represent the resources in the process map?
   - What statistics need to be collected for each resource?

APPENDIX C
Simulation Tool Suppliers

Vendor	Tools	Web Address
CACI Products Company	SIMPROCESS MODSIM III	www.modsim.com
Edge Software, Inc.	WorkDraw Design/ Analyst	www.workdraw.com
High Performance Systems, Inc.	ithink	www.hps-inc.com
Imagine That, Inc.	Extend	www.imaginethatinc.com
Micro Analysis Design, Inc.	Micro Saint	www.madboulder.com
Micrografx, Inc.	GrafxProcess	www.micrografx.com
ProModel Corporation	ProModel	www.promodel.com
Process Model Corporation	ProcessModel I	www.processmodel.com
Scitor Corporation	Scitor Process	www.scitor.com
Symix, Inc.	AweSim!	www.pritsker.com
Systems Modeling Corporation	Arena	www.sm.com

Note: Company names and product names change due to mergers, acquisitions, and other reasons. You may have to check an Internet search engine for the most up-to-date company and product information.

APPENDIX 

Standard Theoretical Probability Distributions

This appendix describes common standard theoretical probability distributions that have application in simulation. Most of these distributions are built into current simulation products and only the defining parameters need to be specified.

Exponential—Sometimes referred to as the *Negative Exponential*, this distribution has widespread use in queuing systems. It is used to generate random values for the time between arrivals of customers into a system. The term "customers" can cover an infinite number of possibilities, ranging from packages arriving at a delivery dock to job requests on a computer system. Other possible applications are the time to complete a task and the time to failure of electronic components.

Gamma—The Gamma distribution can be used to represent the time needed to complete a task or group of tasks. Suppose that an Exponential distribution with a mean parameter of 1.2 hours describes the time to complete a given task. The Gamma distribution could be employed to generate values representing the total time required to complete N independent performances of that task. The a value would equal N for this scenario.

Normal—The Normal distribution is often utilized to measure various types of error. Receiving/inspection operations frequently require the use of calibrated instruments to measure the dimensions of various components. The measurements revealed by an instrument are assumed to be normally distributed about the true dimensions of the component. A Normal distribution could be used to represent the readings obtained on each individual measurement.

Uniform—A Uniform distribution over the range of zero to one is the basis for generating values from standard probability distributions. It can also be utilized to generate random values from customized algorithms. Another common application is for representing the duration of a task when minimal information is known about the actual task times. Sometimes the time to complete a task is believed to vary randomly and evenly between two values. Given these conditions, the Uniform distribution is a good preliminary estimation for the cycle time duration.

Weibull—Reliability issues are often represented with a Weibull distribution. It can be used to generate values for the time to failure of a piece of equipment or the average life of an electronic component. The time to complete a task can also be reflected by this distribution.

Triangular—The Triangular distribution is particularly useful for situations where only three pieces of information are known about a task. Ask assemblers on a production line how long it takes to perform an operation and their response will likely be "Most of the time it is y, but it can range from x to z." The minimum (x), mode (y), and maximum (z) can be used as the defining parameters of a Triangular distribution.

Lognormal—A Lognormal distribution can be used to represent the time to perform a task. An example might be the cycle time for competing a carrousel storage/retrieval operation in an automated stores system. The parameter values for this distribution are generally calculated from the natural logarithms of the empirical data. Given these conditions, values generated from a Lognormal distribution might be expressed in terms of the natural logarithms of the desired random values. If this is true, then the generated values must be converted to non-logarithmic values in order to obtain random variates that will be representative of the empirical data.

Erlang—The Erlang distribution is a special case of the Gamma distribution that is frequently used in queuing systems to represent service-time distributions for various tasks. The K parameter value is equivalent to the A parameter in a Gamma distribution, but the values of K are restricted to integer values greater than zero. The distribution becomes an Exponential distribution when K = 1. Suppose an operation consists of performing a single task 10 times and the time to complete each task is described by an Exponential distribution with a mean parameter of 2. Given these circumstances, the time to complete the entire operation can be represented by an Erlang distribution with a mean parameter equal to 20 (calculated 2 x 10) and a K parameter equal to 10.

Beta—Two parameters are needed to define the Beta distribution, A1 and A2. Varying their values will produce a variety of distribution shapes. Values generated from a Beta distribution will have a range of zero to one. For this reason, it is particularly useful for representing phenomena pertaining to proportions. The proportion of defective items found in a given lot size could be described by this distribution. The Beta distribution is also used to represent the time to complete an activity, when very little or no information is available about the duration of the activity.

Poisson—The Poisson distribution is usually associated with arrival rates. It reflects the probability associated with a finite number of successes (arrivals) occurring in a given arrival time interval or specified area. For each integer value of a random variable X, there is a unique probability of occurrence. In queuing models, the arrival rate of customers into a system is referred to as a Poisson input process. This implies that the inter-arrival times of customers are exponentially distributed. The number of phone calls arriving at a switchboard each hour might be represented by a Poisson distribution. The mean value parameter reflects the average arrival rate per hour. Values generated from this distribution will be integer values greater than or equal to zero.

Binomial—Consider an experiment that can produce two possible outcomes, success or failure. "P" denotes the probability of success and "q" denotes the probability of failure (q = 1-p). If the probability of success remains constant with each independent repetition of the experiment, then the number of successes in N independent trials can be described by a Binomial distribution. The number of defective items in a batch of size N is sometimes represented by this distribution. The random values produced will reflect the number of defects per batch.

Discrete Uniform—Suppose an automated storage and retrieval system consists of six individual carrousels, with parts distributed among them uniformly. A Discrete Uniform distribution with values from 1 to 6 might be used to determine the carrousel in which any given part is stored. Each value for the random variable X (carrousel in which a part is stored) will be an integer within that range.

Bernoulli Distribution

The Bernoulli distribution (sometimes called the Bernoulli trial) is a discrete distribution that applies to situations where there are two possible states (e.g., reject, non-reject). The probability of one state occurring is p and the probability of the other state occurring is $1 - p$. Examples of phenomena that might be defined using a Bernoulli distribution include:

- The output of a process is either defective or nondefective.
- An employee shows up for work or not.
- An operation will require a secondary process or not.

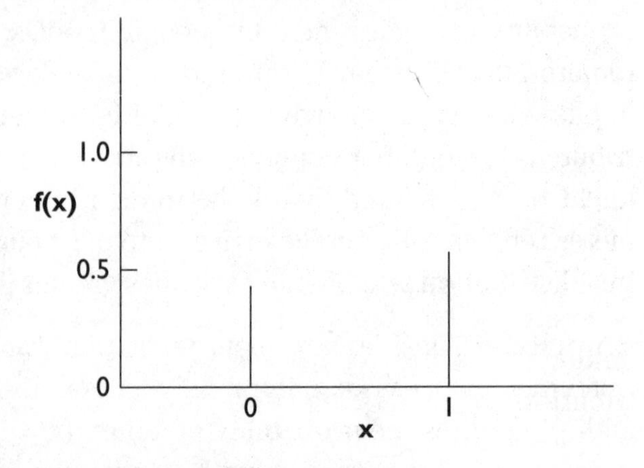

Bernoulli distribution with $p = 0.60$

Binomial Distribution

The Binomial distribution is a discrete distribution that expresses the number of outcomes in n trials. It is essentially the sum of n Bernoulli trials. A binomial distribution is defined by the probability (p) of a particular outcome occurring in a number (n) of trials. Examples of phenomena that might be defined using a binomial distribution include:

- The number of defective items in a batch.
- The number of customers of a particular type that enter the system.
- The number of employees out of a group of employees who call in sick on a given day.

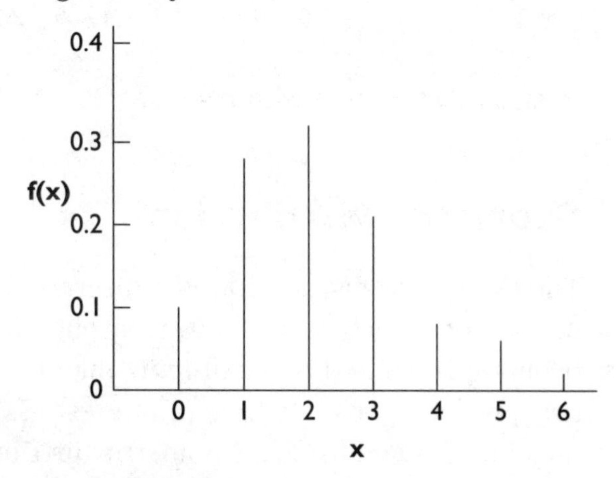

Binomial distribution with $p = 0.30$ and $n = 6$

Poisson Distribution

The Poisson distribution is a discrete distribution used to model a rate of occurrences (i.e. the number of times an event or characteristic occurs per interval of time or per entity unit). It is used most often to define arrival rates, particularly in service systems. In a Poisson distribution, the mean is equal to the variance. It is therefore defined only by the average rate of occurrence. Examples of phenomena that might be defined using a Poisson distribution include:

- The number of entities arriving each hour.
- The number of defects per item.
- The number of times a resource is interrupted each hour.

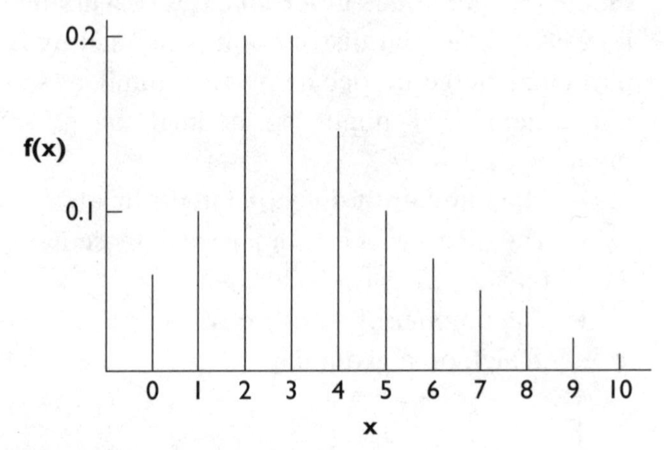

Poisson distribution with $p = 4.0$

Geometric Distribution

The Geometric distribution is a discrete distribution that defines the number of trials before a particular outcome occurs. A Geometric distribution is defined by identifying the probability (p) of any potential trial producing the outcome of interest. Examples of phenomena that might be defined using a Geometric distribution include:

- The number of machine cycles before a failure occurs.
- The number of items inspected before a defective item is found.
- The number of customers processed before a customer of a particular type is encountered.

Uniform Distribution

The Uniform distribution is a continuous distribution used to define a value that is equally likely to fall anywhere within a specified range. A Uniform distribution is defined by specifying the lower limit (a) and the upper limit (b) of the range. Alternatively, it is defined by specify-

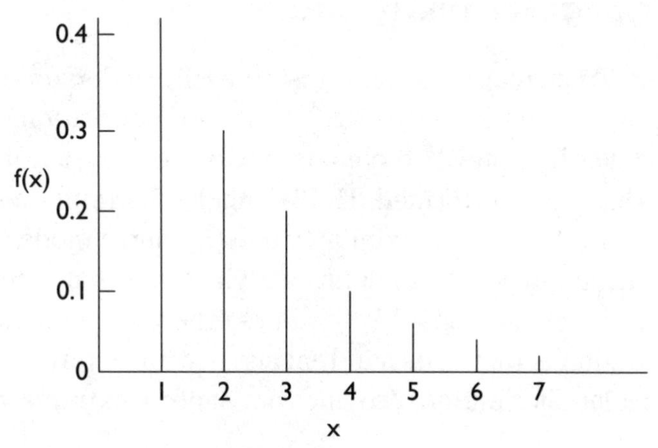

Geometric distribution with $p = 0.5$

ing the midpoint and half range. The Uniform distribution is seldom a valid representation of phenomena that occur in manufacturing and service systems. It is sometimes used when the underlying distribution is unknown.

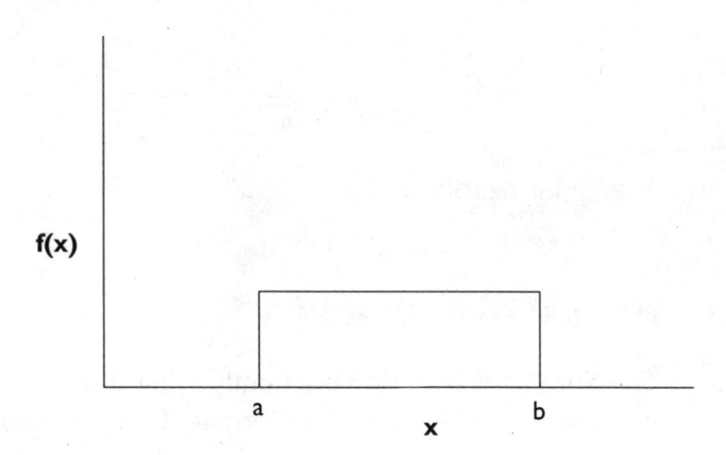

Uniform distribution

Triangular Distribution

The Triangular distribution is an easily understood and definable distribution that provides a good first approximation of the true underlying distribution when data are sparse and no distribution fitting analysis has been performed. The Triangular distribution is defined by a minimum value (a), a maximum value (b), and a mode (m). The Triangular distribution is used to define activity times that tend to have minimum, maximum, and most likely values. The weakness of the Triangular distribution is that values in real activity times rarely taper linearly. A triangular distribution also does not capture extreme values that are rare.

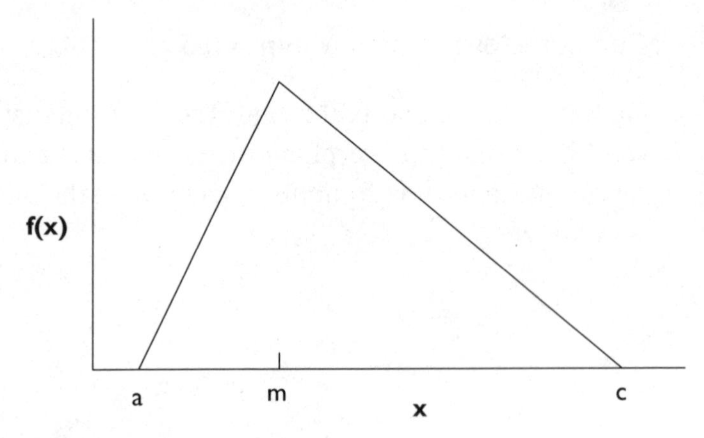

Triangular distribution

Normal Distribution

The Normal distribution is a familiar distribution and relatively easy to understand and define. The Normal distribution is defined by a mean ($\bar{X}$ or μ) and standard deviation (σ). The Normal distribution is used to define activity times that tend to be symmetrical about a central tendency (hence the bell shape). Contrary to what might at first seem to be the case, there are very few activities whose times fit a normal distribution. This is because most activities tend to be skewed (stretched out) to the right, so that times are often quite longer than they are shorter from the mean.

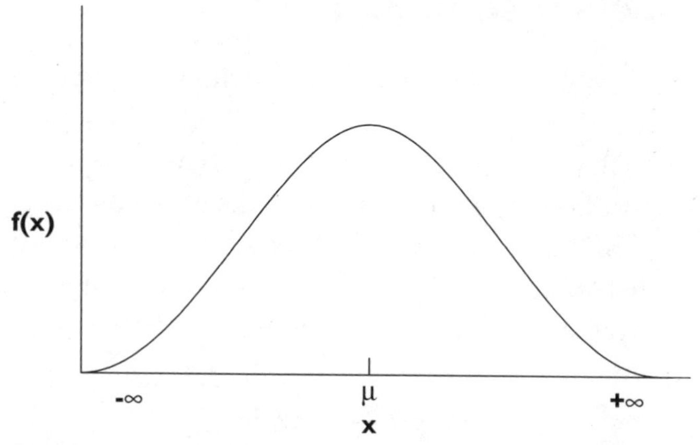

Normal distribution

Exponential Distribution

The Exponential distribution, sometimes called the Negative Exponential distribution, is closely related to the Poisson distribution in that, if an occurrence happens at a rate that is Poisson distributed, the time between occurrences is exponentially distributed. The Exponential distribution is defined by the mean time ($\bar{X}$). The Exponential distribution has a memoryless property that allows completely random occurrences to take place. The Exponential distribution is used primarily to define intervals between occurrences, such as the time between customer arrivals. Some activity times, such as repair times or the duration of telephone conversations, may also be exponentially distributed.

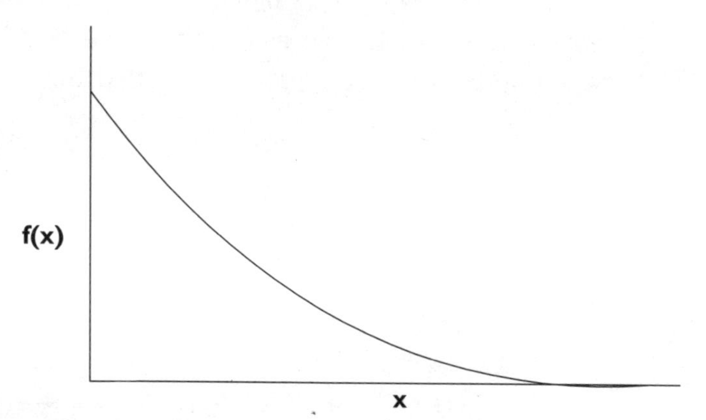

Exponential distribution

Beta Distribution

The Beta distribution is used when the data available are insufficient to define a more accurate distribution. It defines random proportions, such as the percentage of defective items in a lot and activity times, particularly when multiple tasks make up the activity, as in a project. (PERT network activity times assume a Beta distribution.) The Beta distribution is defined by two shape parameters and must be scaled to provide ranges greater than 1.

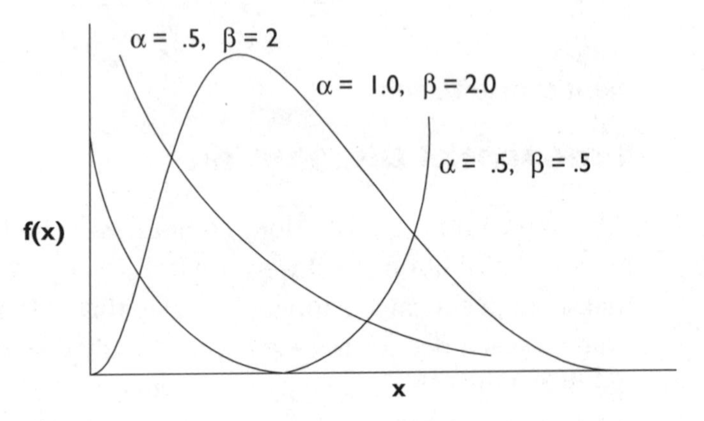

Beta distribution

Lognormal Distribution

The Lognormal distribution is a useful distribution that is characteristic of activities having multiple subactivities. It is often used to define manual activities such as assembly, inspection, or repair. The time between failures is often lognormally distributed.

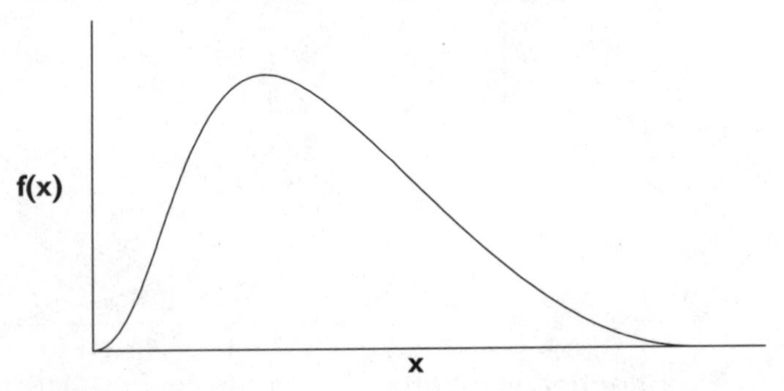

Lognormal distribution

Gamma Distribution

The Gamma distribution takes on a variety of different shapes and is therefore useful for describing time values for many different types of activities. Typical activities whose time may be defined by a Gamma distribution include manual tasks, such as service times or repair times. A special case of the Gamma distribution is the Erlang distribution.

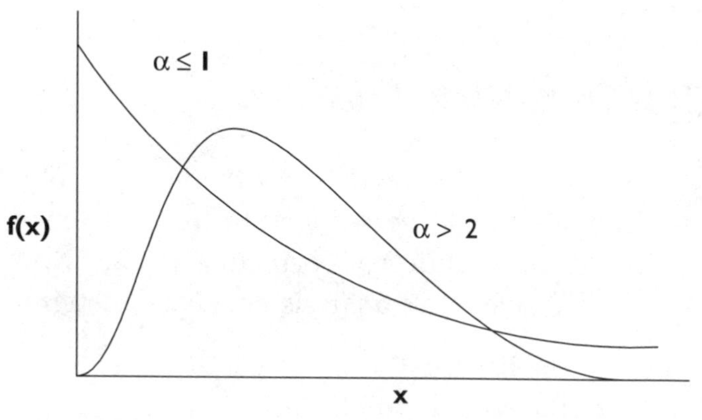

Gamma distribution

Weibull Distribution

The Weibull distribution is similar to the Gamma distribution, having many different shapes. It is often used in reliability theory for defining the time until failure, particularly due to wear (e.g., bearings, tooling, etc.).

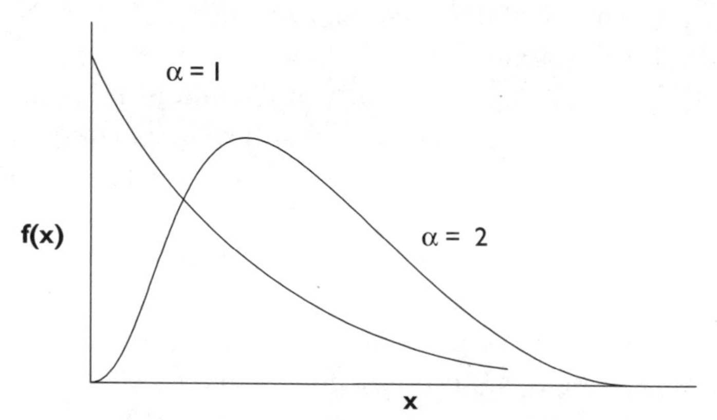

Weibull distribution

APPENDIX E
Best-Value Future-State Solution Analysis

Benefits/Cost/Risk Analysis

As a result of the modeling activities, the potential list of future-state solutions should be reduced to three or fewer, each of which could include many different corrective actions. Now is the time to make a detailed qualitative analysis of each, to determine:

- the benefits
- the costs of implementation
- the associated risk
- disadvantages

This task is not as difficult as it may seem at first. Much of the information can be or was obtained from your benchmarking partner. (Examples: How much did it cost them to implement it? What approach did they use to implement it? What difficulties did they have? What impact did it have on the critical measurements?) Another source of cost and implementation data is the supplier used by the benchmarking process that helped with particular changes and/or potential suppliers that you plan on using (software packages, information technology, automation equipment, etc.). In preparing the implementation cost estimate, make good use of the support departments within your organization. Departments such as Information Systems, Industrial Engineering, and Finance can be very helpful in developing implementation costs, cycle time, benefits, and potential risk estimates. It's particularly important to involve these departments in this analysis if they are going to be involved in the implementation.

Develop an Assumptions List

To help prepare these estimates, we recommend that you rely heavily on help from your internal experts in the area that you are evaluating (finance, industrial engineering, sales and marketing, product engineering, etc.). A list of working assumptions should be prepared and reviewed with key management personnel to get their agreement before the assumptions are used as part of the estimating process. This can eliminate a great deal of rework and false starts. Typical working assumptions could be:

- A percentage point improvement in customer satisfaction is worth $100,000 in profits.
- An equivalent employee hour (EEH) saved is worth the individual's salary plus $35 in variable overhead.
- Inventory floor space saved is worth $15 per square foot per month.
- For every 24 hours' reduction in cycle time, sales would increase 0.1%.
- Mainframe computer processing time costs $87 per minute.
- Reduced annual inventory value results in bottom-line savings of $18 per $1,000 reduction.

Your organization should not be making changes for the sake of change alone. We change to improve the organization's performance. We all understand that any change costs money to implement and if the cost of implementing the change is not offset by improved performance that is more valuable to the organization than the costs (dollars and emotional) the change should not be made. Every improvement opportunity should be looked at to determine its impact on performance. If reducing cycle time doesn't improve customer satisfaction so that the customers buy more products or doesn't increase the organization's market share or doesn't reduce cost, there's no reason to do it. Too often a manager will pursue implementing best practices only for self-gratification, without providing any benefit to the organization. This is all right as long as it does not cost the organization any money or time. Otherwise, these no-payback improvements should not be made, since they often detract from another improvement that will have a positive impact on the organization's performance. It's extremely important to define the benefits that the organization will gain from each measurement improvement so that the process improvement team can make the correct trade-offs. Often some of these benefits will reflect opportunities that are missed if the measurement is not improved.

Work with Finance and key internal experts in establishing these assumptions and getting upper management's agreement with them. This will save a lot of heartburn when you try to get upper management's approval to implement the selected future-state solution.

Benefits Analysis

Once the assumption list is approved, the benchmarking team needs to estimate dollar savings related to each proposed improvement and to estimate the additional cost incurred as a result of implementing the proposed improvement. Typical added implementation costs are:

- Implementation team salary and overhead
- Training costs
- Consulting fees
- Travel costs
- Information system support costs
- New equipment and software costs
- Pilot program's cost
- Added costs that result from running parallel operations during implementation
- Organizational change management costs
- Moving and layout costs
- Communication costs
- Costs of productivity lost while learning the new process
- Cost of maintaining the change after it is implemented (which can be greater than the implementation cost in the case of information technology and automation changes)

Be very careful to document the process you use in preparing all of the estimates, since it is almost certain that someone will challenge the benchmarking team during the approval process. If you cannot reconstruct the numbers, the entire benchmarking project's credibility is in jeopardy and everyone will probe into every assumption and estimate.

As you prepare your implementation estimates, remember that some improvements require only a one-time implementation cost while others have a one-time implementation cost and a yearly cost. Include both in your cost estimates. We like to estimate savings based upon a three-year period. Using a one-year cycle estimating approach provides a more conservative view of the return on investment and highlights improvements that can be implemented quickly. This can lead to accepting changes that are less important to the organization's long-term performance.

In making this analysis look at each potential improvement independently and estimate the following:

- Cost of implementation
  - Equivalent employee days to implement
  - Equivalent employee days added to operating cost due to interruptions of normal activities
  - Consulting cost
  - Equipment and software cost
  - Relocation cost
  - Organizational change management cost
  - Training cost
  - Miscellaneous costs
- Cost to maintain the change after implementation
- Cycle time from the start of the implementation process to complete implementation
- Estimated improvement in performance measurements
- Estimated negative impact on performance measurements
- List of problems associated with the improvement (e.g., How will the additional workload be handled when each person attends a 40-hour class and the area is already working overtime?)

- Estimation of the risks associated with successful implementation (normally stated as a probability that the improvement will not meet estimated performance levels and/or implementation cost and schedule estimates)

It is often necessary to develop a preliminary implementation strategy before the benefits/cost/risk analysis can be made. Both the cost and cycle time of implementation and the risk involved can vary greatly if the improvement needs to be piloted before it is fully implemented.

Once the individual improvements that make up a future-state solution have been evaluated independently, their combined impact should be estimated. (Note: one future-state solution may be made up of a number of individual improvements.) For example, in one future-state solution, the benchmarking team could recommend:

- combining two departments
- moving the activities to a hub city
- eliminating review activities at three points in the process
- bar-coding the receipts so that they could be automatically sorted and filed
- reorganizing department 032 into five employee work teams
- installing a toll-free hotline on the scheduler's desk

In this case we have six improvements that need to be evaluated independently. Each potential improvement may or may not have an impact on more than one measurement, and that impact can be either positive or negative. Here is where the interactive charts (Figure 1) and the analysis of impact (Figure 2) will provide a very significant input. The benchmarking team now has to estimate the total impact of the combined future-state solution. The data collected during the modeling are very helpful in developing these combined performance improvement projections. Figure 3 shows a typical improvement analysis chart for one future-state solution.

Corrective Actions	Measurements							
	1	2	3	4	5	6	7	8
A	0	+	0	0	+	–	+	0
B	+	0	0	0	0	0	0	0
C	+	–	+	0	+	0	0	–
D	–	0	0	+	0	–	0	+
E	0	0	0	–	0	+	+	0
F	0	+	+	–	0	+	+	0
G	0	0	0	+	+	0	0	0

FIGURE 1. Measurement interaction chart

Cycle Time (Hrs)	Corrective Action #	Estimated Time to Implement (Hrs)	Applic-ability	Ease to Implement	Cost to Implement	Status
2	1	10	B	B	B	R
6	21	7	G	F	G	A
9	12	2	F	G	F	R
9	13	5	G	G	G	A
9	10	3	F	F	G	R

G = Good
F = Fair
B = Bad

A = Accepted Corrective Action
R = Rejected Corrective Action

FIGURE 2. Gap/corrective action impact chart

Cost Analysis

Figure 4 shows a typical implementation cost analysis chart. You will note that the sum of the costs of doing the six improvements individually is higher than the total cost of doing them all. This difference results because resources can be better used when a number of improvements are implemented simultaneously. You will also note that as part of the cost analysis the cost of the organizational change

Measurement	Improvement						Original Value	New Value
	1	2	3	4	5	6		
Cycle Time (days)	-9.0	-0.5	-3.0	-10.0	+5.0	0	35.0	17.5
Processing Time (hrs)	-1.0	-4.0	-1.1	0	+3.1	0	10.0	7.5
Error Rate (errors/1000)	0	0	0	0	-5	-2	8.0	3.0

FIGURE 3. Improvement analysis chart for future-state solution #3

management (OCM) process that will be used to support the implementation is added to the total cost.

Group	Improvement Cost (in $1000)						Total Cost
	1	2	3	4	5	6	
Implementation Team	10	20	.5	60	10	5	101
Target Group	3	0	4	10	0		17.0
Consulting	0	0	0	100	0	0	100.0
Equipment	0	0	0	100	0	0	100.0
Software	10	0	0	50	0	0	60.0
OCM	4.0	0	0	50	3.5	0	57.5
Total	27.0	20.0	4.5	370	13.5	0.5	435.5

FIGURE 4. Cost analysis chart for future-state solution #3

Figure 4. Cost analysis chart for future-state solution #3

Risk Analysis

Typically, risk-analysis percentages are developed for each individual improvement. This is an analysis of the probability that the improvement may not be implemented successfully or not obtain the projected results if nothing is done to minimize the risks. Figure 5 shows a typical risk analysis chart.

Once the process improvement team has identified the risk for each improvement, it develops a corrective action plan to minimize these risks. This plan should be documented and included in the project file. Then, it should develop a total risk percentage for the future-state solution, based upon the risk corrective action plan. You will note that in most cases the future-state solution risk percentage is less than the sum of the individual improvement risks even if no corrective action plan is prepared. This is because each improvement has a different level of impact on the total future-state item's performance. In most cases, the total risk percentage will not be greater than the highest individual risk percentage unless the amount of change already going on in the area is so great that the area goes into "future shock" when all of the improvements are implemented. (For example, improvement #6 in Figure 5 shows a 20% risk factor, because the improvement could overrun costs, but the total implementation cost of improvement #6 is only $500, whereas the implementation cost of future-state solution #4 is $370,000. As you can see, a risk of greater than 20% in the $500 estimate has little impact upon the total risk for future-state solution #3.)

Often when risk percentages are assigned, the assigned risk is based upon an allowable deviation from projections. For example, a risk analysis could be based upon the following question: What is the risk that the projected performance improvement and costs are over or under estimated values by more than 20%?

Improvement No.	Risk Percent	Reason
1	20%	Too little data to verify the effectiveness of the improvement
2	5%	High workload area
3	0%	—
4	20%	New computer and software that we have not used
5	10%	No sustaining sponsor
6	20%	Could be a cost overrun
Total	12%	Corrective action plan did not eliminate all the risks.

Figure 5. Risk analysis chart for future-state solution #3

Looking at the Total

A typical example of a benefits/cost/risk analysis chart for three alternative future-state solutions can be seen in Figure 6.

You will note that in this case the process improvement team has identified three potential future-state solutions that have very different levels of impact on the organization, all of which represent a minimum of a 30% improvement to the organization. The big challenge for the benchmarking team now is to identify which offers the best overall value to the organization.

Classification of Future-State Solutions

Any improvement or combination of improvements can be put into one of four classifications.

1. **Refinement.** This type of change results in improvement that reduces cost, cycle time, and defect rates between 5% and 15%

Benefit

	Original Process	Solution 1	Solution 2	Solution 3
Effectiveness (Quality)	0.2	0.02	0.01	0.009
Efficiency (Productivity)	12.9 hrs/cycle	7.5 hrs/cycle	6.3 hrs/cycle	5.3 hrs/cycle
Adaptability Measurement	25%	not measured	80%	65%
Cycle Time	305 hrs	105 hrs	105 hrs	85 hrs
Cost per Cycle	$605	not measured	$410	$380

Cost

	Solution 1	Solution 2	Solution 3
Cost	$1,300,000	$20,000	$280,000
Implementation Cycle Time	24 months	6 months	15 months
Probability of Success	50%	95%	85%
Major Problem	Need more data	Training time	New org. structure

FIGURE 6. Benefit/cost/risk analysis chart for three alternative future-state solutions

per year. Most activities of a department improvement team or a natural work team fall into this classification. On occasion, a benchmarking project will fall into this classification.

2. **Copycat.** This type of change usually occurs when a change is implemented that makes an item similar to some other organization's item. Typically, this emulation occurs when a process improvement team develops its future-state solution based solely on the country's best-in-class. The typical improvement reduces cost, cycle time, and error rates between 20% and 40%.
3. **Breakthrough.** This type of change usually occurs when the process improvement team develops its future-state solution by

combining the best features related to the item under study from each of the world-class organizations in the industry to create a new and better design. Typical improvements reduce cost, cycle time, and error rates between 30% and 60%.

4. **Revolutionary.** This type of change occurs when the process improvement team benchmarks worldwide best in all classes. It requires a shift in thinking within the organization, as all of the sacred cows are challenged. The old rules are discarded. Major paradigm shift and culture change are required to support the redesigned item. These changes are difficult and often fail because they are not in line with the organization's operational activities and culture. They require a large investment in organizational change management and even then the risk of failure is high. Seldom do you see revolutionary future-state solutions come out of benchmarking projects. Often these types of changes occur as a result of reengineering projects that, by their nature, are very risky. Michael Hammer and James Champy, in their book *Reengineering the Corporation*, reported that between 50% and 70% of the reengineering projects fail. Typically, revolutionary change results in improvement that reduces cost, cycle time, and error rates between 60% and 90%.

The team should look closely at each of the potential future-state solutions and identify it as a class 1, 2, 3, or 4 type of improvement. The risks, cost, and return go up as the numbers get higher.

Index

A

B

C

Q

R

ERNST & YOUNG LLP/SYSTEMCORP INC.

GUIDED TOUR

Included with this book is Ernst & Young LLP's/SystemCorp Inc.'s Multimeida Guided Tour CD-ROM called *Simulation Modeling Methods*

System Requirements

- Windows 3.1 or higher
- Sound Blaster or similar sound card
- CD-ROM Drive
- 8MB RAM
- 4MB free disk space

Installation Instructions:

1. Start Windows.
2. Load Guided Tour CD-ROM into CD-ROM drive.
3. Select Run from the file or Start menu.
4. Type in **<drive>:\setup** where **<drive>** is the drive letter of your CD-ROM drive.
5. Follow instructions given in setup program.

CONTENTS OF CD-ROM GUIDED TOUR

1. **Multimedia overview of the methodology**

2. **Author's biographies**

3. **Other books in this series**

4. **Word Draw**
   This is an advanced process modeling application developed by Edge Software Inc.

4. **High Tech Enablers Examples**
   To compete, today's organizations need to make effective use of technologies. Included are examples that we find helpful.
   - **ISO 9000 Step-by-Step**
     An interactive multimedia application designed to help small, medium, and large corporations attain ISO 9000 registration much faster and at an affordable cost.
   - **PMI's Managing Projects**
     A interactive multimedia application, based on PMI's latest version of A Guide to PMBOK, that allows you to customize your organization's project management methodology and maximizes your ability to standardize, communicate, and control all aspects of your project through groupware task management.
   - **Office Control Web**
     it is a brower-based document management solution for single or multisite organizations. Integrate existing electronic documents or design powerful forms processing capabilities in full compliance with ISO or QS-9000.

ANY QUESTIONS?

In you need any technical assistance or for more detailed product information or any of the programs demonstrated, contact **SystemCorp** at (514) 339-1067.

Fax a copy of this page to get a 10% discount on any of our products.